DECKER'S PATTERNS OF EXPOSITION 12

DECKER'S PATTERNS OF EXPOSITION 12

Randall E. Decker

Robert A. Schwegler
University of Rhode Island

SCOTT, FORESMAN/LITTLE, BROWN HIGHER EDUCATION
A Division of Scott, Foresman and Company
Glenview, Illinois   London, England

An Instructor's Edition of *Decker's Patterns of Exposition* 12 is available through your local Scott, Foresman/Little, Brown representative or by writing the English Editor, College Division, Scott, Foresman and Company, 1900 East Lake Avenue, Glenview, Illinois 60025.

Library of Congress Cataloging-in-Publication Data

Patterns of exposition / [edited by] Randall E. Decker, Robert A. Schwegler.—12th ed.
    p. cm.
  Rev. ed. of: Patterns of exposition 11. c1988.
  ISBN 0-673-52016-1 (Student's ed.)—ISBN 0-673-49861-1 (Instructor's ed.)
  1. College readers. 2. Exposition (Rhetoric) I. Decker, Randall E. II. Schwegler, Robert A. III. Patterns of exposition 11.
PE1417.P386   1990
808'.0427—dc20   89-37832
                                               CIP

ISBN: 0-673-52016-1 (Student's Edition)
ISBN: 0-673-49861-1 (Instructor's Edition)

23456–RRN–9493929190

"*Checks #2*" by Rebecca Shore, Chicago, Illinois, 1984, 87 × $67\frac{1}{2}$ inches, machine-pieced and hand-quilted quilt. Collection of Carolyn Jahn and James Kramer. Permission granted by The Quilt Digest Press, San Francisco.

To the Instructor

Patterns of Exposition 12 retains the basic principles and the general format of previous editions. Use of the book remains high, and we continue to poll instructor-users for evaluations of the selections and about the need for basic changes in the framework. We also reviewed the responses of students who returned questionnaires like the one at the back of this book. Although obviously we are unable to comply with all requests, we have seriously considered and fully appreciated all of them, and we have incorporated many suggestions into this new edition.

The annotated demonstration paragraphs located at the end of introductory sections are now supplemented by an additional example (two in the case of Section 11, illustrating induction and deduction). The new paragraphs are drawn from a variety of publications and illustrate some of the structural and stylistic variations professional writers often add while employing the basic patterns. Some of these authors are well known for their work; others less so, though the sample paragraphs may call attention to the quality of their writing.

A revised "Introduction" incorporates current theories of reading as a basis for practical advice about reading the selections in the text both for comprehension and as a bridge into writing. The discussion also describes specific reading/writing activities that instructors may wish to assign or students may decide to employ on their own.

Because so many instructors find it useful, we have retained the table of contents listing pairs of essays. Each pair provides contrasts (or similarities) in theme, approach, and style that are worth study. The essay pairs can form the focus of class discussion or writing assignments.

Although the focus of the text as a whole is on exposition and the rhetorical patterns it employs, we recognize that many instructors like to include a section on argument in their courses, and that argument often uses the same rhetorical patterns as exposition. Selections from the argument section may be added to those in the expository chapters to further illustrate the usefulness of the patterns. The argument chapter is similar in arrangement and approach to the other sections of the text.

The "Further Readings" section provides a classic essay and two fine contemporary selections chosen to provoke discussion of ideas and strategies. The pieces have also been chosen to suggest some of the intriguing forms and goals essays can pursue in the hands of skilled and daring writers. The essays in this section can be used on their own or along with the other sections of the book. They provide stimulus for writing and discussion as well as illustrations of strategies for students to use in their own writing.

But throughout *Patterns of Exposition 12* we have tried, as always, to make possible the convenient use of all materials in whatever ways instructors think best for their own classes. With a few exceptions, only complete essays or freestanding units of larger works have been included. With their inevitable overlap of patterns, they are more complicated than excerpts illustrating single principles, but they are also more realistic examples of exposition and more useful for other classroom purposes. Versatility has been an important criterion in choosing materials.

Twenty-eight of the selections best liked in previous editions have been retained. Twenty-four selections are new, and all but a few of these are anthologized for the first time.

Their arrangement is but one of many workable orders; instructors can easily develop another if they so desire. The Thematic Table of Contents and the table of Essay Pairs also suggest a variety of arrangements.

We have tried to vary the study questions—and undoubtedly have included far more than any one teacher will want—from the purely objective to those calling for some serious self-examination by students. (The Instructor's Manual supplements these materials.)

Suggestions for writing assignments to be developed from ideas in the essays are located immediately after each selection. But for classes in which the instructor prefers writing to be done according to the expository pattern under study at the time, regardless of subject matter, topic suggestions are located at the end of each section.

"A Guide to Terms," where matters from *Abstract* to *Unity* are briefly discussed, refers whenever possible to the essays themselves for illustrations. To permit unity and easy access, it is located at the back of the book, but there are cross-references to it in the study questions.

In all respects—size, content, arrangement, format—we have tried to keep *Patterns of Exposition 12* uncluttered and easy to use.

ACKNOWLEDGMENTS

For their help and support, the editors would like to thank the staff of Scott, Foresman/Little, Brown College Division: Ted Simpson, Marisa L. L'Heureux, Anne Smith, Constance Rajala, and Elizabeth Fresen.

The second editor wishes to thank Brian Schwegler for his ideas and responses; Christopher Schwegler for his smiles; and Nancy Newman Schwegler for her love, insight, and support.

The continued success of *Patterns of Exposition* is due to a great extent to the many students and instructors who respond to questionnaires and offer helpful suggestions, making the job of revision easier. For their invaluable assistance with the twelfth edition we would especially like to thank James T. Anderson, Calla Andres, D. L. Arendt, Beth Bean, Kelley Jo Burke, Marion Butler, Tracey Cozman, Alex Dumanowski, Suzanne Eovaldi, Jay Garver, Terry Goodtrack, Eric Hufnagel, Chris M. Izzolino, Michael Kane, Meaghan Ketcheson, Lila N. Meeks, Dr. Barbara Powell, J. A. Schaffer, Ruth Elizabeth Shore, Henning Tannis, and R. A. Zerr.

Table of Contents

> Our clothing, our personal possessions, our behavior, and our attitudes can all be signs of our membership in modern tribes. And these tribes provide a sense of identity and belonging, says this writer, who looks at some fashionable tribes from the last decade.

3 Explaining by Means of *Comparison* and *Contrast* / 77

> What happens when you start looking at a thing of beauty in terms of its use?

> A famous historian identifies these two great Civil War generals as the embodiments of the passing and rising orders.

> Our experiences and those of our parents can create very different perspectives. The result can be disagreements and misunderstandings mingled with affection, as this writer's experiences illustrate.

> For this Hispanic-American writer, growing up bilingual meant living in two worlds: one of home and family and the other of school and public places.

7   Using *Definition* to Help Explain   /   215

Thematic Table of Contents

Society and Social Change

Culture and Customs

Politics and Leaders

Personality and Behavior

Nature and the Environment

Morals, Crime, and Punishment

Growing Up/Getting Old

Differences

Essay Pairs

Among the selections in *Patterns of Exposition* are a number of essay pairs whose similarities in topic or theme and contrasts in perspective or style offer interesting insights. These relationships show that the strategies a writer chooses can affect the way readers come to view the subject matter of an essay. The following list identifies some sets of essays that are particularly well suited for study and discussion; there are, of course, many other interesting and revealing ways of pairing the selections in the text.

A few of the pairs illustrate different ways of using the same pattern, such as example or definition. In other sets, the patterns offer contrasting strategies for expression or alternate ways of viewing a subject.

Introduction

Exposition is one of the basic aims of communication, more important in many situations than the other aims—entertainment, persuasion, or self-expression. Sometimes we may write to entertain, as do the novelist and to a certain extent the sports writer; or we may try to persuade in the manner of the lawyer, the salesperson, or the preacher. We may even choose to express our beliefs and feelings in personal letters and conversation. Yet much of the writing and speaking everyday activities call for is expository in purpose, requiring us to share our knowledge of a subject. People in specialized professions are also frequent users of exposition.

Exposition means explanation, simply an *exposing* of information or ideas. Its primary function is not to tell a story or create vivid pictures for the reader, although exposition often *uses* narration and description among many other techniques. Its primary function is not to convey an author's feelings about a subject, though this perspective may at times be a valuable element in exposition. The primary function of exposition is not to convince or persuade, though argumentative and expository writing share many techniques and may each contain elements of the other. The primary function of exposition itself is merely *to explain*.

Beyond our need for informally written and spoken explanations, we use the processes of written exposition throughout college—in reports, term papers, essay examinations. Most of us use exposition throughout our working lives—in letters, in memoranda, in business and professional reports. Hence there are practical reasons most college composition courses are devoted primarily to study and practice in exposition. For the same reasons, this book concentrates on patterns of expository writing and other techniques commonly used. But because argument is closely related to exposition and shares many techniques with it, this book also contains a section on argument, arranged according to those expository patterns that appear frequently in argumentative writing. (The last part, ''Further Readings,'' offers an even wider variety of composition forms and subject matter.) There is nothing new about the ten basic patterns of exposition; we have been using most of them since we first tried to explain why birds fly south in the winter. But mature writing depends partly on the author's being able to use *deliberately* whichever techniques will do the job best, with the least chance of misunderstanding. We study these techniques to get a clearer view of their functions and possibilities, with the aim of being able to use them more effectively in our own writing.

We examine and practice these techniques separately, realizing that they are seldom used separately in practical writing. After all, when we observe and practice for hours a skill involved in tennis or golf, we are not assuming that an entire game will be made up of serving or putting. In writing, we know there is no reason a process analysis should not be used to assist comparison in some explanations, no reason an illustration might not be valuably aided in certain developments by narration. In good writing, if the patterns do not overlap, it is simply because one alone is sufficient for the purpose.

The patterns of exposition are useful techniques in other kinds of writing as well, particularly in argument. The editorial writer arguing against a proposed government project might compare it to other such projects in the past that have been expensive failures or might analyze cause-and-effect relationships and use a series of examples to show that the project will not meet the needs of those it is supposed to serve. In the argument section of this book, we see how the expository patterns work in a different kind of writing. One of the goals of this book is to create an awareness of the patterns and of the roles they can play in different kinds of expression.

But besides the study of writing techniques in a college anthology, we have a right to expect real benefit from the reading itself. Reading and thinking about new ideas or experiences are excellent ways to widen horizons, to broaden our interests—and this broadening is an important phase of becoming educated. In general, each set of essays in this book progresses in complexity and depth. Challenges help our understanding to reach an ever higher level.

Reading is not a simple act, however, and may have several purposes. In both these qualities it resembles the act of writing. Moreover, like composing, reading is active, not passive. Even when our sole concern is to perceive an author's message or to glean facts and ideas from a text, we are not simply recipients of information but discoverers as well. To comprehend a piece of writing, we need to pay attention to the signals it contains and to follow their directions. We need to recognize patterns and to take note of distinctions between generalizations and supporting detail.

Comprehension is seldom the sole aim of reading, except, perhaps, when we are searching for specific information to complete a task—a set of figures to include in a graph, the next step in assembling a model airplane, or the ingredients for a special punch at a holiday party. In casual reading we let our imaginations roam for the pleasure of the activity. In more serious reading, when a writer challenges us with fresh ideas and arguments, we speculate on the consequences or create impassioned counterarguments, some of which we may even share in writing of our own.

One sign of good writing, then, is that it invites response. It asks readers to call on their experiences in order to understand the text and the author's vision, and it encourages (or provokes) further ideas and rejoinders from the reader. To read as a writer means to be open to the imaginative responses a text provokes and to capture them in some form—marginal notes, a writer's journal—so they can be seeds for written expression.

Writers read (or reread) in practical ways as well, often with pen in hand. They admire a particular way of closing the discussion or a strategy for explaining complex causes and effects. They make note of phrases to employ as quotations or as models for their own sentences. And they remember in particular the overall patterns of development and ways the strategies are employed or combined.

Any single reading of a text, whether the first or the fifth, likely combines several activities. An instructor, moreover, may suggest the manner of approaching a reading and the ways to study it. Instead of a system for reading, therefore, we offer students some suggestions to be employed according to the reading situation, the reader's/writer's needs and abilities, as well as the nature of the text being examined.

1. For the first reading, relax. Read the selection casually, as you would a magazine article, for whatever enjoyment or new ideas you get without straining. Do not stop to look up new words unless the sentences in which they are used are meaningless until you do. But have a pen or pencil in hand and mark all words or passages you are doubtful about, and then go on.

2. When you have finished the first reading, put the book down; for a few minutes think over what you have read. Do not worry too much at this point about figuring out exactly what the writer has to say. The memories, feelings, and opinions that come to mind at this stage are an important part of the reading process. They can be the basis for detailed comprehension or for writing of your own.

3. Then use the dictionary to help you understand the words you have marked. Do not make the mistake of finding and trying to memorize the first or the shortest definition of a word. Instead, look at the various meanings, and for the word's uses as a noun, verb, and modifier. *Think* about them. Pronounce the word. Use it in a few sentences. Identify it with similar words you already know. Then see how the author has used it.

4. Read and think briefly about the assigned questions and remarks following the selection. (The paragraphs in each selection are numbered for easy reference.)

5. Reread the essay, pausing at times to think and to *question*, underlining important ideas, marking sentences or phrases that seem to you especially interesting, misleading, amusing, or well expressed.

6. Return to the questions at the end. You will probably find you have already provided most of the answers. If not, give the questions further thought, referring again to the essay and to ''A Guide to Terms'' or earlier explanations wherever necessary for thorough understanding.

7. *Evaluate* the selection. What was the author trying to explain? Was the author successful in explaining? Was the endeavor worthwhile? For what point of view was the author arguing? Was

the argument convincing? What lessons for writers can be drawn from the selection?

For writing activities to accompany reading, we have several suggestions as well:

Marginal notes: Use the margins of the text to record disagreements and agreements with what the author has to say or to hold shorthand references to memories and ideas that might be developed in essays of your own. As we read, many ideas for our own compositions come to mind, but unless they are recorded, even in brief form, they are likely to disappear by the time we get down to writing.

Reading logs: Keep a notebook of ideas, feelings, and experiences that come to mind either as you read or later as you reflect on your reading. The log you create can be a source of ideas for essays or parts essays in the future.

Double-entry notebooks: Draw a vertical line down the middle of the pages of a notebook. On the left side of the page, make brief notes summarizing the content of what you read. On the right side, record questions that occur to you as you read. The questions can be trivial or serious. They may be about the author, about what is coming next in the selection, or about a subject related to that under discussion. The summaries aid your understanding of what the author has to say and can be a source of information for your writing. The questions tell you about your reading process, provide insight into the ideas and problems that concern you, and can be springboards for essays of your own.

Useful as the selections in this text can be, they are not intended as models for imitation by students. Each was written, as all expository projects should be, to give a particular audience a particular explanation. (Or, in the case of argument essays, to persuade a particular audience.) The style of some selections is much too informal for most college writing. Other styles, perhaps from a slower and more sedate age than ours, would be too stately for today. Pure imitation is not the purpose of our study.

But each of the selections does demonstrate one or more of the *patterns* of exposition and argument, which are as useful now as ever. Each can provide, too, some profitable study of other sound principles of writing—principles of effective sentences and paragraphs, mature diction, forceful introductions and closings. The consideration of all these principles, instead of being handled in separate sections, is a continuing study within the basic framework of the expository patterns. The book is designed so that instructors and students can use it in several ways.

1

Illustrating Ideas by Use of *Example*

The use of examples to illustrate an idea under discussion is the most common, and frequently the most efficient, pattern of exposition. It is a method we use almost instinctively; for instance, instead of talking in generalities about the qualities of a good city manager, we cite Harry Hibbons as an example. We may go further and illustrate Harry's virtues by a specific account of his handling of a crucial situation during the last power shortage or hurricane. In this way we put our abstract ideas into concrete form—a process that is always an aid to clarity. (As a matter of fact, with the "for instance" in this very paragraph, examples are employed to illustrate even the *use* of example.)

Lack of clear illustrations may leave readers with only a hazy conception of the points the writer has tried to make. Even worse, readers may try to supply examples from their own knowledge or experience, and these might do the job poorly or even lead them to an impression different from that intended by the author. Since writers are the ones trying to communicate, clarity is primarily their responsibility.

Not only do good examples put into clear form what otherwise might remain vague and abstract, but the writing also becomes more interesting, with a better chance of holding the reader's attention. With something specific to be visualized, a statement also becomes more convincing—but convincing within certain limitations. If we use the Volvo as an example of Swedish workmanship, the reader is probably aware that this car may not be entirely typical. Although isolated examples will not hold up well in logical argument, for ordinary purposes of explanation the Volvo example could make its point convincingly enough. In supporting an argument, however, we need either to choose an example that is clearly typical or to present several examples to show we have represented the situation fairly.

As in the selection and use of all materials for composition, of course, successful writers select and use examples cautiously, always keeping in mind the nature of their reader-audience and their own specific purpose for communicating. To be effective, each example must be pertinent, respecting the chief qualities of the generality it illustrates. Its function as an example must be either instantly obvious to the readers or fully enough developed so that they learn exactly what it illustrates, and how. Sometimes, however, illustration may be provided best by something other than a real-life example—a fictional anecdote, an analogy, or perhaps a parable that demonstrates the general idea. Here even greater care is needed to be sure these examples are both precise and clear.

Illustration is sometimes used alone as the basic means of development, but it also frequently assists other basic techniques, such as comparison and contrast. In either of its functions, authors may find their purpose best served by one well-developed example, possibly with full background information and descriptive details. But sometimes citing several shorter examples is best, particularly if the authors are attempting to show a trend or a prevalence. In more difficult explanations, of course, a careful combination of the two techniques—using both one well-developed example and several shorter examples—may be worth the extra time and effort required.

Whichever method is used, the writers are following at least one sound principle of writing: they are trying to make the general more specific, the abstract more concrete.

Sample Paragraph (Annotated)

The topic sentence, what paragraph is about. Also happens to be the *generality* in need of specific examples.

Many Ilona Valley people prefer to support local charitable organizations, rather than the big, impersonal agencies. One of the local favorites, Ilona Relief Service, is a model of efficiency and compassion and enjoys an un-

Developed example.

blemished reputation. Last year, for instance, on May 18, a hurricane at noon devastated six blocks of a Casey residential area; but by nightfall well-trained volunteers had every one of the homeless provided with shelter and bed; an emergency kitchen was set up at the local fairground and was dispensing soup, cheese, bread and molasses, and apples.

Use of *minor examples.*

All children under age six had something tangible to hold on to: a rag doll, a toy truck, a fuzzy panda—all donated.

Several *undeveloped examples,* to show prevalence. (Author has used combination of illustrative techniques.)

And hardly a month goes by without a similar demonstration of compassion and efficiency: Ilona Relief promptly on the scene after a boating accident or chemical spill, a record freezing temperature, an apartment house fire in Waldoville, the food poisoning at Valley View Elementary School, or the disastrous flood of 1979. It is no mystery why Ilona Relief is the favored charity of the Valley.

Sample Paragraph (Example)

Something strange is happening to our weather. And it didn't just begin last summer. During the past decade, the United States has seen three of the coldest winters and four of the warmest average years ever recorded, a string of weather extremes that would occur by chance less than once in 1000 years. Elsewhere, weather has also run to extremes—with the Soviet Union and India experiencing their highest temperatures. Last winter, snow fell on the gondolas of Venice, the usually sunny beaches of the French Riviera, arid South Africa and even subtropical Brazil.

ANDREW A. ROONEY was born in 1920, in Albany, New York. He was drafted into the army while still a student at Colgate University; he served in the European theatre of operations as a *Stars and Stripes* reporter. After the war Rooney began what has been a prolific and illustrious career as a writer-producer for various television networks—chiefly for CBS—and has won numerous awards, including the Writers Guild Award for Best Script of the Year (six times—more than any other writer in the history of the medium) and three National Academy Emmy awards. In 1965 Rooney wrote the script for the first Telstar transatlantic satellite broadcast, which was carried by all three networks and translated into eleven other languages. As well as being the author of seven books, Rooney has contributed to *Esquire, Harper's, Playboy, Saturday Review,* and several other magazines. Rooney also writes a syndicated column, which appears in more than 250 newspapers, and has lectured on documentary writing at various universities. His most recent books are *A Few Minutes with Andy Rooney* (1981), *And More by Andy Rooney* (1982), *Pieces of My Mind* (1984), and *Word for Word* (1986). He now lives in Rowayton, Connecticut.

In and of Ourselves We Trust

"In and of Ourselves We Trust" was one of Rooney's syndicated column. Rooney's piece uses one simple example to illustrate a generality. He draws from it a far-reaching set of conclusions: that we have a "contract" with each other to stop for red lights—and further, that our whole system of trust depends on everyone doing the right thing.

Last night I was driving from Harrisburg to Lewisburg, Pa., a distance of about 80 miles. It was late, I was late, and if anyone asked me how fast I was driving, I'd have to plead the Fifth Amendment to avoid self-incrimination. 1

"In and of Ourselves We Trust" by Andy Rooney. Reprinted by permission of Tribune Media Services.

At one point along an open highway, I came to a crossroads   2
with a traffic light. I was alone on the road by now, but as I approached the light, it turned red, and I braked to a halt. I looked
left, right, and behind me. Nothing. Not a car, no suggestion of
headlights, but there I sat, waiting for the light to change, the only
human being, for at least a mile in any direction.

I started wondering why I refused to run the light. I was not   3
afraid of being arrested, because there was obviously no cop anywhere around and there certainly would have been no danger in
going through it.

Much later that night, after I'd met with a group in Lewisburg   4
and had climbed into bed near midnight, the question of why I'd
stopped for that light came back to me. I think I stopped because
it's part of a contract we all have with each other. It's not only the
law, but it's an agreement we have, and we trust each other to
honor it: We don't go through red lights. Like most of us, I'm
more apt to be restrained from doing something bad by the social
convention that disapproves of it than by any law against it.

It's amazing that we ever trust each other to do the right thing,   5
isn't it? And we do, too. Trust is our first inclination. We have to
make a deliberate decision to mistrust someone or to be suspicious
or skeptical.

It's a darn good thing, too, because the whole structure of our   6
society depends on mutual trust, not distrust. This whole thing we
have going for us would fall apart if we didn't trust each other
most of the time. In Italy they have an awful time getting any
money for the government because many people just plain don't
pay their income tax. Here, the Internal Revenue Service makes
some gestures toward enforcing the law, but mostly they just have
to trust that we'll pay what we owe. There has often been talk of
a tax revolt in this country, most recently among unemployed auto
workers in Michigan, and our government pretty much admits
that if there were a widespread tax revolt here, they wouldn't be
able to do anything about it.

We do what we say we'll do. We show up when we say we'll   7
show up.

I was so proud of myself for stopping for that red light. And   8
inasmuch as no one would ever have known what a good person
I was on the road from Harrisburg to Lewisburg, I had to tell
someone.

Meanings and Values

1a. Explain the concept of a "contract we all have with each other" (par. 4).

 b. How is the "agreement" achieved (par. 4)?

2. Why do you suppose exceeding the speed limit (par. 1) would not also be included in the "contract"? Or is there some other reason for Rooney's apparent inconsistency?

3. Explain the significance of the title of this selection.

Expository Techniques

1a. What generality is exemplified by the solution to Rooney's red-light enigma?

 b. In this instance, what does the generality have to do with the central theme? (See Guide to Terms: *Unity.*)

 c. Is there any disadvantage in this generality's location? Explain.

 d. Does the example prove anything?

 e. Do you think it is a good example of what it illustrates? Is it typical?

2. What other uses of example do you find in the selection?

3. How effective do you consider Rooney's closing? Why? (Guide: *Closings.*)

4. What, if anything, do the brief examples in paragraph 6 add to this piece? (Guide: *Evaluation.*)

Diction and Vocabulary

1. Does it seem to you that the diction and vocabulary levels of this selection are appropriate for the purpose intended? Why, or why not? (Guide: *Diction.*)

2. Could this be classified as a formal essay? Why? (Guide: *Essay.*)

Suggestions for Writing and Discussion

Choose one of the following passages from this selection to develop for further discussion. You may agree or disagree, or both, but organize your ideas for most effective presentation:

1.   "[Most of us are] more apt to be restrained from doing something bad by the social convention that disapproves of it than by any law against it."

2.   "Trust is our first inclination."

3.   ". . . the whole social structure of our society depends on mutual trust, not distrust."

(NOTE: Suggestions for topics requiring development by use of EXAMPLE are on page 37, at the end of this section.)

JOHN LANGONE

JOHN LANGONE was born in 1929 in Cambridge, Massachusetts. He has been an academic fellow at several universities and taught medical ethics in the Department of Social Medicine at the Harvard Medical School. Langone was also a United Press International bureau manager, science editor of the *Boston Herald* newspaper, and senior editor of *Discover* magazine. Currently, he is associate editor for medicine at *Time* magazine. Langone's many books include *Long Life, Vital Signs: How We Die in America,* and most recently, *Aids: The Facts* (1988).

There's Always a Catch

"There's Always a Catch," first published in the *New York Times Magazine,* explores a theme similar to that of the Rooney selection: the way social and personal constraints shape our behavior. Langone, however, takes a more psychological and subjective approach and, among other strategies, makes effective use of dialogue, a narrative technique. The light touches of irony in his work should also serve as gentle reminders to readers to view examples critically, no matter how believable they seem.

Commit a crime, they say, and the world is made of glass. I have   1
long believed it. As a teenager in the Navy, I walked off my ship one shore liberty with half-a-dozen blank notebooks, property of Uncle Sam, hidden beneath the civilian clothes in my bag. At the end of the gangway, a crusty master-of-arms singled me out of the stream of shorebound sailors (most of them, I thought, with a lot more evil in their eyes than I), glared at the bag and asked me to open it. Caught red-handed, I mumbled something about my mother having sent the notebooks, an excuse dismissed immedi-

ately by the M.A., who merely pointed at Uncle's initials on the covers. I was sent back aboard to spend the glorious San Francisco weekend chipping paint off the old carrier's sides.

As a young reporter for United Press International, I drew the dreaded assignment of visiting a woman to ask for a photograph of her husband, who had just gone down with the liner *Andrea Doria*. I sat in my car outside her home for half an hour, trying to raise the courage to go in. I did not, and went sheepishly back to my office, where I announced to my editor that there had been no answer to my persistent ringing of the doorbell. "Oh yeah?" said the editor, who actually had but one eye that was all-seeing, and who always reminded me of my old master-at-arms. "That was probably because she was on the phone with us."

I am used to getting caught. In my youth, I would go to confession at the Italian or the Portuguese or the Lithuanian churches in my neighborhood, always searching for priests who didn't speak English. But even in those foreign, dark cubicles, the priests found me out because they gave me whole rosaries to recite (they could say that in English, all right, along with an ominous, "Be good boy").

If I left work early—taking a slide, we used to call it—I'd always run into my boss, even if I was 10 blocks from the office on some obscure street, or he was supposed to be on assignment in China. I could be having an affair at the South Pole, I began to believe, and my 80-year-old mother would turn out to be the base chef. Even when I wasn't really doing anything wrong, but was in a situation that looked as though I were, I would invariably be confronted by someone I knew, who would think the worst.

When I am caught, I don't find it easy to lie. On the few occasions when I have told a bald-faced whopper, I have blushed and sweated, telegraphing my dishonesty like a semaphoreman. So when obligated to explain my actions, I give a varnished form of the truth, which allows me to justify my actions while covering up the possibility (do I mean probability?) that I did what I did because I wanted to. I must say I delight in an occasional transgression. If I could get away with it, there's no telling what I might do. But whether it is paranoia or a guilty conscience, I always look over my shoulder. Someone is watching, or if they are not, they soon will be.

Recently, I went to a bar with a young female friend, a coworker I have known for years. Honestly, she was not just some pickup. We had a couple of wines apiece, no more than that, I swear. We left the bar very early—at 7 o'clock which, in Manhattan, is like not even going out. I walked my friend to her bus stop, and we waited. This is a fact. I mean, it wasn't as though we had gone to a hotel room to wait for the bus. It was rainy and cold, so we stepped in a doorway. Because of the weather, we had our arms around each other, just trying to keep warm. You know how that is. (It did feel nice, standing there like that. This friend is definitely someone who rates a second glance.)

After a few minutes, I spotted the bus coming, and gave her an extra hard hug—meaning goodbye and I'll see you later—and heard a voice in back of me.   7

It said, "Dad?"   8

It was him, all right, my son, towering over me, his girlfriend on his arm. She was staring at me, he was staring at me. They could see it wasn't mom I was with. Since my friend was leaning against the doorway, I had a tough time getting my arm from around her. I remember swinging it in a wide arc over my head in a movement that was as subtle as a crutch. Under my breath, I cursed daylight savings time. I had a sudden vision of Biff walking in on his dad, Willy Loman, shacked up with the woman he'd brought hosiery to. Of Jimmy Swaggart blubbering on television over his dalliance. Scarlet, I mumbled an introduction, inanities. I sighed.   9

The rest was a blur. My son and his girlfriend excused themselves (too quickly, I thought) and left. I looked at him hunched over, apparently whispering something to her. My friend kissed me on the cheek, that's all it was, and I recoiled (of course!). She ran for her bus. In shame, I slumped toward my apartment.   10

Honest John, they used to call me, and Honest John it would always be, I told myself after two quick vodka martinis before my wife got home. I had to be. If my son didn't acknowledge to his mother that he had run into me, that would mean he thought old dad was fooling around. If I didn't mention the meeting to my wife, and my son did, they both might have suspected it. So head 'em off at the pass. Come clean. But, as always, temper it a bit. As St. Paul said, tell the truth, but with charity.   11

I told my wife the whole story, naturally leaving out the part about my enjoying standing there in the damp with my friend. My wife laughed. She kidded me, saying she was glad I had been having fun. "Fun?" I shouted. "Who's having fun?" I felt like Peter   12 going for his third denial. I played the wounded swan. I hung my head, shocked that she would think I was, well, you know. I told her this was serious, that our son might have suffered severe emotional trauma. She said he was 30 years old and had been around—more than you, she added with a grin. I ignored her barb.

"Call him up," I demanded. "See if he says anything."

"He won't," she assured me.

"But that's the problem," I said. "He has to say something or there'll be big trouble."

My wife called him—I'm still not sure why. She said, "I hear you ran into your dad tonight." He must have said something funny, because my wife let out one of those delighted shrieks of hers. Cradling the phone against her shoulder, she told me, "He says you had some chick leaning against the wall, his words, and he says he hopes you had a great time." I could hear my son cackling into the phone. I think I also heard him cheering.

Meanings and Values

1a. This selection opens with a proverb: "Commit a crime, . . . and the world is made of glass" (par. 1). What does the saying mean?

  b. Can the opening sentence be considered the generality that the essay illustrates?

  c. If so, is it restated elsewhere in the essay?

  d. If not, what generality does the essay illustrate?

2a. What authority figures does the author describe in the course of the essay?

  b. How does he react to them?

3a. Explain why you find the author's excuses for his behavior with the young woman either believable or hard to believe (par. 6).

  b. How would you characterize the tone of paragraph 6? (See Guide to Terms: *Style/Tone.*)

Expository Techniques

1a. What strategy does the author employ to begin this essay? (Guide: *Introductions.*)

  b. Explain why you consider the introduction either effective or ineffective.

2a. Identify the relatively long examples presented in this essay.

  b. Are there any brief examples in the essay? If so, where are they presented?

3a.   What are the topic sentences in paragraphs 1, 3, and 5? (Guide: *Unity*.)

b.   Do paragraphs 6–16 contain topic sentences? If so, in what ways do they differ from those in paragraphs 1–3 and 5?

4.   How does Langone use parallelism to help introduce the examples in paragraphs 1 and 2? (Guide: *Parallel Structure*.)

5a.   How does the narrative in paragraphs 6–16 contribute to the effectiveness of the essay? (Guide: *Evaluation*.)

b.   How might the purpose of this essay change if the narrative were omitted and in its place the author provided several more examples like those in the opening paragraphs? (Guide: *Purpose*.)

Diction and Vocabulary

1.   Explain the meaning of each of the following phrases, consulting a dictionary as necessary to understand the words:

a.   "telegraphing my dishonesty like a semaphoreman" (par. 5)

b.   "a varnished form of the truth" (par. 5)

c.   "I cursed daylight savings time" (par. 9)

d.   "I ignored her barb" (par. 12)

2a.   What are the allusions in paragraph 9, and how do they add to the reader's understanding of the events? (Guide: *Figures of Speech*.)

b.   What meaning does the allusion to "Peter" in paragraph 12 convey?

3.   Discuss how the author's use of quotations and dialogue in paragraphs 8 and 12–16 adds to the drama and humor of the example.

Suggestions for Writing and Discussion

1.   How much of what the author says about himself and the events can we take at face value? To what extent is he being ironic, either poking fun at himself or disguising his real motives and feelings? (Guide: *Irony*.)

2.   As a way of developing ideas for an essay of your own, list some situations or events that often make you feel guilty or uncomfortable. Then try to arrive at some generalizations about these feelings and to identify some examples that might explain the feelings to others.

(NOTE: Suggestions for topics requiring development by use of EXAMPLE are on page 37, at the end of this section.)

BRENT STAPLES

BRENT STAPLES was born in 1951 in Chester, Pennsylvania. He received his B.A. in 1973 from Widener University and his Ph.D. (in psychology) in 1982 from the University of Chicago. He has been first assistant metropolitan editor of the *New York Times* since 1985 and was formerly a reporter for the *Chicago Sun-Times* and an editor of the *New York Times Book Review*.

Just Walk on By

The power of examples to enable a reader to see through some-one else's eyes is evident in this selection. Though many of the examples in the essay draw on a reader's sympathy, their main purpose appears to be explanatory; hence, the author accom-panies them with detailed discussions. The result is a piece that is both enlightening and moving.

My first victim was a woman—white, well dressed, probably in her early twenties. I came upon her late one evening on a deserted street in Hyde Park, a relatively affluent neighborhood in an other-wise mean, impoverished section of Chicago. As I swung onto the avenue behind her, there seemed to be a discreet, uninflammatory distance between us. Not so. She cast back a worried glance. To her, the youngish black man—a broad six feet two inches with a beard and billowing hair, both hands shoved into the pockets of a bulky military jacket—seemed menacingly close. After a few more quick glimpses, she picked up her pace and was soon running in earnest. Within seconds she disappeared into a cross street.

That was more than a decade ago. I was 22 years old, a gradu-ate student newly arrived at the University of Chicago. It was in the echo of that terrified woman's footfalls that I first began to know the unwieldy inheritance I'd come into—the ability to alter public space in ugly ways. It was clear that she thought herself the quarry of a mugger, a rapist, or worse. Suffering a bout of insomnia, however, I was stalking sleep, not defenseless wayfarers. As a softy who is scarcely able to take a knife to a raw chicken—let alone hold it to a person's throat—I was surprised, embarrassed, and dismayed all at once. Her flight made me feel like an accomplice in tyranny. It also made it clear that I was indistinguishable from the muggers who occasionally seeped into the area from the surrounding ghetto. That first encounter, and those that followed, signified that a vast, unnerving gulf lay between nighttime pedestrians—particularly women—and me. And I soon gathered that being perceived as dangerous is a hazard in itself. I only needed to turn a corner into a dicey situation, or crowd some frightened, armed person in a foyer somewhere, or make an errant move after being pulled over by a policeman. Where fear and weapons meet— and they often do in urban America—there is always the possibility of death.

In that first year, my first away from my hometown, I was 3 to become thoroughly familiar with the language of fear. At dark, shadowy intersections in Chicago, I could cross in front of a car stopped at a traffic light and elicit the *thunk, thunk, thunk, thunk* of the driver—black, white, male, or female—hammering down the door locks. On less traveled streets after dark, I grew accustomed to but never comfortable with people who crossed to the other side of the street rather than pass me. Then there were the standard unpleasantries with police, doormen, bouncers, cab drivers, and others whose business it is to screen out troublesome individuals *before* there is any nastiness.

I moved to New York nearly two years ago and I have re- 4 mained an avid night walker. In central Manhattan, the near-constant crowd cover minimizes tense one-on-one street encounters. Elsewhere—visiting friends in SoHo, where sidewalks are narrow and tightly spaced buildings shut out the sky—things can get very taut indeed.

Black men have a firm place in New York mugging literature. 5 Norman Podhoretz in his famed (or infamous) 1963 essay, ''My Negro Problem—And Ours,'' recalls growing up in terror of black males; they ''were tougher than we were, more ruthless,'' he writes—and as an adult on the Upper West Side of Manhattan, he continues, he cannot constrain his nervousness when he meets black men on certain streets. Similarly, a decade later, the essayist and novelist Edward Hoagland extols a New York where once "Negro bitterness bore down mainly on other Negroes." Where some see mere panhandlers, Hoagland sees "a mugger who is clearly screwing up his nerve to do more than just *ask* for money." But Hoagland has "the New Yorker's quick-hunch posture for broken-field maneuvering," and the bad guy swerves away.

I often witness that "hunch posture," from women after dark   6
on the warrenlike streets of Brooklyn where I live. They seem to set their faces on neutral and, with their purse straps strung across their chests bandolier style, they forge ahead as though bracing themselves against being tackled. I understand, of course, that the danger they perceive is not a hallucination. Women are particularly vulnerable to street violence, and young black males are drastically overrepresented among the perpetrators of that violence. Yet these truths are no solace against the kind of alienation that comes of being ever the suspect, against being set apart, a fearsome entity with whom pedestrians avoid making eye contact.

It is not altogether clear to me how I reached the ripe old age   7
of 22 without being conscious of the lethality nighttime pedestrians attributed to me. Perhaps it was because in Chester, Pennsylvania, the small, angry industrial town where I came of age in the 1960s, I was scarcely noticeable against a backdrop of gang warfare, street knifings, and murders. I grew up one of the good boys, had perhaps a half-dozen fist fights. In retrospect, my shyness of combat has clear sources.

Many things go into the making of a young thug. One of those   8
things is the consummation of the male romance with the power to intimidate. An infant discovers that random flailings send the baby bottle flying out of the crib and crashing to the floor. Delighted, the joyful babe repeats those motions again and again, seeking to duplicate the feat. Just so, I recall the points at which some of my boyhood friends were finally seduced by the perception of themselves as tough guys. When a mark cowered and surrendered his money without resistance, myth and reality merged— and paid off. It is, after all, only manly to embrace the power to frighten and intimidate. We, as men, are not supposed to give an

inch of our lane on the highway; we are to seize the fighter's edge in work and in play and even in love; we are to be valiant in the face of hostile forces.

Unfortunately, poor and powerless young men seem to take all this nonsense literally. As a boy, I saw countless tough guys locked away; I have since buried several, too. They were babies, really—a teenage cousin, a brother of 22, a childhood friend in his mid-twenties—all gone down in episodes of bravado played out in the streets. I came to doubt the virtues of intimidation early on. I chose, perhaps even unconsciously, to remain a shadow—timid, but a survivor.   9

The fearsomeness mistakenly attributed to me in public places often has a perilous flavor. The most frightening of these confusions occurred in the late 1970s and early 1980s when I worked as a journalist in Chicago. One day, rushing into the office of a magazine I was writing for with a deadline story in hand, I was mistaken for a burglar. The office manager called security and, with an ad hoc posse, pursued me through the labyrinthine halls, nearly to my editor's door. I had no way of proving who I was. I could only move briskly toward the company of someone who knew me.   10

Another time I was on assignment for a local paper and killing time before an interview. I entered a jewelry store on the city's affluent Near North Side. The proprietor excused herself and returned with an enormous red Doberman pinscher straining at the end of a leash. She stood, the dog extended toward me, silent to my questions, her eyes bulging nearly out of her head. I took a cursory look around, nodded, and bade her good night. Relatively speaking, however, I never fared as badly as another black male journalist. He went to nearby Waukegan, Illinois, a couple of summers ago to work on a story about a murderer who was born there. Mistaking the reporter for the killer, police hauled him from his car at gunpoint and but for his press credentials would probably have tried to book him. Such episodes are not uncommon. Black men trade tales like this all the time.   11

In "My Negro Problem—And Ours," Podhoretz writes that the hatred he feels for blacks makes itself known to him through a variety of avenues—one being his discomfort with that "special brand of paranoid touchiness" to which he says blacks are prone.   12

No doubt he is speaking here of black men. In time, I learned to smother the rage I felt at so often being taken for a criminal. Not to do so would surely have led to madness—via that special "paranoid touchiness" that so annoyed Podhoretz at the time he wrote the essay.

I began to take precautions to make myself less threatening. I move about with care, particularly late in the evening. I give a wide berth to nervous people on subway platforms during the wee hours, particularly when I have exchanged business clothes for jeans. If I happen to be entering a building behind some people who appear skittish, I may walk by, letting them clear the lobby before I return, so as not to seem to be following them. I have been calm and extremely congenial on those rare occasions when I've been pulled over by the police.

And on late-evening constitutionals along streets less traveled by, I employ what has proved to be an excellent tension-reducing measure: I whistle melodies from Beethoven and Vivaldi and the more popular classical composers. Even steely New Yorkers hunching toward nighttime destinations seem to relax, and occasionally they even join in the tune. Virtually everybody seems to sense that a mugger wouldn't be warbling bright, sunny selections from Vivaldi's *Four Seasons.* It is my equivalent of the cowbell that hikers wear when they know they are in bear country.

Meanings and Values

1a. What does the author have to say about his personality and values in paragraphs 2, 7, and 9?

b. For what reasons does he walk at night?

c. How is it likely that his "victim" (par. 1) viewed him?

2. In your own words—not those of the essay—explain what each of the following passages means or refers to:

a. "unwieldy inheritance" (par. 2)

b. "an accomplice in tyranny" (par. 2)

c. "being perceived as dangerous is a hazard in itself" (par. 2)

3a. Does the author's presence (or the presence of other young black males) affect only women? If not, who else does it affect?

b. How does the author now avoid frightening people?

4a. What cause or causes does Staples identify for the fearful reactions he describes in the essay?

b. Identify the evidence he presents to show that such fears are at least partially justifiable.

Expository Techniques

1a. What expectations about the subject and purpose of the selection are most readers likely to hold after reading the opening sentences?

b. Describe the ways in which the rest of the essay bears out or reverses these expectations.

2. Identify the examples in paragraphs 1, 3, 4, 10, and 11.

3. The quotations in paragraph 5 contribute to the essay in what ways?

4a. Discuss the strategies the author employs to explain why he and other black males can be considered victims of stereotyping and of the surroundings in which they grew up.

b. Characterize the author's response to Podhoretz's comment about the "special brand of paranoid touchiness" (par. 12) of blacks.

c. Tell why it is appropriate that the paragraph quoting Podhoretz on "paranoid touchiness" (par. 12) comes after the two examples presented in paragraphs 10 and 11.

Diction and Vocabulary

1. The diction of this essay is often quite formal: for example, "The fearsomeness mistakenly attributed to me in public places often has a perilous flavor" (par. 10). Discuss the likely effect of such diction on the way readers view the author's character and values. (See Guide to Terms: *Diction.*)

2. Examine paragraphs 1, 11, and 14 and then discuss Staples's use of concrete diction in them. (Guide: *Concrete/Abstract.*)

3. Tell why the following sentence from the end of the essay can be considered a summary of some of its themes: "It is my equivalent of the cowbell that hikers wear when they know they are in bear country" (par. 14).

4. If you find any of the following words puzzling, look them up in a dictionary: quarry, unnerving, dicey (par. 2); taut (4); warrenlike, bandolier (6); lethality (7); consummation (8); perilous, ad hoc (10); cursory (11); constitutionals (14).

Suggestions for Writing and Discussion

1. Discuss any experiences you have had that were similar either to those of the author or of the people who reacted fearfully to him. Does the essay help you to interpret them in a different way?

2. Are the experiences Staples describes more likely to happen in an urban than a suburban setting? Why?

3. To what extent are the tensions Staples explores the result of social class as well as race?

(NOTE: Suggestions for topics requiring development by use of EXAMPLE are on page 37, at the end of this section.)

WILLIAM F. BUCKLEY, JR.

WILLIAM F. BUCKLEY, JR., was born in 1925, in New York, where
he now lives with his wife and son. He graduated from Yale
University and holds honorary degrees from a number of universities, including Seton Hall, Syracuse University, Notre
Dame, and Lafayette College. He has been editor-in-chief of *National Review* since 1955, a syndicated columnist since 1962, and
a host of public television's "Firing Line" since 1966. Generally
considered one of the most articulate conservative writers,
Buckley has published in various general circulation magazines
and has received numerous honors and awards. He lectures
widely and is the author of several novels and nonfiction books,
among them *God and Man at Yale: The Superstitions of "Academic
Freedom"* (1951), *Saving the Queen* (1976), *Stained Glass* (1978),
Who's on First (1980), *Marco Polo, If You Can* (1982), *Atlantic High*
(1982), *Overdrive: A Personal Documentary* (1983), *The Story of
Henri Tod* (1984), *The Tall Ships* (1986), *See You Later, Alligator*
(1985), *High Jinx* (1986), *Racing Through Paradise: A Pacific Passage*
(1987), and Mongoose R.I.P. (1988).

Why Don't We Complain?

First published in *Esquire,* "Why Don't We Complain?" is a
good illustration of the grace and wit that characterize most of
Buckley's writing. For students of composition, it can also provide another demonstration of the use of varied examples—
some well developed, others scarcely at all—to make a single
generality more specific. And the generality itself, as we can see
toward the end, is of considerably broader significance than it
appears at first.

It was the very last coach and the only empty seat on the entire   1
train, so there was no turning back. The problem was to breathe.
Outside, the temperature was below freezing. Inside the railroad

car the temperature must have been about 85 degrees. I took off my overcoat, and a few minutes later my jacket, and noticed that the car was flecked with the white shirts of the passengers. I soon found my hand moving to loosen my tie. From one end of the car to the other, as we rattled through Westchester County, we sweated; but we did not moan.

I watched the train conductor appear at the head of the car. "Tickets, all tickets, please!" In a more virile age, I thought, the passengers would seize the conductor and strap him down on a seat over the radiator to share the fate of his patrons. He shuffled down the aisle, picking up tickets, punching commutation cards. *No one addressed a word to him.* He approached my seat, and I drew a deep breath of resolution. "Conductor," I began with a considerable edge to my voice. . . . Instantly the doleful eyes of my seatmate turned tiredly from his newspaper to fix me with a resentful stare: what question could be so important as to justify my sibilant intrusion into his stupor? I was shaken by those eyes. I am incapable of making a discreet fuss, so I mumbled a question about what time were we due in Stamford (I didn't even ask whether it would be before or after dehydration could be expected to set in), got my reply, and went back to my newspaper and to wiping my brow.

The conductor had nonchalantly walked down the gauntlet of eighty sweating American freemen, and not one of them had asked him to explain why the passengers in that car had been consigned to suffer. There is nothing to be done when the temperature *outdoors* is 85 degrees, and indoors the air conditioner has broken down; obviously when that happens there is nothing to do, except perhaps curse the day that one was born. But when the temperature outdoors is below freezing, it takes a positive act of will on somebody's part to set the temperature *indoors* at 85. Somewhere a valve was turned too far, a furnace overstocked, a thermostat maladjusted: something that could easily be remedied by turning off the heat and allowing the great outdoors to come indoors. All this is so obvious. What is not obvious is what has happened to the American people.

It isn't just the commuters, whom we have come to visualize as a supine breed who have got on to the trick of suspending their sensory faculties twice a day while they submit to the creeping dissolution of the railroad industry. It isn't just they who have given up trying to rectify irrational vexations. It is the American people everywhere.

A few weeks ago at a large movie theater I turned to my wife   5
and said, "The picture is out of focus." "Be quiet," she answered.
I obeyed. But a few minutes later I raised the point again, with mounting impatience. "It will be all right in a minute," she said apprehensively. (She would rather lose her eyesight than be around when I make one of my infrequent scenes.) I waited. It was *just* out of focus—not glaringly out, but out. My vision is 20–20, and I assume that is the vision, adjusted, of most people in the movie house. So, after hectoring my wife throughout the first reel, I finally prevailed upon her to admit that it *was* off, and very annoying. We then settled down, coming to rest on the presumption that: (a) someone connected with the management of the theater must soon notice the blur and make the correction; or (b) that someone seated near the rear of the house would make the complaint in behalf of those of us up front; or (c) that—any minute now—the entire house would explode into catcalls and foot stamping, calling dramatic attention to the irksome distortion.

What happened was nothing. The movie ended, as it had be-   6
gun, *just* out of focus, and as we trooped out, we stretched our faces in a variety of contortions to accustom the eye to the shock of normal focus.

I think it is safe to say that everybody suffered on that occa-   7
sion. And I think it is safe to assume that everyone was expecting someone else to take the initiative in going back to speak to the manager. And it is probably true even that if we had supposed the movie would run right through the blurred image, someone surely would have summoned up the purposive indignation to get up out of his seat and file his complaint.

But notice that no one did. And the reason no one did is be-   8
cause we are all increasingly anxious in America to be unobtrusive, we are reluctant to make our voices heard, hesitant about claiming our rights; we are afraid that our cause is unjust, or that if it is not unjust, that it is ambiguous; or if not even that, that it is too trivial to justify the horrors of a confrontation with Authority; we still sit in an oven or endure a racking headache before undertaking a head-on, I'm-here-to-tell-you complaint. That tendency to passive

compliance, to a heedless endurance, is something to keep one's eyes on—in sharp focus.

I myself can occasionally summon the courage to complain, but I cannot, as I have intimated, complain softly. My own instinct is so strong to let the thing ride, to forget about it—to expect that someone will take the matter up, when the grievance is collective, in my behalf—that it is only when the provocation is at a very special key, whose vibrations touch simultaneously a complexus of nerves, allergies, and passions, that I catch fire and find the reserves of courage and assertiveness to speak up. When that happens, I get quite carried away. My blood gets hot, my brow wet, I become unbearably and unconscionably sarcastic and bellicose; I am girded for a total showdown.

Why should that be? Why could not I (or anyone else) on that railroad coach have said simply to the conductor, "Sir"—I take that back: that sounds sarcastic—"Conductor, would you be good enough to turn down the heat? I am extremely hot. In fact, I tend to get hot every time the temperature reaches 85 degr—" Strike that last sentence. Just end it with the simple statement that you are extremely hot, and let the conductor infer the cause.

Every New Year's Eve I resolve to do something about the Milquetoast in me and vow to speak up, calmly, for my rights, and for the betterment of our society, on every appropriate occasion. Entering last New Year's Eve, I was fortified in my resolve because that morning at breakfast I had had to ask the waitress three times for a glass of milk. She finally brought it—after I had finished my eggs, which is when I don't want it any more. I did not have the manliness to order her to take the milk back, but settled instead for a cowardly sulk, and ostentatiously refused to drink the milk— though I later paid for it—rather than state plainly to the hostess, as I should have, why I had not drunk it, and would not pay for it.

So by the time the New Year ushered out the Old, riding in on my morning's indignation and stimulated by the gastric juices of resolution that flow so faithfully on New Year's Eve, I rendered my vow. Henceforward I would conquer my shyness, my despicable disposition to supineness. I would speak out like a man against the unnecessary annoyances of our time.

Forty-eight hours later, I was standing in line at the ski repair store in Pico Peak, Vermont. All I needed, to get on with my skiing, was the loan, for one minute, of a small screwdriver, to tighten a loose binding. Behind the counter in the workshop were two men. One was industriously engaged in servicing the complicated requirements of a young lady at the head of the line, and obviously he would be tied up for quite a while. The other—"Jiggs," his workmate called him—was a middle-aged man, who sat in a chair puffing a pipe, exchanging small talk with his working partner. My pulse began its telltale acceleration. The minutes ticked on. I stared at the idle shopkeeper, hoping to shame him into action, but he was impervious to my telepathic reproof and continued his small talk with his friend, brazenly insensitive to the nervous demands of six good men who were raring to ski.

Suddenly my New Year's Eve resolution struck me. It was   14
now or never. I broke from my place in line and marched to the counter. I was going to control myself. I dug my nails into my palms. My effort was only partially successful:

"If you are not too busy," I said icily, "would you mind hand-   15
ing me a screwdriver?"

Work stopped and everyone turned his eyes on me, and I ex-   16
perienced that mortification I always feel when I am the center of centripetal shafts of curiosity, resentment, perplexity.

But the worst was yet to come. "I am sorry, sir," said Jiggs   17
deferentially, moving the pipe from his mouth. "I am not supposed to move. I have just had a heart attack." That was the signal for a great whirring noise that descended from heaven. We looked, stricken, out the window, and it appeared as though a cyclone had suddenly focused on the snowy courtyard between the shop and the ski lift. Suddenly a gigantic army helicopter materialized, and hovered down to a landing. Two men jumped out of the plane carrying a stretcher, tore into the ski shop, and lifted the shopkeeper onto the stretcher. Jiggs bade his companion good-by, was whisked out the door, into the plane, up to the heavens, down— we learned—to a nearby army hospital. I looked up manfully—into a score of man-eating eyes. I put the experience down as a reversal.

As I write this, on an airplane, I have run out of paper and   18
need to reach into my briefcase under my legs for more. I cannot do this until my empty lunch tray is removed from my lap. I arrested the stewardess as she passed empty-handed down the aisle

on the way to the kitchen to fetch the lunch trays for the passengers up forward who haven't been served yet. "Would you please take my tray?" "Just a *moment*, sir!" she said, and marched on sternly. Shall I tell her that since she is headed for the kitchen *anyway*, it could not delay the feeding of the other passengers by more than two seconds necessary to stash away my empty tray? Or remind her that not fifteen minutes ago she spoke unctuously into the loudspeaker the words undoubtedly devised by the airline's highly paid public relations counselor: "If there is anything I or Miss French can do for you to make your trip more enjoyable, *please* let us—" I have run out of paper.

I think the observable reluctance of the majority of Americans to assert themselves in minor matters is related to our increased sense of helplessness in an age of technology and centralized political and economic power. For generations, Americans who were too hot, or too cold, got up and did something about it. Now we call the plumber, or the electrician, or the furnace man. The habit of looking after our own needs obviously had something to do with the assertiveness that characterized the American family familiar to readers of American literature. With the technification of life goes our direct responsibility for our material environment, and we are conditioned to adopt a position of helplessness not only as regards the broken air conditioner, but as regards the overheated train. It takes an expert to fix the former, but not the latter; yet these distinctions, as we withdraw into helplessness, tend to fade away.

Our notorious political apathy is a related phenomenon. Every year, whether the Republican or the Democratic Party is in office, more and more power drains away from the individual to feed vast reservoirs in far-off places; and we have less and less say about the shape of events which shape our future. From this alienation of personal power comes the sense of resignation with which we accept the political dispensations of a powerful government whose hold upon us continues to increase.

An editor of a national weekly news magazine told me a few years ago that as few as a dozen letters of protest against an editorial stance of his magazine was enough to convene a plenipotentiary meeting of the board of editors to review policy. "So few people complain, or make their voices heard," he explained to me, ''that we assume a dozen letters represent the inarticulated views of thousands of readers.'' In the past ten years, he said, the volume of mail has noticeably decreased, even though the circulation of his magazine has risen.

When our voices are finally mute, when we have finally suppressed the natural instinct to complain, whether the vexation is trivial or grave, we shall have become automatons, incapable of feeling. When Premier Khrushchev first came to this country late in 1959, he was primed, we are informed, to experience the bitter resentment of the American people against his tyranny, against his persecutions, against the movement which is responsible for the great number of American deaths in Korea, for billions in taxes every year, and for life everlasting on the brink of disaster; but Khrushchev was pleasantly surprised, and reported back to the Russian people that he had been met with overwhelming cordiality (read: apathy), except, to be sure, for ''a few fascists who followed me around with their wretched posters, and should be horsewhipped.''   22

I may be crazy, but I say there would have been lots more   23 posters in a society where train temperatures in the dead of winter are not allowed to climb to 85 degrees without complaint.

Meanings and Values

1. By what means, if any, does Buckley's scolding of the American people avoid being disagreeable?

2. Restate completely what you believe to be the meaning of the last sentence of paragraph 8.

3. Why do you think the author said to ''strike that last sentence'' of the quoted matter in paragraph 10?

4. Explain the connection between anti-Khrushchev posters and complaining about the heat in a train (par. 23).

5a. State in your own words the central theme of this selection. (See Guide to Terms: *Unity.*)

  b. Does it seem to you that this is the best way to have developed the theme? If not, what might have been a better way?

6. On a specific-to-general continuum, where would you place ''Why Don't We Complain?'' Why? (Guide: *Specific/General.*)

Expository Techniques

1a.   Which of the standard methods of introduction does the first para-
        graph demonstrate? (Guide: *Introductions*.)

b.   How successful is its use?

2a.   What generality do Buckley's examples illustrate? (You may use
        his words or your own.)

b.   In what way, if at all, does this statement differ from his central
        theme?

c.   In this respect, how does the writing differ from most?

3.   Why do you think the Khrushchev example is kept until last?
        (Guide: *Emphasis*.)

4.   What seems to be the purpose, or purposes, of paragraphs 4 and
        12?

5.   Assuming that this piece is typical of Buckley's writing, what as-
        pects of his style or tone will probably make his writing identifiable
        when you next encounter it? (Guide: *Style/Tone*.)

Diction and Vocabulary

1.   Explain the meaning (in par. 22) of Khrushchev's being "met with
        overwhelming cordiality (read: apathy)."

2.   Explain the illusion to Milquetoast in paragraph 11. (Guide: *Figures
        of Speech*.)

3a.   Were you annoyed by Buckley's liberal use of "dictionary-type"
        words? To what extent? Why were you annoyed?

b.   Cite any such words that were used without good reason.

c.   To what extent is this use a matter of style?

4.   Use a dictionary as needed to understand the meanings of the fol-
        lowing words: virile, doleful, sibilant, discreet (par. 2); gauntlet,
        consigned (3); supine, faculties, dissolution, rectify (4); hectoring
        (5); purposive (7); unobtrusive, ambiguous (8); provocation, com-
        plexus, unconscionably, bellicose, girded (9); infer (10); ostenta-
        tiously (11); impervious, reproof (13); centripetal (16); deferentially
        (17); unctuously (18); technification (19); apathy, phenomenon,
        dispensations (20); stance, plenipotentiary, inarticulated (21); au-
        tomatons (22).

Suggestions for Writing and Discussion

1.   Discuss, if you can, the idea that readers of American literature are
        familiar with the "assertiveness that characterized the American
        family" (par. 19).

2. An apathy such as Buckley describes, if permitted to develop to its extreme, could have disastrous results. Explore what some of these might be.

3. Buckley is generally thought to be one of the most effective spokespeople for the conservative right. Explain how you could have guessed his political views by what he says in this largely nonpolitical essay. Be specific.

4. Does the response of the American public to recent social and political issues indicate an increase or decrease in apathy? Give examples. If you are familiar with some other country, Canada or Mexico, for instance, indicate whether its citizens are as apathetic as the people Buckley describes.

(NOTE: Suggestions for topics requiring development by use of EXAMPLE are on page 37, at the end of this section.)

BARBARA EHRENREICH

BARBARA EHRENREICH received a B.A. from Reed College and a Ph.D. from Rockefeller University in biology. She has been active in the women's movement and other movements for social change for a number of years and has taught women's issues at several universities, including New York University and the State University of New York—Old Westbury. She is a Fellow of the Institute for Policy Studies in Washington, D.C., and is active in the Democratic Socialists of America. A prolific author, Ehrenreich is a regular columnist for *Ms.* and *Mother Jones* and has published articles in a wide range of magazines, among them *Esquire, Atlantic Monthly, Vogue, New Republic, The Wall Street Journal, TV Guide, New York Times Magazine, Social Policy,* and *The Nation.* Her books include *For Her Own Good: 150 Years of the Experts' Advice to Women* (with Deidre English)(1978); *The Hearts of Men: American Dreams and the Flight from Commitment* (1983); and *Remaking Love: The Feminization of Sex* (with Elizabeth Hess and Gloria Jacobs) (1986).

What I've Learned from Men

The theme and strategies of this essay (first published in *Ms.*) are similar in some striking ways to those of Buckley's piece. Nonetheless, the essays' perspectives are clearly different, reflecting the social and political outlooks of their authors. Yet Ehrenreich, like Buckley, provides numerous illustrations of the skillful use of examples in support of a generality. In addition, she demonstrates the role of examples in definition as she contrasts "lady" with "woman."

For many years I believed that women had only one thing to learn from men: how to get the attention of a waiter by some means

"What I've Learned from Men: Lessons for a Full-Grown Feminist" by Barbara Ehrenreich, *Ms.* August, 1985, vol. 14, no. 2. Copyright © 1985 by Matilda Publications, Inc. Reprinted by permission.

short of kicking over the table and shrieking. Never in my life have I gotten the attention of a waiter, unless it was an off-duty waiter whose car I'd accidentally scraped in a parking lot somewhere. Men, however, can summon a maître d' just by thinking the word "coffee," and this is a power women would be well-advised to study. What else would we possibly want to learn from them? How to interrupt someone in mid-sentence as if you were performing an act of conversational euthanasia? How to drop a pair of socks three feet from an open hamper and keep right on walking? How to make those weird guttural gargling sounds in the bathroom?

But now, at mid-life, I am willing to admit that there are some   2
real and useful things to learn from men. Not from all men—in fact, we may have the most to learn from some of the men we like the least. This realization does not mean that my feminist principles have gone soft with age: what I think women could learn from men is how to get *tough*. After more than a decade of consciousness-raising, assertiveness training, and hand-to-hand combat in the battle of the sexes, we're still too ladylike. Let me try that again—we're just too *damn* ladylike.

Here is an example from my own experience, a story that I   3
blush to recount. A few years ago, at an international conference held in an exotic and luxurious setting, a prestigious professor invited me to his room for what he said would be an intellectual discussion on matters of theoretical importance. So far, so good. I showed up promptly. But only minutes into the conversation—held in all-too-adjacent chairs—it emerged that he was interested in something more substantial than a meeting of minds. I was disgusted, but not enough to overcome 30-odd years of programming in ladylikeness. Every time his comments took a lecherous turn, I chattered distractingly; every time his hand found its way to my knee, I returned it as if it were something he had misplaced. This went on for an unconscionable period (as much as 20 minutes); then there was a minor scuffle, a dash for the door, and I was out—with nothing violated but my self-esteem. I, a full-grown feminist, conversant with such matters as rape crisis counseling and sexual harassment at the workplace, had behaved like a ninny—or, as I now understand it, like a lady.

The essence of ladylikeness is a persistent servility masked as   4
"niceness." For example, we (women) tend to assume that it is our

responsibility to keep everything "nice" even when the person we are with is rude, aggressive, or emotionally AWOL. (In the above example, I was so busy taking responsibility for preserving the veneer of "niceness" that I almost forgot to take responsibility for myself.) In conversations with men, we do almost all the work: sociologists have observed that in male-female social interactions it's the woman who throws out leading questions and verbal encouragements ("So how did you *feel* about that?" and so on) while the man, typically, says "Hmmmm." Wherever we go, we're perpetually smiling—the on-cue smile, like the now-outmoded curtsy, being one of our culture's little rituals of submission. We're trained to feel embarrassed if we're praised, but if we see a criticism coming at us from miles down the road, we rush to acknowledge it. And when we're feeling aggressive or angry or resentful, we just tighten up our smiles or turn them into rueful little moues. In short, we spend a great deal of time acting like wimps.

For contrast, think of the macho stars we love to watch. Think, for example, of Mel Gibson facing down punk marauders in "The Road Warrior" . . . John Travolta swaggering his way through the early scenes of "Saturday Night Fever" . . . or Marlon Brando shrugging off the local law in "The Wild One." Would they simper their way through tight spots? Chatter aimlessly to keep the conversation going? Get all clutched up whenever they think they might—just might—have hurt someone's feelings? No, of course not, and therein, I think, lies their fascination for us.

The attraction of the "tough guy" is that he has—or at least seems to have—what most of us lack, and that is an aura of power and control. In an article, feminist psychiatrist Jean Baker Miller writes that "a woman's using self-determined power for herself is equivalent to selfishness [and] destructiveness"—an equation that makes us want to avoid even the appearance of power. Miller cites cases of women who get depressed just when they're on the verge of success—and of women who do succeed and then bury their achievement in self-deprecation. As an example, she describes one company's periodic meetings to recognize outstanding salespeople: when a woman is asked to say a few words about her achievement, she tends to say something like, "Well, I really don't know how it happened. I guess I was just lucky this time." In contrast, the men will cheerfully own up to the hard work, intelligence, and so on, to which they owe their success. By putting herself down, a woman avoids feeling brazenly powerful and potentially "selfish"; she also does the traditional lady's work of trying to make everyone else feel better ("She's not really so smart, after all, just lucky").

So we might as well get a little tougher. And a good place to start is by cutting back on the small acts of deference that we've been programmed to perform since girlhood. Like unnecessary smiling. For many women—waitresses, flight attendants, receptionists—smiling is an occupational requirement, but there's no reason for anyone to go around grinning when she's not being paid for it. I'd suggest that we save our off-duty smiles for when we truly feel like sharing them, and if you're not sure what to do with your face in the meantime, study Clint Eastwood's expressions—both of them.

Along the same lines, I think women should stop taking responsibility for every human interaction we engage in. In a social encounter with a woman, the average man can go 25 minutes saying nothing more than "You don't say?" "Izzat so?" and, of course, "Hmmmm." Why should we do all the work? By taking so much responsibility for making conversations go well, we act as if we had much more at stake in the encounter than the other party—and that gives him (or her) the power advantage. Every now and then, we deserve to get more out of a conversation than we put into it: I'd suggest not offering information you'd rather not share ("I'm really terrified that my sales plan won't work") and not, out of sheer politeness, soliciting information you don't really want ("Wherever did you get that lovely tie?"). There will be pauses, but they don't have to be awkward for *you*.

It is true that some, perhaps most, men will interpret any decrease in female deference as a deliberate act of hostility. Omit the free smiles and perky conversation-boosters and someone is bound to ask, "Well, what's come over *you* today?" For most of us, the first impulse is to stare at our feet and make vague references to a terminally ill aunt in Atlanta, but we should have as much right to be taciturn as the average (male) taxi driver. If you're taking a vacation from smiles and small talk and some fellow is moved to inquire about what's "bothering" you, just stare back levelly and say, the international debt crisis, the arms race, or the death of God.

There are all kinds of ways to toughen up—and potentially move up—at work, and I leave the details to the purveyors of assertiveness training. But Jean Baker Miller's study underscores a fundamental principle that anyone can master on her own. We can stop acting less capable than we actually are. For example, in the matter of taking credit when credit is due, there's a key difference between saying "I was just lucky" and saying "I had a plan and it worked." If you take the credit you deserve, you're letting people know that you were confident you'd succeed all along, and that you fully intend to do so again.

Finally, we may be able to learn something from men about what to do with anger. As a general rule, women get irritated: men get *mad*. We make tight little smiles of ladylike exasperation; they pound on desks and roar. I wouldn't recommend emulating the full basso profundo male tantrum, but women do need ways of expressing justified anger clearly, colorfully, and, when necessary, crudely. If you're not just irritated, but *pissed off*, it might help to say so.

I, for example, have rerun the scene with the prestigious professor many times in my mind. And in my mind, I play it like Bogart. I start by moving my chair over to where I can look the professor full in the face. I let him do the chattering, and when it becomes evident that he has nothing serious to say, I lean back and cross my arms, just to let him know that he's wasting my time. I do not smile, neither do I nod encouragement. Nor, of course, do I respond to his blandishments with apologetic shrugs and blushes. Then, at the first flicker of lechery, I stand up and announce coolly, "All right, I've had enough of this crap." Then I walk out—slowly, deliberately, confidently. Just like a man.

Or—now that I think of it—just like a woman.

Meanings and Values

1. How are most women likely to respond to the opening paragraph? How are most men likely to respond? Why?

2. The author "blush[es] to recount" her encounter with the "prestigious professor" (par. 3). Why?

3a. Define the psychological and moral problem that women face in grasping and exercising power (outlined in paragraph 6).

 b. Does the explanation of the problem and its causes offered by Ehrenreich seem reasonable to you? Be ready to explain your answer and to cite examples from your experience, if possible.

4. Is the main purpose of this essay expository or argumentative? If you have read the Buckley piece earlier in this section, you may wish to compare his aim in writing with Ehrenreich's. (See Guide to Terms: *Purpose, Argument.*)

Expository Techniques

1a. Why do you think the author chose to wait until paragraph 2 to state the essay's theme? (Guide: *Unity.*)

  b. What purpose is served by the brief examples in paragraph 1, including those in the form of rhetorical questions? (Guide: *Rhetorical Questions.*)

2a. In your own words, state the problem identified in paragraph 2.

  b. In what way is the example in paragraph 3 related to the statement of the problem in the preceding paragraph?

  c. Specify the contrasts explored in the long example in paragraph 3.

  d. Tell how this example is central to the expository purposes of the essay.

3a. Besides paragraph 3, which other parts of the essay discuss the definition of "lady" and "woman"?

  b. Examine the use of contrasting pairs of quotations in paragraphs 4, 8, and 10 and be ready to explain how the author uses them to make generalities more forceful or convincing.

4a. If you have read Buckley's "Why Don't We Complain?" compare the strategies Ehrenreich and Buckley use to open their essays. (Guide: *Introductions.*)

  b. To conclude their essays. (Guide: *Closings.*)

Diction and Vocabulary

1a. Discuss the ways in which the diction in paragraph 3 emphasizes the contrast between the professor's reputation and intellectual achievements and his behavior (Guide: *Diction.*)

  b. Identify the contrasts in diction in paragraph 11 and indicate the ways in which parallelism adds emphasis to them. (Guide: *Parallel Structure.*)

2. List the connotations that "lady" is likely to have for most readers and compare them with the connotations the word acquires in the course of this selection. (Guide: *Connotation/Denotation.*)

3. The following words may be unfamiliar to many readers. Use your dictionary, if necessary, to discover their meanings: maître d', guttural (par. 1); adjacent, lecherous, unconscionable, conversant (3);

servility, veneer (4); simper (5); self-deprecation, brazenly (6); deference (7); taciturn (9); basso profundo (11); blandishments (12).

Suggestions for Writing and Discussion

1.   If you have read Buckley's essay in this section, compare the political and social values in Ehrenreich's essay with those in Buckley's.
2.   To what extent are the explanations and advice in this selection applicable solely or primarily to women? To whom else might they apply?
3.   How accurate are the examples Ehrenreich provides of the way men and women converse?

(NOTE: Suggestions for topics requiring development by use of EXAMPLE follow.)

Writing Suggestions for Section 1
Example

Use one of the following statements or another suggested by them as your central theme. Develop it into a unified composition, using examples from history, current events, or personal experience to illustrate your ideas. Be sure to have your reader-audience clearly in mind, as well as your specific purpose for the communication.

1. Successful businesses keep employees at their highest level of competence.

2. In an age of working mothers, fathers spend considerable time and effort helping raise the children.

3. Family life can create considerable stress.

4. Laws holding parents responsible for their children's crimes would (or would not) result in serious injustices.

5. Letting people decide for themselves which laws to obey and which to ignore would result in anarchy.

6. Many people find horror movies entertaining.

7. Service professions are often personally rewarding.

8. Religion in the United States is not dying.

9. Democracy is not always the best form of government.

10. A successful career is worth the sacrifices it requires.

11. "An ounce of prevention is worth a pound of cure."

12. The general quality of television commercials may be improving (or deteriorating).

13. An expensive car can be a poor investment.

14. "Some books are to be tasted; others swallowed; and some few to be chewed and digested." (*Francis Bacon,* English scientist-author, 1561–1626.)

15. Most people are superstitious in one way or another.

16. Relationships within the family are much more important than relationships outside the family.

17. New government-sponsored social welfare programs are necessary in spite of their cost (or are not necessary enough to warrant the huge costs).

2

Analyzing a Subject by *Classification*

People naturally like to sort and classify things. The untidiest urchin, moving into a new dresser of his own, will put his handkerchiefs together, socks and underwear in separate stacks, and perhaps his toads and snails (temporarily) into a drawer of their own. He may classify animals as those with legs, those with wings, and those with neither. As he gets older, he finds that schoolteachers have ways of classifying *him*, not only into a reading group but, periodically, into an "A" or "F" category, or somewhere in between. On errands to the grocery store, he discovers the macaroni in the same department as the spaghetti, the pork chops somewhere near the ham. In reading the local newspaper, he observes that its staff has done some classifying for him, putting most of the comics together and seldom mixing sports stories with the news of bridal showers. Eventually he finds courses neatly classified in the college catalogue, and he knows enough not to look for biology courses under "Social Science." (Examples again—used to illustrate a "prevalence.")

Our main interest in classification here is its use as a structural pattern for explanatory writing. Many subjects about which either students or graduates may need to write will remain a hodgepodge of facts and opinions unless they can find some system of analyzing the material, dividing the subject into categories, and classifying individual elements into those categories. Here we have the distinction usually made between the rhetorical terms *division* and *classification*—for example, dividing "meat" into pork, beef, mutton, and fowl, then classifying ham and pork chops into the category of "pork." But this distinction is one we need scarcely pause for here; once the need for analysis is recognized, the dividing and classifying become inevitable companions and result in the single scheme of "classification" itself, as we have been discussing it. The original division into parts merely sets up the system that, if well chosen, best serves our purpose.

Obviously, no single system of classification is best for all purposes. Our untidy urchin may at some point classify girls according to athletic prowess, then later by size or shape or hair color. (At the same time, of course, the girls may be placing him into one or more categories.) Other people may need entirely different systems of classification: the music instructor classifies girls as sopranos, altos, contraltos; the psychologist, according to their behavior patterns; the sociologist, according to their ethnic origins.

Whatever the purpose, for the more formal uses of classification ("formal," that is, to the extent of most academic and on-the-job writing), we should be careful to use a logical system that is complete and that follows a consistent principle throughout. It would not be logical to divide Protestantism into the categories of Methodist, Baptist, and Lutheran, because the system would be incomplete and misleading. But in classifying Protestants attending some special conference—a different matter entirely—such a limited system might be both complete and logical. In any case, the writer must be careful that classes do not overlap: to classify the persons at the conference as Methodists, Baptists, Lutherans, and clergy would be illogical, because some are undoubtedly both Lutheran, for instance, and clergy.

In dividing and classifying, we are really using the basic process of outlining. Moreover, if we are dealing with classifiable *ideas*, the resulting pattern *is* our outline, which has been our aim all along—a basic organizational plan.

This process of classification frequently does, in fact, organize much less tangible things than the examples mentioned. We might wish to find some orderly basis for discussing the South's post–Civil War problems. Division might give us three primary categories of information: economic, political, and social. But for a full-scale consideration of these, the major divisions themselves may be subdivided for still more orderly explanation: the economic information may be further divided into agriculture and industry. Now it is possible to isolate and clarify such strictly industrial matters as shortage of investment capital, disrupted transportation systems, and lack of power development.

Any plan like this seems almost absurdly obvious, of course—*after* the planning is done. It appears less obvious, however, to inexperienced writers who are dealing with a jumble of information they must explain to someone else. This is when they should be aware of the patterns at their disposal, and one of the most useful of these, alone or combined with others, is classification.

Sample Paragraph (Annotated)

(Topic sentence, the main stream to which everything else must serve as tributary.)

Division, into four basic categories.

("Throat" is a metaphor.)

Classification, into the general category of "commerce."

For the most part Ilona Valley enjoys a well-balanced economy. Young people graduating from one of the two big high schools, if they prefer not to go to college, still have some choice as to the kind of work they will do. They might get a job on one of the Valley's numerous ranches, with the hope of becoming a foreman or even owner; they might work in the woods or in one of the eight sawmills; or they might, especially if they live near the lower end, the throat where the Valley constricts before entering the mountain passes, work on one of the many fishing boats based "outside" in Bayport. A fourth category of employment, of course, is commerce: the various retail stores and service stations, restaurants, taverns, banks, and a big retail lumber yard that advertises as the only one in the country located in a river. (It's on an island, of course, connected by bridge to the rest of Waldoville.) Opportunities are not exactly unlimited in the Valley, to be sure, but many people have built happy and prosperous lives here for themselves and their families.

Sample Paragraph (Classification)

Rock and roll is old enough now to have its generations. Some of you reading this may be part of the first (those who grew up in the fifties on Elvis and Chuck Berry), or the second (fans of the British Invasion and the Motown sound), or even the third generation (kids in the seventies for whom the members of Led Zepplin were *eminences grises* and the Beatles were Paul McCartney's *old* band). But no matter what wave you rode in on, the chances are pretty good that your parents didn't listen to rock, that they in fact detested it and regarded everything you listened to with the utmost disdain. I can still recall my mother's reaction to the first 45 I ever bought with my own money, the Rolling Stones' "Paint It Black," with "Stupid Girl" on the flip side. Staring in outrage at the photograph that adorned the sleeve—Mick, Keith, and the boys in their foppish, Edwardian finest—she finally exclaimed, "I suppose *that's* how you want to look!"

From "Talking 'Bout Their Generation," *Parenting Magazine* (September 1988). Reprinted by permission.

ERIC BERNE

ERIC BERNE (1910–1970) was a graduate of McGill University's School of Medicine. A psychiatrist, he wrote extensively in that field, lectured at various universities, and served on the psychiatric staff of Mount Sinai Hospital in New York City. He later engaged in private practice and research in California. His books include *Games People Play* (1964), *The Happy Valley* (1968), *Sex in Human Loving* (1970), and *What Do You Say After You Say Hello?* (1972).

Can People Be Judged by Their Appearance?

"Can People Be Judged by Their Appearance?" was originally published in Berne's *Mind in Action* (1947) and was later included in a revised edition of his book *A Layman's Guide to Psychiatry and Psychoanalysis* (1947). This explanation of one theory of basic human types is an example of a scientific subject made readable for nonscientists. Using division and classification as his primary pattern of development, Berne also relies to varying extents on most of the other expository patterns: illustration, comparison and contrast, process analysis, cause and effect, definition, and description.

Everyone knows that a human being, like a chicken, comes from   1
an egg. At a very early stage, the human embryo forms a three-layered tube, the inside layer of which grows into the stomach and lungs, the middle layer into bones, muscles, joints, and blood vessels, and the outside layer into the skin and nervous system.

Usually these three grow about equally, so that the average   2
human being is a fair mixture of brains, muscles, and inward organs. In some eggs, however, one layer grows more than the oth-

ers, and when the angels have finished putting the child together, he may have more gut than brain, or more brain than muscle. When this happens, the individual's activities will often be mostly with the overgrown layer.

We can thus say that while the average human being is a mix-   3 ture, some people are mainly "digestion-minded," some "muscle-minded," and some "brain-minded," and correspondingly digestion-bodied, muscle-bodied, or brain-bodied. The digestion-bodied people look thick; the muscle-bodied people look wide; and the brain-bodied people look long. This does not mean the taller a man is, the brainier he will be. It means that if a man, even a short man, looks long rather than wide or thick, he will often be more concerned about what goes on in his mind than about what he does or what he eats; but the key factor is slenderness and not height. On the other hand, a man who gives the impression of being thick rather than long or wide will usually be more interested in a good steak than in a good idea or a good long walk.

Medical men use Greek words to describe these types of body-   4 build. For the man whose body shape mostly depends on the inside layer of the egg, they use the word *endomorph*. If it depends mostly upon the middle layer, they call him a *mesomorph*. If it depends mostly upon the outside layer, they call him an *ectomorph*. We can see the same roots in our English words "enter," "medium," and "exit," which might just as easily have been spelled "ender," "mesium," and "ectit."

Since the inside skin of the human egg, or endoderm, forms   5 the inner organs of the belly, the viscera, the endomorph is usually belly-minded; since the middle skin forms the body tissues, or soma, the mesomorph is usually muscle-minded; and since the outside skin forms the brain, or cerebrum, the ectomorph is usually brain-minded. Translating this into Greek, we have the viscerotonic endomorph, the somatotonic mesomorph, and the cerebrotonic ectomorph.

Words are beautiful things to a cerebrotonic, but a viscerotonic   6 knows you cannot eat a menu no matter what language it is printed in, and a somatotonic knows you cannot increase your chest expansion by reading a dictionary. So it is advisable to leave these words and see what kinds of people they actually apply to, remembering again that most individuals are fairly equal mixtures and that what we have to say concerns only the extremes. Up to the present, these types have been thoroughly studied only in the male sex.

Viscerotonic Endomorph. If a man is definitely a thick type rather than a broad or long type, he is likely to be round and soft, with a big chest but a bigger belly. He would rather eat than breathe comfortably. He is likely to have a wide face, short, thick neck, big thighs and upper arms, and small hands and feet. He has overdeveloped breasts and looks as though he were blown up a little like a balloon. His skin is soft and smooth, and when he gets bald, as he does usually quite early, he loses the hair in the middle of his head first. 7

The short, jolly, thickset, red-faced politician with a cigar in his mouth, who always looks as though he were about to have a stroke, is the best example of this type. The reason he often makes a good politician is that he likes people, banquets, baths, and sleep; he is easygoing, soothing, and his feelings are easy to understand. 8

His abdomen is big because he has lots of intestines. He likes to take in things. He likes to take in food, and affection and approval as well. Going to a banquet with people who like him is his idea of a fine time. It is important for a psychiatrist to understand the natures of such men when they come to him for advice. 9

Somatotonic Mesomorph. If a man is definitely a broad type rather than a thick or long type, he is likely to be rugged and have lots of muscle. He is apt to have big forearms and legs, and his chest and belly are well formed and firm, with the chest bigger than the belly. He would rather breathe than eat. He has a bony head, big shoulders, and a square jaw. His skin is thick, coarse, and elastic, and tans easily. If he gets bald, it usually starts on the front of the head. 10

Dick Tracy, Li'l Abner, and other men of action belong to this type. Such people make good lifeguards and construction workers. They like to put out energy. They have lots of muscles and they like to use them. They go in for adventure, exercise, fighting, and getting the upper hand. They are bold and unrestrained, and love to master the people and things around them. If the psychia- 11 trist knows the things which give such people satisfaction, he is able to understand why they may be unhappy in certain situations.

Cerebrotonic Ectomorph. The man who is definitely a long type is likely to have thin bones and muscles. His shoulders are apt to sag and he has a flat belly with a dropped stomach, and long, weak legs. His neck and fingers are long, and his face is shaped like a long egg. His skin is thin, dry, and pale, and he rarely gets bald. He looks like an absent-minded professor and often is one.

Though such people are jumpy, they like to keep their energy and don't fancy moving around much. They would rather sit quietly by themselves and keep out of difficulties. Trouble upsets them, and they run away from it. Their friends don't understand them very well. They move jerkily and feel jerkily. The psychiatrist who understands how easily they become anxious is often able to help them get along better in the sociable and aggressive world of endomorphs and mesomorphs.

In the special cases where people definitely belong to one type or another, then, one can tell a good deal about their personalities from their appearance. When the human is engaged in one of its struggles with itself or with the world outside, the individual's way of handling the struggle will be partly determined by his type. If he is a viscerotonic, he will often want to go to a party where he can eat and drink and be in good company at a time when he might be better off attending to business; the somatotonic will want to go out and do something about it, master the situation, even if what he does is foolish and not properly figured out, while the cerebrotonic will go off by himself and think it over, when perhaps he would be better off doing something about it or seeking good company to try to forget it.

Since these personality characteristics depend on the growth of the layers of the little egg from which the person developed, they are very difficult to change. Nevertheless, it is important for the individual to know about these types, so that he can have at least an inkling of what to expect from those around him, and can make allowances for the different kinds of human nature, and so that he can become aware of and learn to control his own natural tendencies, which may sometimes guide him into making the same mistakes over and over again in handling his difficulties.

Meanings and Values

1. Consider people you have known who fit, or nearly fit, into one or another of the three categories of build.

   a. Do they also have the traits described by Berne in paragraphs 8, 9, 11, and 13? Or do you know, perhaps, a "thick" person who hates banquets, a "wide" person who writes poetry, or a "long" person who bullies other people?

   b. If so, should we assume that these are learned characteristics? Explain.

2. Illustrate clearly how an understanding of basic types of people can be important to the layperson.

3. In view of the fact that so many of a person's characteristics are determined before birth, what room does the author leave for the possibility of altering or controlling these natural tendencies?

Expository Techniques

1a. Most people, according to the author, are not classifiable in the categories he discusses. Is the classification system then faulty, since it does not include everyone?

   b. Explain the difference, if any, between this system and the faulty classification of Protestants mentioned in the introduction to this section.

2. Study the general organization of this essay.

   a. Which paragraphs give an overall preview of Berne's classification system?

   b. Which paragraphs are devoted to explanations of individual categories?

   c. Where does the author bring the categories together again to show the importance of the whole analysis?

   d. Can you work out another plan that would have presented his material as meaningfully?

3. The author ends each detailed account of type characteristics with a statement of why the psychiatrist needs to know these things (pars. 9, 11, 13). Why is this a valuable technique, even though the essay was not written for psychiatrists?

4. Show the value of the parallel structures in paragraphs 4 and 5. (See Guide to Terms: *Parallel Structure*.)

5. In your opinion, do Berne's occasional attempts at humor—e.g., "the angels" and "cannot eat a menu"—benefit or detract from his explanation? Why?

Diction and Vocabulary

1a. Are the numerous Greek words as bothersome as you expected them to be when you first glanced at the essay? Why, or why not?

b. Do you think the author expects us really to master them? If not, why did he use them?

2. Aside from the Greek words, you probably found no words with which you were not already familiar. Is this a result of the subject matter, the author's concern for his audience, or something else? Explain.

Suggestions for Writing and Discussion

1. At the time this essay was written, the types had been "thoroughly studied only in the male sex." Even if the same general traits were characteristic of women, might tradition and social pressures tend to modify the natural tendencies more in women than in men (e.g., women are "not supposed" to go around flexing their muscles or getting into fist fights)? Explain any differences that you would expect.

2. Using examples for illustration, show that basic nature can be changed—or, if you prefer, that such change is very difficult or impossible.

3. Show the practical importance—especially for success in your future career—of understanding people and why they act as they do.

4. Develop the thesis that people of opposite types can sometimes get along more congenially than those of the same type.

(NOTE: Suggestions for topics requiring development by use of CLASSIFICATION are on page 76, at the end of this section.)

JUDITH VIORST

JUDITH VIORST was born in Newark, New Jersey, and attended
Rutgers University. A contributing editor of *Redbook* magazine,
for which she writes a monthly column, she has also been a
newspaper columnist, and in 1970 she received an Emmy award
for her contributions to a CBS television special. She has written
numerous fiction and nonfiction books for children, including
Alexander and the Terrible, Horrible, No Good, Very Bad Day (1982).
Among her various books of verse and prose for adults are *It's
Hard to Be Hip Over Thirty and Other Tragedies of Married Life* (1968)
(a collection of poems), *Yes, Married: A Saga of Love and Complaint*
(1972) (prose pieces), and, more recently, *If I Were in Charge of
the World and Other Worries* (1981), *Love and Guilt and the Meaning
of Life* (1984), and *Necessary Losses* (1986).

What, Me? Showing Off?

In "What, Me? Showing Off?" first published in *Redbook,* Viorst
uses classification to explore a behavior that most of us notice
readily enough in other people but may be reluctant to acknowledge in our own actions—showing off. Though its tone is breezy
and it contains frequent touches of humor, this essay is carefully
organized and serious in purpose. Besides classification, Viorst
makes good use of examples, definition, brief narratives, and
even a short dramatic episode.

We're at the Biedermans' annual blast, and over at the far end of   1
the living room an intense young woman with blazing eyes and
a throbbing voice is decrying poverty, war, injustice and human
suffering. Indeed, she expresses such anguish at the anguish of
mankind that attention quickly shifts from the moral issues she is
expounding to how very, very, very deeply she cares about them.

She's showing off.

Down at the other end of the room an insistently scholarly fellow has just used *angst, hubris,* Kierkegaard and *epistemology* in the same sentence. Meanwhile our resident expert in wine meditatively sips, then pushes away, a glass of unacceptable Beaujolais.

They're showing off.

And then there's us, complaining about how tired we are today because we went to work, rushed back to see our son's school play, shopped at the market and hurried home in order to cook gourmet, and then needlepointed another dining-room chair.

And what we also are doing is showing off.

Indeed everyone, I would like to propose, has some sort of need to show off. No one's completely immune. Not you. And not I. And although we've been taught that it's bad to boast, that it's trashy to toot our own horn, that nice people don't strut their stuff, seek attention or name-drop, there are times when showing off may be forgivable and maybe even acceptable.

But first let's take a look at showing off that *is* obnoxious, that's *not* acceptable, that's *never* nice. Like showoffs motivated by a fierce, I'm-gonna-blow-you-away competitiveness. And like narcissistic showoffs who are willing to do anything to be—and stay—the center of attention.

Competitive showoffs want to be the best of every bunch. Competitive showoffs must outshine all others. Whatever is being discussed, they have more—expertise or money or even aggravation—and better—periodontists or children or marriages or recipes for pesto—and deeper—love of animals or concern for human suffering or orgasms. Competitive showoffs are people who reside in a permanent state of sibling rivalry, insisting on playing Hertz to everyone else's Avis.

(You're finishing a story, for instance, about the sweet little card that your five-year-old recently made for your birthday when the CSO interrupts to relate how *her* daughter not only made her a sweet little card, but also brought her breakfast in bed and saved her allowance for months and months in order to buy her—obviously much more beloved—mother a beautiful scarf for her birthday. *Grrr.*)

Narcissistic showoffs, however, don't bother to compete because they don't even notice there's anyone there to compete with. They talk nonstop, they brag, they dance, they sometimes quote Homer in Greek, and they'll even go stand on their head if attention should flag. Narcissistic showoffs want to be the star while everyone else is the audience. And yes, they are often adorable and charming and amusing—but only until around the age of six.

(I've actually seen an NSO get up and leave the room when the conversation shifted from his accomplishments. "What's the matter?" I asked when I found him standing on the terrace, brooding darkly. "Oh, I don't know," he replied, "but all of a sudden the talk started getting so superficial." *Aagh!*) 12

Another group of showoffs—much more sympathetic types— are showoffs who are basically insecure. And while there is no easy way to distinguish the insecure from the narcissists and competitors, you may figure out which are which by whether you have the urge to reassure or to strangle them. 13

Insecure showoffs show off because, as one close friend explained, "How will they know that I'm good unless I tell them about it?" And whatever the message—I'm smart, I'm a fine human being, I'm this incredibly passionate lover—showoffs have many different techniques for telling about it. 14

Take smart, for example. 15

A person can show off explicitly by using flashy words, like the hubris-Kierkegaard fellow I mentioned before. 16

Or a person can show off implicitly, by saying not a word and just wearing a low-cut dress with her Phi Beta Kappa key gleaming softly in the cleavage. 17

A person can show off satirically, by mocking showing off: "My name is Bill Sawyer," one young man announces to every new acquaintance, "and I'm bright bright bright bright bright." 18

Or a person can show off complainingly: "I'm sorry my daughter takes after me. Men are just so frightened of smart women." 19

Another way showoffs show off about smart is to drop a Very Smart Name—if this brain is my friend, goes the message, I must be a brain too. And indeed, a popular showing-off ploy—whether you're showing off smartness or anything else—is to name-drop a glittery name in the hope of acquiring some gilt by association. 20

The theory seems to be that Presidents, movie stars, Walter Cronkite and Princess Di could be friends, if they chose, with anyone in the world, and that if these luminaries have selected plain old Stanley Stone to be friends with, Stanley Stone must be one hell of a guy. (Needless to say, old Stanley Stone might also be a very dreary fellow, but if Walt and Di don't mind him, why should I?) 21

Though no one that I know hangs out with Presidents and movie stars, they do (I too!) sometimes drop famous names.

As in: "I go to John Travolta's dermatologist."

Or: "I own the exact same sweater that Jackie Onassis wore in a newspaper photograph last week."

Or: "My uncle once repaired a roof for Sandra Day O'Connor."

Or: "My cousin's neighbor's sister-in-law has a child who is Robert Redford's son's best friend."

We're claiming we've got gilt—though by a very indirect association. And I think that when we do, we're showing off.

Sometimes showoffs ask for cheers to which they're not entitled. Sometimes showoffs earn the praise they seek. And sometimes folks achieve great things and nonetheless do not show off about it.

Now *that's* impressive.

Indeed, when we discover that the quiet mother of four with whom we've been talking intimately all evening has recently been elected to the state senate—*and she never even mentioned it!*—we are filled with admiration, with astonishment, with awe.

What self-restraint!

For we know damn well—*I* certainly know—that if we'd been that lucky lady, we'd have worked our triumph into the conversation. As a matter of fact, I'll lay my cards right on the table and confess that the first time some poems of mine were published, I not only worked my triumph into every conversation for months and months, but I also called almost every human being I'd ever known to proclaim the glad tidings both local and long distance. Furthermore—let me really confess—if a stranger happened to stop me on the street and all he wanted to know was the time or directions, I tried to detain him long enough to enlighten him with the news that the person to whom he was speaking was a Real Live Genuine Honest-to-God Published Poet.

Fortunately for everyone, I eventually—it took me awhile—calmed down.

Now, I don't intend to defend myself—I was showing off, I was bragging and I wasn't the slightest bit shy or self-restrained, but a golden, glowing, glorious thing had happened in my life and I had an overwhelming need to exult. Exulting, however (as I intend to argue farther on), may be a permissible form of showing off.

Exulting is what my child does when he comes home with an   35
A on his history paper (''Julius Caesar was 50,'' it began, ''and his
good looks was pretty much demolished'') and wants to read me
the entire masterpiece while I murmur appreciative comments at
frequent intervals.

Exulting is what my husband does when he cooks me one of   36
his cheese-and-scallion omelets and practically does a tap dance as
he carries it from the kitchen stove to the table, setting it before me
with the purely objective assessment that this may be the greatest
omelet ever created.

Exulting is what my mother did when she took her first grand-   37
son to visit all her friends, and announced as she walked into the
room, ''Is he gorgeous? Is that a gorgeous baby? Is that the most
gorgeous baby you ever saw?''

And exulting is what that mother of four would have done if   38
she'd smiled and said, ''Don't call me 'Marge' any more. Call me
'Senator.'''

Exulting is shamelessly shouting our talents or triumphs to the   39
world. It's saying: I'm taking a bow and I'd like to hear clapping.
And I think if we don't overdo it (stopping strangers to say you've
been published is overdoing it), and I think if we know when to
quit (''Enough about me. Let's talk about you. So what do you
think about me?'' does not count as quitting), and I think if we
don't get addicted (i.e., crave a praise-fix for every poem or A or
omelet), and I think if we're able to walk off the stage (and clap
and cheer while others take their bows), then I think we're allowed, from time to time, to exult.

Though showing off can range from very gross to very subtle,   40
and though the point of showing off is sometimes nasty, sometimes needy, sometimes nice, showoffs always run the risk of being thought immodest, of being harshly viewed as . . . well . . .
showoffs. And so for folks who want applause without relinquish-
ing their sense of modesty, the trick is keeping quiet and allowing
someone else to show off *for* you.

And I've seen a lot of marriages where wives show off for   41
husbands and where husbands, in return, show off for wives.
Where Joan, for instance, mentions Dick's promotion and his running time in the marathon. And where Dick, for instance, mentions all the paintings Joanie sold at her last art show. And where
both of them lean back with self-effacing shrugs and smiles and
never once show off about themselves.

Friends also may show off for friends, and parents for their children, though letting parents toot our horns is risky. Consider, for example, this sad tale of Elliott, who was a fearless and feisty public-interest lawyer:

"My son," his proud mother explained to his friends, "has always been independent." (Her son blushed modestly.)

"My son," his proud mother continued, "was the kind of person who always knew his own mind." (Her son blushed modestly.)

"My son," his proud mother went on, "was never afraid. He never kowtowed to those in authority." (Her son blushed modestly.)

"My son," his proud mother concluded, "was so independent and stubborn and unafraid of authority that we couldn't get him toilet-trained—he wet his pants till he was well past four." (Her son . . .)

But showing off is always a risk, whether we do it ourselves or whether somebody else is doing it for us. And perhaps we ought to consider the words Lord Chesterfield wrote to his sons: "Modesty is the only sure bait when you angle for praise."

And yes, of course he's right, we know he's right, he must be right. But sometimes it's so hard to be restrained. For no matter what we do, we always have a lapse or two. So let's try to forgive each other for showing off.

Meanings and Values

1a. Name the categories into which Viorst divides showoffs. (Note: In doing this you will need to decide if Viorst views people who say nothing about their achievements as a category of showoffs.)

 b. Which of the categories does Viorst divide into subcategories? What are the subcategories?

2a. Where, if anywhere, do the categories in this essay overlap? For example, can showoffs who have a real achievement to brag about be *both* competitive and exulting?

 b. If the categories overlap, is the result confusing and misleading? Why? Or is some overlap inevitable in any classification that attempts to explain human behavior?

 c. Are the categories identified clearly enough in the essay? If not, how might they be made more obvious?

3. According to the examples in paragraphs 36 and 37, exulting may sometimes mean exaggerating or stretching the truth. Do you

agree with Viorst that exulting should be permissible even if it means inflating one's accomplishments? Be ready to defend your answer.

4a. What is meant by the passage "people who reside in a permanent state of sibling rivalry, insisting on playing Hertz to everyone else's Avis" (par. 9)?

  b. What does Viorst imply about the personalities of narcissistic showoffs when she says "they are often adorable and charming and amusing—but only until around the age of six" (par. 11)?

  c. What message is the woman with the Phi Beta Kappa key conveying (par. 17)?

  d. Who is "the hubris-Kierkegaard fellow I mentioned before" (par. 16)?

Expository Techniques

1a. In what order are the categories arranged? Worst to best? Most forgivable to least forgivable? Some other order?

  b. Where and how is this arrangement announced to the reader?

  c. Is the arrangement appropriate and effective? How else might the essay be organized?

2a. The introduction to this essay is relatively long (pars. 1–8). What does Viorst do to get readers interested in the subject? (See Guide to Terms: *Introductions.*)

  b. Where in the introduction does she announce the central theme? Where else in the essay does she speak directly about the central theme?

  c. Where in the introduction does she indicate the plan of organization?

  d. What role do the one-sentence paragraphs play in the introduction? Do they add to its effectiveness or detract from it? (Guide: *Evaluation.*)

3a. At several places in the essay Viorst comments on its organization and summarizes the categories. Identify these places.

  b. Is this commentary disruptive or does it help the reader better understand the essay? Explain.

4a. Why does paragraph 10 seem to be addressed to a female reader?

  b. Can the example be easily understood by male readers or might it alienate them?

  c. In the rest of the essay does Viorst take care to balance examples more likely to appeal to men with those more likely to appeal to women? Be ready to support your answer.

5a.   For some of the categories the discussion consists of a general def-
      inition followed by examples. Which discussions follow this ar-
      rangement?

 b.   Describe briefly the organization of the remaining discussions.

 c.   Is this variety of approaches confusing? Helpful? Interesting? Ex-
      plain your answer.

6a.   Identify a section of the essay where Viorst uses parallel para-
      graphs and discuss their effect. (Guide: *Parallel Structure.*)

 b.   Do the same with parallel sentences.

 c.   Do the same with parallel sentence parts.

7.   Examine the complicated syntax of the sentence beginning, "And
      I think if we don't . . ." in paragraph 39. Indicate why you think
      this is an appropriate or inappropriate strategy for conveying the
      author's point. (Guide: *Syntax.*)

Diction and Vocabulary

1a.   What words or kinds of words does Viorst repeat frequently in the
      course of the essay?

 b.   What purposes does the repetition serve?

2a.   To what does the phrase "gilt by association" allude? (Guide: *Fig-
      ures of Speech—Allusion.*)

 b.   Identify as many as you can of the direct references and allusions
      to people, ideas, or events in paragraphs 3, 9, 11, 21, and 23–26.

 c.   Discuss the purposes of these references.

3.   How is irony (understatement) used in paragraph 36? (Guide:
      Irony.) How is exaggeration used in paragraph 32?

4a.   Viorst uses some devices that in many essays would seem exces-
      sively informal or careless: unusual or made-up words (*"Grr,"* par.
      10; *"Aagh,"* 12); informal phrases ("strut their stuff," 7); exclama-
      tion points and parentheses surrounding an entire paragraph,
      among other things. In what ways do such devices contribute to
      the humor of the essay? to its overall tone? (Guide: *Style/Tone.*)

 b.   How do these devices help make readers willing to pay attention
      to the serious points about human behavior the essay makes?

5.   If you are unfamiliar with any of the following words, consult your
      dictionary as necessary: decrying, expounding (par. 1); *angst, hu-
      bris, epistemology* (3); narcissistic (8); periodontists, sibling (9);
      brooding (12); cleavage (17); dermatologist (23); enlighten (32); ex-
      ult (34); appreciative (35); assessment (36); shamelessly, crave (39);
      gross, immodest, relinquishing (40); feisty (42); kowtowed (45).

Suggestions for Writing and Discussion

1. Are there times when it might be useful or appropriate to be a competitive (narcissistic, insecure) showoff? Be ready to justify your answer and to provide specific examples.

2. Prepare an essay of your own that classifies some other human behavior according to its acceptable and unacceptable forms, like losing one's temper, being afraid, or being envious.

3. At several places in the essay, the author pokes fun at her own behavior or that of members of her family. Discuss how important this strategy is to the success of the essay and to the willingness of readers to view their own behavior in the ways Viorst describes.

4. If you have read Berne's essay at the beginning of this chapter, compare the two essays according to how well each author has avoided overlapping categories and according to how successful each is in conveying a sense of the complexity of human motivations and actions.

(NOTE: Suggestions for topics requiring development by use of CLASSIFICATION are on page 76, at the end of this section.)

DESMOND MORRIS

DESMOND MORRIS was born in 1928, in England, and educated at Birmingham University (B.S.) and Oxford (Ph.D.). He was later researcher in animal behavior at the Department of Zoology, Oxford, and for several years served as curator of mammals at the Zoological Society of London. Morris has increasingly specialized in human behavior and now holds a Research Fellowship at Oxford, where he spends much of his time writing. He is the author of some fifty scientific papers and a dozen books. In 1967 he published *The Naked Ape*, which has sold over 8 million copies and been translated into twenty-three languages. Other recent books have been *The Human Zoo* (1970); *Intimate Behaviour* (1972); *Manwatching* (1977); as co-author, *Gestures: Their Origins and Distribution* (1979); *Animal Days* (1980); *The Book of Ages* (1984); *Dogwatching* (1986); and *Catwatching* (1986).

Territorial Behaviour

"Territorial Behaviour" is a chapter from *Manwatching*. The selection is straightforward in purpose and execution: Morris's divisions of territorial behaviour, though simple and obvious, provide a firm and valid structure for the writing.

A territory is a defended space. In the broadest sense, there are 1 three kinds of human territory: tribal, family and personal.

It is rare for people to be driven to physical fighting in defence 2 of these "owned" spaces, but fight they will, if pushed to the limit. The invading army encroaching on national territory, the gang moving into a rival district, the trespasser climbing into an orchard, the burglar breaking into a house, the bully pushing to the front of a queue, the driver trying to steal a parking space, all of these intruders are liable to be met with resistance varying from the vigorous to the savagely violent. Even if the law is on the side of the intruder, the urge to protect a territory may be so strong that otherwise peaceful citizens abandon all their usual controls and inhibitions. Attempts to evict families from their homes, no matter how socially valid the reasons, can lead to siege conditions reminiscent of the defence of a medieval fortress.

The fact that these upheavals are so rare is a measure of the   3
success of Territorial Signals as a system of dispute prevention. It is sometimes cynically stated that "all property is theft," but in reality it is the opposite. Property, as owned space which is *displayed* as owned space, is a special kind of sharing system which reduces fighting much more than it causes it. Man is a co-operative species, but he is also competitive, and his struggle for dominance has to be structured in some way if chaos is to be avoided. The establishment of territorial rights is one such structure. It limits dominance geographically. I am dominant in my territory and you are dominant in yours. In other words, dominance is shared out spatially, and we all have some. Even if I am weak and unintelligent and you can dominate me when we meet on neutral ground, I can still enjoy a thoroughly dominant role as soon as I retreat to my private base. Be it ever so humble, there is no place like a home territory.

Of course, I can still be intimidated by a particularly dominant   4
individual who enters my home base, but his encroachment will be dangerous for him and he will think twice about it, because he will know that here my urge to resist will be dramatically magnified and my usual subservience banished. Insulted at the heart of my own territory, I may easily explode into battle—either symbolic or real—with a result that may be damaging to both of us.

In order for this to work, each territory has to be plainly adver-   5
tised as such. Just as a dog cocks its leg to deposit its personal scent on the trees in its locality, so the human animal cocks its leg symbolically all over his home base. But because we are predominantly visual animals, we employ mostly visual signals, and it is worth asking how we do this at the three levels: tribal, family and personal.

First: the Tribal Territory. We evolved as tribal animals, living   6
in comparatively small groups, probably of less than a hundred, and we existed like that for millions of years. It is our basic social

unit, a group in which everyone knows everyone else. Essentially, the tribal territory consisted of a home base surrounded by extended hunting grounds. Any neighbouring tribe intruding on our social space would be repelled and driven away. As these early tribes swelled into agricultural super-tribes, and eventually into industrial nations, their territorial defence systems became increasingly elaborate. The tiny, ancient home base of the hunting tribe became the great capital city, the primitive war-paint became the flags, emblems, uniforms and regalia of the specialized military, and the war-chants became national anthems, marching songs and bugle calls. Territorial boundary-lines hardened into fixed borders, often conspicuously patrolled and punctuated with defensive structures—forts and look-out posts, checkpoints and great walls, and, today, customs barriers.

Today each nation flies its own flag, a symbolic embodiment of its territorial status. But patriotism is not enough. The ancient tribal hunter lurking inside each citizen finds himself unsatisfied by membership in such a vast conglomeration of individuals, most of whom are totally unknown to him personally. He does his best to feel that he shares a common territorial defence with them all, but the scale of the operation has become inhuman. It is hard to feel a sense of belonging with a tribe of fifty million or more. His answer is to form sub-groups, nearer to his ancient pattern, smaller and more personally known to him—the local club, the teenage gang, the union, the specialist society, the sports association, the political party, the college fraternity, the social clique, the protest group, and the rest. Rare indeed is the individual who does not belong to at least one of these splinter groups, and take from it a sense of tribal allegiance and brotherhood. Typical of all these groups is the development of Territorial Signals—badges, costumes, headquarters, banners, slogans, and all the other displays of group identity. This is where the action is, in terms of tribal territorialism, and only when a major war breaks out does the emphasis shift upwards to the higher group level of the nation.

Each of these modern pseudo-tribes sets up its own special kind of home base. In extreme cases non-members are totally excluded, in others they are allowed in as visitors with limited rights and under a control system of special rules. In many ways they are like miniature nations, with their own flags and emblems and their own border guards. The exclusive club has its own "customs barrier": the doorman who checks your "passport" (your membership card) and prevents strangers from passing in unchallenged. There is a government: the club committee; and often special displays of the tribal elders: the photographs or portraits of previous officials on the walls. At the heart of the specialized territories there is a powerful feeling of security and importance, a sense of shared defence against the outside world. Much of the club chatter, both serious and joking, directs itself against the rottenness of everything outside the club boundaries—in that "other world" beyond the protected portals.

In social organizations which embody a strong class system, 9 such as military units and large business concerns, there are many territorial rules, often unspoken, which interfere with the official hierarchy. High-status individuals, such as officers or managers, could in theory enter any of the regions occupied by the lower levels in the pecking order, but they limit this power in a striking way. An officer seldom enters a sergeant's mess or a barrack room unless it is for a formal inspection. He respects those regions as alien territories even though he has the power to go there by virtue of his dominant role. And in businesses, part of the appeal of unions, over and above their obvious functions, is that with their officials, headquarters and meetings they add a sense of territorial power for the staff workers. It is almost as if each military organization and business concern consists of two warring tribes: the officers versus the other ranks, and the management versus the workers. Each has its special home base within the system, and the territorial defence pattern thrusts itself into what, on the surface, is a pure social hierarchy. Negotiations between managements and unions are tribal battles fought out over the neutral ground of a boardroom table, and are as much concerned with territorial display as they are with resolving problems of wages and conditions. Indeed, if one side gives in too quickly and accepts the other's demands, the victors feel strangely cheated and deeply suspicious that it may be a trick. What they are missing is the protracted sequence of ritual and counter-ritual that keeps alive their group territorial identity.

Likewise, many of the hostile displays of sports fans and teen- 10 age gangs are primarily concerned with displaying their group image to rival fan-clubs and gangs. Except in rare cases, they do not attack one another's headquarters, drive out the occupants, and reduce them to a submissive, subordinate condition. It is enough to have scuffles on the borderlands between the two rival territories. This is particularly clear at football matches, where the fan-club headquarters becomes temporarily shifted from the club-house to a section of the stands, and where minor fighting breaks out at the unofficial boundary line between the massed groups of rival supporters. Newspaper reports play up the few accidents and injuries which do occur on such occasions, but when they are studied in relation to the total numbers of displaying fans involved, it is clear that the serious incidents represent only a tiny fraction of the overall group behaviour. For every actual punch or kick there are a thousand war-cries, war-dances, chants and gestures.

Second: the Family Territory. Essentially, the family is a breeding unit and the family territory is a breeding ground. At the centre of this space, there is the nest—the bedroom—where, tucked up in bed, we feel at our most territorially secure. In a typical house the bedroom is upstairs, where a safe nest should be. This puts it farther away from the entrance hall, the area where contact is made, intermittently, with the outside world. The less private reception rooms, where intruders are allowed access, are the next line of defence. Beyond them, outside the walls of the building, there is often a symbolic remnant of the ancient feeding grounds—a garden. Its symbolism often extends to the plants and animals it contains, which cease to be nutritional and become merely decorative—flowers and pets. But like a true territorial space it has a conspicuously displayed boundary-line, the garden fence, wall, or railings. Often no more than a token barrier, this is the outer territorial demarcation, separating the private world of the family from the public world beyond. To cross it puts any visitor or intruder at an immediate disadvantage. As he crosses the threshold, his dominance wanes, slightly but unmistakably. He is entering an area where he senses that he must ask permission to do simple things that he would consider a right elsewhere. Without lifting a finger, the territorial owners exert their dominance. This is done by all the hundreds of small ownership "markers" they have deposited on their family territory: the ornaments, the "possessed" objects positioned in the rooms and on the walls; the furnishings, the furniture, the colours, the patterns, all owner-chosen and all making this particular home base unique to them.

It is one of the tragedies of modern architecture that there has been a standardization of these vital territorial living units. One of the most important aspects of a home is that it should be similar to other homes only in a general way, and that in detail it should have many differences, making it a *particular* home. Unfortunately, it is cheaper to build a row of houses, or a block of flats, so that all the family living-units are identical, but the territorial urge rebels against this trend and house-owners struggle as best they can to make their mark on their mass-produced properties. They do this with garden-design, with front-door colours, with curtain patterns, with wallpaper and all the other decorative elements that together create a unique and different family environment. Only when they have completed this nest-building do they feel truly "at home" and secure.

When they venture forth as a family unit, they repeat the process in a minor way. On a day-trip to the seaside, they load the car with personal belongings and it becomes their temporary, portable territory. Arriving at the beach, they stake out a small territorial claim, marking it with rugs, towels, baskets and other belongings to which they can return from their seaboard wanderings. Even if they all leave it at once to bathe, it retains a characteristic territorial quality and other family groups arriving will recognize this by setting up their own "home" bases at a respectful distance. Only when the whole beach has filled up with these marked spaces will newcomers start to position themselves in such a way that the inter-base distance becomes reduced. Forced to pitch between several existing beach territories, they will feel a momentary sensation of intrusion, and the established "owners" will feel a similar sensation of invasion, even though they are not being directly inconvenienced. 13

The same territorial scene is being played out in parks and fields and on riverbanks, wherever family groups gather in their clustered units. But if rivalry for spaces creates mild feelings of hostility, it is true to say that without the territorial system of sharing and space-limited dominance, there would be chaotic disorder. 14

Third: the Personal Space. If a man enters a waiting-room and sits at one end of a long row of empty chairs, it is possible to predict where the next man to enter will seat himself. He will not sit next to the first man, nor will he sit at the far end, right away from him. He will choose a position about halfway between these two points. The next man to enter will take the largest gap left, and sit roughly in the middle of that, and so on, until eventually the latest newcomer will be forced to select a seat that places him right next 15 to one of the already seated men. Similar patterns can be observed in cinemas, public urinals, airplanes, trains and buses. This is a reflection of the fact that we all carry with us, everywhere we go, a portable territory called a Personal Space. If people move inside this space, we feel threatened. If they keep too far outside it, we feel rejected. The result is a subtle series of spatial adjustments, usually operating quite unconsciously and producing ideal compromises as far as this is possible. If a situation becomes too crowded, then we adjust our reactions accordingly and allow our personal space to shrink. Jammed into an elevator, a rush-hour compartment, or a packed room, we give up altogether and allow body-to-body contact, but when we relinquish our Personal Space in this way, we adopt certain special techniques. In essence, what we do is to convert these other bodies into "nonpersons." We studiously ignore them, and they us. We try not to face them if we can possibly avoid it. We wipe all expressiveness from our faces, letting them go blank. We may look up at the ceiling or down at the floor, and we reduce body movements to a minimum. Packed together like sardines in a tin, we stand dumbly still, sending out as few social signals as possible.

Even if the crowding is less severe, we still tend to cut down our social interactions in the presence of large numbers. Careful observations of children in play groups revealed that if they are high-density groupings there is less social interaction between the individual children, even though there is theoretically more opportunity for such contacts. At the same time, the high-density groups show a higher frequency of aggressive and destructive behaviour patterns in their play. Personal Space—"elbow room"—is a vital commodity for the human animal, and one that cannot be ignored without risking serious trouble.

Of course, we all enjoy the excitement of being in a crowd, and this reaction cannot be ignored. But there are crowds and crowds. It is pleasant enough to be in a "spectator crowd," but not also appealing to find yourself in the middle of a rush-hour crush. The difference between the two is that the spectator crowd is all facing in the same direction and concentrating on a distant point of interest. Attending a theatre, there are twinges of rising hostility towards the stranger who sits down immediately in front of you or the one who squeezes into the seat next to you. The shared armrest can become a polite, but distinct, territorial boundary-dispute region. However, as soon as the show begins, these invasions of Personal Space are forgotten and the attention is focused beyond the small space where the crowding is taking place. Now, each member of the audience feels himself spatially related, not to his cramped neighbours, but to the actor on the stage, and this distance is, if anything, too great. In the rush-hour crowd, by contrast, each member of the pushing throng is competing with his neighbours all the time. There is no escape to a spatial relation with a distant actor, only the pushing, shoving bodies all around.

Those of us who have to spend a great deal of time in crowded 18 conditions become gradually better able to adjust, but no one can ever become completely immune to invasions of Personal Space. This is because they remain forever associated with either powerful hostile or equally powerful loving feelings. All through our childhood we will have been held to be loved and held to be hurt, and anyone who invades our Personal Space when we are adults is, in effect, threatening to extend his behaviour into one of these two highly charged areas of human interaction. Even if his motives are clearly neither hostile nor sexual, we still find it hard to suppress our reactions to his close approach. Unfortunately, different countries have different ideas about exactly how close is close. It is easy enough to test your own "space reaction": when you are talking to someone in the street or in any open space, reach out with your arm and see where the nearest point on his body comes. If you hail from western Europe, you will find that he is at roughly fingertip distance from you. In other words, as you reach out, your fingertips will just about make contact with his shoulder. If you come from eastern Europe, you will find you are standing at "wrist distance." If you come from the Mediterranean region, you will find that you are much closer to your companion, a little more than "elbow distance."

Trouble begins when a member of one of these cultures meets 19 and talks to one from another. Say a British diplomat meets an Italian or an Arab diplomat at an embassy function. They start talking in a friendly way, but soon the fingertips man begins to feel uneasy. Without knowing quite why, he starts to back away gently from his companion. The companion edges forward again. Each tries in his way to set up a Personal Space relationship that suits his own background. But it is impossible to do. Every time the

Mediterranean diplomat advances to a distance that feels comfortable for him, the British diplomat feels threatened. Every time the Briton moves back, the other feels rejected. Attempts to adjust this situation often lead to a talking pair shifting slowly across a room, and many an embassy reception is dotted with western-European fingertip-distance men pinned against the walls by eager elbow-distance men. Until such differences are fully understood and allowances made, these minor differences in "body territories" will continue to act as an alienation factor which may interfere in a subtle way with diplomatic harmony and other forms of international transaction.

If there are distance problems when engaged in conversation, then there are clearly going to be even bigger difficulties where people must work privately in a shared space. Close proximity of others, pressing against the invisible boundaries of our personal body-territory, makes it difficult to concentrate on non-social matters. Flat-mates, students sharing a study, sailors in the cramped quarters of a ship, and office staff in crowded work-places, all have to face this problem. They solve it by "cocooning." They use a variety of devices to shut themselves off from the others present. The best possible cocoon, of course, is a small private room—a den, a private office, a study or a studio—which physically obscures the presence of other nearby territory-owners. This is the ideal situation for non-social work, but the space-sharers cannot enjoy this luxury. Their cocooning must be symbolic. They may, in certain cases, be able to erect small physical barriers, such as screens and partitions, which give substance to their invisible Personal Space boundaries, but when this cannot be done, other means must be sought. One of these is the "favoured object." Each space-sharer develops a preference, repeatedly expressed until it becomes a fixed pattern, for a particular chair, or table, or alcove. Others come to respect this, and friction is reduced. This system is often formally arranged (this is my desk, that is yours), but even where it is not, favoured places soon develop. Professor Smith has a favourite chair in the library. It is not formally his, but he always uses it and others avoid it. Seats around a messroom table, or a boardroom table, become almost personal property for specific individuals. Even in the home, father has his favourite chair for reading the newspaper or watching television. Another device is the blinkers-posture. Just as a horse that over-reacts to other horses and the distractions of the noisy race-course is given a pair of blinkers to shield its eyes, so people studying privately in a public place put on pseudo-blinkers in the form of shielding hands. Resting their elbows on the table, they sit with their hands screening their eyes from the scene on either side.

A third method of reinforcing the body-territory is to use per- 21
sonal markers. Books, papers and other personal belongings are scattered around the favoured site to render it more privately owned in the eyes of companions. Spreading out one's belongings is a well-known trick in public-transport situations, where a travel-ler tries to give the impression that seats next to him are taken. In many contexts carefully arranged personal markers can act as an effective territorial display, even in the absence of the territory owner. Experiments in a library revealed that placing a pile of mag-azines on the table in one seating position successfully reserved that place for an average of 77 minutes. If a sports-jacket was added, draped over the chair, then the "reservation effect" lasted for over two hours.

In these ways, we strengthen the defences of our Personal 22
Spaces, keeping out intruders with the minimum of open hostility. As with all territorial behaviour, the object is to defend space with signals rather than with fists and at all three levels—the tribal, the family and the personal—it is a remarkably efficient system of space-sharing. It does not always seem so, because newspapers and newscasts inevitably magnify the exceptions and dwell on those cases where the signals have failed and wars have broken out, gangs have fought, neighbouring families have feuded, or col-leagues have clashed, but for every territorial signal that has failed, there are millions of others that have not. They do not rate a men-tion in the news, but they nevertheless constitute a dominant fea-ture of human society—the society of a remarkably territorial an-imal.

Meanings and Values

1. What are the characteristics that enable you to classify this selec-tion as formal, informal, or familiar? (See Guide to Terms: *Essay.*)

2a. What are some of the "socially valid" reasons that justify evicting a family from its home (par. 2)?

b. If you think there are no such valid reasons, justify your stand.

3a. List other subgroups that give members a "powerful feeling of security and importance" (par. 8).

b.   What are the territorial signals of each group?

4a. In one sentence, state the central theme of this selection. (Guide: *Unity.*)

b.   Does the writing have unity? Why, or why not?

5a. What was the author's apparent purpose?

b.   How successfully does he accomplish this purpose?

c.   How worthwhile was it? Why?

Expository Techniques

1a. Is this classification system logical, complete, and consistent in all respects? Cite any exceptions and state what is wrong.

b.   What other basis can you suggest for organizing the discussion of the territorial behavior of humans? Which do you prefer? Why?

2a. Into how many categories does the author divide the solutions of people sharing cramped living or working quarters?

b.   Cite two of the solutions in each division.

3a. Demonstrate the value of using examples by eliminating them entirely from any one portion of this selection, leaving only the generalities.

b.   What would be the effect on the reader?

4a. It is possible (but not very rewarding) to argue about whether this selection has a one-paragraph or a five-paragraph introduction. Assuming the latter to be the author's intention, which of the standard introductory techniques does he use? (Guide: *Introductions.*)

b.   How successfully does he perform the four potential functions of an introduction? Be specific.

Diction and Vocabulary

1.   How can you account for the unusual spelling of some of the words, such as "behaviour" (title), "defence" (par. 2), and "colours" (par. 11)?

2.   Why do you think the author considered the word *"displayed"* important enough to be italicized (par. 3)?

3a. Of what might a "symbolic" exploding into battle consist (par. 4)?

b.   What makes some of the barriers listed in paragraph 20 "symbolic"?

c.   Explain how the uses of "symbolic" and "symbolically" in these paragraphs and in paragraphs 5, 7, and 11 are, or are not, consistent with the discussion of "symbol" in this book. (Guide: *Symbol.*)

4a. What, if anything, is noteworthy about the diction or syntax of this selection? (Guide: *Diction and Syntax.*)

b. To what extent, if at all, is Morris's writing characterized by his style? (Guide: *Style/Tone.*) You may want to compare his style, or lack of it, with that of an author previously read.

Suggestions for Writing and Discussion

1. Select one of the subgroups listed in answering question 3 of "Meanings and Values" and discuss it more fully—explaining, perhaps, just what the members get out of belonging.

2. The owners of a home also assert their dominance through subtle and unconscious actions as well as objects. Discuss these actions and explain why such asserted dominance is not resented by the average visitor.

3. Most of Morris's discussion of family territory seems to refer to family-owned homes. What are the limitations on renters, especially of apartments, in displaying their territorial signals? To what extent do you suppose a desire for greater territorial display contributes to most people's dream of one day owning their own home?

(NOTE: Suggestions for topics requiring development by use of CLASSIFICATION are on page 76, at the end of this section.)

PETER MARSH

PETER MARSH has devoted his career to studying and writing about patterns of human behavior. Currently, he is senior lecturer in social psychology at Oxford Polytechnic and co-director of the Contemporary Violence Research Unit at Oxford University. Marsh has written or co-authored numerous books, including *Rules of Disorder* (1968), *Aggro: The Illusion of Violence* (1978), *Gestures: Their Origins and Distribution* (1979) (with Desmond Morris and others), *Driving Passion: The Psychology of the Car* (1986), and *Tribes* (1988).

Tribes[1]

"Tribes," a section from Marsh's book with the same title, looks in depth at one of the categories discussed by Desmond Morris in the preceding essay. The tribes identified in this piece, however, are not formal organizations but informal (and short-lived) social groupings based on similarities in fashion and lifestyle. The economic and cultural impact of such groups is often considerable, however, and they are characteristic features of modern society. For the student of composition, this selection demonstrates the importance of specific detail in establishing and explaining categories.

Many modern societies are now fast approaching their limits in terms of size and the impersonality which that size creates. Increasingly we witness violent reactions in massive urban developments to the alienation experienced by their inhabitants. Many young people, in particular, find no source of identity or sense of belonging in a world which often disowns them, and so turn in-

1

"Social Groupings in Modern Society" from *Tribes* by Peter Marsh. Copyright © 1988 by Peter Marsh. Reprinted by permission of the author.
[1]Editors' title.

creasingly to alternative youth cultures in which they can be *some-body*. In the harshness of economic recession, this quest for identity, coupled with the anger engendered by disadvantage, is expressed in the aggression of the youth gang or in declarations of solidarity which require a clearly defined enemy. Racism, anti-Semitism, and other types of victimization of "out-groups" occur when a sense of frustration is fuelled by feelings of anonymity and detachment. For some members of our 20th-century cultures, the only way of fully understanding themselves is to establish whom they are against.

While on the one hand a sense of injustice and disenchant- 2
ment gives rise to tribalism, sometimes with destructive consequences, the same drive for social bonding is equally evident among the more affluent and successful members of our societies—so much so that social labelling among the new professional groups has become increasingly common. The term "Yuppie" (young, upwardly mobile professional) originated in the 1980s in the United States as a description of a new breed of rising entrepreneurs. Once the term had been coined, people started to identify with this distinctive label and positively to aspire to the lifestyle it denoted. Soon the Yuppies became a tribe of people with similar jobs, style of language, interests, tastes and attitudes. The Filofax, or "personal organizer," became more than just a high-priced diary and address book: now it was a symbol of allegiance to a cultural unit.

In the wake of the Yuppies have come other middle-class 3
tribes, each with equally distinctive acronymic nicknames, and it is now fashionable to describe people in terms of their social tribe. Up-market glossy magazines regularly carry features informing their readers about the current labels and the groups to which they refer. Although such articles are usually quite trivial, they reveal the rising need for people to define themselves in terms of their lifestyles and to feel a sense of affiliation with those who share them.

In Britain, this trend towards tribal definitions and labels was 4
undoubtedly given a boost by Peter York and his reported "discovery" of the Sloane Rangers—affluent young people who lived in fashionable areas such as that around London's Sloane Square. Writing with an appropriate sense of cynicism, he described the world of this particular section of British upper-middle-class society in the way an anthropologist might talk of a distinctive African

culture. Sloanes could be identified by the fact that they wore green wellington boots and waxed jackets, drove Golf GTIs and virtually lived out their lives in wine bars. A simplistic but not totally inaccurate caricature, this description soon became much more of a reality as young people in that stratum of society identified themselves with the image and adopted both the Sloane style and the attitudes that went with it.

Young Fogeys have of course always been around in the rarefied atmosphere of Oxford, Cambridge, Harvard and other ''prestige'' universities, but it was only in the 1980s that the name began to be applied. Their reactionary views, traditional styles of dress and feigned disinterest in the real world of work and the professions typified them, and their distinctiveness was reinforced by the emergence of brash, stylish and energetic groups of upstarts.

Yuppies were, and still are, the antithesis of the establishment order, relying on their talents and business acumen rather than on inherited wealth or the old school tie. It is through such clear contrasts that tribal unity is made concrete. While the Yuppie, the Sloane and the Young Fogey do indeed have common interests and values, this commonality is enhanced by the experience of distance from other clearly defined collectives. As one tribe emerges, others are spawned in its shadow.

Dinkies, for example, emerged as a Yuppie splinter group, embracing an especially single-minded segment of the new professional classes. ''Double Income, No Kids'' couples were able to carve out a particularly identifiable stylish lifestyle because their considerable disposable income was not squandered on raising offspring and sending them to smart schools. In contrast were the Drabbies, the staid but ideologically sound tribe with several children and socially useful jobs as teachers, social workers, etc. Yummies (Young Urban Mothers), Swells (Single Women Earning Lots in London) and Spoolers (Stripped Pine, Olive Oil, Laura Ashley) also became the subject of dinner-table talk.

While the terms used to describe such tribes are rather ephemeral, they reflect the ever-increasing need for people to define themselves as members of distinct subgroups of the population. The reality of such groupings is revealed not only in the plethora of labels but more directly in new trends in market-research techniques. In order to market and sell goods effectively, major companies have to identify particular segments of the population and target their advertising accordingly. There is little point, for example, in advertising expensive designer-label jewellery in mass-circulation magazines bought by people who cannot possibly afford such luxury items; by contrast, an advertisement placed in a low-circulation "quality" magazine may produce an impressive response. Increasingly, however, the marketing people are finding that the traditional demographic measures, based primarily on social class and income levels, are not sufficiently sensitive or sophisticated. The aim of the newer methods is to identify the social tribes to which people belong and the size and characteristic features of each of those tribes. Known as "values and lifestyles analysis," the approach is little interested in knowledge simply of people's income or social background: that does not permit a sufficient distinction between the various types of potential customer, and nor does it predict with any degree of accuracy which newspapers people read, what they watch on television, or the range of articles they might be interested in purchasing.

Identifying people in terms of the discrete social groupings [9] they belong to, defined in terms of aspirations, tastes, values and particular lifestyles, allows marketing departments to determine very easily the size of the market for various products and the channels through which advertising should be directed. Where there are several segments of the population to whom a particular product might appeal, the manner in which an item is advertised can be tailored to each of them so that it appeals directly to their tribal affiliations.

This commercial realization of patterns of collective bonding [10] is, perhaps, the best evidence for tribalism in modern societies. We may make jokes about the names of trendy middle-class groupings, or prefer to think of ourselves as free, independent spirits, owing allegiance to no group in particular, but most of us in actuality find it hard to escape categorization. Modern tribes consist not merely of the ostentatious youth cults, with their elaborate hairstyles and seemingly perverse tastes in clothing. Nor is it only members of esoteric institutions, secret societies, clubs and associations who strive to achieve distinctive collective unity. All of us rely on others for our sense of self and identity. Where the scale of our culture denies us a true sense of belonging, we conspire to scale things down—to create units in which we can be human. In other words, tribes.

Meanings and Values

1a.   What three main groups does Marsh discuss in this selection?

  b.   In what ways are the groups similar? (In answering this question consider traits such as social class, age, and moral or social values.)

  c.   What groups does Marsh mention briefly?

2.   Summarize the explanation Marsh offers in paragraphs 8–10 to support his conclusion that "the best evidence for tribalism in modern societies" is the "commercial realization" of social groups (par. 10).

3.   If you have read Desmond Morris's essay "Territorial Behaviour," discuss how the kinds of tribes he identifies differ from those outlined in this selection.

4.   Why does the author believe that people in modern society form tribes?

Expository Techniques

1.   Where in the second paragraph is the central theme of this selection stated? (See Guide to Terms: *Unity.*)

2a.   Identify the specific details Marsh uses to characterize each of the following groups: Yuppies, Sloane Rangers, Drabbies, Spoolers.

  b.   What objects or activities are identified in paragraphs 2, 4, and 7 that might be said to symbolize particular groups? (Guide: *Symbol.*)

3.   Are the categories Marsh presents distinct enough and clear enough for the purposes of this piece? Does it matter, for example, that Dinkies might be considered a kind of Yuppie and not a distinct group? (Guide: *Purpose, Evaluation.*)

4.   Groupings like those described by Marsh come and go rapidly. Is the effectiveness of the writing or the central theme of the selection likely to be undermined if some or all of its categories seem dated to a reader? Why, or why not? (Guide: *Evaluation.*)

Diction and Vocabulary

1a.   To what does the name "Sloane Rangers" allude? (Guide: *Figures of Speech.*)

  b.   What evidence is there that Marsh or the originator of the term, Peter York, intended it to be applied ironically? (Guide: *Irony.*)

2a.   In what ways is the vocabulary in this selection characteristic of writing in the social sciences, such as anthropology, sociology, or psychology?

  b.   In paragraphs 1, 2, and 8–10 the author employs a number of relatively technical terms. How, if at all, do they add to or reinforce the meaning of the paragraphs?

   c.   Do technical terms detract from the meaning or clarity of any passages, at least for the average reader? If so, which sections are most likely to trouble readers? (Guide: *Diction*.)

3.   If you do not know the meaning of any of the following words, look them up in a dictionary: alienation, engendered, disadvantage, solidarity (par. 1); entrepreneurs (2); acronymic (3); cynicism, simplistic, caricature (4); rarefied, reactionary, feigned, disinterest (5); antithesis, acumen (6); staid (7); ephemeral, plethora (8); ostentatious, esoteric (10).

Suggestions for Writing and Discussion

1.   Identify and discuss any new social groups based on lifestyle that have arisen since this essay was published.

2.   Many would argue that it is unfair to characterize people according to the kinds of groupings Marsh presents because individuals are much more complex than his categories suggest. Based on the essay, how do you think Marsh might respond to this criticism? To what extent do you agree or disagree with the criticism?

3.   Prepare an essay of your own dividing artists, entertainers, politicians, physicians, or other professionals into groups based on categories appropriate to their activities. You might, for example, decide to classify physicians according to their skill in dealing with patients or politicians according to their ability to inspire people.

(NOTE: Suggestions for topics requiring development by CLASSIFICATION follow.)

Writing Suggestions for Section 2
Classification

Use division and classification (into at least three categories) as your basic method of analyzing one of the following subjects from one interesting point of view. (Your instructor may have good reason to place limitations on your choice of subject.) Narrow the topic as necessary to enable you to do a thorough job.

1. College students.
2. College teachers.
3. Athletes.
4. Coaches.
5. Salespeople.
6. Hunters (or fishermen).
7. Parents.
8. Drug users.
9. Police officers.
10. Summer (or part-time) jobs.
11. Sailing vessels.
12. Game show hosts.
13. Friends.
14. Careers.
15. Horses (or other animals).
16. Television programs.
17. Motivations for study.
18. Methods of studying for exams.
19. Lies.
20. Selling techniques.
21. Tastes in clothes.
22. Contemporary music.
23. Love.
24. Ways to spend money.
25. Attitudes toward life.
26. Fast foods (or junk foods).
27. Smokers.
28. Investments.
29. Actors.
30. Books or magazines.

3

Explaining by Means of *Comparison* and *Contrast*

One of the first expository methods we used as children was *comparison*, noticing similarities of objects, qualities, and actions, or *contrast*, noticing their differences. We compared the color of the new puppies with that of their mother, contrasted our father's height with our own. Then the process became more complicated. Now we employ it frequently in college essay examinations or term papers when we compare or contrast forms of government, reproductive systems of animals, or ethical philosophies of humans. Later, in the business or professional world, we may prepare important reports based on comparison and contrast—between kinds of equipment for purchase, the personnel policies of different departments, or precedents in legal matters. Nearly all people use the process, though they may not be aware of this, many times a day—in choosing a head of lettuce, in deciding what to wear to school, in selecting a house or a friend or a religion.

In the more formal scholastic and professional uses of comparison and contrast, however, an ordered plan is needed to avoid having a mere list of characteristics or a frustrating jumble of similarities and differences. If authors want to avoid communication blocks that will prevent their "getting through" to their readers, they will observe a few basic principles of selection and development. These principles apply mostly to comparisons between two subjects only; if three or more are to be considered, they should be grouped to make the discussion easy to follow.

A *logical* comparison or contrast can be made only between subjects of the same general type. (Analogy, a special form of comparison used for another purpose, is discussed in the next section.)

For example, contrasting a pine and a maple could be useful or meaningful, but little would be gained, except exercise in sentence construction, by contrasting the pine and the pansy.

Of course, logical but informal comparisons that are merely incidental to the basic structure, and hence follow no special pattern, may be made in any writing. Several of the preceding selections make limited use of comparison and contrast; Viorst does some contrasting of types of showoffs, and Desmond Morris uses some comparison between tribal territorial behavior now and in prehistoric times. But once committed to a formal, full-scale analysis by comparison and contrast, the careful writer ordinarily gives the subjects similar treatment. Points used for one should also be used for the other, and usually in the same order. All pertinent points should be explored—pertinent, that is, to the purpose of the comparison.

The purpose and the complexity of materials will usually indicate their arrangement and use. Sometimes the purpose is merely to point out *what* the likenesses and differences are, sometimes it is to show the *superiority* of one thing over another—or possibly to convince the reader of the superiority, as this is also a technique of argumentation. The purpose may be to explain the *unfamiliar* (wedding customs in Ethiopia) by comparing it to the *familiar* (wedding customs in Kansas). Or it may be to explain or emphasize some other type of *central idea,* as in most of the essays in this section.

One of the two basic methods of comparison is to present all the information on the two subjects, one at a time, and to summarize by combining their most important similarities and differences. This method may be desirable if there are few points to compare, or if the individual points are less important than the overall picture they present. Therefore, this procedure might be a satisfactory means of showing the relative difficulty of two college courses or of comparing two viewpoints concerning an automobile accident. (Of course, as in all other matters of expository arrangement, the last subject discussed is in the most emphatic position.)

However, if there are several points of comparison to be considered, or if the points are of individual importance, alternation of the material would be a better arrangement. Hence, in a detailed comparison of Oak Valley and Elm Hill hospitals, we might compare their sizes, locations, surgical facilities, staffs, and so on, always in the same order. To tell all about Oak Valley and then all about Elm Hill would create a serious communication block, requiring readers constantly to call on their memory of what was cited earlier or to turn back to the first group of facts again and again in order to make the meaningful comparisons that the author should have made for them.

Often the subject matter or the purpose itself will suggest a more casual treatment, or some combination or variation of the two basic methods. We might present the complete information on the first subject, then summarize it point by point within the complete information on the second. In other circumstances (as in "The Spider and the Wasp" in Section 5), it may be desirable simply to set up the thesis of likeness or difference, and then to explain a *process* that demonstrates this thesis. And although expository comparisons and contrasts are frequently handled together, it is sometimes best to present all similarities first, then all differences—or vice versa, depending on the emphasis desired. In argument, the arrangement we choose is that which best demonstrates the superiority of one thing (or plan of action) over another. This may mean a point-by-point contrast or the presentation of a weaker alternative before a stronger one.

In any basic use of comparison (conveniently, the term is most often used in a general sense to cover both comparison and contrast), the important thing is to have a plan that suits the purpose and material thoughtfully worked out in advance.

Sample Paragraph (Annotated)

(Topic sentence of paragraph. Also a very vague generality, to be made more specific by examples.)

Comparison, noting likenesses, using the point-by-point method.

("Apple-pie . . . art": metaphor.)

("Booze": colloquial usage, consistent only with an informal style.)

Who can tell what a town is really like by looking at it! Riverton is a prosperous place of 3,127 people, three miles from the river; ten miles further up, on the other side, is equally prosperous Eden, population, 3,120 people. Both places are good to look at, could easily be models for some apple-pie calendar art. And they are alike in another respect: nobody in either place knows what makes their people so different. Riverton's six churches are full on Sundays and Wednesday nights. The sale of booze was banned

Transitional, to other side of contrast.

Contrast, noting differences. Discusses several aspects of one town, then turns to the other.

("Shady ladies": colloquial.)

Simple, direct use of *contrast*.

in 1960; there are no dance halls, card games, or shady ladies. But anyone who wants a wilder time than the square dance sponsored monthly by the Town Board can always go up to Eden, where there's only one church, poorly attended and in need of paint, but five thriving taverns. Most of these feature shady ladies, dark dance floors, and wicked-looking card rooms in back. Several broad-minded couples even formed a "free-trade society" called the Swinging Dingles. But last year in Riverton when a new dentist tried to start a similar diversion, they promptly arrested him for disturbing the peace and took him to the county jail over on the coast.

Sample Paragraph (Comparison/Contrast)

Large computers have some essential attributes of an intelligent brain: they have large memories, and they have gates whose connections can be modified by experience. However, the thinking of these computers tends to be narrow. The richness of human thought depends to a considerable degree on the enormous number of wires, or nerve fibers, coming into each gate in the human brain. A gate in a computer has two, or three, or at most four wires entering on one side, and one wire coming out the other side. In the brain of an animal, the gates may have thousands of wires entering one side, instead of two or three. In the human brain, a gate may have as many as 100,000 wires entering it. Each wire comes from another gate or nerve cell. This means that every gate in the human brain is connected to as many as 100,000 other gates in other parts of the brain. During the process of thinking innumerable gates open and close throughout the brain. When one of these gates ''decides'' to open, the decision is the result of a complicated assessment involving inputs from thousands of other gates. This circumstance explains much of the difference between human thinking and computer thinking.

MARK TWAIN was the pen name of Samuel Clemens (1835–1910). He was born in Missouri and became the first author of importance to emerge from "beyond the Mississippi." Although best known for bringing humor, realism, and Western local color to American fiction, Mark Twain wanted to be remembered as a philosopher and social critic. Still widely read, in most languages and in all parts of the world, are his numerous short stories (his "tall tales," in particular), autobiographical accounts, and novels, especially *Adventures of Huckleberry Finn* (1884). Ernest Hemingway called the last "the best book we've had," an appraisal with which many critics agree.

Two Ways of Seeing a River

"Two Ways of Seeing a River" (editors' title) is from Mark Twain's "Old Times on the Mississippi," which was later expanded and published in book form as *Life on the Mississippi* (1883). It is autobiographical. The prose of this selection is vivid, as in all of Mark Twain's writing, but considerably more reflective in tone than most.

Now when I had mastered the language of this water and had come to know every trifling feature that bordered the great river as familiarly as I knew the letters of the alphabet, I had made a valuable acquisition. But I had lost something, too. I had lost something which could never be restored to me while I lived. All the grace, the beauty, the poetry, had gone out of the majestic river! I still kept in mind a certain wonderful sunset which I witnessed when steamboating was new to me. A broad expanse of the river was turned to blood; in the middle distance the red hue brightened into gold, through which a solitary log came floating, black and conspicuous; in one place a long, slanting mark lay sparkling upon the water; in another the surface was broken by boiling, tumbling

1

rings that were as many-tinted as an opal; where the ruddy flush was faintest was a smooth spot that was covered with graceful circles and radiating lines, ever so delicately traced; the shore on our left was densely wooded, and the somber shadow that fell from this forest was broken in one place by a long, ruffled trail that shone like silver; and high above the forest wall a clean-stemmed dead tree waved a single leafy bough that glowed like a flame in the unobstructed splendor that was flowing from the sun. There were graceful curves, reflected images, woody heights, soft distances, and over the whole scene, far and near, the dissolving lights drifted steadily, enriching it every passing moment with new marvels of coloring.

I stood like one bewitched. I drank it in, in a speechless rapture. The world was new to me and I had never seen anything like this at home. But as I have said, a day came when I began to cease from noting the glories and the charms which the moon and the sun and the twilight wrought upon the river's face; another day came when I ceased altogether to note them. Then, if that sunset scene had been repeated, I should have looked upon it without rapture and should have commented upon it inwardly after this fashion: ''This sun means that we are going to have wind tomorrow; that floating log means that the river is rising, small thanks to it; that slanting mark on the water refers to a bluff reef which is going to kill somebody's steamboat one of these nights, if it keeps on stretching out like that; those tumbling 'boils' show a dissolving bar and a changing channel there; the lines and circles in the slick water over yonder are a warning that that troublesome place is shoaling up dangerously; that silver streak in the shadow of the forest is the 'break' from a new snag and he has located himself in the very best place he could have found to fish for steamboats; that tall dead tree, with a single living branch, is not going to last long, and then how is a body ever going to get through this blind place at night without the friendly old landmark?''

No, the romance and beauty were all gone from the river. All the value any feature of it had for me now was the amount of usefulness it could furnish toward compassing the safe piloting of a steamboat. Since those days, I have pitied doctors from my heart. What does the lovely flush in a beauty's cheek mean to a doctor but a ''break'' that ripples above some deadly disease? Are not all her visible charms sown thick with what are to him the signs and symbols of hidden decay? Does he ever see her beauty at all, or doesn't he simply view her professionally and comment upon her unwholesome condition all to himself? And doesn't he sometimes wonder whether he has gained most or lost most by learning his trade?

Meanings and Values

1. No selection could better illustrate the intimate relationship of several skills with which students of writing should be familiar, especially the potentials in *point of view* (and attitude), *style,* and *tone.*

   a. What is the point of view in paragraph 1? (See Guide to Terms: *Point of View.*)

   b. Where, and how, does it change in paragraph 2?

   c. Why is the shift important to the author's contrast?

   d. Show how the noticeable change of tone is related to this change in point of view. (Guide: *Style/Tone.*)

   e. Specifically, what changes in style accompany the shift in tone and attitude?

   f. How effectively do they all relate to the central theme itself? (Remember that such effects seldom just "happen"; the writer *makes* them happen.)

   2a. Is the first paragraph primarily objective or subjective? (Guide: *Objective/Subjective.*)

   b. How about the latter part of paragraph 2?

   c. Are your answers to 2a and 2b related to point of view? If so, how?

   3a. Does the author permit himself to engage in sentimentality? (Guide: *Sentimentality.*) If so, how could it have been avoided without damage to his theme's development?

   b. If not, what restraints does the author use?

4. Do you think the last sentence refers only to doctors? Why, or why not?

5. List other vocations in which you assume (or perhaps know) that the beauty and romance eventually give way to practical realities; state briefly, for each, why this hardening should be expected.

Expository Techniques

1a. Where do you find a second comparison or contrast? Which is it?

   b. Is the comparison/contrast made within itself, with something external, or both? Explain.

c.   Is this part of the writing closely enough related to the major contrast to justify its use? Why, or why not?

2a.   In developing the numerous points of the major contrast, would an alternating, point-to-point system have been better? Why, or why not?

b.   Show how the author uses organization within the groups to assist in the overall contrast.

3a.   What is the most noteworthy feature of syntax in paragraphs 1 and 2? (Guide: *Syntax*.)

b.   How effectively does it perform the function intended?

4.   What is gained by the apparently deliberate decision to use rhetorical questions only toward the end? (Guide: *Rhetorical Questions*.)

Diction and Vocabulary

1.   Why would the colloquialism in the last sentence of paragraph 2 have been inappropriate in the first paragraph? (Guide: *Colloquial Expressions*.)

2a.   Compare the quality of metaphors in the quotation of paragraph 2 with the quality of those preceding it. (Guide: *Figures of Speech*.)

b.   Is the difference justified? Why, or why not?

Suggestions for Writing and Discussion

1.   Select for further development one of the vocations in your answer to question 5 of "Meanings and Values." How would one's attitude be apt to change from the beginning romantic appeal?

2.   Show how, if at all, Mark Twain's contrast might be used to show parallels to life itself—e.g., differences in the idealism and attitudes of youth and maturity.

3.   Explore the possibility, citing examples if possible, of being able to retain *both* the "rapture" and the "usefulness."

(NOTE: Suggestions for topics requiring development by use of COMPARISON and CONTRAST are on page 114, at the end of this section.)

BRUCE CATTON

BRUCE CATTON (1899–1978) was a Civil War specialist whose early career included reporting for various newspapers. In 1954 he received both the Pulitzer Prize for historical work and the National Book Award. He served as director of information for the United States Department of Commerce and wrote many books, including *Mr. Lincoln's Army* (1951), *Glory Road* (1952), *A Stillness at Appomattox* (1953), *The Hallowed Ground* (1956), *America Goes to War* (1958), *The Coming Fury* (1961), *Terrible Swift Sword* (1963), *Never Call Retreat* (1966), *Waiting for the Morning Train: An American Boyhood* (1972), and *Gettysburg: The Final Fury* (1974). For five years, Catton edited *American Heritage*.

Grant and Lee: A Study in Contrasts

''Grant and Lee: A Study in Contrasts'' was written as a chapter of *The American Story*, a collection of essays by noted historians. In this study, as in most of his other writing, Catton does more than recount the facts of history: he shows the significance within them. It is a carefully constructed essay, using contrast and comparison as the entire framework for his explanation.

When Ulysses S. Grant and Robert E. Lee met in the parlor of a 1 modest house at Appomattox Court House, Virginia, on April 9, 1865, to work out the terms for the surrender of Lee's Army of Northern Virginia, a great chapter in American life came to a close, and a great new chapter began.

These men were bringing the Civil War to its virtual finish. To 2 be sure, other armies had yet to surrender, and for a few days the fugitive Confederate government would struggle desperately and vainly, trying to find some way to go on living now that its chief

From *The American Story*, Earl Schenck Miers, editor. © 1956 by Broadcast Music, Inc. Copyright renewed 1984. Reprinted by permission of the U.S. Capitol Historical Society.

support was gone. But in effect it was all over when Grant and Lee signed the papers. And the little room where they wrote out the terms was the scene of one of the poignant, dramatic contrasts in American history.

They were two strong men these oddly different generals, and they represented the strengths of two conflicting currents that, through them, had come into final collision. 3

Back of Robert E. Lee was the notion that the old aristocratic concept might somehow survive and be dominant in American life. 4

Lee was tidewater Virginia, and in his background were family, culture, and tradition . . . the age of chivalry transplanted to a New World which was making its own legends and its own myths. He embodied a way of life that had come down through the age of knighthood and the English country squire. America was a land that was beginning all over again, dedicated to nothing much more complicated than the rather hazy belief that all men had equal rights and should have an equal chance in the world. In such a land Lee stood for the feeling that it was somehow of advantage to human society to have a pronounced inequality in the social structure. There should be a leisure class, backed by ownership of land; in turn, society itself should be keyed to the land as the chief source of wealth and influence. It would bring forth (according to this ideal) a class of men with a strong sense of obligation to the community; men who lived not to gain advantage for themselves, but to meet the solemn obligations which had been laid on them by the very fact that they were privileged. From them the country would get its leadership; to them it could look for the higher values—of thought, of conduct, or personal deportment—to give it strength and virtue. 5

Lee embodied the noblest elements of this aristocratic ideal. Through him, the landed nobility justified itself. For four years, the Southern states had fought a desperate war to uphold the ideals for which Lee stood. In the end, it almost seemed as if the Confederacy fought for Lee; as if he himself was the Confederacy . . . the best thing that the way of life for which the Confederacy stood could ever have to offer. He had passed into legend before Appomattox. Thousands of tired, underfed, poorly clothed Confederate soldiers, long since past the simple enthusiasm of the early days of the struggle, somehow considered Lee the 6 symbol of everything for which they had been willing to die. But they could not quite put this feeling into words. If the Lost Cause, sanctified by so much heroism and so many deaths, had a living justification, its justification was General Lee.

Grant, the son of a tanner on the Western frontier, was every-   7
thing Lee was not. He had come up the hard way and embodied nothing in particular except the eternal toughness and sinewy fiber of the men who grew up beyond the mountains. He was one of a body of men who owed reverence and obeisance to no one, who were self-reliant to a fault, who cared hardly anything for the past but who had a sharp eye for the future.

These frontier men were the precise opposites of the tidewater   8
aristocrats. Back of them, in the great surge that had taken people over the Alleghenies and into the opening Western country, there was a deep, implicit dissatisfaction with a past that had settled into grooves. They stood for democracy, not from any reasoned conclusion about the proper ordering of human society, but simply because they had grown up in the middle of democracy and knew how it worked. Their society might have privileges, but they would be privileges each man had won for himself. Forms and patterns meant nothing. No man was born to anything, except perhaps to a chance to show how far he could rise. Life was competition.

Yet along with this feeling had come a deep sense of belonging   9
to a national community. The Westerner who developed a farm, opened a shop, or set up in business as a trader could hope to prosper only as his own community prospered—and his community ran from the Atlantic to the Pacific and from Canada down to Mexico. If the land was settled, with towns and highways and accessible markets, he could better himself. He saw his fate in terms of the nation's own destiny. As its horizons expanded, so did his. He had, in other words, an acute dollars-and-cents stake in the continued growth and development of his country.

And that, perhaps, is where the contrast between Grant and   10
Lee becomes most striking. The Virginia aristocrat, inevitably, saw himself in relation to his own region. He lived in a static society which could endure almost anything except change. Instinctively, his first loyalty would go to the locality in which that society existed. He would fight to the limit of endurance to defend it, be-

cause in defending it he was defending everything that gave his own life its deepest meaning.

The Westerner, on the other hand, would fight with an equal 11 tenacity for the broader concept of society. He fought so because everything he lived by was tied to growth, expansion, and a constantly widening horizon. What he lived by would survive or fall with the nation itself. He could not possibly stand by unmoved in the face of an attempt to destroy the Union. He would combat it with everything he had, because he could only see it as an effort to cut the ground out from under his feet.

So Grant and Lee were in complete contrast, representing two 12 diametrically opposed elements in American life. Grant was the modern man emerging; beyond him, ready to come on the stage, was the great age of steel and machinery, of crowded cities and a restless burgeoning vitality. Lee might have ridden down from the old age of chivalry, lance in hand, silken banner fluttering over his head. Each man was the perfect champion of his cause, drawing both his strengths and his weaknesses from the people he led.

Yet it was not all contrast, after all. Different as they were— 13 in background, in personality, in underlying aspiration—these two great soldiers had much in common. Under everything else, they were marvelous fighters. Furthermore, their fighting qualities were really very much alike.

Each man had, to begin with, the great virtue of utter tenacity 14 and fidelity. Grant fought his way down the Mississippi Valley in spite of acute personal discouragement and profound military handicaps. Lee hung on in the trenches at Petersburg after hope itself had died. In each man there was an indomitable quality . . . the born fighter's refusal to give up as long as he can still remain on his feet and lift his two fists.

Daring and resourcefulness they had, too: the ability to think 15 faster and move faster than the enemy. These were the qualities which gave Lee the dazzling campaigns of Second Manassas and Chancellorsville and won Vicksburg for Grant.

Lastly, and perhaps greatest of all, there was the ability, at the 16 end, to turn quickly from war to peace once the fighting was over. Out of the way these two men behaved at Appomattox came the possibility of a peace of reconciliation. It was a possibility not wholly realized, in the years to come, but which did, in the end,

help the two sections to become one nation again . . . after a war
whose bitterness might have seemed to make such a reunion
wholly impossible. No part of either man's life became him more
than the part he played in their brief meeting in the McLean house
at Appomattox. Their behavior there put all succeeding generations of Americans in their debt. Two great Americans, Grant and
Lee—very different, yet under everything very much alike. Their
encounter at Appomattox was one of the great moments of American history.

Meanings and Values

1a.   Clarify the assertions that through Lee "the landed nobility justi-
      fied itself" and that "if the Lost Cause . . . had a living justifica-
      tion," it was General Lee (par. 6).

 b.   Why are these assertions pertinent to the central theme?

2a.   Does it seem reasonable that "thousands of tired, underfed, poorly
      clothed Confederate soldiers" (par. 6) had been willing to fight for
      the aristocratic system in which they would never have had even
      a chance to be aristocrats? Why, or why not?

 b.   Can you think of more likely reasons why they were willing to
      fight?

3.   Under any circumstances today might such a social structure as
      the South's be best for a country? Explain.

4a.   What countries of the world have recently been so torn by internal
      war and bitterness that reunion has seemed, or still seems, impos-
      sible?

 b.   Do you see any basic differences between the trouble in those
      countries and that in America at the time of the Civil War?

5a.   The author calls Lee a symbol (par. 6). Was Grant also a symbol?
      If so, of what? (See Guide to Terms: *Symbol*.)

 b.   How would you classify this kind of symbolism?

Expository Techniques

1.   Make an informal list of paragraph numbers from 3 to 16, and note
      by each number whether the paragraph is devoted primarily to
      Lee, to Grant, or to direct comparison or contrast of the two. This
      chart will show you Catton's basic pattern of development. (No-
      tice, for instance, how the broad information of paragraphs 4–6

and 7–9 seems almost to "funnel" down through the narrower summaries in paragraphs 10 and 11 and into paragraph 12, where the converging elements meet and the contrast is made specific.)

2. What new technique of development is started in paragraph 13?

3a. What is gained, or lost, by using one sentence for paragraph 3?

 b. For paragraph 4?

4a. How many paragraphs does the introduction comprise?

 b. How successfully does it fulfill the three basic requirements of a good introduction? (Guide: *Introductions.*)

5. Show how Catton has constructed the beginning of each paragraph so that there is a smooth transition from the one preceding it. (Guide: *Transition.*)

6. The author's conclusion is really only the explanation of one of his integral points—and this method, if not carefully planned, runs the risk of ending too abruptly and leaving the reader unsatisfied. How has Catton avoided this hazard? (Guide: *Closings.*)

7a. What seems to be the author's attitude toward Grant and Lee?

 b. Show how his tone reflects this attitude. (Guide: *Style/Tone.*)

Diction and Vocabulary

1. Why would a use of colloquialisms have been inconsistent with the tone of this writing?

2a. List or mark all metaphors in paragraphs 1, 3, 5, 7–11, 16. (Guide: *Figures of Speech.*)

 b. Comment on their general effectiveness.

3. If you are not already familiar with the following words, study their meanings as given in the dictionary and as used in this essay: virtual, poignant (par. 2); concept (4); sinewy, obeisance (7); implicit (8); tenacity (11); diametrically, burgeoning (12); aspiration (13); fidelity, profound, indomitable (14); succeeding (16).

4. Explain how the word "poignant" aptly describes this contrast of two men (par. 2).

Suggestions for Writing and Discussion

1. Find, by minor research, an incident in the life of Grant or Lee that will, in suitable essay form, illustrate one of Catton's points.

2. Select some other dramatic moment in history and show its long-range significance.

3.   Select some important moment in your life and show its long-range significance.

4.   Explain how someone you know symbolizes a philosophy or way of life.

(NOTE: Suggestions for topics requiring development by use of COMPARISON and CONTRAST are on page 114, at the end of this section.)

FRANK S. CROCE

FRANK S. CROCE is a practicing attorney in New Jersey. He was born in Camden, New Jersey, in 1949. Following his graduation from St. Joseph's University in 1971 he taught high school English and attended law school in the evenings at Rutgers University—Camden. Croce has published mystery stories in a variety of magazines, including *Woman's World*.

Scrambled Eggs and Cross-Purposes

Comparison and contrast is an appropriate strategy for exploring disagreements over values, particularly when no easy resolution seems possible. In this essay, taken from the *New York Times Magazine,* Frank Croce uses careful exposition both to explain a conflict and to point the way toward reconciliation. Students of writing may be especially interested in the way he gives each side a full hearing without favoring either one.

Ten years ago my mother and father split up. In the uneasy truce that has followed, my father's Sunday morning visits have become a ritual. I scramble some eggs. The kids play in their pajamas. My wife dresses for Mass.

Retired now, he is youthful-appearing since he gave up the chemotherapy. But he walks and speaks with a look only those who have had the cancer cut out of them can possess. The surgeon said there was a 75 percent chance the cancer would return in the next five years. If my father gets by that, he's cured. He's into his fourth year, but being a fatalist by nature, he talks loosely of when he will "check out." We don't dwell on the possibility, but maybe it accounts for the edgy overtones that accompany our conversations.

My father is still a strong union man. For nearly 43 years he cut meat for a large supermarket chain. I have a clear memory of his leaving the house one night back in those black-and-white late 1950s, grim, pale-faced, baseball bat in hand, to protect the picket line, his job, me. Inevitably, our talk turns to unions and politics and sports.

Family talk is taboo. And just as inevitably, we end up on opposite sides—as we did 20 years ago when my hair was long. Experience versus formal education; a Depression-haunted childhood versus an adolescence in relative affluence. The debate is as predictable as a bad sit-com. We can't agree. Only the issues have changed.

He has remained a die-hard Democrat—the party of the little man. He has nothing but scorn for those who cry that unions have ruined our industry. My feeble explanation for why corporations seek cheaper labor in Taiwan and Korea only infuriate him further. He defends free agency and the players' outrageous salaries as if defending John L. Lewis' struggling coal miners. I point out the contradictions in the players' stance; what kind of union allows men with the same time on the job to make such grossly different salaries for the same job? They are only masquerading as laborers, I say. He refuses to budge. Our voices rise. He examines me—his son, the college graduate, the schoolteacher, the newly admitted attorney—and sums up his feelings in one killing phrase: ''You're for the bosses.''

I struggle to defend myself. A silent alarm sounds, and he pushes away the coffee cup, searching for the grandchildren who will demand only that he perform his disappearing penny trick. We retreat to the living room and the Sunday papers scattered on the floor.

I sit and contemplate. I tell myself his feelings are understandable. After 30 years, his union surrendered to the supermarket's tactical bankruptcy—$4 chopped off the hourly rate, vacation time reduced to two weeks and the demise of a union man's greatest accomplishment and weapon, seniority. Then the cancer. My positions are correct. I am not wrong. He simply does not understand the complexity of it all.

He looks up from the grandchildren swamping his chair and talks wistfully about his father, the shoemaker, who always whittled. I recall the winter visits to the county hospital, my grandfather's home for five years after the Christmas Eve stroke left him paralyzed and nearly speechless. "My father was a good shoemaker," he says, "but no businessman." He says a few words in Italian I don't understand. I offer him another cup of coffee but he shakes it off.

A look of tired puzzlement crosses his face. He kisses the children, tells my wife she is looking beautiful and we walk to what he calls his last car, a youthful, silver Camaro. 9

"Look," he says, pointing with his car key toward the front door. "Just worry about those kids and your wife, you hear? Don't worry about me, your mother, or nobody." 10

I nod and ask him if he needs anything, the password for money. He lies and says his pension check will come on Wednesday. He tells me for the hundredth time that the payments on the Camaro are insured so that when he "croaks," I'll get the car. I laugh and tell him he's going to live another 20 years. 11

It is only after closing the front door behind me that I feel the hollowness of my debating victory in the kitchen. The use of verbal acrobatics learned in law school makes me feel like a petty thief. I was arguing issues; he was talking beliefs. The anecdotes of those beliefs haunt me—his indignance at the Philadelphia supervisors who fired a man for stealing a steak while corporate bigshots drained the company dry; the childhood acquaintances who moved to suburbia and forgot "when we all ate salami sandwiches"; his admiration for Humphrey Bogart, who said he only wanted money so he could tell the bigshots to go to hell. 12

And the most bitter, most sustaining lesson in the life of a man whose marriage has failed and who has little money in the bank— it is one he is forever telling me—the power of money to hide a multitude of sins, how it soothes and excuses and defends callous manners, cheap tactics and even crime. It is the lesson of America, his voice seems to chant. He has learned it well. 13

The kids are chaotic. I bark an order, half-obeyed. The tuition is due. We need to move. There is the law school loan to pay. My wife needs cash for the collection basket. I am almost 40. I have a mortgage. 14

At 19, my father manned a PT boat in the Pacific, fighting the Japanese Empire. At the same age, I sat in a college dining hall drinking bad coffee from a Styrofoam cup, debating the issues raised by another Asian war about as familiar to me as a television 15

program. I once believed that the contrast in our experiences symbolized a true gap. No more. Book learning has fooled me. Daily
the boundaries of the gap draw closer, merging into a single line—
an arc—traveling as it must, backward to its beginnings and its
end.

Meanings and Values

1a. About what issues do the author and his father disagree?

 b. On what other matters do they have different perspectives?

2. What is the tone of this essay, and what does it reveal about the
author's attitude toward the conflicts over values he has with his
father? (See Guide to Terms: *Tone.*)

3. To what extent do the values and emotions expressed in paragraphs 13–15 at the end of the essay differ from those conveyed
earlier in the selection?

4. Is the main purpose of this essay to explore and explain the difference between parent and child? To identify grounds for resolving
the differences? To help readers see in the author's experience an
image of relationships with their own parents? Explain.

Expository Techniques

1a. Why should paragraphs 1 and 2 be regarded as introductory? What
kinds of information do they provide? (Guide: *Introductions.*)

 b. Should paragraph 3 be regarded as part of the introduction? Why?

2. Which sections of the essay focus primarily on contrasts? Which
look also at similarities and agreements?

3. Are there any indications in paragraph 12 that readers should consider it a turning point in the development of the essay? If so, what
are they?

4. Discuss the use Croce makes of parallel examples, sentences, and
phrases in paragraphs 4, 5, and 15 to emphasize contrasts. (Guide:
Emphasis, Parallel Structure.)

Diction and Vocabulary

1. What evidence is there in the diction of paragraph 4 of the author's
profession as a lawyer? (Guide: *Diction.*)

2. Choose a section of the essay in which the author reports his and
his father's words indirectly and compare it to a section in which
direct quotation is used. Are different purposes served by these

strategies? What are they? Is one technique more effective than the other? Why? (Guide: *Purpose, Evaluation.*)

3.   Identify the figures of speech in the following passages and discuss their purposes and effects (Guide: *Figures of Speech*):

a.   "The debate is as predictable as a bad sit-com." (par. 4)

b.   " . . . as if defending John L. Lewis' struggling coal miners." (par. 5)

c.   " . . . another Asian war about as familiar to me as a television program." (par. 15)

4.   What use does the father make of slang and colloquial expressions in his speech? How does this contrast with the language his son employs in writing the essay? (Guide: *Slang, Colloquial Expressions.*)

Suggestions for Writing and Discussion

1.   Do conflicts between people born in the 1970s and their parents revolve around different matters than those discussed in this essay? Or is there less conflict than characterizes the relationships of the baby boom generation to which Croce belongs?

2.   Can some contemporary social or political issues be viewed as the result of differences in age, experience, or social class? Consider exploring an issue and its causes in a paper of your own.

(NOTE: Suggestions for topics requiring development by COMPARISON and CONTRAST are on page 114, at the end of this section.)

RICHARD RODRIGUEZ

RICHARD RODRIGUEZ was born in 1944 in San Francisco. His parents were Mexican-Americans and he did not learn to speak English until he attended grammar school. He eventually attended Stanford University and the University of California at Berkeley, from which he received a Ph.D. in English literature. He also studied at Columbia University and the Warburg Institute in London. He currently works as a writer, editor, and lecturer. His articles have appeared in *Saturday Review, College English, Change, American Scholar,* and *Harper's*. His prize-winning memoir *Hunger of Memory* (1982) traces his experiences growing up in two cultures: the immigrant culture of which his family was a part and the American culture into which he was born.

Aria

This selection is the opening section of a chapter entitled "Aria" in *Hunger of Memory*. In it, Rodriguez explains what it is like to grow up caught between two cultures and two languages. Although this experience may be unfamiliar to many readers, Rodriguez makes careful use of comparison and contrast and other patterns such as narrative and description to re-create the tensions he and other children of immigrants felt as they grew up.

I remember to start with that day in Sacramento—a California now nearly thirty years past—when I first entered a classroom, able to understand some fifty stray English words.

The third of four children, I had been preceded to a neighborhood Roman Catholic school by an older brother and sister. But neither of them had revealed very much about their classroom experiences. Each afternoon they returned, as they left in the morning, always together, speaking in Spanish as they climbed the five steps of the porch. And their mysterious books, wrapped in shopping-bag paper, remained on the table next to the door, closed firmly behind them.

An accident of geography sent me to a school where all my classmates were white, many the children of doctors and lawyers and business executives. All my classmates certainly must have been uneasy on that first day of school—as most children are uneasy—to find themselves apart from their families in the first institution of their lives. But I was astonished. 3

The nun said, in a friendly but oddly impersonal voice, 'Boys and girls, this is Richard Rodriguez.' (I heard her sound out: *Rich-heard Road-ree-guess.*) It was the first time I had heard anyone name me in English. 'Richard,' the nun repeated more slowly, writing my name down in her black leather book. Quickly I turned to see my mother's face dissolve in a watery blur behind the pebbled glass door. 4

Many years later there is something called bilingual education—a scheme proposed in the late 1960s by Hispanic-American social activists, later endorsed by a congressional vote. It is a program that seeks to permit non-English-speaking children, many from lower-class homes, to use their family language as the language of school. (Such is the goal its supporters announce.) I hear them and am forced to say no: It is not possible for a child—any child—ever to use his family's language in school. Not to understand this is to misunderstand the public uses of schooling and to trivialize the nature of intimate life—a family's 'language.' 5

Memory teaches me what I know of these matters; the boy reminds the adult. I was a bilingual child, a certain kind—socially disadvantaged—the son of working-class parents, both Mexican immigrants. 6

In the early years of my boyhood, my parents coped very well in America. My father had steady work. My mother managed at home. They were nobody's victims. Optimism and ambition led them to a house (our home) many blocks from the Mexican south side of town. We lived among *gringos* and only a block from the biggest, whitest houses. It never occurred to my parents that they couldn't live wherever they chose. Nor was the Sacramento of the 7 fifties bent on teaching them a contrary lesson. My mother and father were more annoyed than intimidated by those two or three neighbors who tried initially to make us unwelcome. ('Keep your brats away from my sidewalk!') But despite all they achieved, perhaps because they had so much to achieve, any deep feeling of ease, the confidence of 'belonging' in public was withheld from them both. They regarded the people at work, the faces in crowds, as very distant from us. They were the others, *los gringos*. That term was interchangeable in their speech with another, even more telling, *los americanos.*

I grew up in a house where the only regular guests were my relations. For one day, enormous families of relatives would visit and there would be so many people that the noise and the bodies would spill out to the backyard and front porch. Then, for weeks, no one came by. (It was usually a salesman who rang the doorbell.) Our house stood apart. A gaudy yellow in a row of white bungalows. We were the people with the noisy dog. The people who raised pigeons and chickens. We were the foreigners on the block. A few neighbors smiled and waved. We waved back. But no one in the family knew the names of the old couple who lived next door; until I was seven years old, I did not know the names of the kids who lived across the street.

In public, my father and mother spoke a hesitant, accented, not always grammatical English. And they would have to strain— their bodies tense—to catch the sense of what was rapidly said by *los gringos*. At home they spoke Spanish. The language of their Mexican past sounded in counterpoint to the English of public society. The words would come quickly, with ease. Conveyed through those sounds was the pleasing, soothing, consoling reminder of being at home.

During those years when I was first conscious of hearing, my mother and father addressed me only in Spanish; in Spanish I learned to reply. By contrast, English (*inglés*), rarely heard in the house, was the language I came to associate with *gringos*. I learned my first words of English overhearing my parents speak to strangers. At five years of age, I knew just enough English for my mother to trust me on errands to stores one block away. No more.

I was a listening child, careful to hear the very different sounds of Spanish and English. Wide-eyed with hearing, I'd listen to sounds more than words. First, there were English (*gringo*) sounds. So many words were still unknown that when the butcher or the lady at the drugstore said something to me, exotic polysyllabic sounds would bloom in the midst of their sentences. Often the speech of people in public seemed to me very loud, booming with confidence. The man behind the counter would literally ask, 'What can I do for you?' But by being so firm and so clear, the sound of his voice said that he was a *gringo;* he belonged in public society.

I would also hear then the high nasal notes of middle-class 12 American speech. The air stirred with sound. Sometimes, even now, when I have been traveling abroad for several weeks, I will hear what I heard as a boy. In hotel lobbies or airports, in Turkey or Brazil, some Americans will pass, and suddenly I will hear it again—the high sound of American voices. For a few seconds I will hear it with pleasure, for it is now the sound of *my* society—a reminder of home. But inevitably—already on the flight headed for home—the sound fades with repetition. I will be unable to hear it anymore.

When I was a boy, things were different. The accent of *los grin-* 13 *gos* was never pleasing nor was it hard to hear. Crowds at Safeway or at bus stops would be noisy with sound. And I would be forced to edge away from the chirping chatter above me.

I was unable to hear my own sounds, but I knew very well 14 that I spoke English poorly. My words could not stretch far enough to form complete thoughts. And the words I did speak I didn't know well enough to make into distinct sounds. (Listeners would usually lower their heads, better to hear what I was trying to say.) But it was one thing for *me* to speak English with difficulty. It was more troubling for me to hear my parents speak in public: their high-whining vowels and guttural consonants; their sentences that got stuck with 'eh' and 'ah' sounds; the confused syntax; the hesitant rhythm of sounds so different from the way the *gringos* spoke. I'd notice, moreover, that my parents' voices were softer than those of *gringos* we'd meet.

I am tempted now to say that none of this mattered. In adult- 15 hood I am embarrassed by childhood fears. And, in a way, it didn't matter very much that my parents could not speak English with ease. Their linguistic difficulties had no serious consequences. My mother and father made themselves understood at the county hospital clinic and at government offices. And yet, in another way, it mattered very much—it was unsettling to hear my parents struggle with English. Hearing them, I'd grow nervous, my clutching trust in their protection and power weakened.

There were many times like the night at a brightly lit gasoline station (a blaring white memory) when I stood uneasily, hearing my father. He was talking to a teenaged attendant. I do not recall what they were saying, but I cannot forget the sounds my father made as he spoke. At one point his words slid together to form one word—sounds as confused as the threads of blue and green oil in the puddle next to my shoes. His voice rushed through what he had left to say. And, toward the end, reached falsetto notes, appealing to his listener's understanding. I looked away to the lights of passing automobiles. I tried not to hear anymore. But I heard only too well the calm, easy tones in the attendant's reply. Shortly afterward, walking toward home with my father, I shivered when he put his hand on my shoulder. The very first chance that I got, I evaded his grasp and ran on ahead into the dark, skipping with feigned boyish exuberance.

But then there was Spanish. *Español:* my family's language. *Español:* the language that seemed to me a private language. I'd hear strangers on the radio and in the Mexican Catholic church across town speaking in Spanish, but I couldn't really believe that Spanish was a public language, like English. Spanish speakers, rather, seemed related to me, for I sensed that we shared—through our language—the experience of feeling apart from *los gringos.* It was thus a ghetto Spanish that I heard and I spoke. Like those whose lives are bound by a barrio, I was reminded by Spanish of my separateness from *los otros, los gringos* in power. But more intensely than for most barrio children—because I did not live in a barrio—Spanish seemed to me the language of home. (Most days it was only at home that I'd hear it.) It became the language of joyful return.

A family member would say something to me and I would feel myself specially recognized. My parents would say something to me and I would feel embraced by the sounds of their words. Those sounds said: *I am speaking with ease in Spanish. I am addressing you in words I never use with* los gringos. *I recognize you as someone special, close, like no one outside. You belong with us. In the family.*

(*Ricardo.*)

At the age of five, six, well past the time when most other

children no longer easily notice the difference between sounds uttered at home and words spoken in public, I had a different experience. I lived in a world magically compounded of sounds. I remained a child longer than most; I lingered too long, poised at the edge of language—often frightened by the sounds of *los gringos,* delighted by the sounds of Spanish at home. I shared with my family a language that was startlingly different from that used in the great city around us.

For me there were none of the gradations between public and private society so normal to a maturing child. Outside the house was public society; inside the house was private. Just opening or closing the screen door behind me was an important experience. I'd rarely leave home all alone or without reluctance. Walking down the sidewalk, under the canopy of tall trees, I'd warily notice the—suddenly—silent neighborhood kids who stood warily watching me. Nervously, I'd arrive at the grocery store to hear there the sounds of the *gringo*—foreign to me—reminding me that in this world so big, I was a foreigner. But then I'd return. Walking back toward our house, climbing the steps from the sidewalk, when the front door was open in summer, I'd hear voices beyond the screen door talking in Spanish. For a second or two, I'd stay, linger there, listening. Smiling, I'd hear my mother call out, saying in Spanish (words): 'Is that you, Richard?' All the while her sounds would assure me: *You are home now; come closer; inside. With us.* 21

'*Si,*' I'd reply. 22

Once more inside the house I would resume (assume) my place in the family. The sounds would dim, grow harder to hear. Once more at home, I would grow less aware of that fact. It required, however, no more than the blurt of the doorbell to alert me to listen to sounds all over again. The house would turn instantly still while my mother went to the door. I'd hear her hard English sounds. I'd wait to hear her voice return to soft-sounding Spanish, which assured me, as surely as did the clicking tongue of the lock on the door, that the stranger was gone. 23

Plainly, it is not healthy to hear such sounds so often. It is not healthy to distinguish public words from private sounds so easily. I remained cloistered by sounds, timid and shy in public, too dependent on voices at home. And yet it needs to be emphasized: I was an extremely happy child at home. I remember many nights when my father would come back from work, and I'd hear him 24 call out to my mother in Spanish, sounding relieved. In Spanish, he'd sound light and free notes he never could manage in English. Some nights I'd jump up just at hearing his voice. With *mis hermanos* I would come running into the room where he was with my mother. Our laughing (so deep was the pleasure!) became screaming. Like others who know the pain of public alienation, we transformed the knowledge of our public separateness and made it consoling—the reminder of intimacy. Excited, we joined our voices in a celebration of sounds. *We are speaking now the way we never speak out in public. We are alone—together,* voices sounded, surrounded to tell me. Some nights, no one seemed willing to loosen the hold sounds had on us. At dinner, we invented new words. (Ours sounded Spanish, but made sense only to us.) We pieced together new words by taking, say, an English verb and giving it Spanish endings. My mother's instructions at bedtime would be lacquered with mock-urgent tones. Or a word like *si* would become, in several notes, able to convey added measures of feeling. Tongues explored the edges of words, especially the fat vowels. And we happily sounded that military drum roll, the twirling roar of the Spanish *r.* Family language: my family's sounds. The voices of my parents and sisters and brother. Their voices insisting: *You belong here. We are family members. Related. Special to one another. Listen!* Voices singing and sighing, rising, straining, then surging, teeming with pleasure that burst syllables into fragments of laughter. At times it seemed there was steady quiet only when, from another room, the rustling whispers of my parents faded and I moved closer to sleep.

Meanings and Values

1a. This essay presents a number of contrasts or oppositions, the most important of which is the contrast between public and private language. What are some of the others?

 b. Summarize the author's view of the differences between public and private language, making sure to indicate what meanings each held for him as a boy.

2. When the author speaks of a "language," he seems to mean more than a particular set of words used to talk about ideas, actions, or things. What else, for him, makes up a language?

3. What evidence is there in the essay that despite its being based on the author's experience and directed toward problems often faced

by other Mexican-Americans, its conclusions are meant to apply to readers in general?

4a.   What does the author mean when he says "it is not healthy to hear such sounds so often" or "to distinguish public words from private sounds so easily" (par. 24)?

b.   Does the paragraph that follows these conclusions undermine them entirely or simply moderate and qualify them? Explain.

Expository Techniques

1a.   What does the author do to distinguish his experience on the first day of school from that of the average pupil attending school for the first time?

b.   How is the author's experience as an adult hearing American voices in foreign countries (par. 12) unified with the discussion that focuses on his experience as a child (pars. 11 and 13) and with the themes of the essay as a whole? (See Guide to Terms: *Unity.*)

2a.   Why does the author make an effort in paragraph 7 to show that his parents did not suffer to any great extent from racial discrimination or economic hardship?

b.   What evidence does he provide in the essay to show that he and his family were different from the other people in his neighborhood and school, and where in the essay are these contrasts discussed?

3a.   What transitional devices are used in paragraphs 9, 10, 15, and 17 to introduce comparisons or contrasts?

b.   Discuss the various uses of parallelism in paragraph 21.

c.   For what special effect does the author use italics in paragraphs 18 and 19?

4a.   Where in the essay are the following patterns used as a means to develop the basic pattern of comparison and contrast: narration, example, cause–effect, and description?

b.   What other patterns, if any, are used in the essay?

Diction and Vocabulary

1a.   What figure of speech is used in paragraph 16 to convey the emotional impact of the event on the author as a young boy? (Guide: *Figures of Speech.*)

b.   What other elements of diction or figures of speech contribute to the ability of the paragraph to describe vividly the events and their emotional impact? (Guide: *Diction.*)

2a.   For what purposes does the author use the Spanish words in paragraphs 7, 10, 17, 22, and 24?

b.   Which of the words mentioned above, if any, would be difficult to understand for someone who does not speak Spanish?

c.   Discuss the probable effect of these words on readers with an English (or non-Spanish) speaking background. On readers who grew up with a Hispanic cultural background.

3.   If you do not know the meaning of some of the following words, look them up in your dictionary: impersonal (par. 4); intimidated (7); counterpoint (9); guttural, syntax (14); falsetto (16); barrio (17); gradations, warily (21); lacquered (24).

Suggestions for Writing and Discussion

1.   In what sense can each of us be said to have public and private languages?

2.   Are two categories (public and private) enough for understanding the roles language plays in our lives? Suggest and illustrate some other important categories of language such as the language of business or of sports and recreation.

3.   If you have had the experience of learning a second language in school, by moving to a foreign country, or through some other circumstance, compare your learning experiences to those Rodriguez reports.

4.   If you spoke at home a different language from that used at school, or if the religious, cultural, or racial makeup of your family was markedly different from that of the surrounding community, explore in an essay the contrasts or conflicts you observed as a child.

(NOTE: Suggestions for topics requiring development by COMPARISON and CONTRAST are on page 114, at the end of this section.)

ALICE WALKER

ALICE WALKER was born in Georgia in 1944, the youngest in a family of eight. Her parents were sharecroppers, and she attended rural schools as a child, going on eventually to attend Spelman College and Sarah Lawrence College, from which she graduated. She worked as an editor of *Ms.* magazine and taught at several colleges. At present she teaches at the University of California at Berkeley and lives in northern California. Her work as a poet, novelist, and essayist has been highly acclaimed, and one of her novels, *The Color Purple* (1982), received both a Pulitzer Prize and the American Book Award for fiction. Some of her other works are *Revolutionary Petunias and Other Poems* (1973); *In Love and Trouble* (1973), short stories; *Meridian* (1976), a novel; *In Search of Our Mothers' Gardens* (1983); and *Living by the Word* (1988), essays.

Am I Blue?

Humans and horses might seem at first so different that any comparison would have to take the form of an analogy—a pairing of essentially unlike subjects whose limited similarities can be used for explanatory purposes (see Section 4). Walker's strategy in this essay from *Living by the Word* is just the opposite, however. She explains that despite their obvious differences, humans and animals are essentially alike, at least in important matters such as the capacity to love and to communicate.

"Ain't these tears in these
eyes tellin' you?"

For about three years my companion and I rented a small house in
the country that stood on the edge of a large meadow that appeared to run from the end of our deck straight into the mountains. The mountains, however, were quite far away, and between
us and them there was, in fact, a town. It was one of the many
pleasant aspects of the house that you never really were aware of
this.

It was a house of many windows, low, wide, nearly floor to
ceiling in the living room, which faced the meadow, and it was
from one of these that I first saw our closest neighbor, a large white
horse, cropping grass, flipping its mane, and ambling about—not
over the entire meadow, which stretched well out of sight of the
house, but over the five or so fenced-in acres that were next to the
twenty-odd that we had rented. I soon learned that the horse,
whose name was Blue, belonged to a man who lived in another
town, but was boarded by our neighbors next door. Occasionally,
one of the children, usually a stocky teen-ager, but sometimes a
much younger girl or boy, could be seen riding Blue. They would
appear in the meadow, climb up on his back, ride furiously for ten
or fifteen minutes, then get off, slap Blue on the flanks, and not
be seen again for a month or more.

There were many apple trees in our yard, and one by the fence
that Blue could almost reach. We were soon in the habit of feeding
him apples, which he relished, especially because by the middle
of summer the meadow grasses—so green and succulent since January—had dried out from lack of rain, and Blue stumbled about
munching the dried stalks half-heartedly. Sometimes he would
stand very still just by the apple tree, and when one of us came
out he would whinny, snort loudly, or stamp the ground. This
meant, of course: I want an apple.

It was quite wonderful to pick a few apples, or collect those
that had fallen to the ground overnight, and patiently hold them,
one by one, up to his large, toothy mouth. I remained as thrilled
as a child by his flexible dark lips, huge, cubelike teeth that
crunched the apples, core and all, with such finality, and his high,
broad-breasted *enormity;* beside which, I felt small indeed. When I
was a child, I used to ride horses, and was especially friendly with

one named Nan until the day I was riding and my brother deliberately spooked her and I was thrown, head first, against the trunk of a tree. When I came to, I was in bed and my mother was bending worriedly over me; we silently agreed that perhaps horseback riding was not the safest sport for me. Since then I have walked, and prefer walking to horseback riding—but I had forgotten the depth of feeling one could see in horses' eyes.

I was therefore unprepared for the expression in Blue's. Blue was lonely. Blue was horribly lonely and bored. I was not shocked that this should be the case; five acres to tramp by yourself, endlessly, even in the most beautiful of meadows—and his was—cannot provide many interesting events, and once rainy season turned to dry that was about it. No, I was shocked that I had forgotten that human animals and nonhuman animals can communicate quite well; if we are brought up around animals as children we take this for granted. By the time we are adults we no longer remember. However, the animals have not changed. They are in fact *completed* creations (at least they seem to be, so much more than we) who are not likely *to* change; it is their nature to express themselves. What else are they going to express? And they do. And, generally speaking, they are ignored. 6

After giving Blue the apples, I would wander back to the house, aware that he was observing me. Were more apples not forthcoming then? Was that to be his sole entertainment for the day? My partner's small son had decided he wanted to learn how to piece a quilt; we worked in silence on our respective squares as I thought . . . 7

Well, about slavery: about white children, who were raised by black people, who knew their first all-accepting love from black women, and then, when they were twelve or so, were told they must "forget" the deep levels of communication between themselves and "mammy" that they knew. Later they would be able to relate quite calmly, "My old mammy was sold to another good family." "My old mammy was —— ——." Fill in the blank. Many more years later a white woman would say: "I can't understand these Negroes, these blacks. What do they want? They're so different from us." 8

And about the Indians, considered to be "like animals" by the "settlers" (a very benign euphemism for what they actually were), who did not understand their description as a compliment. 9

And about the thousands of American men who marry Japa- 1•
nese, Korean, Filipina, and other non-English-speaking women
and of how happy they report they are, *"blissfully,"* until their
brides learn to speak English, at which point the marriages tend to
fall apart. What then did the men see, when they looked into the
eyes of the women they married, before they could speak English?
Apparently only their own reflections.

I thought of society's impatience with the young. "Why are 11
they playing the music so loud?" Perhaps the children have listened to much of the music of oppressed people their parents
danced to before they were born, with its passionate but soft cries
for acceptance and love, and they have wondered why their parents failed to hear.

I do not know how long Blue had inhabited his five beautiful, 12
boring acres before we moved into our house; a year after we had
arrived—and had also traveled to other valleys, other cities, other
worlds—he was still there.

But then, in our second year at the house, something hap- 13
pened in Blue's life. One morning, looking out the window at the
fog that lay like a ribbon over the meadow, I saw another horse, a
brown one, at the other end of Blue's field. Blue appeared to be
afraid of it, and for several days made no attempt to go near. We
went away for a week. When we returned, Blue had decided to
make friends and the two horses ambled or galloped along together, and Blue did not come nearly as often to the fence underneath the apple tree.

When he did, bringing his new friend with him, there was a 14
different look in his eyes. A look of independence, of self-
possession, of inalienable *horse*ness. His friend eventually became
pregnant. For months and months there was, it seemed to me, a
mutual feeling between me and the horses of justice, of peace. I
fed apples to them both. The look in Blue's eyes was one of un-
abashed "this is *it*ness."

It did not, however, last forever. One day, after a visit to the 15
city, I went out to give Blue some apples. He stood waiting, or so
I thought, though not beneath the tree. When I shook the tree and
jumped back from the shower of apples, he made no move. I carried some over to him. He managed to half-crunch one. The rest
he let fall to the ground. I dreaded looking into his eyes—because
I had of course noticed that Brown, his partner, had gone—but I

did look. If I had been born into slavery, and my partner had been sold or killed, my eyes would have looked like that. The children next door explained that Blue's partner had been "put with him" (the same expression that old people used, I had noticed, when speaking of an ancestor during slavery who had been impregnated by her owner) so that they could mate and she conceive. Since that was accomplished, she had been taken back by her owner, who lived somewhere else.

Will she be back? I asked.   16

They didn't know.   17

Blue was like a crazed person. Blue *was*, to me, a crazed person.   18
He galloped furiously, as if he were being ridden, around and around his five beautiful acres. He whinnied until he couldn't. He tore at the ground with his hooves. He butted himself against his single shade tree. He looked always and always toward the road down which his partner had gone. And then, occasionally, when he came up for apples, or I took apples to him, he looked at me. It was a look so piercing, so full of grief, a look so *human*, I almost laughed (I felt too sad to cry) to think there are people who do not know that animals suffer. People like me who have forgotten, and daily forget, all that animals try to tell us. "Everything you do to us will happen to you; we are your teachers, as you are ours. We are one lesson" is essentially it, I think. There are those who never once have even considered animals' rights: those who have been taught that animals actually want to be used and abused by us, as small children "love" to be frightened, or women "love" to be mutilated and raped. . . . They are the great-grandchildren of those who honestly thought, because someone taught them this: "Women can't think," and "niggers can't faint." But most disturbing of all, in Blue's large brown eyes was a new look, more painful than the look of despair: the look of disgust with human beings, with life; the look of hatred. And it was odd what the look of hatred did. It gave him, for the first time, the look of a beast. And what that meant was that he had put up a barrier within to protect himself from further violence; all the apples in the world wouldn't change that fact.

And so Blue remained, a beautiful part of our landscape, very   19
peaceful to look at from the window, white against the grass. Once a friend came to visit and said, looking out on the soothing view: "And it *would* have to be a *white* horse; the very image of free-

dom." And I thought, yes, the animals are forced to become for
us merely "images" of what they once so beautifully expressed.
And we are used to drinking milk from containers showing "con-
tented" cows, whose real lives we want to hear nothing about,
eating eggs and drumsticks from "happy" hens, and munching
hamburgers advertised by bulls of integrity who seem to command
their fate.

As we talked of freedom and justice one day for all, we sat
down to steaks. I am eating misery, I thought, as I took the first
bite. And spit it out.

Meanings and Values

1a.   In which paragraphs does Walker describe what she believes to be
      Blue's thoughts and feelings?

 b.   According to Walker, in what ways is Blue similar to a human? In
      what ways is he different?

2.   What thematic purposes are served by the following phrases:

 a.   "human animals and nonhuman animals" (par. 6)

 b.   "who did not understand their description as a compliment"
      (par. 9)

 c.   "Am I Blue?" (title)

 d.   "If I had been born into slavery, and my partner had been sold or
      killed, my eyes would have looked like that." (par. 15)

 e.   "It gave him, for the first time, the look of a beast." (par. 18)

3.   To what other groups does the author compare Blue and his rela-
      tionships with humans in paragraphs 8–11?

Expository Techniques

1a.   Why do you think Walker chose to wait until near the end of the
      essay (paragraph 18) for a detailed discussion of its theme? (Guide
      to Terms: *Unity.*)

 b.   To what extent does the placement of this discussion give the essay
      an expository rather than argumentative purpose? (Guide: *Argu-
      ment.*)

2.   Discuss how the "'images'" presented in paragraph 19 can be re-
      garded as ironic symbols. (Guide: *Symbol, Irony.*)

3a. Describe the way Walker alters the tempo of the sentences and builds to a climax in the concluding paragraph of the essay. (Guide: *Closings.*)

b. Some readers might consider the ending effective. Others might consider it overly dramatic or distasteful. Explain which reaction you consider most appropriate. (Guide: *Evaluation.*)

Diction and Vocabulary

1. Describe the ways in which Walker uses syntax and figurative language (simile) for thematic purposes in this passage: "Blue was like a crazed person. Blue *was*, to me, a crazed person" (par. 18). (Guide: *Syntax, Figures of Speech.*)

2. In speaking of the "'settlers,'" Walker says that this term is "a very benign euphemism for what they actually were" (par. 9). What does she mean by this comment? What other terms might be applied to them (from Walker's point of view)? Why might she have chosen not to use such terms?

3a. The title of this essay is taken from a song of the same name. In terms of the content of the essay, to what ideas or themes does it refer? Can it be considered a paradox? (Guide: *Paradox.*)

b. The quotation from the song that opens the essay points to some of the ideas discussed in the essay. What are they?

Suggestions for Writing and Discussion

1. Prepare a paper of your own explaining the regulations that safeguard the rights of animals used in experiments or outlining some common abuses in animal experimentation.

2. Walker links racism and disregard for the rights of animals. Is she correct in doing this, or is the connection farfetched?

3. Should people adopt vegetarianism for moral as well as health reasons?

4. Many people claim that in attributing human personalities to animals, we are simply fooling ourselves or being egocentric in assuming that the real meaning of events can be understood in human terms. What do you think?

(NOTE: Suggestions for topics requiring development by COMPARISON and CONTRAST follow.)

Writing Suggestions for Section 3
Comparison and *Contrast*

Base your central theme on one of the following, and develop your composition primarily by use of comparison and/or contrast. Use examples liberally for clarity and concreteness, chosen always with your purpose and reader-audience in mind.

1. Two kinds of home life.
2. The sea at two different times.
3. The innate qualities needed for success in two different careers.
4. The natural temperaments of two acquaintances.
5. Two musicians.
6. The teaching techniques of two instructors or former teachers.
7. Two methods of parental handling of teenage problems.
8. Two family attitudes toward the practice of religion.
9. Two "moods" of the same town at different times.
10. The personalities (or atmospheres) of two cities or towns of similar size.
11. Two politicians with different leadership styles.
12. Two people who approach problems in different ways.
13. Two different attitudes toward the same thing or activity: one "practical," the other romantic or aesthetic.
14. The beliefs and practices of two religions or denominations concerning *one* aspect of religion.
15. Two courses on the same subject: one in high school and one in college.
16. The differing styles of two players of some sport or game.
17. The hazards of frontier life and those of life today.
18. Two companies with very different styles or business philosophies.
19. Two recent movies or rock videos.
20. Two magazines focusing on similar subjects but directed at different audiences.

4

Using *Analogy* as
an Expository Device

Analogy is a special form of comparison that is used for a specific purpose: to explain something abstract or difficult to understand by showing its similarity to something concrete or easy to understand. A much less commonly used technique than logical comparison (and contrast), analogy is, nonetheless, a highly efficient means of explaining some difficult concepts or of giving added force to the explanations.

Logical comparison is made between two members of the same general class, usually assuming the same kind of interest in the subject matter of both. But in analogy we are really concerned only with the subject matter of one, using a second just to help explain the first. The two subjects, quite incomparable in most respects, are never of the same general class; if they are, we then have logical comparison, not analogy.

If the analogy is to be effective, the writer should be able to assume that the reader is familiar enough with the easier subject, or can quickly be made so, that it really helps explain the more difficult one. A common example is the explanation of the human circulatory system, which we may have trouble comprehending, by comparing the heart and arteries with a pump forcing water through the pipes of a plumbing system. This analogy has been carried further to liken the effect of cholesterol deposits on the inner walls of the arteries to mineral deposits that accumulate inside water pipes and eventually close them entirely. Although there is little logical similarity between a steel pipe and a human artery, the *analogical* similarity would be apparent to most readers—but the analogy might cause even greater confusion for anyone who did not know about pumps.

Distinguishing between analogy and metaphor is sometimes difficult. The difference is basically in their purpose: the function of a metaphor is merely *to describe,* to create a brief, vivid image for the reader; the function of analogy is primarily one of exposition, *to explain,* rather than to describe. In this sense, however, the function of a metaphor is actually *to suggest* an analogy: instead of showing the similarities of the heart and the pump, a metaphor might simply refer to "that faithful pump inside my chest," implying enough of a comparison to serve its purpose as description. (We can see here why some people refer to analogy as "extended" metaphor.) The analogist, when trying to explain the wide selection of college subjects and the need for balance in a course of study, could use the easily understood principle of a cafeteria, which serves Jell-O and lemon meringue pie, as well as meat and potatoes. If his purpose had been only to create an image, to describe, he might have referred simply to the bewildering variety in "the cafeteria of college courses"—and that would have been a metaphor. (For still another example of the more conventional type of analogy, see the explanation of *Unity,* in the Guide to Terms.)

But as useful as analogy can be in exposition, it is a difficult technique to use in logical argument. The two subjects of an analogy, although similar in one or more ways useful for illustration, may be basically too different for any reliable conclusions to be drawn from their similarity.

Sample Paragraph (Annotated)

Sets up, in first sentence, the *analogical* comparison. (They cannot form a logical comparison, however, as towns and a family are of different classes.)

("Broad" is a slang term, usually further classified as a vulgarity. Suitable only for very informal writing.)

Sometimes the local poets-at-heart think of Valley towns as members of a family—diverse, scrappy, but loyal and loving too, each with its own characteristics. Casey, for instance, is the plain old daddy of all, unimaginative, hard-working, but also a notorious brawler on paycheck nights. The eldest daughter is Riverton, a pale and beautiful woman with her head bowed in prayer. But across the river is a pretty lady of a different sort: sister Eden, a good-hearted broad with lips

If used for descriptive rather than explanatory, purposes, various portions of the analogy could be classed as metaphors: e.g., "plain old daddy" and "head bowed in prayer."

("Fellow": colloquial.)

("Kid": colloquial.)

("Picks on" is colloquial and would not be suitable in formal writing.)

painted red and earrings clinking, living on the verge of scandal but never quite in it. And there's Waldoville, the wise older brother, a prosperous country type but tolerant of diversities, first to sail in with both fists flying when any of the rest is attacked. But off to the north lives the peculiar brother, Camelot, an artistic fellow, not much for socializing, mostly content in his own little world. And several smaller stepchildren are scattered around: like Rejoice, that untidy kid who is probably anemic as well; Little Lost Ben, still nearly lost in the woods; New Cambria, a pretty little retarded lass; and, on the far south side, sturdy young Stephen's Mill, who may be the best athlete of all. True, this country family may fight and bicker among themselves—but woe to the outside bully who picks on any one of them.

Sample Paragraph (Analogy)

If distant galaxies are really receding from the earth, and if more distant galaxies are receding faster than nearby ones, a remarkable picture of the universe emerges. Imagine that the galaxies were raisins scattered through a rising lump of bread dough. As the dough expanded, the raisins would be carried farther and farther apart from each other. If you were standing on one of the raisins, how would things look? You wouldn't feel any motion yourself, of course, just as you don't feel the effects of the earth's motion around the sun, but you would notice that your nearest neighbor was moving away from you. This motion would be due to the fact that the dough between you and your nearest neighbor would be expanding, pushing the two of you apart.

TOM WOLFE

TOM WOLFE was born in 1931 and grew up in Richmond, Virginia, was graduated from Washington and Lee University, and took his doctorate at Yale. After working for several years as a reporter for the *Washington Post*, he joined the staff of the *New York Herald Tribune* in 1962. He has won two Washington Newspaper Guild Awards, one for humor and the other for foreign news. Wolfe has been a regular contributor to *New York*, *Esquire*, and other magazines. His books include *The Kandy-Kolored Tangerine-Flake Streamline Baby* (1965), *The Electric Kool-Aid Acid Test* (1968), *The Pump House Gang* (1968), *Radical Chic and Mau-Mauing the Flak Catchers* (1970), *The New Journalism* (1973), *The Painted Word* (1975), *The Right Stuff* (1977), *In Our Time* (1980), *Underneath the I-Beams: Inside the Compound* (1981), *From Bauhaus to Our House* (1981), *The Purple Decades: A Reader* (1984), and *The Bonfire of the Vanities* (1986).

O Rotten Gotham—Sliding Down into the Behavioral Sink

"O Rotten Gotham—Sliding Down into the Behavioral Sink," as used here, is excerpted from a longer selection by that title in Wolfe's book *The Pump House Gang* (1968). Here, as he frequently does, the author investigates an important aspect of modern life—seriously, but in his characteristic and seemingly freewheeling style. It is a style that is sometimes ridiculed by scholars but is far more often admired. (Wolfe, as the serious student will discover, is always in complete control of his materials and methods, using them to create certain effects, to reinforce his ideas.) In this piece his analogy is particularly noteworthy for the extensive usage he is able to get from it.

I just spent two days with Edward T. Hall, an anthropologist, watching thousands of my fellow New Yorkers short-circuiting themselves into hot little twitching death balls with jolts of their own adrenalin. Dr. Hall says it is overcrowding that does it. Overcrowding gets the adrenalin going, and the adrenalin gets them queer, autistic, sadistic, barren, batty, sloppy, hot-in-the-pants, chancred-on-the-flankers, leering, puling, numb—the usual in New York, in other words, and God knows what else. Dr. Hall has the theory that overcrowding has already thrown New York into a state of behavioral sink. Behavioral sink is a term from ethology, which is the study of how animals relate to their environment. Among animals, the sink winds up with a "population collapse" or "massive die-off." O rotten Gotham.

It got to be easy to look at New Yorkers as animals, especially 2 looking down from some place like a balcony at Grand Central at the rush hour Friday afternoon. The floor was filled with the poor white humans, running around, dodging, blinking their eyes, making a sound like a pen full of starlings or rats or something.

"Listen to them skid," says Dr. Hall.   3

He was right. The poor old etiolate animals were out there 4 skidding on their rubber soles. You could hear it once he pointed it out. They stop short to keep from hitting somebody or because they are disoriented and they suddenly stop and look around, and they skid on their rubber-soled shoes, and a screech goes up. They pour out onto the floor down the escalators from the Pan-Am Building, from 42nd Street, from Lexington Avenue, up out of subways, down into subways, railroad trains, up into helicopters—

"You can also hear the helicopters all the way down here," 5 says Dr. Hall. The sound of the helicopters using the roof of the Pan-Am Building nearly fifty stories up beats right through. "If it weren't for this ceiling"—he is referring to the very high ceiling in Grand Central—"this place would be unbearable with this kind of crowding. And yet they'll probably never 'waste' space like this again."

They screech! And the adrenal glands in all those poor white 6 animals enlarge, micrometer by micrometer, to the size of cantaloupes. Dr. Hall pulls a Minox camera out of a holster he has on his belt and starts shooting away at the human scurry. The Sink!

Dr. Hall has the Minox up to his eye—he is a slender man, 7 calm, 52 years old, young-looking, an anthropologist who has worked with Navajos, Hopis, Spanish-Americans, Negroes, Trukese. He was the most important anthropologist in the government during the crucial years of the foreign aid program, the 1950s. He directed both the Point Four training program and the Human Relations Area Files. He wrote *The Silent Language* and *The Hidden Dimension*, two books that are picking up the kind of "underground" following his friend Marshall McLuhan started picking up about five years ago. He teaches at the Illinois Institute of Technology, lives with his wife, Mildred, in a high-ceilinged town house on one of the last great residential streets in downtown Chicago, Astor Street; he has a grown son and daughter, loves good food, good wine, the relaxed, civilized life—but comes to New York with a Minox at his eye to record!—perfect—The Sink.

We really got down in there by walking down into the Lexington Avenue line subway stop under Grand Central. We inhaled those nice big fluffy fumes of human sweat, urine, effluvia, and sebaceous secretions. One old female human was already stroked out on the upper level, on a stretcher, with two policemen standing by. The other humans barely looked at her. They rushed into line. They bellied each other, haunch to paunch, down the stairs. Human heads shone through the gratings. The species North European tried to create bubbles of space around themselves, about a foot and a half in diameter—

"See, he's reacting against the line," says Dr. Hall.

—but the species Mediterranean presses on in. The hell with bubbles of space. The species North European resents that, this male human behind him presses forward toward the booth . . . *breathing* on him, he's disgusted, he pulls out of the line entirely, the species Mediterranean resents him for resenting it, and neither of them realizes what the hell they are getting irritable about exactly. And in all of them the old adrenals grow another micrometer.

Dr. Hall whips out the Minox. Too perfect! The bottom of The Sink.

It is the sheer overcrowding, such as occurs in the business sections of Manhattan five days a week and in Harlem, Bedford-Stuyvesant, southeast Bronx every day—sheer overcrowding is converting New Yorkers into animals in a sink pen. Dr. Hall's argument runs as follows: all animals, including birds, seem to have a built-in inherited requirement to have a certain amount of territory, space, to lead their lives in. Even if they have all the food they need, and there are no predatory animals threatening them, they cannot tolerate crowding beyond a certain point. No more than two hundred wild Norway rats can survive on a quarter acre of ground, for example, even when they are given all the food they can eat. They just die off.

But why? To find out, ethologists have run experiments on all sorts of animals, from stickleback crabs to Sika deer. In one major experiment, an ethologist named John Calhoun put some domesti-cated white Norway rats in a pen with four sections to it, con-nected by ramps. Calhoun knew from previous experiments that the rats tend to split up into groups of ten to twelve and that the pen, therefore, would hold forty to forty-eight rats comfortably, assuming they formed four equal groups. He allowed them to re-produce until there were eighty rats, balanced between male and female, but did not let it get any more crowded. He kept them supplied with plenty of food, water, and nesting materials. In other words, all their more obvious needs were taken care of. A less obvious need—space—was not. To the human eye, the pen did not even look especially crowded. But to the rats, it was crowded beyond endurance.

The entire colony was soon plunged into a profound behav-ioral sink. ''The sink,'' said Calhoun, ''is the outcome of any be-havioral process that collects animals together in unusually great numbers. The unhealthy connotations of the term are not acciden-tal: a behavioral sink does act to aggravate all forms of pathology that can be found within a group.''

For a start, long before the rat population reached eighty, a status hierarchy had developed in the pen. Two dominant male rats took over the two end sections, acquired harems of eight to ten females each, and forced the rest of the rats into the two middle pens. All the overcrowding took place in the middle pens. That was where the ''sink'' hit. The aristocrat rats at the end grew big-ger, sleeker, healthier, and more secure the whole time.

In The Sink, meanwhile, nest building, courting, sex behavior, reproduction, social organization, health—all of it went to pieces. Normally, Norway rats have a mating ritual in which the male chases the female, the female ducks down into a burrow and sticks her head up to watch the male. He performs a little dance outside the burrow, then she comes out, and he mounts her, usually for a few seconds. When The Sink set in, however, no more than three males—the dominant males in the middle sections—kept up the old customs. The rest tried everything from satyrism to homosexuality or else gave up on sex altogether. Some of the subordinate males spent all their time chasing females. Three or four might chase one female at the same time, and instead of stopping at the burrow entrance for the ritual, they would charge right in. Once mounted, they would hold on for minutes instead of the usual seconds.

Homosexuality rose sharply. So did bisexuality. Some males would mount anything—males, females, babies, senescent rats, anything. Still other males dropped sexual activity altogether, wouldn't fight and, in fact, would hardly move except when the other rats slept. Occasionally, a female from the aristocrat rats' harems would come over the ramps and into the middle sections to sample life in The Sink. When she had had enough, she would run back up the ramp. Sink males would give chase up to the top of the ramp, which is to say, to the very edge of the aristocratic preserve. But one glance from one of the king rats would stop them cold and they would return to The Sink. 17

The slumming females from the harems had their adventures and then returned to a placid, healthy life. Females in The Sink, however, were ravaged, physically and psychologically. Pregnant rats had trouble continuing pregnancy. The rate of miscarriages increased significantly, and females started dying from tumors and other disorders of the mammary glands, sex organs, uterus, ovaries, and Fallopian tubes. Typically, their kidneys, livers, and adrenals were also enlarged or diseased or showed other signs associated with stress. 18

Child-rearing became totally disorganized. The females lost the interest or the stamina to build nests and did not keep them up if they did build them. In the general filth and confusion, they would not put themselves out to save offspring they were momentarily separated from. Frantic, even sadistic competition among the males was going on all around them and rendering their lives chaotic. The males began unprovoked and senseless assaults upon one another, often in the form of tail-biting. Ordinarily, rats will suppress this kind of behavior when it crops up. In The Sink, male rats gave up all policing and just looked out for themselves. The ''pecking order'' among males in The Sink was never stable. Normally, male rats set up a three-class structure. Under the pressure of overcrowding, however, they broke up into all sorts of unstable 19 subclasses, cliques, packs—and constantly pushed, probed, explored, tested one another's power. Anyone was fair game, except for the aristocrats in the end pens.

Calhoun kept the population down to eighty, so that the next stage, "population collapse" or "massive die-off," did not occur. But the autopsies showed that the pattern—as in the diseases among the female rats—was already there.

The classic study of die-off was John J. Christian's study of Sika deer on James Island in the Chesapeake Bay, west of Cambridge, Maryland. Four or five of the deer had been released on the island, which was 280 acres and uninhabited, in 1916. By 1955 they had bred freely into a herd of 280 to 300. The population density was only about one deer per acre at this point, but Christian knew that this was already too high for the Sikas' inborn space requirements, and something would give before long. For two years the number of deer remained 280 to 300. But suddenly, in 1958, over half the deer died; 161 carcasses were recovered. In 1959 more deer died and the population steadied at about 80.

In two years, two-thirds of the herd had died. Why? It was not starvation. In fact, all the deer collected were in excellent condition, with well-developed muscles, shining coats, and fat deposits between the muscles. In practically all the deer, however, the adrenal glands had enlarged by 50 percent. Christian concluded that the die-off was due to "shock following severe metabolic disturbance, probably as a result of prolonged adrenocortical hyperactivity. . . . There was no evidence of infection, starvation, or other obvious cause to explain the mass mortality." In other words, the constant stress of overpopulation, plus the normal stress of the cold of the winter, had kept the adrenalin flowing so constantly in the deer that their systems were depleted of blood sugar and they died of shock.

Well, the white humans are still skidding and darting across the floor of Grand Central. Dr. Hall listens a moment longer to the skidding and the darting noises, and then says, "You know, I've been on commuter trains here after everyone has been through one of these rushes, and I'll tell you, there is enough acid flowing in the stomachs in every car to dissolve the rails underneath."

Just a little invisible acid bath for the linings to round off the day. The ulcers the acids cause, of course, are the one disease people have already been taught to associate with the stress of city life. But overcrowding, as Dr. Hall sees it, raises a lot more hell with the body than just ulcers. In everyday life in New York—just the usual, getting to work, working in massively congested areas like 42nd Street between Fifth Avenue and Lexington, especially now that the Pam-Am Building is set in there, working in cubicles such as those in the editorial offices at Time-Life, Inc., which Dr. Hall cites as typical of New York's poor handling of space, working in cubicles with low ceilings and, often, no access to a window, while construction crews all over Manhattan drive everybody up the Masonite wall with air-pressure generators with noises up to the boil-a-brain decibel level, then rushing to get home, piling into subways and trains, fighting for time and for space, the usual day in New York—the whole now-normal thing keeps shooting jolts of adrenalin into the body, breaking down the body's defenses and winding up with the work-a-daddy human animal stroked out at the breakfast table with his head apoplexed like a cauliflower out of his $6.95 semi-spread Pima-cotton shirt, and nosed over into a plate of No-Kloresto egg substitute, signing off with the black thrombosis, cancer, kidney, liver, or stomach failure, and the adrenals ooze to a halt, the size of eggplants in July.

One of the people whose work Dr. Hall is interested in on this score is Rene Dubos at the Rockefeller Institute. Dubos's work indicates that specific organisms, such as the tuberculosis bacillus or a pneumonia virus, can seldom be considered "the cause" of a disease. The germ or virus, apparently, has to work in combination with other things that have already broken the body down in some way—such as the old adrenal hyperactivity. Dr. Hall would like to see some autopsy studies made to record the size of adrenal glands in New York, especially of people crowded into slums and people who go through the full rush-hour-work-rush-hour cycle every day. He is afraid that until there is some clinical, statistical data on how overcrowding actually ravages the human body, no one will be willing to do anything about it. Even in so obvious a thing as air pollution, the pattern is familiar. Until people can actually see the smoke or smell the sulphur or feel the sting in their eyes, politicians will not get excited about it, even though it is well known that many of the lethal substances polluting the air are invisible and odorless. For one thing, most politicians are like the aristocrat rats. They are insulated from The Sink by practically sultanic buffers—limousines, chauffeurs, secretaries, aides-de-camp, doormen, shuttered houses, high-floor apartments. They almost never ride subways, fight rush hours, much less live in the slums or work in the Pam-Am Building.

Meanings and Values

1a.   Who are members of the ''species Mediterranean''?

b.   Who belong to the ''species North European''?

c.   What could account for their difference in space requirements (pars. 8–10)?

2.   Is this writing primarily objective or subjective? (See Guide to Terms: *Objective/Subjective.*) Why?

3a.   Do you get the impression that the author is being unkind, ''making fun'' of the harried New Yorkers?

b.   How, if at all, does he prevent such an impression?

4a.   Compare Wolfe's style, tone, and point of view with those of Catton (Sec. 3). (Guide: *Style/Tone* and *Point of View.*)

b.   Do these features necessarily make one author less effective than another in achieving his purposes? Explain.

Expository Techniques

1a.   Using whatever criteria we have available for judging the success of analogy, appraise the effectiveness of this one.

b.   Does the author work it *too* hard? Be prepared to defend your answer.

2.   What are the benefits of the frequent return to what Dr. Hall is doing or saying (e.g., in pars. 3, 5, 7, 9, 11, 23)?

3.   Paragraph 12 has a useful function beyond the simple information it imparts—a sort of organic relation to the coming development. Explain how this is accomplished.

4.   How is the switch to Sika deer (par. 21) prepared for, and a bumpy transition avoided?

5.   The preceding three questions are related in some manner to the problems of transition. How, if at all, are such problems also matters of coherence? (Guide: *Coherence.*)

6.   Wolfe is adept at creating just the effect he wants, and the careful student of writing can detect a subtle change of style and pace with each change of subpurpose. (Guide: *Style/Tone.*)

a.   Analyze stylistic differences, with resulting effects, between the description of chaos at Grand Central and the information about Dr. Hall in paragraph 7.

b.   Analyze such differences between the Grand Central scene and the account of the laboratory experiment with rats.

c.   Analyze the differences between the Grand Central scene and the final paragraph.

7.   Explain how the style of the more descriptive portions is also a matter of emphasis. (Guide: *Emphasis.*)

8a.   Illustrate as many as possible of the elements of effective syntax (itself a matter of style) by examples from this selection. (Guide: *Syntax.*)

b.   What is gained or lost by the unusual length and design of the last sentence of paragraph 24? (We can be sure that it did not ''just happen'' to Wolfe—and equally sure that one of such length would be disastrous in most writing.)

Diction and Vocabulary

1.   What is the significance of the word ''Gotham''?

2a.   Why do you think the author refers (deliberately, no doubt) to ''my fellow New Yorkers'' in the first sentence?

b.   What soon could have been the effect if he had not taken such a step?

3.   Why does he consistently, after paragraph 2, refer to the people as ''poor white humans,'' ''poor human animals,'' etc.?

4.   In paragraph 14 he refers to the connotations of the word ''sink.'' What are its possible connotations? (Guide: *Connotation/Denotation.*)

5.   Cite examples of verbal irony to be found in paragraphs 5, 8, 24. (Guide: *Irony.*)

6.   Which of the elements of style mentioned in your answer to question 4a of ''Meanings and Values'' are also matters of diction?

7.   Consult your dictionary as needed for full understanding of the following words: autistic, puling (par. 1); etiolate (4); effluvia, sebaceous (8); pathology (14); satyrism (16); senescent (17); decibel, thrombosis (24); lethal (25).

Suggestions for Writing and Discussion

1.   Carrying Wolfe's analogy still further, trace the steps by which a rise in serious crime must result from the overcrowding of ''poor human animals.''

2. If you are familiar with another city, particularly during rush hours, which appears to you much like New York in this respect, describe it.

3. If you are familiar with some area of high-density population that has solved its problem of overcrowding, explain the solution.

4. What practical steps can the *individual* take, if forced to live and/or work in overcrowded conditions, to avoid becoming the victim of his or her own adrenals?

(NOTE: Suggestions for topics requiring development by use of ANALOGY are on page 148, at the end of this section.)

LOREN C. EISELEY

LOREN C. EISELEY (1907–1977) was professor of anthropology and the history of science at the University of Pennsylvania, where he also served as provost from 1959 to 1961. He was a Guggenheim Foundation Fellow and was in charge of anthropological expeditions for various universities and for the Smithsonian Institution. Eiseley, a respected naturalist and conservationist, also served on many public service boards and commissions and was awarded many honorary degrees and medals. Widely published in both scholarly and popular magazines, Eiseley also wrote several books, including *The Immense Journey* (1957), *Darwin's Century* (1959), *The Firmament of Time* (1960), *The Unexpected Universe* (1969), and *The Night Country* (1971).

The Brown Wasps

"The Brown Wasps" was selected from Eiseley's book *The Night Country*. It is an essay with a simple theme, developed through a rather intricate web of simple analogies. In reading this selection, you will see why Eiseley was—and is—widely admired for his lucid, almost poetic style, as well as for his sensitive philosophical approach to all living things.

There is a corner in the waiting room of one of the great Eastern 1
stations where women never sit. It is always in the shadow and overhung by rows of lockers. It is, however, always frequented—not so much by genuine travelers as by the dying. It is here that a certain element of the abandoned poor seeks a refuge out of the weather, clinging for a few hours longer to the city that has fathered them. In a precisely similar manner I have seen, on a sunny day in midwinter, a few old brown wasps creep slowly over an

abandoned wasp nest in a thicket. Numbed and forgetful and frost-blackened, the hum of the spring hive still resounded faintly in their sodden tissues. Then the temperature would fall and they would drop away into the white oblivion of the snow. Here in the station it is in no way different save the city is busy in its snows. But the old ones cling to their seats as though these were symbolic and could not be given up. Now and then they sleep, their gray old heads resting with painful awkwardness on the backs of the benches.

Also they are not at rest. For an hour they may sleep in the gasping exhaustion of the ill-nourished and aged who have to walk in the night. Then a policeman comes by on his round and nudges them upright.

"You can't sleep here," he growls.

A strange ritual then begins. An old man is difficult to waken. After a muttered conversation the policeman presses a coin into his hand and passes fiercely along the benches prodding and gesturing toward the door. In his wake, like birds rising and settling behind the passage of a farmer through a cornfield, the men totter up, move a few paces and subside once more upon the benches.

One man, after a slight, apologetic lurch, does not move at all. Tubercularly thin, he sleeps on steadily. The policeman does not look back. To him, too, this has become a ritual. He will not have to notice it again officially for another hour.

Once in a while one of the sleepers will not awaken. Like the brown wasps, he will have had his wish to die in the great droning center of the hive rather than in some lonely room. It is not so bad here with the shuffle of footsteps and the knowledge that there are others who share the bad luck of the world. There are also the whistles and the sounds of everyone, everyone in the world, starting on journeys. Amidst so many journeys somebody is bound to come out all right. Somebody.

Maybe it was on a like thought that the brown wasps fell away from the old paper nest in the thicket. You hold till the last, even if it is only to a public seat in a railroad station. You want your place in the hive more than you want a room or a place where the aged can be eased gently out of the way. It is the place that matters, the place at the heart of things. It is life that you want, that bruises your gray old head with the hard chairs; a man has a right to his place.

But sometimes the place is lost in the years behind us. Or 8
sometimes it is a thing of air, a kind of vaporous distortion above
a heap of rubble. We cling to a time and place because without
them man is lost, not only man but life. This is why the voices,
real or unreal, which speak from the floating trumpets at spiritual-
ist seances are so unnerving. They are voices out of nowhere
whose only reality lies in their ability to stir the memory of a living
person with some fragment of the past. Before the medium's cabi-
net both the dead and the living revolve endlessly about an episode, a place, an event that has already been engulfed by time.

This feeling runs deep in life; it brings stray cats running over 9
endless miles, and birds homing from the ends of the earth. It is
as though all living creatures, and particularly the more intelligent,
can survive only by fixing or transforming a bit of time into space
or by securing a bit of space with its objects immortalized and
made permanent in time. For example, I once saw, on a flower
pot in my own living room, the efforts of a field mouse to build a
remembered field. I have lived to see this episode repeated in a
thousand guises, and since I have spent a large portion of my life
in the shade of a nonexistent tree, I think I am entitled to speak
for the field mouse.

One day as I cut across the field, which at that time extended 10
on one side of our suburban shopping center, I found a giant slug
feeding from a runnel of pink ice cream in an abandoned Dixie
cup. I could see his eyes telescope and protrude in a kind of dim,
uncertain ecstasy as his dark body bunched and elongated in the
curve of the cup. Then, as I stood there at the edge of the concrete,
contemplating the slug, I began to realize it was like standing on
a shore where a different type of life creeps up and fumbles tentatively among the rocks and sea wrack. It knows its place and will
only creep so far until something changes. Little by little as I stood
there, I began to see more of this shore that surrounds the place
of man. I looked with sudden care and attention at things I had
been running over thoughtlessly for years. I even waded out a
short way into the grass and the wild-rose thickets to see more.
A huge black-belted bee went droning by and there were some
indistinct scurryings in the underbrush.

Then I came to a sign which informed me that this field was 11
to be the site of a new Wanamaker suburban store. Thousands of
obscure lives were about to perish, the spores of puffballs would

go smoking off to new fields, and the bodies of little white-footed mice would be crunched under the inexorable wheels of the bulldozers. Life disappears or modifies its appearances so fast that everything takes on an aspect of illusion—a momentary fizzing and boiling with smoke rings, like pouring dissident chemicals into a retort. Here man was advancing, but in a few years his plaster and bricks would be disappearing once more into the insatiable maw of the clover. Being of an archaeological cast of mind, I thought of this fact with an obscure sense of satisfaction and waded back through the rose thickets to the concrete parking lot. As I did so, a mouse scurried ahead of me, frightened of my steps if not of that ominous Wanamaker sign. I saw him vanish in the general direction of my apartment house, his little body quivering with fear in the great open sun on the blazing concrete. Blinded and confused, he was running straight away from his field. In another week scores would follow him.

I forgot the episode then and went home to the quiet of my living room. It was not until a week later, letting myself into the apartment, that I realized I had a visitor. I am fond of plants and had several ferns standing on the floor in pots to avoid the noon glare by the south window.

As I snapped on the light and glanced carelessly around the room, I saw a little heap of earth on the carpet and a scrabble of pebbles that had been kicked merrily over the edge of one of the flower pots. To my astonishment I discovered a full-fledged burrow delving downward among the fern roots. I waited silently. The creature who had made the burrow did not appear. I remembered the wild field then, and the flight of the mice. No house mouse, no *Mus domesticus*, had kicked up this little heap of earth or sought refuge under a fern root in a flower pot. I thought of the desperate little creature I had seen fleeing from the wild-rose thicket. Through intricacies of pipes and attics, he, or one of his fellows, had climbed to this high green solitary room. I could visualize what had occurred. He had an image in his head, a world of seed pods and quiet, of green sheltering leaves in the dim light among the weed stems. It was the only world he knew and it was gone.

Somehow in his flight he had found his way to this room with drawn shades where no one would come till nightfall. And here he had smelled green leaves and run quickly up the flower pot to dabble his paws in common earth. He had even struggled half the afternoon to carry his burrow deeper and had failed. I examined the hole, but no whiskered twitching face appeared. He was gone. I gathered up the earth and refilled the burrow. I did not expect to find traces of him again.

Yet for three nights thereafter I came home to the darkened room and my ferns to find the dirt kicked gaily about the rug and the burrow reopened, though I was never able to catch the field mouse within it. I dropped a little food about the mouth of the burrow, but it was never touched. I looked under beds or sat reading with one ear cocked for rustlings in the ferns. It was all in vain; I never saw him. Probably he ended in a trap in some other tenant's room. 15

But before he disappeared, I had come to look hopefully for his evening burrow. About my ferns there had begun to linger the insubstantial vapor of an autumn field, the distilled essence, as it were, of a mouse brain in exile from its home. It was a small dream, like our dreams, carried a long and weary journey along pipes and through spider webs, past holes over which loomed the shadows of waiting cats, and finally, desperately, into this room where he had played in the shuttered daylight for an hour among the green ferns on the floor. Every day these invisible dreams pass us on the street, or rise from beneath our feet, or look out upon us from beneath a bush. 16

Some years ago the old elevated railway in Philadelphia was torn down and replaced by a subway system. This ancient El with its barnlike stations containing nut-vending machines and scattered food scraps had, for generations, been the favorite feeding ground of flocks of pigeons, generally one flock to a station along the route of the El. Hundreds of pigeons were dependent upon the system. They flapped in and out of its stanchions and steel work or gathered in watchful little audiences about the feet of anyone who rattled the peanut-vending machines. They even watched people who jingled change in their hands, and prospected for food under the feet of the crowds who gathered between trains. Probably very few among the waiting people who tossed a crumb to an eager pigeon realized that this El was like a food-bearing river, and that the life which haunted its banks was dependent upon the running of the trains with their human freight. 17

I saw the river stop. 18

The time came when the underground tubes were ready; the
traffic was transferred to a realm unreachable by pigeons. It was
like a great river subsiding suddenly into desert sands. For a day,
for two days, pigeons continued to circle over the El or stand close
to the red vending machines. They were patient birds, and surely
this great river which had flowed through the lives of unnumbered
generations was merely suffering from some momentary drought.

They listened for the familiar vibrations that had always her-
alded an approaching train; they flapped hopefully about the head
of an occasional workman walking along the steel runways. They
passed from one empty station to another, all the while growing
hungrier. Finally, they flew away.

I thought I had seen the last of them about the El, but there
was a revival and it provided a curious instance of the memory of
living things for a way of life or a locality that has long been cherished. Some weeks after the El was abandoned, workmen began
to tear it down. I went to work every morning by one particular
station, and the time came when the demolition crews reached this
spot. Acetylene torches showered passers-by with sparks, pneu-
matic drills hammered at the base of the structure, and a blind man
who, like the pigeons, had clung with his cup to a stairway leading
to the change booth, was forced to give up his place.

It was then, strangely, momentarily, one morning that I witnessed the return of a little band of the familiar pigeons. I even
recognized one or two members of the flock that had lived around
this particular station before they were dispersed into the streets.
They flew bravely in and out among the sparks and the hammers
and the shouting workmen. They had returned—and they had returned because the hubbub of the wreckers had convinced them
that the river was about to flow once more. For several hours they
flapped in and out through the empty windows, nodding their
heads and watching the fall of girders with attentive little eyes. By
the following morning the station was reduced to some burned-off
stanchions in the street. My bird friends had gone. It was plain,
however, that they retained a memory for an insubstantial structure now compounded of air and time. Even the blind man clung
to it. Someone had provided him with a chair, and he sat at the
same corner staring sightlessly at an invisible stairway where, so
far as he was concerned, the crowds were still ascending to the
trains.

I have said my life has been passed in the shade of a non-existent tree, so that such sights do not offend me. Prematurely I am one of the brown wasps and I often sit with them in the great droning hive of the station, dreaming sometimes of a certain tree. It was planted sixty years ago by a boy with a bucket and a toy spade in a little Nebraska town. That boy was myself. It was a cottonwood sapling and the boy remembered it because of some words spoken by his father and because everyone died or moved away who was supposed to wait and grow old under its shade. The boy was passed from hand to hand, but the tree for some intangible reason had taken root in his mind. It was under its branches that he sheltered; it was from this tree that his memories, which are my memories, led away into the world.   23

After sixty years the mood of the brown wasps grows heavier upon one. During a long inward struggle I thought it would do me good to go and look upon that actual tree. I found a rational excuse in which to clothe this madness. I purchased a ticket and at the end of two thousand miles I walked another mile to an address that was still the same. The house had not been altered.   24

I came close to the white picket fence and reluctantly, with great effort, looked down the long vista of the yard. There was nothing there to see. For sixty years that cottonwood had been growing in my mind. Season by season its seeds had been floating farther on the hot prairie winds. We had planted it lovingly there, my father and I, because he had a great hunger for soil and live things growing, and because none of these things had long been ours to protect. We had planted the little sapling and watered it faithfully, and I remembered that I had run out with my small bucket to drench its roots the day we moved away. And all the years since, it had been growing in my mind, a huge tree that somehow stood for my father and the love I bore him. I took a grasp on the picket fence and forced myself to look again.   25

A boy with the hard bird eye of youth pedaled a tricycle slowly up beside me.   26

"What'cha lookin' at?" he asked curiously.   27

"A tree," I said.   28

"What for?" he said.   29

"It isn't there," I said, to myself mostly, and began to walk away at a pace just slow enough not to seem to be running.   30

"What isn't there?" the boy asked. I didn't answer. It was   31 obvious I was attached by a thread to a thing that had never been there, or certainly not for long. Something that had to be held in the air, or sustained in the mind, because it was part of my orientation in the universe and I could not survive without it. There was more than an animal's attachment to a place. There was something else, the attachment of the spirit to a grouping of events in time; it was part of our morality.

So I had come home at last, driven by a memory in the brain as surely as the field mouse who had delved long ago into my flower pot or the pigeons flying forever amidst the rattle of nut-vending machines. These, the burrow under the greenery in my living room and the red-bellied bowls of peanuts now hovering in midair in the minds of pigeons, were all part of an elusive world that existed nowhere and yet everywhere. I looked once at the real world about me while the persistent boy pedaled at my heels.

It was without meaning, though my feet took a remembered path. In sixty years the house and street had rotted out of my mind. But the tree, the tree that no longer was, that had perished in its first season, bloomed on in my individual mind, unblemished as my father's words. "We'll plant a tree here, son, and we're not going to move any more. And when you're an old, old man you can sit under it and think how we planted it here, you and me, together."

I began to outpace the boy on the tricycle.

"Do you live here, Mister?" he shouted after me suspiciously. I took a firm grasp on airy nothing—to be precise, on the bole of a great tree. "I do," I said. I spoke for myself, one field mouse, and several pigeons. We were all out of touch but somehow permanent. It was the world that had changed.

Meanings and Values

1a.   How would you describe the tone of this selection? (See Guide to Terms: *Style/Tone.*)

b.   Are the tone and the pace suitable to the subject matter? Why, or why not?

c.   Is Eiseley's style compatible with the tone?

2a.   What was Eiseley's apparent purpose in writing this essay? (Guide: *Evaluation.*) ("Purpose" is the key question in this evaluation: it is significant that the essay was written for inclusion in a book.)

b.   How well did he achieve his purpose?

c.   Was it worthwhile?

3.   Explain how the seats were "symbolic" to the old men (par. 1). (Guide: *Symbol.*)

4.   Paragraphs 2–5 give us a small but well-rounded picture of the policeman. Use your own words to describe him as fully as possible.

5a. Clarify the meaning, or meanings, of paragraph 8.

b.   How does spending much of his life in the shade of a nonexistent tree entitle Eiseley to speak for the field mouse (par. 9)?

c.   What was it, precisely, that caused Eiseley's "obscure sense of satisfaction" (par. 11)? Why?

6a. Where would you place this essay on an objective-to-subjective continuum? Why? (Guide: *Objective/Subjective.*)

b.   Could you classify it as formal? Why? (Guide: *Essay.*)

7.   Select at least one passage that would be, in the hands of many writers, particularly subject to sentimentalism. (Guide: *Sentimentalism.*) Explain why you consider it overly sentimental, or how Eiseley was able to avoid that fault.

Expository Techniques

1a. What are the three major analogies that are linked in this essay?

b.   Do they all have the same analogical purpose? If not, what is their relationship?

c.   With what particular act does Eiseley analogically equate his own return to Nebraska, or is it an outgrowth of the whole theme to that point?

d.   How effectively does each analogy achieve its purpose?

2a. The transition between paragraphs 7 and 8 is especially important. Why? (Guide: *Transitions.*)

b.   By what means does Eiseley assure a smooth connection?

3.   Is unity damaged by the introduction of the boy toward the end? (Guide: *Unity.*) Show how it is damaged, or explain what you think was Eiseley's purpose in using him. (The fact that the child happened along in "real life" would not have justified including him here; the author *selects* his own details.)

4a. Study the second sentence of paragraph 23 and the first sentence of paragraph 24. What, exactly, do they have in common?

b.   What, if anything, is gained by this change?

5a. Did you find it difficult to get at the essence of Eiseley's mean-ings—in other words, did you find the essay hard to read? If so, try to determine just what caused your difficulties.

b. Could these difficulties have been readily avoided by the author without sacrificing anything of quality or message?

c. Do you think a more experienced reader than you would have had any difficulty at all?

Diction and Vocabulary

1a. How would you describe the diction of this writing? (Guide: *Diction.*)

b. How would you describe the syntax? (Guide: *Syntax.*)

c. Explain why the diction and syntax, and the pace of the writing, would, or would not, be appropriate for most college papers. For most newspaper writing.

2. Why does the author refer to the old "paper" nest in the thicket (par. 7)?

3a. Demonstrate the meaning of the term *metaphor* by use of one or more examples from this selection. (Guide: *Figures of Speech.*)

b. The meaning of *simile.*

c. The meaning of *personification.*

4. If you are not familiar with the meaning of any of the following words, consult your dictionary: sodden (par. 1); subside (4); vapor-ous (8); guises (9); runnel, wrack (10); inexorable, dissident, retort, insatiable, maw (11); dispersed (22).

Suggestions for Writing and Discussion

Plan and discuss, in oral or written form, one of the following pas-sages, clarifying its meanings and implications.

1. "We cling to a time and place because without them man is lost, not only man but life."

2. "Life disappears or modifies its appearances so fast that every-thing takes on an aspect of illusion. . . ."

3. "Every day these invisible dreams pass us on the street, or rise from beneath our feet, or look out upon us from beneath a bush."

4. ". . . the attachment of the spirit to a grouping of events in time; it was part of our morality."

(NOTE: Suggestions for topics requiring development by use of ANALOGY are on page 148, at the end of this section.)

JAMES C. RETTIE

JAMES C. RETTIE was an employee of the National Forest Service's experimental station at Upper Darby, Pennsylvania, in 1948 when he adapted this fable from a United States Department of Agriculture pamphlet entitled "To Hold This Soil." At the time, he was a member of The Society of the Friends of the Land and an ardent conservationist.

"But a Watch in the Night": A Scientific Fable

"But a Watch in the Night"[1] is a highly innovative analogy and illustrates, among other things, the extreme versatility of this pattern of exposition. The analogy itself (a "scientific fable," as the author has called it) is composed almost entirely of narration (a pattern to be studied further in Section 9). While Rettie has taken numerous creative liberties not often available to the student in ordinary college writing, he apparently was very much aware of the same goal we all need to keep in mind when writing: the desired effect, for *his* purposes, on *his* reader-audience.

"But a Watch in the Night" by James C. Rettie from *Forever the Land*, edited by Russell and Kate Lord. Copyright 1950 by Harper & Row, Publishers, Inc. Reprinted by permission of Harper & Row, Publishers, Inc.

[1]From the Bible, Psalm 90, apparently either slightly altered or using a translation other than the King James version, which reads:

Lord, thou hast been our dwelling place
In all generations.
Before the mountains were brought forth,
Or ever thou hadst formed the earth and the world,
Even from everlasting, thou art God.
Thou turnest man to destruction;
And sayest, "Return, ye children of men."
For a thousand years in thy sight
Are but as yesterday when it is past,
And as a watch in the night. . . .   —EDS.

Out beyond our solar system there is a planet called Copernicus. It came into existence some four or five billion years before the birth of our Earth. In due course of time it became inhabited by a race of intelligent men.

About 750 million years ago the Copernicans had developed the motion picture machine to a point well in advance of the stage that we have reached. Most of the cameras that we now use in motion picture work are geared to take twenty-four pictures per second on a continuous strip of film. When such film is run through a projector, it throws a series of images on the screen and these change with a rapidity that gives the visual impression of normal movement. If a motion is too swift for the human eye to see it in detail, it can be captured and artificially slowed down by means of the slow-motion camera. This one is geared to take many more shots per second—ninety-six or even more than that. When the slow-motion film is projected at the normal speed of twenty-four pictures per second, we can see just how the jumping horse goes over a hurdle.

What about motion that is too slow to be seen by the human eye? That problem has been solved by the use of the time-lapse camera. In this one, the shutter is geared to take only one shot per second, or one per minute, or even one per hour—depending upon the kind of movement that is being photographed. When the time-lapse film is projected at the normal speed of twenty-four pictures per second, it is possible to see a bean sprout growing up out of the ground. Time-lapse films are useful in the study of many types of motion too slow to be observed by the unaided, human eye.

The Copernicans, it seems, had time-lapse cameras some 757 million years ago and they also had superpowered telescopes that gave them a clear view of what was happening upon this Earth. They decided to make a film record of the life history of Earth and to make it on the scale of one picture per year. The photography has been in progress during the last 757 million years.

In the near future, a Copernican interstellar expedition will arrive upon our Earth and bring with it a copy of the time-lapse film. Arrangements will be made for showing the entire film in one continuous run. This will begin at midnight of New Year's eve and continue day and night without a single stop until midnight of December 31. The rate of projection will be twenty-four pictures per second. Time on the screen will thus seem to move at the rate of 24 years per second; 1,440 years per minute; 86,400 years per hour; approximately 2 million years per day; and 62 million years per month. The normal life-span of individual man will occupy about three seconds. The full period of Earth history that will be unfolded on the screen (some 757 million years) will extend from what the geologists call Pre-Cambrian times up to the present. This will, by no means, cover the full time-span of the Earth's geological history, but it will embrace the period since the advent of living organisms.

During the months of January, February and March the picture will be desolate and dreary. The shape of the land masses and the oceans will bear little or no resemblance to those that we know. The violence of geological erosion will be much in evidence. Rains will pour down on the land and promptly go booming down to the seas. There will be no clear streams anywhere except where the rains fall upon hard rock. Everywhere on the steeper ground the stream channels will be filled with boulders hurled down by rushing waters. Raging torrents and dry stream beds will keep alternating in quick succession. High mountains will seem to melt like so much butter in the sun. The shifting of land into the seas, later to be thrust up as new mountains, will be going on at a grand scale. 6

Early in April there will be some indication of the presence of single-celled living organisms in some of the warmer and sheltered coastal waters. By the end of the month it will be noticed that some of these organisms have become multicellular. A few of them, including the Trilobites, will be encased in hard shells. 7

Toward the end of May, the first vertebrates will appear, but they will still be aquatic creatures. In June about 60 percent of the land area that we know as North America will be under water. One broad channel will occupy the space where the Rocky Mountains now stand. Great deposits of limestone will be forming under some of the shallower seas. Oil and gas deposits will be in process of formation—also under shallow seas. On land there will still be no sign of vegetation. Erosion will be rampant, tearing loose particles and chunks of rock and grinding them into sand and silt to be spewed out by the streams into bays and estuaries. 8

About the middle of July the first land plants will appear and take up the tremendous job of soil building. Slowly, very slowly, 9 the mat of vegetation will spread, always battling for its life against the power of erosion. Almost foot by foot, the plant life will advance, lacing down with its root structures whatever pulverized rock material it can find. Leaves and stems will be giving added protection against the loss of the soil foothold. The increasing vegetation will pave the way for the land animals that will live upon it.

Early in August the seas will be teeming with fish. This will be what geologists call the Devonian period. Some of the races of these fish will be breathing by means of lung tissue instead of through gill tissues. Before the month is over, some of the lung fish will go ashore and take on a crude lizard-like appearance. Here are the first amphibians.

In early September the insects will put in their appearance. Some will look like huge dragon flies and will have a wingspread of 24 inches. Large portions of the land masses will now be covered with heavy vegetation that will include the primitive spore-propagating trees. Layer upon layer of this plant growth will build up, later to appear as the coal deposits. About the middle of this month, there will be evidence of the first seed-bearing plants and the first reptiles. Heretofore, the land animals will have been amphibians that could reproduce their kind only by depositing a soft egg mass in quiet waters. The reptiles will be shown to be freed from the aquatic bond because they can reproduce by means of a shelled egg in which the embryo and its nurturing liquids are sealed in and thus protected from destructive evaporation. Before September is over, the first dinosaurs will be seen—creatures destined to dominate the animal realm for about 140 million years and then to disappear.

In October there will be a series of mountain uplifts along what is now the eastern coast of the United States. A creature with feathered limbs—half bird and half reptile in appearance—will take itself into the air. Some small and rather unpretentious animals will be seen to bring forth their young in a form that is a miniature replica of the parents and to feed these young on milk secreted by mammary glands in the female parent. The emergence of this mammalian form of animal life will be recognized as one of the great events in geologic time. October will also witness the high water mark of the dinosaurs—creatures ranging in size from that of the modern goat to monsters like Brontosaurus that weighed some 40 tons. Most of them will be placid vegetarians, but a few will be hideous-looking carnivores, like Allosaurus and Tyrannosaurus. Some of the herbivorous dinosaurs will be clad in bony armor for protection against their flesh-eating comrades.

November will bring pictures of a sea extending from the Gulf of Mexico to the Arctic in space now occupied by the Rocky Mountains. A few of the reptiles will take to the air on bat-like wings. One of these, called Pteranodon, will have a wingspread of 15 feet. There will be a rapid development of the modern flowering plants, modern trees, and modern insects. The dinosaurs will disappear. Toward the end of the month there will be a tremendous land disturbance in which the Rocky Mountains will rise out of the sea to assume a dominating place in the North American landscape.

As the picture runs on into December, it will show the mammals in command of the animal life. Seed-bearing trees and grasses will have covered most of the land with a heavy mantle of vegetation. Only the areas newly thrust up from the sea will be barren. Most of the streams will be crystal clear. The turmoil of geologic erosion will be confined to localized areas. About December 25 will begin the cutting of the Grand Canyon of the Colorado River. Grinding down through layer after layer of sedimentary strata, this stream will finally expose deposits laid down in Pre-Cambrian times. Thus in the walls of that canyon will appear geological formations dating from recent times to the period when the earth had no living organisms upon it.

The picture will run on through the latter days of December and even up to its final day with still no sign of mankind. The spectators will become alarmed in the fear that man has somehow been left out. But not so; sometime about noon on December 31 (one million years ago) will appear a stooped, massive creature of man-like proportions. This will be Pithecanthropus, the Java ape man. For tools and weapons he will have nothing but crude stone and wooden clubs. His children will live a precarious existence threatened on the one side by hostile animals and on the other by tremendous climatic changes. Ice sheets—in places 4000 feet deep—will form in the northern parts of North America and Eurasia. Four times this glacial ice will push southward to cover half the continents. With each advance the plant and animal life will be swept under or pushed southward. With each recession of the ice, life will struggle to reestablish itself in the wake of the retreating glaciers. The wooly mammoth, the musk ox, and the caribou all will fight to maintain themselves near the ice line. Sometimes they will be caught and put into cold storage—skin, flesh, blood, bones and all.

The picture will run on through supper time with still very little evidence of man's presence on the Earth. It will be about 11 o'clock when Neanderthal man appears. Another half hour will go by before the appearance of Cro-Magnon man living in caves and painting crude animal pictures on the walls of his dwelling. Fifteen minutes more will bring Neolithic man, knowing how to chip stone and thus produce sharp cutting edges for spears and tools. In a few minutes more it will appear that man has domesticated the dog, the sheep and, possibly, other animals. He will then begin the use of milk. He will also learn the arts of basket weaving and the making of pottery and dugout canoes.

The dawn of civilization will not come until about five or six minutes before the end of the picture. The story of the Egyptians, the Babylonians, the Greeks, and the Romans will unroll during the fourth, the third and the second minute before the end. At 58 minutes and 43 seconds past 11:00 P.M. (just 1 minute and 17 seconds before the end) will come the beginning of the Christian era. Columbus will discover the new world 20 seconds before the end. The Declaration of Independence will be signed just 7 seconds before the final curtain comes down.

In those few moments of geologic time will be the story of all that has happened since we became a nation. And what a story it will be! A human swarm will sweep across the face of the continent and take it away from the primitive red men. They will change it far more radically than it has ever been changed before in a comparable time. The great virgin forests will be seen going down before ax and fire. The soil, covered for aeons by its protective mantle of trees and grasses, will be laid bare to the ravages of water and wind erosion. Streams that had been flowing clear will, once again, take up a load of silt and push it toward the seas. Humus and mineral salts, both vital elements of productive soil, will be seen to vanish at a terrifying rate. The railroads and highways and cities that will spring up may divert attention, but they cannot cover up the blight of man's recent activities. In great sections of Asia, it will be seen that man must utilize cow dung and every scrap of available straw or grass for fuel to cook his food. The forests that once provided wood for this purpose will be gone without a trace. The use of these agricultural wastes for fuel, in place of returning them to the land, will be leading to increasing soil impoverishment. Here and there will be seen a dust storm darkening the landscape over an area a thousand miles across. Man-creatures will be shown counting their wealth in terms of bits of printed paper representing other bits of a scarce but comparatively useless yellow metal that is kept buried in strong vaults. Meanwhile, the soil, the only real wealth that can keep mankind alive on the face of this Earth, is savagely being cut loose from its ancient moorings and washed into the seven seas.

We have just arrived upon this Earth. How long will we stay? 19

Meanings and Values

1a.   What is the significance of the quotation, as it is used in the title of this essay?

b.   Is the title itself an allusion? Why, or why not? (See Guide to Terms: *Figures of Speech.*)

c.   Explain why you personally do, or do not, like the title.

2a.   What do you find ironic in the latter part of paragraph 18? (Guide: *Irony.*)

b.   What kind of irony is it?

3a.   Compare the effectiveness of Rettie's unique handling of the soil-loss problem with the methods commonly used for environmental propaganda.

b.   Could he have enlarged it effectively to include other environmental problems? Why, or why not?

Expository Techniques

1a.   In what respects does "But a Watch in the Night" qualify as analogy?

b.   Why could the author not have achieved his purpose as well by showing us more simply, in actual year spans, the brevity of human existence on earth, rather than by this condensed movie version?

2a.   The author devotes five paragraphs just to setting up his analogy. In what way, or ways, might this slow beginning be justified?

b.   Does the analogy benefit by such a detailed explanation of the camera's capabilities? Why, or why not?

c.   Why do you suppose Rettie created a fictional planet?

d.   Should he have told us at some point that the whole thing is make-believe? Why, or why not?

3a.   Why do you think the author took the trouble to work out the rate of projection to fit exactly into one year?

b.   What is gained, or lost, by learning as early as paragraph 5 that the normal life span of individual man would occupy only about three seconds?

4a.   What did you believe at first to be the central theme? (Guide: *Unity.*)

b.   How did your impression of the theme become modified in paragraph 5?

c.   In view of the overall essay, state what you now believe to have been the author's theme.

d.   Does the composition have unity—i.e., do all parts serve as tributaries, however indirect, into the central theme?

5a.   Explain fully, in terms of "emphasis," why this slow unfolding of the real theme helps, or hinders, in achieving the author's apparent purpose. (Guide: *Emphasis.*)

b.   This is a more "creative" piece than most expositions. Why would such a slow unfolding be inappropriate to most college and workaday writing?

6.   What advantage is gained, if any, by the parallel beginnings of most paragraphs? (Guide: *Parallel Structure.*)

7a.   What criteria did Rettie apparently use in selecting, from among thousands, the details to be included in the various time periods?

b.   Would it have been better to use some other criteria? Why, or why not?

8a.   A rhetorical question is used here in a highly strategic position. Where is it? (Guide: *Rhetorical Questions.*)

b.   How effective is its use?

Diction and Vocabulary

1a.   The naming of the planet makes use, rather indirectly, of an allusion. To what does it refer? (Guide: *Figures of Speech.*)

b.   Why is it appropriate, or inappropriate, for this piece?

2a.   What kind of figure of speech do you find in paragraph 6?

  b.   In paragraph 17 there is a figure of speech that is also a cliché. What is it? (Guide: *Figures of Speech* and *Clichés.*)

  c.   What kind of figure of speech is it?

  d.   Why is it also classifiable as a cliché?

Suggestions for Writing and Discussion

1.   What practical steps could be taken now to prevent the rest of our "only real wealth" from being washed into the sea? What are the chances of such steps being taken seriously enough, soon enough?

2.   Assuming that our food-production technology continues to advance rapidly, is it conceivable that humankind might manage to survive without much soil? Discuss this possibility.

3.   If you are particularly interested in the Bible, for either literary or religious reasons, discuss more fully the meanings of the part of Psalm 90 quoted in the introduction. If you like, you may enlarge your discussion to include the entire psalm.

(NOTE: Suggestions for topics requiring development by use of ANALOGY follow.)

Writing Suggestions for Section 4
Analogy

In any normal situation, the analogy is chosen to help explain a theme-idea that already exists—such as those in the first group below. But for classroom training, which even at best is bound to be somewhat artificial, it is sometimes permissible to work from the other direction, to develop a theme that fits some preselected analogy-symbol. Your instructor will indicate which of the groups to use.

1. State a central theme about one of the following general topics or a suitable one of your own, and develop it into a composition by use of an analogy of your own choosing.
   a. A well-organized school system.
   b. Starting a new business or other enterprise.
   c. The long-range value of programs for underprivileged children.
   d. Learning a new skill.
   e. The need for cooperation between management and labor.
   f. Today's intense competition for success.
   g. Dealing with stress.
   h. The results of ignorance.
2. Select an analogy-symbol from the following list and fashion a worthwhile theme that it can illustrate. Develop your composition as instructed.
   a. A freeway at commuting time.
   b. Building a road through a wilderness.
   c. Building a bridge across a river.
   d. A merry-go-round.
   e. A wedding.
   f. A car wash.
   g. Flood destruction of a levee.
   h. The tending of a young orchard.
   i. An animal predator stalking prey.
   j. A medical clinic.
   k. A juggling act.
   l. An oasis.
   m. A duel.
   n. An airport.

5

Explaining Through *Process Analysis*

Process analysis explains how the steps of an operation lead to its completion. Although in one narrow sense it may be considered a kind of narration, process analysis has an important difference in purpose, and hence in approach. Other narration is mostly concerned with the story itself, or with a general concept illustrated by it, but process tells of methods that end in specified results. We might narrate a story about a rifle—its purchase, its role in colorful episodes, perhaps its eventual retirement from active service. (We could, for other purposes, *define* "rifle," or *classify* the types of rifles, and no doubt *compare* and *contrast* these types and *illustrate* by examples.) But showing how a rifle works, or how it is manufactured, or how it should be cared for—this is process, and it sometimes becomes the basic pattern of an exposition.

Most writers are especially concerned with two kinds of process, both of them apparent in the preceding example of rifles: the directional, which explains how to *do* something (how to shoot a gun or how to clean it); and the informational, which explains how something is or was *done* (how guns are manufactured). The directional process can range from the instructions on a shampoo bottle to a detailed plan showing how to make the United Nations more effective, and will often contain detailed justification for individual steps or for the process itself. The informational process, on the other hand, might explain the steps of a wide variety of operations or actions, of mental or evolutionary processes, with no how-to-do-it purpose at all—how someone went about choosing a college or how the planet Earth was formed. Informational process analysis has been seen in earlier selections: Staples explained how he keeps from frightening other people when he takes his evening walks, and Wolfe explained how the experiment with Norway rats was conducted.

Most process analyses are explained in simple, chronological steps. Indeed, the exact order is sometimes of greatest importance, as in a recipe. But occasionally there are problems in organization. The step-by-step format may need to be interrupted for descriptions, definitions, and other explanatory asides. If the process is a proposed solution, part of a problem-solution argument, then it may be necessary to justify each of the steps in turn and dismiss alternatives. And, still more of a problem, some processes defy a strict chronological treatment, because several things occur simultaneously. To explain the operating process of a gasoline engine, for example, the writer would be unable to convey at once everything that happens at the same time. Some way must be found to present the material in *general* stages, organized as subdivisions, so that the reader can see the step-by-step process through the confusion of interacting relationships.

Another difficulty in explaining by process analysis is estimating what knowledge the reader may already have. Presuming too little background may quickly lead to boredom or even irritation, with a resulting communication block; presuming too much will almost certainly leave the reader bewildered. Like a chain dependent on its weakest link for its strength, the entire process analysis can fail because of just one unclear point that makes the rest incomprehensible.

Sample Paragraph (Annotated)

Background information. *Process* objective is specified.

("Sort of": colloquial.)

Outsiders marvel at how Valley people are always of one opinion on public matters. But locally it's called "predisposition," a process having no legal status but used since early days when the Caseys still ran things. (In Valley isolation, folks had developed a sort of poor-cousins complex, had become highly defensive against Outside

Begins *informational process* itself, how the specified objective is achieved. Uses simple chronological steps.

Ends *informational process.*

Example, used to illustrate generality in preceding sentence.

("Guy": slang expression, not suitable in formal writing.)

Result of the process.

("Mess around": colloquial.) ("Hornets" is used metaphorically.)

Authority.) The process begins with ten local forums throughout the Valley, where everyone can voice an opinion. Arguments are loud, sometimes physical, but in the end each major faction at each meeting elects its own share of delegates to the District Assembly. This convenes later in Grange Hall—and it all starts over, but on a generally more decorous level. Once the final vote is taken, that verdict becomes THE Valley opinion, come what may, with no exceptions. Anyone wanting to be an exception, in public, will certainly never want to again—like that new realtor in Eden. Recently the State decided to put a four-lane road through the Valley, a move opposed by local "predisposition." But this guy went to a hearing in Bayport to relate how much the road was needed. A month later, when his last realty listings had evaporated, he changed his mind and went back to the city. And the State, recalling past experience, wisely decided not to mess around just now with those Valley hornets.

Sample Paragraph (Process Analysis)

It's not the wind, though, that's the most dangerous part of a hurricane. It's the water, especially when something called the "storm surge" occurs. As the low-pressure eye of the hurricane sits over the ocean, the sea level literally rises into a dome of water. For every inch drop in barometric pressure, the ocean rises a foot higher. Now, out at sea, that means nothing. The rise is not even noticeable. But when that mound of water starts moving toward land, the situation becomes crucial. As the water approaches a shallow beach, the dome of water rises. It may rise ten to fifteen feet in an hour and span fifty miles. Like a marine bulldozer, the surge may rise up twenty feet high, crash onto land, and wash everything away. Then with six- to eight-foot waves riding atop this mound of water, the storm surge destroys buildings, trees, cars, and anything else in its path. It's this storm surge that accounts for 90 percent of the deaths during a hurricane.

DONALD M. MURRAY

DONALD M. MURRAY, born in 1924 in Boston, is himself a writer and until recently taught writing at the University of New Hampshire. He has served as an editor of *Time* and, in 1954, was awarded the Pulitzer Prize for editorials written for the Boston *Herald*. Among his published works are novels, books of nonfiction, stories, poetry, and both textbooks and articles on the teaching of writing.

The Maker's Eye: Revising Your Own Manuscripts

"The Maker's Eye: Revising Your Own Manuscripts," first published in slightly different form in *The Writer*, provides an example of directional process. The author presents his information in chronological steps, most of them supported by direct quotations from professional writers. Much of the advice is applicable to student writing as well as to professional work.

When students complete a first draft, they consider the job of writing done—and their teachers too often agree. When professional writers complete a first draft, they usually feel that they are at the start of the writing process. When a draft is completed, the job of writing can begin.   1

   That difference in attitude is the difference between amateur   2
and professional, inexperience and experience, journeyman and craftsman. Peter F. Drucker, the prolific business writer, calls his first draft "the zero draft"—after that he can start counting. Most writers share the feeling that the first draft, and all of those which follow, are opportunities to discover what they have to say and how best they can say it.

To produce a progression of drafts, each of which says more and says it more clearly, the writer has to develop a special kind of reading skill. In school we are taught to decode what appears on the page as finished writing. Writers, however, face a different category of possibility and responsibility when they read their own drafts. To them the words on the page are never finished. Each can be changed and rearranged, can set off a chain reaction of confusion or clarified meaning. This is a different kind of reading, which is possibly more difficult and certainly more exciting.

Writers must learn to be their own best enemy. They must accept the criticism of others and be suspicious of it; they must accept the praise of others and be even more suspicious of it. Writers cannot depend on others. They must detach themselves from their own pages so that they can apply both their caring and their craft to their own work.

Such detachment is not easy. Science fiction writer Ray Bradbury supposedly puts each manuscript away for a year to the day and then rereads it as a stranger. Not many writers have the discipline or the time to do this. We must read when our judgment may be at its worst, when we are close to the euphoric moment of creation.

Then the writer, counsels novelist Nancy Hale, ''should be critical of everything that seems to him most delightful in his style. He should excise what he most admires, because he wouldn't thus admire it if he weren't . . . in a sense protecting it from criticism.'' John Ciardi, the poet, adds, ''The last act of the writing must be to become one's own reader. It is, I suppose, a schizophrenic process, to begin passionately and to end critically, to begin hot and to end cold; and, more important, to be passion-hot and critic-cold at the same time.''

Most people think that the principal problem is that writers are too proud of what they have written. Actually, a greater problem for most professional writers is one shared by the majority of students. They are overly critical, think everything is dreadful, tear up page after page, never complete a draft, see the task as hopeless.

The writer must learn to read critically but constructively, to cut what is bad, to reveal what is good. Eleanor Estes, the children's book author, explains: ''The writer must survey his work critically, coolly, as though he were a stranger to it. He must be willing to prune, expertly and hard-heartedly. At the end of each revision, a manuscript may look . . . worked over, torn apart, pinned together, added to, deleted from, words changed and words changed back. Yet the book must maintain its original freshness and spontaneity.''

Most readers underestimate the amount of rewriting it usually   9
takes to produce spontaneous reading. This is a great disadvantage to the student writer, who sees only a finished product and never watches the craftsman who takes the necessary step back, studies the work carefully, returns to the task, steps back, returns, steps back, again and again. Anthony Burgess, one of the most prolific writers in the English-speaking world, admits, ''I might revise a page twenty times.'' Roald Dahl, the popular children's writer, states, ''By the time I'm nearing the end of a story, the first part will have been reread and altered and corrected at least 150 times. . . . Good writing is essentially rewriting. I am positive of this.''

Rewriting isn't virtuous. It isn't something that ought to be   10
done. It is simply something that most writers find they have to do to discover what they have to say and how to say it. It is a condition of the writer's life.

There are, however, a few writers who do little formal rewrit-   11
ing, primarily because they have the capacity and experience to create and review a large number of invisible drafts in their minds before they approach the page. And some writers slowly produce finished pages, performing all the tasks of revision simultaneously, page by page, rather than draft by draft. But it is still possible to see the sequence followed by most writers most of the time in rereading their own work.

Most writers scan their drafts first, reading as quickly as possi-   12
ble to catch the larger problems of subject and form, then move in closer and closer as they read and write, reread and rewrite.

The first thing writers look for in their drafts is *information*.   13
They know that a good piece of writing is built from specific, accurate, and interesting information. The writer must have an abundance of information from which to construct a readable piece of writing.

Next writers look for *meaning* in the information. The specifics   14
must build to a pattern of significance. Each piece of specific information must carry the reader toward meaning.

Writers reading their own drafts are aware of *audience*. They   15
put themselves in the reader's situation and make sure that they

deliver information which a reader wants to know or needs to know in a manner which is easily digested. Writers try to be sure that they anticipate and answer the questions a critical reader will ask when reading the piece of writing.

Writers make sure that the *form* is appropriate to the subject and the audience. Form, or genre, is the vehicle which carries meaning to the reader, but form cannot be selected until the writer has adequate information to discover its significance and an audience which needs or wants that meaning.

Once writers are sure the form is appropriate, they must then look at the *structure,* the order of what they have written. Good writing is built on a solid framework of logic, argument, narrative, or motivation which runs through the entire piece of writing and holds it together. This is the time when many writers find it most effective to outline as a way of visualizing the hidden spine by which the piece of writing is supported.

The element on which writers may spend a majority of their time is *development*. Each section of a piece of writing must be adequately developed. It must give readers enough information so that they are satisfied. How much information is enough? That's as difficult as asking how much garlic belongs in a salad. It must be done to taste, but most beginning writers underdevelop, underestimating the reader's hunger for information.

As writers solve development problems, they often have to consider questions of *dimension.* There must be a pleasing and effective proportion among all the parts of the piece of writing. There is a continual process of subtracting and adding to keep the piece of writing in balance.

Finally, writers have to listen to their own voices. *Voice* is the force which drives a piece of writing forward. It is an expression of the writer's authority and concern. It is what is between the words on the page, what glues the piece of writing together. A good piece of writing is always marked by a consistent, individual voice.

As writers read and reread, write and rewrite, they move closer and closer to the page until they are doing line-by-line editing. Writers read their own pages with infinite care. Each sentence, each line, each clause, each phrase, each word, each mark of punctuation, each section of white space between the type has to contribute to the clarification of meaning.

Slowly the writer moves from word to word, looking through   22
language to see the subject. As a word is changed, cut, or added,
as a construction is rearranged, all the words used before that moment and all those that follow that moment must be considered
and reconsidered.

Writers often read aloud at this stage of the editing process,   23
muttering or whispering to themselves, calling on the ear's experience with language. Does this sound right—or that? Writers edit,
shifting back and forth from eye to page to ear to page. I find I
must do this careful editing in short runs, no more than fifteen or
twenty minutes at a stretch, or I become too kind with myself. I
begin to see what I hope is on the page, not what actually is on
the page.

This sounds tedious if you haven't done it, but actually it is   24
fun. Making something right is immensely satisfying, for writers
begin to learn what they are writing about by writing. Language
leads them to meaning, and there is the joy of discovery, of understanding, of making meaning clear as the writer employs the technical skills of language.

Words have double meanings, even triple or quadruple mean-   25
ings. Each word has its own potential for connotation and denotation. And when writers rub one word against the other, they are
often rewarded with a sudden insight, an unexpected clarification.

The maker's eye moves back and forth from word to phrase   26
to sentence to paragraph to sentence to phrase to word. The maker's eye sees the need for variety and balance, for a firmer structure, for a more appropriate form. It peers into the interior of the
paragraph, looking for coherence, unity, and emphasis, which
make meaning clear.

I learned something about this process when my first bifocals   27
were prescribed. I had ordered a larger section of the reading portion of the glass because of my work, but even so, I could not contain my eyes within this new limit of vision. And I still find myself
taking off my glasses and bending my nose towards the page, for
my eyes unconsciously flick back and forth across the page, back
to another page, forward to still another, as I try to see each evolv-
ing line in relation to every other line.

When does this process end? Most writers agree with the great   28
Russian writer Tolstoy, who said, ''I scarcely ever reread my published writings, if by chance I come across a page, it always strikes

me: all this must be rewritten; this is how I should have written it.''

The maker's eye is never satisfied, for each word has the potential to ignite new meaning. This article has been twice written all the way through the writing process, and it was published four years ago. Now it is to be republished in a book. The editors make a few small suggestions, and then I read it with my maker's eye. Now it has been re-edited, re-revised, re-read, re-re-edited, for each piece of writing to the writer is full of potential and alternatives.

A piece of writing is never finished. It is delivered to a deadline, torn out of the typewriter on demand, sent off with a sense of accomplishment and shame and pride and frustration. If only there were a couple more days, time for just another run at it, perhaps then. . . .

Meanings and Values

1a. What is the author's point of view in this selection? (See Guide to Terms: *Point of View.*)

 b. What is the relationship between his tone and the point of view? (Guide: *Style/Tone.*)

2a. What, if anything, prevents this selection from being as fascinating to read as some of the other pieces already studied?

 b. Could (or should) Murray have done anything else to enliven his process analysis? If so, what might it be?

3a. What was the author's purpose in writing this selection? (Guide: *Evaluation.*)

 b. How well did he succeed?

 c. Was it worth doing?

Expository Techniques

1a. What standard techniques of introduction does this author use in his opening paragraph? (Guide: *Introductions.*)

 b. How well does this paragraph meet the requirements of a good introduction?

2. Into which of the two basic types of process analysis can this selection be classed? Why?

3. What, if anything, is gained by the frequent use of quotations from professional writers?

4a.   Are the distinctions among his eight steps of rewriting (pars. 13–20) made clear enough? Be specific.

b.   Does anything about the order of these eight steps seem peculiar to you? If so, explain.

5a.   Cite examples of parallel structure from paragraphs 21 and 26. (Guide: *Parallel Structure.*)

b.   What is gained by such usage?

Diction and Vocabulary

1a.   Cite several uses of figurative language and state what kind they are. (Guide: *Figures of Speech.*)

b.   What is the main advantage in their use?

2a.   What, if anything, do you find unusual about saying "a majority of their time" (par. 18)?

b.   What other way, if any, do you prefer?

3.   Is it clear to you how "each word has its own potential for connotation and denotation" (par. 25)? (Guide: *Connotation/Denotation.*) If it is, explain the assertion.

4.   Use the dictionary as necessary to understand the meanings of the following words: prolific (par. 2); euphoric (5); excise, schizophrenic (6); spontaneity (8); genre (16); potential (29).

Suggestions for Writing and Discussion

1a.   Who was the reader-audience the author apparently had in mind in writing this process analysis?

b.   Explain fully why it would, or would not, be worth all the suggested time and trouble just to produce papers for your college courses.

2.   Discuss the assertion that "writers begin to learn what they are writing about by writing" (par. 24). If it seems more logical (for you) to learn what you are writing about some other way, what is it?

(NOTE: Suggestions for topics requiring development by PROCESS ANALYSIS are on page 182, at the end of this section.)

JOE BUHLER was born in 1950 in Vancouver, Washington. He currently teaches mathematics at Reed College in Portland, Oregon. In addition to numerous scholarly publications in the field of mathematics, Professor Buhler has published a number of essays for more general audiences. His popular writings include essays on science, juggling, and the oriental game Go.

RON GRAHAM was born in Taft, California, and is presently associated with AT&T Bell Labs in Murray Hill, New Jersey. He has had a distinguished career in mathematics, including membership in the National Academy of Sciences, and has published widely in the field. In addition, he is a past president of the International Juggling Association.

Give Juggling a Hand!

Originally published in the magazine *The Sciences*, this simple and straightforward process analysis nonetheless provides a good deal of information to would-be jugglers and admirers of the art. Student writers may wish to note the ways the authors keep their step-by-step directions simple and clear.

Nothing could be simpler than a game of catch. But just add another ball or two and the game turns magical—the juggled balls take on a life of their own. Suddenly, simple motions and common objects blur into one stunning display after another.

In recent years, juggling has experienced a renaissance. Street performers and skilled amateurs are practicing the ancient art in parks, back yards and on campuses around the globe. Membership

"Give Juggling a Hand" by Joe Buhler and Ron Graham.
This article is reprinted by permission of *The Sciences* and is from the January/February 1984 issue. Individual subscriptions are $13.50 per year. Write to The Sciences, 2 East 63rd Street, New York, NY 10021 or call 1-800-THE-NYAS.

in the largely amateur International Jugglers' Association (IJA) has more than doubled since 1979.

Juggling is actually 4000 years young. In Egypt, Asia and the Americas, it was once associated with religious ritual. In medieval Europe, wandering minstrels often juggled; the very term derives from these *jongleurs.* 3

Amazing jugglers imported from the Orient—in particular the "East Indian" Ramo Samee, who was said to string beads in his mouth while turning rings with his fingers and toes, and the Japanese artist Takashima, who manipulated a cotton ball with a stick held in his teeth—convinced 19th-century Europeans that juggling could be extraordinary show business. 4

Perhaps the greatest juggler of all time was variety-show virtuoso Enrico Rastelli. By his death in 1931, he had taught himself to juggle eight clubs, eight plates or ten balls; he could even bounce three balls continuously on his head. 5

Most people assume that a skilled juggler can manage up to 20 objects. In fact, even five-ball juggling is very difficult and requires about a year to master. Only a few jugglers worldwide have perfected seven-ball routines. At the 1986 IJA competition, one entrant separately juggled nine rings, eight balls and seven clubs. 6

Jugglers use a bewildering variety of objects, including bowling balls, whips, plastic swimming pools, cube puzzles, fruit, flaming torches, and playing cards. Performers trying for the largest number of objects usually choose rings, which allow a tighter traffic pattern and are stable when thrown to great heights. Several jugglers can manage ten or 11 rings, and some are trying for 12 or 13. 7

Clubs are the most visually pleasing objects to juggle. They're especially suited for passing back and forth between performers. Because they take up a lot of space when they rotate and must be caught at one end, juggling even five is tricky. Almost nobody can manage seven, even for a few seconds. 8

Throughout history, all jugglers—from South Sea Islanders to Aztec Indians—have used the same fundamental patterns: 9

The Cascade. Here, each ball travels from one hand to the other and back again, following a looping path that looks like a figure eight lying on its side. The juggler starts with two balls in his right hand, using a scooping motion and releasing a ball when his throwing hand is level with his navel. As the first ball reaches its 10 highest point, the other hand scoops and releases a second ball, and as that one reaches *its* apogee, he throws the third. Skilled jugglers can keep three, five, or even seven balls going in a cascade, but never four or six. With an even number, balls collide at the intersection of the figure eight.

The Shower. In this more difficult pattern, the balls follow a circular path as they are thrown upward by the right hand, caught by the left and quickly passed back to the right. Since the right does all the long-distance throwing, the shower is inherently asymmetrical and, therefore, inefficient; it is difficult with more than three objects.

The Fountain. This figure allows for a large number of balls. In a four-ball fountain, each hand juggles two balls independently in a circular motion. For symmetry, the number of balls is usually even. If the hands throw alternately and the two patterns interlock, it is surprisingly hard to discern that the fountain is made of two separate components and not one.

Because gravity causes objects to accelerate as they fall, a juggler has only a short time to catch and throw one ball before another drops into his hand—even if he throws high. A juggler who throws a ball eight feet in the air, for example, must catch it 1.4 seconds later, but throwing it four times that high only doubles the flight time.

The best way to understand juggling is to learn to do it yourself. Some people get the hang of the three-ball cascade in minutes, although most need at least a few days. Limit your sessions to ten minutes rather than frustrate yourself with a two-hour binge.

Step 1: One Ball. Practice throwing a ball from your right hand to your left and back, letting the ball rise to just above your head. Make the ball follow the path of a figure eight lying on its side, by "scooping" the ball and releasing it near the navel. Catch the ball at the side of your body, then repeat the sequence.

Step 2: Two Balls. Put one in each hand. Throw the ball in the left hand as in Step 1, and then, just as the ball passes its high point, throw the right-hand ball. Avoid releasing the second throw too early or tossing the balls to unequal heights.

At first it may be difficult to catch the balls. Don't worry. Focus instead on the accuracy and height of the throws. Catching will

come naturally as soon as the throws are on target. If things seem
hectic, try higher throws.

Step 3: Two Balls Reversed. Reverse the order of throws so that   18
the sequence is right, then left.

Step 4: Three Balls. Now put two balls in your right hand and   19
one in your left. Try to complete Step 2 while simply holding the
extra ball. Pause, then do Step 3.

The third ball can make it difficult to catch the second throw.   20
To solve this, throw the third ball just after the second reaches its
high point. The sequence is thus right, left, right. At first it may
be tough to persuade your right hand to make its second throw.
Remember: catches are irrelevant in the beginning. Throw high,
accurately and *slowly*. Don't rush the tempo, and don't forget the
figure-eight pattern.

Once you've mastered the three-ball cascade you'll want to try   21
other patterns. A juggler is never finished: there is always one
more ball.

Meanings and Values

1a.   If you find this essay interesting, try to explain what it is that you
      like about the piece. The topic? The authors' approach? Make your
      answers as specific as you can. (See Guide to Terms: *Evaluation.*)

 b.   If you do not find the selection interesting, try to explain the rea-
      sons for your response as specifically as you can and suggest some
      ways in which the essay might be improved.

2.   Explain the pun (play on words) in the title.

3a.   Tell how you think most readers are likely to view juggling before
      reading this essay.

 b.   After reading it.

Expository Techniques

1.   Should the discussion in paragraphs 10–13 be considered a direc-
      tional process, an informational process, or both? Be ready to ex-
      plain your answer using evidence from the text.

2a.   What strategies do the authors use to highlight the steps in the
      process described in paragraphs 14–20?

 b.   To highlight the different processes analyzed in paragraphs 9–13?

3.   Discuss the use of transitions and parallel structures in paragraphs 15–17 to help create orderly and clear explanation. (Guide: *Transition, Parallel Structure.*)

4a.   The opening of this essay presents considerable historical information on juggling, at least given the length of the essay. Why do you think the authors chose to begin the piece in this manner? (Guide: *Introductions.*)

b.   Does this material harm the unity of the essay in any way? Why, or why not? (Guide: *Unity.*)

Diction and Vocabulary

1a.   Analyze the diction in paragraph 10 and explain how it contributes to the clarity of the writing. (Guide: *Diction.*)

b.   Are most readers likely to understand the term "apogee" in paragraph 10? Does its presence make the explanation confusing?

2.   How do the objects listed in the first sentence of paragraph 7 and the order in which they are presented emphasize the drama and excitement that jugglers are capable of creating? (Guide: *Emphasis.*)

3.   In explaining how to accomplish a three-ball cascade (pars. 14–20), the authors try to make the process seem reasonably simple and easy. How do their vocabulary choices (especially verbs) help accomplish this? (Guide: *Diction.*)

Suggestions for Writing and Discussion

1.   Prepare a set of directions for some other entertaining and relaxing activity you know about. Games or exercise routines might be good subjects.

2.   Are there any parts of this essay that make the process seem too simple? How might it be improved or expanded to help readers who want to give juggling a try?

3.   Are many readers likely to take up juggling as a result of this essay—or at least to try it once? What elements in the essay might encourage (or discourage) such a reaction?

(NOTE: Suggestions for topics requiring development by PROCESS ANALYSIS are on page 182, at the end of this section.)

ALEXANDER PETRUNKEVITCH

ALEXANDER PETRUNKEVITCH (1875–1964), a Russian-born zoologist, taught at several leading American universities and received honors from others. He was one of the world's foremost authorities on spiders, and his first important book, published in 1911, was *Index Catalogue of Spiders of North, Central, and South America*. He later achieved distinction for his writings on zoological subjects as well as for his translations of English poetry into Russian and Russian poetry into English. Two of his other books are *Choice and Responsibility* (1947) and *Principles of Classification* (1952).

The Spider and the Wasp

"The Spider and the Wasp" was first published in the August 1952 issue of *Scientific American*, and it is reproduced here almost in its entirety. This essay should be particularly interesting to students of composition because it demonstrates not only exposition of natural process but also semiscientific writing that has been made understandable, perhaps even fascinating, for completely nonscientific readers. It is also a good illustration of the successful interweaving of several expository techniques.

In the feeding and safeguarding of their progeny insects and spiders exhibit some interesting analogies to reasoning and some crass examples of blind instinct. The case I propose to describe here is that of the tarantula spiders and their archenemy, the digger wasps of the genus *Pepsis*. It is a classic example of what looks like intelligence pitted against instinct—a strange situation in which the victim, though fully able to defend itself, submits unwittingly to its destruction.

Most tarantulas live in the tropics, but several species occur in the temperate zone and a few are common in the southern U.S. Some varieties are large and have powerful fangs with which they can inflict a deep wound. These formidable-looking spiders do not, however, attack man; you can hold one in your hand, if you are gentle, without being bitten. Their bite is dangerous only to insects and small mammals such as mice; for man it is no worse than a hornet's sting.

Tarantulas customarily live in deep cylindrical burrows, from which they emerge at dusk and into which they retire at dawn. Mature males wander about after dark in search of females and occasionally stray into houses. After mating, the male dies in a few weeks, but a female lives much longer and can mate several years in succession. In a Paris museum is a tropical specimen which is said to have been living in captivity for 25 years.

A fertilized female tarantula lays from 200 to 400 eggs at a time; thus it is possible for a single tarantula to produce several thousand young. She takes no care of them beyond weaving a co-coon of silk to enclose the eggs. After they hatch, the young walk away, find convenient places in which to dig their burrows and spend the rest of their lives in solitude. The eyesight of tarantulas is poor, being limited to a sensing of change in the intensity of light and to the perception of moving objects. They apparently have lit-tle or no sense of hearing, for a hungry tarantula will pay no atten-tion to a loudly chirping cricket placed in its cage unless the insect happens to touch one of its legs.

But all spiders, and especially hairy ones, have an extremely delicate sense of touch. Laboratory experiments prove that tarantu-las can distinguish three types of touch: pressure against the body wall, stroking of the body hair, and riffling of certain very fine hairs on the legs called trichobothria. Pressure against the body, by the finger or the end of a pencil, causes the tarantula to move off slowly for a short distance. The touch excites no defensive re-sponse unless the approach is from above where the spider can see the motion, in which case it rises on its hind legs, lifts its front legs, opens its fangs and holds this threatening posture as long as the object continues to move.

The entire body of a tarantula, especially its legs, is thickly clothed with hair. Some of it is short and wooly, some long and stiff. Touching this body hair produces one of two distinct reactions. When the spider is hungry, it responds with an immediate and swift attack. At the touch of a cricket's antennae the tarantula seizes the insect so swiftly that a motion picture taken at the rate of 64 frames per second shows only the result and not the process of capture. But when the spider is not hungry, the stimulation of its hairs merely causes it to shake the touched limb. An insect can walk under its hairy belly unharmed.

The trichobothria, very fine hairs growing from disklike mem- 7 branes on the legs, are sensitive only to air movement. A light breeze makes them vibrate slowly, without disturbing the common hair. When one blows gently on the trichobothria, the tarantula reacts with a quick jerk of its four front legs. If the front and hind legs are stimulated at the same time, the spider makes a sudden jump. This reaction is quite independent of the state of its appetite.

These three tactile responses—to pressure on the body wall, 8 to moving of the common hair, and to flexing of the trichobothria— are so different from one another that there is no possibility of confusing them. They serve the tarantula adequately for most of its needs and enable it to avoid most annoyances and dangers. But they fail the spider completely when it meets its deadly enemy, the digger wasp *Pepsis*.

These solitary wasps are beautiful and formidable creatures. 9 Most species are either a deep shiny blue all over, or deep blue with rusty wings. The largest have a wing span of about 4 inches. They live on nectar. When excited, they give off a pungent odor— a warning that they are ready to attack. The sting is much worse than that of a bee or common wasp, and the pain and swelling last longer. In the adult stage the wasp lives only a few months. The female produces but a few eggs, one at a time at intervals of two or three days. For each egg the mother must provide one adult tarantula, alive but paralyzed. The mother wasp attaches the egg to the paralyzed spider's abdomen. Upon hatching from the egg, the larva is many hundreds of times smaller than its living but helpless victim. It eats no other food and drinks no water. By the time it has finished its single Gargantuan meal and become ready for wasphood, nothing remains of the tarantula but its indigestible chitinous skeleton.

The mother wasp goes tarantula-hunting when the egg in her 10 ovary is almost ready to be laid. Flying low over the ground late on a sunny afternoon, the wasp looks for its victim or for the mouth of a tarantula burrow, a round hole edged by a bit of silk. The sex of the spider makes no difference, but the mother is highly discriminating as to species. Each species of *Pepsis* requires a certain species of tarantula, and the wasp will not attack the wrong species. In a cage with a tarantula which is not its normal prey, the wasp avoids the spider and is usually killed by it in the night.

Yet when a wasp finds the correct species, it is the other way about. To identify the species the wasp apparently must explore the spider with her antennae. The tarantula shows an amazing tolerance to this exploration. The wasp crawls under it and walks over it without evoking any hostile response. The molestation is so great and so persistent that the tarantula often rises on all eight legs, as if it were on stilts. It may stand this way for several minutes. Meanwhile the wasp, having satisfied itself that the victim is of the right species, moves off a few inches to dig the spider's grave. Working vigorously with legs and jaws, it excavates a hole 8 to 10 inches deep with a diameter slightly larger than the spider's girth. Now and again the wasp pops out of the hole to make sure that the spider is still there.

When the grave is finished, the wasp returns to the tarantula to complete her ghastly enterprise. First she feels it all over once more with her antennae. Then her behavior becomes more aggressive. She bends her abdomen, protruding her sting, and searches for the soft membrane at the point where the spider's legs join its body—the only spot where she can penetrate the horny skeleton. From time to time, as the exasperated spider slowly shifts ground, the wasp turns on her back and slides along with the aid of her wings, trying to get under the tarantula for a shot at the vital spot. During all this maneuvering, which can last for several minutes, the tarantula makes no move to save itself. Finally the wasp corners it against some obstruction and grasps one of its legs in her powerful jaws. Now at last the harassed spider tries a desperate but vain defense. The two contestants roll over and over on the ground. It is a terrifying sight and the outcome is always the same. The wasp finally manages to thrust her sting into the soft spot and holds it there for a few seconds while she pumps in the poison. Almost immediately the tarantula falls paralyzed on its back. Its legs stop twitching; its heart stops beating. Yet it is not dead, as is shown by the fact that if taken from the wasp it can be restored to some sensitivity by being kept in a moist chamber for several months.

After paralyzing the tarantula, the wasp cleans herself by 13 dragging her body along the ground and rubbing her feet, sucks a drop of blood oozing from the wound in the spider's abdomen, then grabs a leg of the flabby, helpless animal in her jaws and drags it down to the bottom of the grave. She stays there for many minutes, sometimes for several hours, and what she does all that time in the dark we do not know. Eventually she lays her egg and attaches it to the side of the spider's abdomen with a sticky secretion. Then she emerges, fills the grave with soil carried bit by bit in her jaws, and finally tramples the ground all around to hide any trace of the grave from prowlers. Then she flies away, leaving her descendant safely started in life.

In all this the behavior of the wasp evidently is qualitatively 14 different from that of the spider. The wasp acts like an intelligent animal. This is not to say that instinct plays no part or that she reasons as man does. But her actions are to the point; they are not automatic and can be modified to fit the situation. We do not know for certain how she identifies the tarantula—probably it is by some olfactory or chemo-tactile sense—but she does it purposefully and does not blindly tackle a wrong species.

On the other hand, the tarantula's behavior shows only confu- 15 sion. Evidently the wasp's pawing gives it no pleasure, for it tries to move away. That the wasp is not simulating sexual stimulation is certain because male and female tarantulas react in the same way to its advances. That the spider is not anesthetized by some odorless secretion is easily shown by blowing lightly at the tarantula and making it jump suddenly. What, then, makes the tarantula behave as stupidly as it does?

No clear, simple answer is available. Possibly the stimulation 16 by the wasp's antennae is masked by a heavier pressure on the spider's body, so that it reacts as when prodded by a pencil. But the explanation may be much more complex. Initiative in attack is not in the nature of tarantulas; most species fight only when cornered so that escape is impossible. Their inherited patterns of behavior apparently prompt them to avoid problems rather than attack them. For example, spiders always weave their webs in three dimensions, and when a spider finds that there is insufficient space to attach certain threads in the third dimension, it leaves the place and seeks another, instead of finishing the web in a single plane. This urge to escape seems to arise under all circumstances, in all phases of life, and to take the place of reasoning. For a spider to change the pattern of its web is as impossible as for an inexperienced man to build a bridge across a chasm obstructing his way.

In a way the instinctive urge to escape is not only easier but often more efficient than reasoning. The tarantula does exactly what is most efficient in all cases except in an encounter with a ruthless and determined attacker dependent for the existence of her own species on killing as many tarantulas as she can lay eggs. Perhaps in this case the spider follows its usual pattern of trying to escape, instead of seizing and killing the wasp, because it is not aware of its danger. In any case, the survival of the tarantula species as a whole is protected by the fact that the spider is much more fertile than the wasp.

Meanings and Values

1. Briefly summarize the "qualitative" differences between the behavior of the tarantula and that of the wasp.

2. What is the likelihood that some humans also have inherited patterns of behavior that "prompt them to avoid problems rather than attack them" (par. 16)? Use concrete examples, if possible, to support your views.

3. What parallels to the tarantula-wasp relationship can you find in the history of nations? Be specific and explain.

4a. Describe the type, or types, of readers to whom you think *Scientific American* is meant to appeal. (Do not jump to conclusions: if not familiar with the magazine, you may have to browse through a few issues.)

b. If you were the editor, why would you have chosen (or not chosen) to publish this piece?

Expository Techniques

1a. Where does the author state his central theme?

b. Is this a desirable location? Why, or why not?

2a. What is the primary function of the process analysis in relation to the central theme?

b. How successfully does it accomplish its purpose?

3. In paragraph 9 the author goes from pure description of the wasp into the narrative account that involves both wasp and spider. How does he arrange the content itself to provide smooth and natural transition, hence ensuring coherence? (See Guide to Terms: *Transition* and *Coherence*.)

4. The author also usually arranges his subject materials to help achieve effective *inter*paragraph transitions so that one gets an echo of the last part of one paragraph when reading the topic sentence of the next. List or mark the uses of this transitional device.

5. Effective coherence also depends to a great extent on smooth sentence-to-sentence transitions. In describing events in a time sequence, it is sometimes hard to avoid a dull list that runs on "and then . . . and then. . . . " List or mark the eight introductory devices showing time relationship in paragraph 12, and notice their variety.

6a. How many paragraphs constitute the closing?

 b. What function do they serve in addition to concluding the selection?

7. This essay utilizes, to varying extents, the expository patterns of cause and effect, definition, induction, and description. It can also be used to illustrate three patterns we have already studied.

 a. What are the patterns?

 b. Explain their use in this essay.

Diction and Vocabulary

1. Do such informal expressions as "pops out of the hole" (par. 11), "for a shot at the vital spot," and "pumps in the poison" (12) help or hinder the essay's success? Why?

2. Consider such expressions as "beautiful and formidable creatures" (par. 9), "ghastly enterprise," and "terrifying sight" (12).

 a. Are these expressions objective or subjective? (Guide: *Objective/Subjective*.) Explain why.

 b. Why would they be, or not be, suitable in a scientific report?

 c. What useful purpose, if any, do they serve here?

3a. What do your answers to questions 1 and 2 indicate about the author's tone? (Guide: *Style/Tone*.)

 b. How would you describe his tone?

 c. Explain why it is, or is not, suitable to his subject matter and to his audience.

4. Any specialist writing on a technical subject for a lay audience (as much of *Scientific American*'s audience is) has a problem with pro-

fessional terminology. Consider this author's use of "trichobothria" (par. 5), "chitinous" (9), "olfactory," and "chemo-tactile"
(14).

a. Does there seem to be an excessive use of technical language?

b. Do you think these words could have been avoided without weak-
ening scientific exactness? If so, how?

c. Does their use create a communication block for the lay reader, or
does the author succeed in avoiding this fault?

d. Why has he bothered to define "trichobothria"—even repeating
his definition—but not the others?

5. The use of "Gargantuan" (par. 9) is an allusion. (Guide: *Figures of
Speech.*) Find the source to which the author alludes and explain
the word's meaning in this essay.

6. Consult the dictionary as needed for a full understanding of the
following words, especially as used in this essay: progeny, archenemy, classic (par. 1); formidable (2); perception (4); riffling (5);
disklike (7); tactile (8); pungent, chitinous (9); discriminating (10);
evoking, molestation (11); harassed (12); secretion (13); qualitatively, olfactory, chemo-tactile (14).

Suggestions for Writing and Discussion

1. Use the tarantula-wasp relationship as the basis of an analogy to
explain the relationship between two persons that you know.

2. Use analogy as suggested above to explain the historical relationship between two specific countries.

3. Using patterns of illustration and comparison, distinguish between
intellectual and instinctive human behavior.

4. Compare or contrast humans' motives for killing with those of animals. Some use of classification might also be helpful in this assignment.

(NOTE: Suggestions for topics requiring development by PROCESS ANALYSIS are on
page 182, at the end of this section.)

JESSICA MITFORD

JESSICA MITFORD was born in 1917, the daughter of an English peer. Her brother was sent to Eton, but she and her six sisters were educated at home by their mother. At the age of nineteen Mitford left home, eventually making her way to the United States in 1939. Since 1944 she has been an American citizen, and is now living in San Francisco. She did not begin her writing career until she was thirty-eight. Her books are *Lifeitselfmanship* (1956); her autobiography, *Daughters and Rebels* (1960); the best-seller *The American Way of Death* (1963); *The Trial of Dr. Spock* (1969); *Kind and Usual Punishment* (1973), a devastating study of the American penal system; *A Fine Old Conflict* (1977); and *Poison Penmanship* (1979). Mitford's articles have appeared in the *Atlantic, Harper's,* and *McCall's.*

To Dispel Fears of Live Burial

"To Dispel Fears of Live Burial" (editors' title) is a portion of *The American Way of Death*, a book described in the *New York Times* as a "savagely witty and well-documented exposé." The "savagely witty" style, evident in this selection, does not obscure the fact of its being a tightly organized, step-by-step process analysis.

Embalming is indeed a most extraordinary procedure, and one   1
must wonder at the docility of Americans who each year pay hundreds of millions of dollars for its perpetuation, blissfully ignorant of what it is all about, what is done, how it is done. Not one in ten thousand has any idea of what actually takes place. Books on the subject are extremely hard to come by. They are not to be found in most libraries or bookshops.

In an era when huge television audiences watch surgical oper-   2 ations in the comfort of their living rooms, when, thanks to the animated cartoon, the geography of the digestive system has become familiar territory even to the nursery school set, in a land where the satisfaction of curiosity about almost all matters is a national pastime, the secrecy surrounding embalming can, surely, hardly be attributed to the inherent gruesomeness of the subject. Custom in this regard has within this century suffered a complete reversal. In the early days of American embalming, when it was performed in the home of the deceased, it was almost mandatory for some relative to stay by the embalmer's side and witness the procedure. Today, family members who might wish to be in attendance would certainly be dissuaded by the funeral director. All others, except apprentices, are excluded by law from the preparation room.

A close look at what does actually take place may explain in   3 large measure the undertaker's intractable reticence concerning a procedure that has become his major *raison d'être*. Is it possible he fears that public information about embalming might lead patrons to wonder if they really want this service? If the funeral men are loath to discuss the subject outside the trade, the reader may, understandably, be equally loath to go on reading at this point. For those who have the stomach for it, let us part the formaldehyde curtain. . . .

The body is first laid out in the undertaker's morgue—or   4 rather, Mr. Jones is reposing in the preparation room—to be readied to bid the world farewell.

The preparation room in any of the better funeral establish-   5 ments has the tiled and sterile look of a surgery, and indeed the embalmer-restorative artist who does his chores there is beginning to adopt the term "dermasurgeon" (appropriately corrupted by some mortician-writers as "demisurgeon") to describe his calling. His equipment, consisting of scalpels, scissors, augers, forceps, clamps, needles, pumps, tubes, bowls and basins, is crudely imitative of the surgeon's as is his technique, acquired in a nine- or twelve-month post-high-school course in an embalming school. He is supplied by an advanced chemical industry with a bewildering array of fluids, sprays, pastes, oils, powders, creams, to fix or soften tissue, shrink or distend it as needed, dry it here, restore the moisture there. There are cosmetics, waxes and paints to fill and cover features, even plaster of Paris to replace entire limbs.

There are ingenious aids to prop and stabilize the cadaver: A Vari-Pose Head Rest, the Edwards Arm and Hand Positioner, the Repose Block (to support the shoulders during the embalming), and the Throop Foot Positioner, which resembles an old-fashioned stocks.

Mr. John H. Eckels, president of the Eckels College of Mortu- 6 ary Science, thus describes the first part of the embalming procedure: "In the hands of a skilled practitioner, this work may be done in a comparatively short time and without mutilating the body other than by slight incision—so slight that it scarcely would cause serious inconvenience if made upon a living person. It is necessary to remove the blood, and doing this not only helps in the disinfecting, but removes the principal cause of disfigurements due to discoloration."

Another textbook discusses the all-important time element: 7 "The earlier this is done, the better, for every hour that elapses between death and embalming will add to the problems and complications encountered. . . ." Just how soon should one get going on the embalming? The author tells us, "On the basis of such scanty information made available to this profession through its rudimentary and haphazard system of technical research, we must conclude that the best results are to be obtained if the subject is embalmed before life is completely extinct—that is, before cellular death has occurred. In the average case, this would mean within an hour after somatic death." For those who feel that there is something a little rudimentary, not to say haphazard, about this advice, a comforting thought is offered by another writer. Speaking of fears entertained in early days of premature burial, he points out, "One of the effects of embalming by chemical injection, however, has been to dispel fears of live burial." How true; once the blood is removed, chances of live burial are indeed remote.

To return to Mr. Jones, the blood is drained out through the 8 veins and replaced by embalming fluid pumped in through the arteries. As noted in *The Principles and Practices of Embalming*, "Every operator has a favorite injection and drainage point—a fact which becomes a handicap only if he fails or refuses to forsake his favorites when conditions demand it." Typical favorites are the carotid artery, femoral artery, jugular vein, subclavian vein. There are various choices of embalming fluid. If Flextone is used, it will produce a "mild, flexible rigidity. The skin retains a velvety softness, the tissues are rubbery and pliable. Ideal for women and children." It may be blended with B. and G. Products Company's Lyf-Lyk tint, which is guaranteed to reproduce "nature's own skin texture . . . the velvety appearance of living tissue." Suntone comes in three separate tints: Suntan; Special Cosmetic Tint, a pink shade "especially indicated for young female subjects"; and Regular Cosmetic Tint, moderately pink.

About three to six gallons of dyed and perfumed solution of formaldehyde, glycerin, borax, phenol, alcohol and water are soon circulating through Mr. Jones, whose mouth has been sewn together with a "needle directed upward between the upper lip and gum and brought out through the left nostril," with the corners raised slightly "for a more pleasant expression." If he should be bucktoothed, his teeth are cleaned with Bon Ami and coated with colorless nail polish. His eyes, meanwhile, are closed with flesh-tinted eye caps and eye cement.

The next step is to have at Mr. Jones with a thing called a trocar. This is a long, hollow needle attached to a tube. It is jabbed into the abdomen, poked around the entrails and chest cavity, the contents of which are pumped out and replaced with "cavity fluid." This done, and the hole in the abdomen sewn up, Mr. Jones's face is heavily creamed (to protect the skin from burns which may be caused by leakage of the chemicals), and he is covered with a sheet and left unmolested for a while. But not for long—there is more, much more, in store for him. He has been embalmed, but not yet restored, and the best time to start the restorative work is eight to ten hours after embalming, when the tissues have become firm and dry.

The object of all this attention to the corpse, it must be remembered, is to make it presentable for viewing in an attitude of healthy repose. "Our customs require the presentation of our dead in the semblance of normality . . . unmarred by the ravages of illness, disease or mutilation," says Mr. J. Sheridan Mayer in his *Restorative Art.* This is rather a large order since few people die in the full bloom of health, unravaged by illness and unmarked by some disfigurement. The funeral industry is equal to the challenge: "In some cases the gruesome appearance of a mutilated or disease-ridden subject may be quite discouraging. The task of restoration may seem impossible and shake the confidence of the embalmer. This is the time for intestinal fortitude and determination. Once the formative work is begun and affected tissues are cleaned or removed, all doubts of success vanish. It is surprising and gratifying to discover the results which may at obtained.''

The embalmer, having allowed an appropriate interval to elapse, returns to the attack, but now he brings into play the skill and equipment of sculptor and cosmetician. Is a hand missing? Casting one in plaster of Paris is a simple matter. "For replacement purposes, only a cast of the back of the hand is necessary; this is within the ability of the average operator and is quite adequate." If a lip or two, a nose or an ear should be missing, the embalmer has at hand a variety of restorative waxes with which to model replacements. Pores and skin texture are simulated by stippling with a little brush, and over this cosmetics are laid on. Head off? Decapitation cases are rather routinely handled. Ragged edges are trimmed, and head joined to torso with a series of splints, wires and sutures. It is a good idea to have a little something at the neck—a scarf or high collar—when time for viewing comes. Swollen mouth? Cut out tissue as needed from inside the lips. If too much is removed, the surface contour can easily be restored by padding with cotton. Swollen necks and cheeks are reduced by removing tissue through vertical incisions made down each side of the neck. "When the deceased is casketed, the pillow will hide the suture incisions . . . as an extra precaution against leakage, the suture may be painted with liquid sealer." 12

The opposite condition is more likely to present itself—that of emaciation. His hypodermic syringe now loaded with massage cream, the embalmer seeks out and fills the hollowed and sunken areas by injection. In this procedure the backs of the hands and fingers and the under-chin area should not be neglected. 13

Positioning the lips is a problem that recurrently challenges the ingenuity of the embalmer. Closed too tightly, they tend to give a stern, even disapproving expression. Ideally, embalmers feel, the lips should give the impression of being ever so slightly parted, the upper lip protruding slightly for a more youthful appearance. This takes some engineering, however, as the lips tend to drift apart. Lip drift can sometimes be remedied by pushing one or two straight pins through the inner margin of the lower lip and then inserting them between the two front upper teeth. If Mr. Jones happens to have no teeth, the pins can just as easily be anchored in his Armstrong Face Former and Denture Replacer. Another 14 method to maintain lip closure is to dislocate the lower jaw, which is then held in its new position by a wire run through holes which have been drilled through the upper and lower jaws at the midline. As the French are fond of saying, *il faut souffrir pour être belle.*[1]

If Mr. Jones has died of jaundice, the embalming fluid will very likely turn him green. Does this deter the embalmer? Not if he has intestinal fortitude. Masking pastes and cosmetics are heavily laid on, burial garments and casket interiors are color-correlated with particular care, and Jones is displayed beneath rose-colored lights. Friends will say, "How *well* he looks." Death by carbon monoxide, on the other hand, can be rather a good thing from the embalmer's viewpoint: "One advantage is the fact that this type of discoloration is an exaggerated form of a natural pink coloration." This is nice because the healthy glow is already present and needs but little attention.

The patching and filling completed, Mr. Jones is now shaved, washed and dressed. Cream-based cosmetic, available in pink, flesh, suntan, brunette and blond, is applied to his hands and face, his hair is shampooed and combed (and, in the case of Mrs. Jones, set), his hands manicured. For the horny-handed son of toil special care must be taken; cream should be applied to remove ingrained grime, and the nails cleaned. "If he were not in the habit of having them manicured in life, trimming and shaping is advised for better appearance—never questioned by kin."

Jones is now ready for casketing (this is the present participle of the verb "to casket"). In this operation, his right shoulder should be depressed slightly "to turn the body a bit to the right and soften the appearance of lying flat on the back." Positioning the hands is a matter of importance, and special rubber positioning blocks may be used. The hands should be cupped slightly for a more lifelike, relaxed appearance. Proper placement of the body requires a delicate sense of balance. It should lie as high as possible in the casket, yet not so high that the lid, when lowered, will hit the nose. On the other hand, we are cautioned, placing the body too low "creates the impression that the body is in a box."

Jones is next wheeled into the appointed slumber room where a few last touches may be added—his favorite pipe placed in his hand or, if he was a great reader, a book propped into position.

---

[1]You have to suffer if you want to be beautiful.—EDS.

(In the case of little Master Jones a Teddy bear may be clutched.)
Here he will hold open house for a few days, visiting hours 10 A.M.
to 9 P.M.

Meanings and Values

1a. What is the author's tone? (See Guide to Terms: *Style/Tone.*)

b. Try to analyze the effect this tone had, at first reading, on your
impressions of the subject matter itself.

c. Form a specific comparison between this effect of tone and the effect of "tone of voice" in spoken language.

2. Why was it formerly "almost mandatory" for some relative to witness the embalming procedure (par. 2)?

3a. Do you believe that public information about this procedure would
cost mortuaries much embalming business (par. 3)? Why, or why
not?

b. Why *do* people subject their dead to such a process?

4. Use the three-part system of evaluation to judge the success of this
process analysis. (Guide: *Evaluation.*)

Expository Techniques

1a. What is the central theme? (Guide: *Unity.*)

b. Which parts of the writing, if any, do not contribute to the theme,
thus damaging unity?

c. What other elements of the writing contribute to, or damage,
unity?

2a. Beginning with paragraph 4, list or mark the transitional devices
that help to bridge paragraphs. (Guide: *Transition.*)

b. Briefly explain how coherence is aided by such interparagraph
transitions.

3. In this selection, far more than in most, emphasis can best be studied in connection with style. In fact, the two are almost indistinguishable here, and few, if any, of the other methods of achieving
emphasis are used at all. (Guide: *Emphasis* and *Style/Tone.*) Consider each of the following stylistic qualities (some may overlap;
others are included in diction) and illustrate, by examples, how
each creates emphasis.

a. Number and selection of details—e.g., the equipment and "aids"
(par. 5).

b. Understatement—e.g., the "chances of live burial" (par. 7).

c.   Special use of quotations—e.g., "that the body is in a box" (par. 17).

d.   Sarcasm and/or other forms of irony—e.g., "How *well* he looks" (par. 15). (Guide: *Irony*.)

Diction and Vocabulary

1.   Much of the essay's unique style (with resulting emphasis) comes from qualities of diction. Use examples to illustrate the following. (Some may be identical to those of the preceding answer, but they need not be.)

a.   Choice of common, low-key words to achieve sarcasm through understatement—e.g., "This is nice . . . " (par. 15).

b.   Terms of violence—e.g., "returns to the attack" (par. 12).

c.   Terms of the living—e.g., "will hold open house" (par. 18).

d.   The continuing use of "Mr. Jones."

2a. Illustrate the meaning of "connotation" with examples of quotations from morticians. (Guide: *Connotation/Denotation*.)

b.   Are these also examples of "euphemism"?

c.   Show how the author uses these facts to her own advantage—i.e., again, to achieve emphasis.

3a. Comment briefly on the quality and appropriateness of the metaphor that ends the introduction. (Guide: *Figures of Speech*.)

b.   Is this, in any sense, also an allusion? Why, or why not?

4.   Use the dictionary as needed to understand the meanings of the following words: docility, perpetuation (par. 1); inherent, mandatory (2); intractable, reticence, *raison d'être* (3); ingenious (5); rudimentary, cellular, somatic (7); carotid artery, femoral artery, subclavian vein (8); semblance (11); simulated, stippling, sutures (12); emaciation (13); dispel (7, title).

Suggestions for Writing and Discussion

1.   What evidence can you find that "the satisfaction of curiosity about almost all matters is a national pastime" (par. 2)? Is this a good thing or not? Why?

2.   Burial customs differ widely from country to country, sometimes from area to area in this country. If you can, describe one of the more distinctive customs and, if possible, show its sources—e.g., the climate, "old country" tradition.

3.   What do you foresee as near- and far-future trends or radical changes in American burial practices? Why?

4.   You may wish to develop further your answers to question 3 of "Meanings and Values"—the rationale of a large majority of people who do use this mortuary "service" for their departed relatives.

5.   If you like, explain your personal preferences and the reasons for them.

(NOTE: Suggestions for topics requiring development by PROCESS ANALYSIS follow.)

Writing Suggestions for Section 5
Process Analysis

1. From one of the following topics develop a central theme into an *informational* process analysis, showing:
   a. How you selected a college.
   b. How you selected your future career or major field of study.
   c. How your family selected a home.
   d. How an unusual sport is played.
   e. How religious faith is achieved.
   f. How gasoline is made.
   g. How the air (or water) in _____ becomes polluted.
   h. How lightning kills.
   i. How foreign policy is made.
   j. How political campaigns are financed.
   k. How _____ Church was rebuilt.
   l. How fruit blossoms are pollinated.
   m. How a computer chip is designed or made.

2. Select a specific reader-audience and write a *directional* process analysis on one of the following topics, showing:
   a. How to *do* any of the processes suggested by topics 1a–e. (This treatment will require a different viewpoint, completely objective, and may require a different organization.)
   b. How to overcome shyness.
   c. How to overcome stage fright.
   d. How to make the best use of study time.
   e. How to write a college composition.
   f. How to sell an ugly house.
   g. How to prepare livestock or any other entry for a fair.
   h. How to start a club (or some other kind of recurring activity).
   i. How to reduce the number of highway accidents in an area.
   j. How to survive a tornado (or other natural disaster).
   k. How to select a car.
   l. How to sail a boat.
   m. How to set up a fish tank and keep the fish alive and healthy.
   n. How to collect baseball cards.

6

Analyzing *Cause and Effect* Relationships

Unlike process analysis, which merely tells *how,* causal analysis seeks to explain *why.* The two may be combined, but they need not be—many people have driven a car successfully after being told how to do it, never knowing or caring why the thing moved when they turned a key and worked a pedal or two.

Some causes and effects are not very complicated; at least their explanation requires only a simple statement. A car may sit in the garage for a while because its owner has no money for a license tag, and sometimes this is explanation enough. But frequently a much more thorough analysis is required, and this may even become the basic pattern of an exposition.

To explain fully the causes of a war or a depression or election results, the writer must seek not only *immediate* causes (the ones encountered first) but also *ultimate* causes (the basic, underlying factors that help to explain the more apparent ones). Business or professional people, as well as students, often have a pressing need for this type of analysis. How else could they fully understand or report on a failing sales campaign, diminishing church membership, a local increase in traffic accidents, or teenage use of drugs? The immediate cause of a disastrous warehouse fire could be faulty electrical wiring, but this might be attributed in turn to the company's unwise economy measures, which might be traced even further to undue pressures on the management to show large profits. The written analysis might logically stop at any point, of course, depending entirely on its purpose and the reader-audience for which it is intended.

Similarly, both the immediate and ultimate *effects* of an action or situation may, or may not, need to be fully explored. If a 5 percent pay raise is granted, what will be the immediate effect on the cost of production, leading to what ultimate effects on prices and, in some cases, on the economy of a business, a town, or perhaps the entire nation?

In earlier selections of this book we have seen several examples of causal analysis. In Section 1, for instance, Buckley gives some attention to both immediate and ultimate causes of American apathy, and in Section 4, Wolfe is concerned with both immediate and ultimate effects of overcrowding.

Causal analysis is one of the chief techniques of reasoning; and if the method is used at all, the reader must always have confidence in its thoroughness and logic. Here are some ways to avoid the most common faults in causal reasoning:

1. Never mistake the fact that something happens with or after another occurrence as evidence of a causal relationship—for example, that a black cat crossing the road caused the flat tire a few minutes later, or that a course in English composition caused a student's nervous breakdown that same semester.

2. Consider all possibly relevant factors before attributing causes. Perhaps studying English did result in a nervous breakdown, but the cause may also have been ill health, trouble at home, the stress of working while attending college, or the anguish of a love affair. (The composition course, by providing an "emotional" outlet, may even have helped *postpone* the breakdown!)

3. Support the analysis by more than mere assertions: offer evidence. It would not often be enough to *tell* why Shakespeare's wise Othello believed the villainous Iago—the dramatist's lines should be used as evidence, possibly supported by the opinions of at least one literary scholar. If you are explaining that capital punishment deters crime, do not expect the reader to take your word for it—give before-and-after statistics or the testimony of reliable authorities.

4. Be careful not to omit any links in the chain of causes or effects unless you are certain that the readers for whom the writing is intended will automatically make the right connections themselves—and this is frequently a dangerous assumption. To un-

wisely omit one or more of the links might leave the reader with only a vague, or even erroneous, impression of the causal connection, possibly invalidating all that follows and thus making the entire writing ineffective.

5. Be honest and objective. Writers (or thinkers) who bring their old prejudices to the task of causal analysis, or who fail to see the probability of *multiple* causes or effects, are almost certain to distort their analyses or to make them so superficial, so thin, as to be almost worthless.

Ordinarily the method of causal analysis is either to work logically from the immediate cause (or effect) down toward the most basic, or to start with the basic and work up toward the immediate. But after at least analyzing the subject and deciding what the purpose requires in the paragraph or entire composition, the writer will usually find that a satisfactory pattern suggests itself.

Sample Paragraph (Annotated)

Most members of Ilona Principals' League agree that Valley young people are far better behaved than most they've encountered. Except for time-hallowed vices—like sneaking a smoke or a beer, or a little fiddling around between sexes—juvenile delinquency is rare. Why? At their last rap session the educators decided these are the most obvious causes: First, being in a basically rural area, most children grow up with work to do, leaving less time and energy for trouble. Because country kids predominate, working has long been "in" among even "townies" who might otherwise be less subject to it. Second, a much higher percentage of families here remain intact, more likely to keep a traditional value system. (Even the swingers of Eden, when they begin to

("Time-hallowed" is used in a somewhat ironic sense.)

("They've," "fiddling around," and "rap session" are colloquial and would not be suitable in more formal writing.)

On analysis, this first *immediate cause* is made up of three causes fitting into each other: the kids get into less trouble *because* they have less time *because* they have to work *because* they live in the country. ("Kids" is colloquial.)

Three *immediate causes*.

raise families, usually settle down and establish rules.) Third, the small, close-knit communities are mostly well stocked with relatives, interested in keeping misbehavior in check. But basic to all of these is the fact of the Valley's isolation, more psychological now than physical, but nonetheless real. By the time kids reach their upper teens, get driver's licenses, and begin to mix freely at school affairs outside the Valley, character is generally well enough formed to take some exposure to the drug-and-crime culture of the "other world."

The *ultimate cause:* the Valley's isolation.

[One paragraph does not permit much support for the assertions. The use of principals, however, does give the assertions some authority.]

Sample Paragraph (Cause/Effect)

Rap [music] started in discos, not the midtown glitter palaces like Studio 54 or New York, New York, but at Mel Quinn's on 42nd Street and Club 371 in the Bronx, where a young Harlemite who called himself D. J. Hollywood spun on the weekends. It wasn't unusual for black club jocks to talk to their audiences in the jive style of the old personality deejays. Two of the top black club spinners of the day, Pete (D. J.) Jones and Maboya, did so. Hollywood, just an adolescent when he started, created a more complicated, faster style, with more rhymes than his older mentors and call-and-response passages to encourage reaction from the dancers. At local bars, discos, and many illegal after-hours spots frequented by street people, Hollywood developed a huge word-of-mouth reputation. Tapes of his par-

ties began appearing around the city
on the then new and incredibly loud
Japanese portable cassette players
flooding into America. In Harlem,
Kurtis Blow, Eddie Cheeba, and D. J.
Lovebug Star-ski; in the Bronx,
Junebug Star-ski, Grandmaster Flash,
and Melle Mel; in Brooklyn, three
kids from the projects called Whodini;
and in Queens, Russell and Joey, the
two youngest sons from the middle-
class Simmons household—all
shared a fascination with Hollywood's
use of the rhythmic breaks in his club
mixes and his verbal dexterity. These
kids would all grow up to play a role
in the local clubs and, later, a few
would appear on the national scene
to spread Hollywood's style. Back in
the 1970s, while disco reigned in the
media, the Black Main Streets of New
York were listening to D. J. Hollywood, and learning.

Nelson George, The Death of Rhythm and Blues.

BOB GREENE

BOB GREENE, born in 1947 in Columbus, Ohio, is a columnist for
the *Chicago Tribune* and writes regularly for *Esquire* magazine.
His daily reports and commentary are syndicated to more than
120 other newspapers in the United States. His articles have appeared in *Newsweek, Harper's, Rolling Stone, New Times,* the *New
York Times,* and other publications, and his commentary has
been featured on the CBS television and radio networks. Greene
has written numerous books, including *We Didn't Have None of
Them Fat Funky Angels on the Wall of Heartbreak Hotel* (1971), *Billion
Dollar Baby* (1974), *Johnny Deadline, Reporter* (1976), *Good Morning, Merry Sunshine* (1984), *Cheeseburgers* (1985), *Be True to Your
School: A Diary of 1964* (1986), *Homecoming: When the Soldiers Returned from Vietnam* (1989).

Thirty Seconds

Much has been written about the broad influence of television
on our lives and culture. In this essay, however, Bob Greene
looks at some of the specific consequences a television commercial had for a man who participated in it. In doing so, he also
attests to the remarkable power of the medium. "Thirty
Seconds" first appeared in Greene's "American Beat" column
in *Esquire.*

It's funny how a man can live his whole life—a life filled with hero-   1
ism and downfalls, fatherhood and courage and pain and introspection—and no one notices. No one outside the man's family
and his small group of friends.

It's funny what television can do. Take the same man. Film a   2
TV commercial that is brilliantly conceived and executed, and the
man becomes known and revered in every corner of the nation. He

is the same person; nothing at all about him has changed. Nothing except the most important thing of all: he has been televised.

Novelists can write one hundred thousand words, two hundred thousand words, and not cause a ripple. For Bill Demby, it took only fifty-seven words, written by someone else and spoken by an announcer during a thirty-second television commercial, to totally revise his life.

Here are the words:

"When Bill Demby was in Vietnam, he dreamed of coming home and playing a little basketball. A dream that all but died when he lost both legs to a Vietcong rocket. But then researchers discovered that a Du Pont plastic could make truly lifelike artificial limbs. Now Bill's back, and some say he hasn't lost a step."

There was a tag line promoting Du Pont. The fifty-seven words about Bill Demby and the Du Pont tag line weren't what was so significant, of course. What was significant was the film footage of Demby—his artificial legs visible to the camera—competing in a game of playground basketball with able-bodied men. It began airing in the fall of 1987, and it became one of those commercials that people think about and talk to their friends about. It won a Clio award from the advertising industry; Demby was featured on the ABC program *20/20*. He went from being completely anonymous to truly famous in a matter of weeks.

When I caught up with him he was heading for a small college in the Midwest to make an address to the students. The basketball arena had been reserved for the event because an overflow crowd was expected.

"I walked into a McDonald's the other day to get something to eat," Bill Demby said. "This guy said hello to me and I said hi back. I thought he was just a friendly guy. But then he said, 'I liked the commercial.'"

Demby, now thirty-eight, was driving a truck on a road outside Quang Tri, Vietnam, on March 26, 1971, when a Vietcong rocket hit the vehicle. A twenty-year-old Army private at the time, he lost both legs below the knee. He spent the next year in Walter Reed hospital in Washington, and then tried to put his life back together.

Nothing very spectacular happened. He had problems with alcohol and drugs. A promising athlete before going to Vietnam, Demby—with the help of artificial legs—began trying to play sports again. He was in Nashville in 1987 at a basketball tournament sponsored by the U.S. Amputee Athletic Association when he was invited to audition for a Du Pont commercial. Du Pont had manufactured some of the materials used in certain prostheses, and had sent representatives of its advertising agency to the amputee tournament.

"I was very wary about doing it," Demby said. "I knew that on television, they can go into the cutting room and put things together any way they want. As far as the world was concerned at that point, Bill Demby didn't exist. As an amputee, usually I kept to myself."

Demby and four other disabled men wearing prostheses played basketball with personnel from the BBD&O ad agency looking on, and all five men submitted to informal interviews. Before long, Demby was told that he had been selected from the five to be the star of the Du Pont spot.

He was far from thrilled. "Actually, I called them up and said I was not interested in doing the commercial," Demby said.

I asked him why that was. For the first time in our conversation, he seemed to hesitate, as if a little embarrassed. Finally he said:

"I don't like to take my pants off in front of people." Meaning he doesn't like people to look at his artificial legs. Any people, much less millions upon millions of television viewers.

But in the end he decided to say yes. The commercial was shot on a basketball court in New York City, on Columbus Avenue between Seventy-sixth and Seventy-seventh streets, in late August 1987. "They told us that we were just supposed to play basketball, and that they'd film it," Demby said. "The other guys weren't actors—they were just players from the neighborhood. Players without physical disabilities.

"We played basketball from 7:00 in the morning until 6:30 at night. I got very tired. They had rented a room for me at the Warwick Hotel, and when the filming was over I just went to my room, took a shower, and fell asleep with the television set on. When I woke up the next morning the TV was still going. I didn't think much about what had happened. I just thought I had played some pickup basketball and they had filmed it, and now I would go back to my regular life. I went home that day. I felt that nothing had changed."

The advertising agency put the commercial together quickly. 17
Demby and his family, who live near Washington, D.C., received
a telephone call advising them to watch the CBS *Sunday Morning*
broadcast on September 13, 1987. That was the day the commercial
first aired.

"My wife and daughter and I sat in front of the TV set," 18
Demby said. "The commercial came on. The wonderful feeling . . .
there are no words to describe it."

The first time Demby realized that something unusual was up 19
came within a few weeks. "I was walking down the street in Washington, and this real huge guy started staring right into my eyes.
I was kind of scared. He said, 'It's you. It's you.' I didn't know
what he was talking about. I thought that maybe he was going to
rob me or something. I said, 'No, no.' And then the guy said,
'You're the one in the commercial. It's the best one I've ever
seen.'"

Since that moment, Demby has become used to the public rec- 20
ognition. Sometimes he doesn't much like it. "On occasion it still
surprises me when people look at me," he said. "It shouldn't, but
it does. Once in a while when someone will ask me about the commercial, I'll find myself saying, 'No, that was my twin brother.'"

There are other times, though . . . 21

"A man came up to me—a man who had been having a lot of 22
troubles. He explained the details of his troubles. He told me he
had given up on everything. He said that seeing me in the commercial had turned him around. He thanked me for changing his
life. Me.

"I walked away so that he wouldn't see me cry." 23

Soon everything was happening for Demby. He went to a 24
New York Knicks basketball game—he had never even been inside
Madison Square Garden before—and the crowd gave him a long
standing ovation. Moses Malone and Patrick Ewing shook his
hand.

He began to be invited to speak before large groups, such as 25
the college audience he was on his way to address when I joined
him. The *20/20* segment was filmed. The irony, of course, was that
he was the same man he had been for the almost twenty years
after he had returned from Vietnam. But because of those thirty

seconds on the Du Pont commercial (a sixty-second version also ran), for the first time in his life people were treating him as if he were special.

"It was very hard to get used to," Demby said. He was interviewed by newspapers and magazines; suddenly people saw him as a symbol of bravery and hope. He knew that if the commercial had not been broadcast, the same people would stare right through him as though he were invisible. Now they adored him.

Not everything made him feel great. "For a long time, I had been hesitant to tell people that I had lost my legs in Vietnam," he said. "I'd always wear long pants, even when I was playing sports. But now everyone knows what my legs look like.

"And my past problem with alcohol and PCP . . . that was my private problem, and now it's out. My daughter was eight years old, and she didn't know about it. She probably never would have, if the commercial hadn't been filmed and people hadn't started talking about me. She was very hurt by it. I tried to explain. I told her, 'It was just a bad part in Daddy's life. He was weak.'"

There is one aspect of the commercial that Demby virtually never volunteers to talk about. The standard line is that the film crew just shot the pickup basketball game and edited the footage down. The most emotional moment in the commercial comes when Demby is knocked to the ground, hard, by an opposing player. On his back, he stares up. Then he gets to his feet. It is one of those magical television instants—a second or two of film that gives the audience goose bumps and stays with them for a long time.

"That didn't happen during the game," Demby said. "We had been playing all day, and finally the director, Rick Levine, called me aside. He said he needed something else. He asked me if I would mind if he had one of the players knock me down."

It must have been quite a question. Imagine saying to a man with artificial legs: "Listen, we know you've been playing basketball for hours, but would it be okay if we had you jump in the air and then we pushed you to the concrete so that you land on your back? We'll only need to do it a few times."

Demby thought about it and said yes. He figured that Levine must know what he was doing. It paid off; without that sequence—especially the expression in Demby's eyes after he hits the ground—the commercial would lose its strongest surge of visceral humanity and power. Still, though: imagine asking the question.

Now, with all that has happened to Demby, you have to remind yourself that there were four other finalists for the starring role in the commercial, and that if BBD&O had selected any one of those four, today no one would know who Bill Demby is. Demby said that he has not heard from or seen the other four since auditioning. He got the thirty seconds; they didn't.   33

He does his best to keep it in perspective. There are days now when he feels it would be impossible to be any more famous and respected. "But I know that just as fast as this has come, it can leave. It could turn out to be a very temporary thing.   34

"I have a tendency to think we're all sort of crazy. The idea that thirty seconds could completely change a man's life." He tries not to lose sight of the fact that with or without the commercial, he would still be Bill Demby.   35

He is finally accepting the idea that strangers will approach him and tell him how much they admire him. "That's just society, though," he said. "That's just people reacting to what they've seen on their television screen.   36

"I keep having this thought. One of these days the commercial is going to stop running. They all do.   37

"And not long after that, someone is going to say to someone else, 'Hey, do you remember that guy—the amputee who played basketball in that commercial?'   38

"And the other guy will hesitate for a second and then say, 'Yeah, I think so. What was his name?'"   39

Meanings and Values

1a.   List the positive effects of the commercial.

b.   The negative effects.

c.   Explain why you think the author wants us to consider the commercial on the whole as either harmful or beneficial.

2a.   Is the primary focus of this essay on what happened to Bill Demby as a result of the commercial? Or is it on the power of television to affect our lives and attitudes? Be ready to support your answer with evidence from the essay.

b. How would you describe the main purpose or purposes of the essay? (See Guide to Terms: *Purpose.*)

c. If you believe the essay has more than one important purpose, explain why it should (or should not) be considered unified. (Guide: *Unity.*)

3. The subject of this essay is one that many writers might be tempted to handle in a sentimental manner. To what extent does Greene's treatment avoid sentimentality, if at all? (Guide: *Sentimentality.*)

4. Do you remember seeing this commercial on television? Does your memory of the commercial and its effectiveness agree with Greene's account?

Expository Techniques

1a. In which parts of the essay does Greene discuss causes?

b. Effects?

2. Should paragraphs 1–3 or 1–6 be considered the introduction to this essay? Why?

3a. Identify the uses of parallelism in the first two paragraphs of the essay. (Guide: *Parallel Structure.*)

b. How does the author use parallel structures to emphasize the central theme of the essay? (Guide: *Emphasis.*)

4. At several places in the essay, Greene talks about the men who were considered for the commercial but not chosen. To what extent do these discussions detract from the essay's unity or contribute to its central theme? (Guide: *Unity.*)

5. In what ways does Greene's frequent use of quotations from Bill Demby add to the effectiveness of the essay? (Guide: *Evaluation.*)

Diction and Vocabulary

1. Discuss how Greene uses diction and sentence structure to create drama and tension in paragraphs 29, 31, and 32. (Guide: *Diction, Syntax.*)

2. If you do not know the meaning of any of the following words, look them up in the dictionary: introspection (par. 1); prostheses (9); visceral (32).

Suggestions for Writing and Discussion

1. The commercial described in this essay may represent a growing interest in the effects of the Vietnam war on both those who fought

in it and those who did not. What other evidence of this growing interest can you identify?

2. Is Demby's prediction about his anonymity after the commercial stops running likely to come true (pars. 37–39)? Why?

3. If you believe television is as powerful as Greene suggests, can you cite some other examples of its effects?

(NOTE: Suggestions for topics requiring development by analysis of CAUSE AND EFFECT are on page 213, at the end of this section.)

GAIL SHEEHY

GAIL SHEEHY (born 1937) is a native New Yorker. After graduating from the University of Vermont, she was a department store consumer representative, a fashion coordinator, newspaper fashion editor, and women's feature writer for the *New York Herald Tribune*. Since 1968 Sheehy has been a contributing editor for *New York* magazine. Her articles have appeared in numerous magazines, including *McCall's, Cosmopolitan, Holiday, Glamour, Good Housekeeping,* and the *New York Times Magazine.* Her books are *Lovesounds* (1970), *Speed Is of the Essence* (1971), *Panthermania* (1971), *Hustling* (1973), *Pathfinders* (1981), *The Spirit of Survival* (1986), *Search for Leadership* (1988), and *Passages* (1976), which was on the nation's best-seller lists for many months.

$70,000 a Year, Tax Free

"$70,000 a Year, Tax Free" (editors' title) was written for NBC's "Comment" series, but the material was incorporated into *Hustling*. Its brevity, due to time limitations on the original presentation, obviously precluded a really thorough analysis of the topic. Observing how the author did use the time at her disposal provides some of the value of studying the selection here.

How many women do you know who can take home seventy 1 thousand dollars a year? A psychiatrist? She might take home half that. A congresswoman? Shirley Chisholm's salary is forty-two-five.

No, the quickest way for a woman to get ahead in this country 2 is to take up the oldest profession: prostitution.

As one veteran streetwalker explained to a runaway she was 3 breaking in: "You have no status, no power, and no way to get it except by using your body. Why give it away? You're sitting on a gold mine."

And so, every summer, in New York City, the hue and cry   4
goes up: Crack down on prostitution! Close the massage parlors!
But why has New York become a boomtown for hustlers? Not because of the increased use of drugs, as most people assume. It began with a change in New York's penal code four years ago. Loiter-
ing for the purpose of prostitution was reduced by former Police
Commissioner Leary from a misdemeanor to a violation. Even girls
found guilty on the more serious ''pross collar'' rarely go to jail.
Most judges let them go for a twenty-five to fifty dollar fine—and
a week to pay. It amounts to a license.

Word of this change spread with interest through the pimp   5
grapevine around the country: New York was wide open. Today,
you'd hardly guess which four states have the largest pipeline
shipping prostitutes to New York: in order, they are Minnesota,
Massachusetts, Michigan, and Ohio. There are lots of fair haired
girls from Minnesota with street names like Little Tiffany, and Marion the Librarian. But why do they come? It couldn't be a more
American phenomenon: The prostitute's dream is the most upward mobile, middle class, American pie dream of all.

Number one: she wants money—high-style clothes, a model   6
apartment, candy color wigs and her teeth capped.

Number two: she's looking for a ''family.'' Most of the girls   7
have one or two children—illegitimate. On top of that, the girl is
often white and her illegitimate child is black. Back home in Minneapolis, she was already a social pariah, and she couldn't make a
go of living and working while dragging a baby from room to
rented room. So she comes to New York, looking for a new kind
of family—exactly what the pimp provides.

He puts up his stable of three or four girls in a high-rise apart-   8
ment, pays their rent, buys their clothes, foots their doctor bills.
Top woman in this ''family''—the pimp's favorite, who brings in
the most money—is called his ''wife.'' The rest are known as
''wife-in-laws.'' Remarkably enough, they all get along quite well.
The tie that really binds is the baby sitter—the girls share one for
seventy-five dollars a week and this is what frees them to work.

As a midtown hooker from Virginia put it to me: ''Most of the   9
girls are here doing it for their kids. I don't want my daughter to
have the kind of childhood I had. She's going to have the best!''

So now the prostitute has money, a family, a baby sitter. The   10
other thing she craves is ''glamour and excitement,'' things she
probably dreamed of finding in a career as a model or actress. But

those fields are fiercely competitive. Besides, as a prostitute sees it, models and actresses are treated like dress hangers or pieces of meat: they give their bodies away to advance their careers, while so-called straight women exchange sex for the financial security of marriage. A "working girl," as the prostitute refers to herself, is the only honest one: she sets the price, delivers the goods, and concludes her business within the hour—no romantic nonsense about it.

And finally, after she is on the street for a few months, the pace of peeping and hiding, the game of stinging johns and ducking police vans, becomes a way of life. It gets into the blood like gambler's fever.

The hooker with the heart of gold? That's a male myth. Many of our street girls can be as vicious and money mad as any corporation president. Moreover, they can be less emotional than men in conducting acts of personal violence. The bulk of their business is not the dispensation of pleasure: it is to mug, rob, swindle, knife and possibly even murder their patrons. Police drags against them are about as effective as pacification programs in Vietnam. Apply police pressure to streetwalkers and robberies generally go up. If a girl doesn't bring in that fixed amount, two hundred and fifty a night, she'll go home to a beating from her pimp.

People are puzzled: why this boom in prostitution when young America is bursting with sexual freedom? They forget about men over forty, men who learned their sexual fantasies from nudie calendars in the gas station. To be fun, the bedmate must be a no-no. "You can't fantasize about your wife or girlfriend," one man explained. "The woman has to be an unknown." And where is this illicit thrill of forbidden flesh still to be found? On the black market, of course. Furthermore, the prostitute makes no emotional demands. She would never call his office the next day. It is her stock in trade to encourage men's sexual fantasies and exploit them. How else can a girl make seventy thousand dollars a year, tax free?

Meanings and Values

1a.   Briefly summarize the author's reasons for a girl's becoming a prostitute.

b. Do you consider these ultimate or immediate causes—or would you classify them somewhere in between? Why?

2a. Why does the author consider these motivations as an "American pie dream" (par. 5)?

b. To which of the causes, if any, does the description seem to you not to apply? Why?

3. Why does she assume that we'd "hardly guess" which four states have the largest pipelines into New York prostitution (par. 5)?

4. Do you see anything ironic in the prostitute's comments in paragraph 9? (See Guide to Terms: *Irony.*) If so, explain.

5a. How can perpetuation of the "male myth" (par. 12) be explained?

b. Why would it be more difficult to "fantasize" about one's wife or girlfriend (par. 13)?

6a. Where would you locate this selection on an objective-to-subjective continuum? (Guide: *Objective/Subjective.*)

b. Is the author guilty of any sentimentality? (Guide: *Sentimentality.*) If so, where?

Expository Techniques

1a. In which paragraphs does the author explain why prostitution has increased greatly in New York City?

b. Does this seem to be a thorough cause-and-effect analysis?

c. Is it sufficient for the purpose? Why, or why not?

2a. In paragraphs 6–11 the author outlines a different set of causes. Would they have been more effective for her purpose if she had gone deeper into the more ultimate causes?

b. Why do you think she did not?

c. What function is served by the first sentence of paragraph 10? Why would the author have considered it a useful device in this particular exposition?

3a. What is Sheehy's central theme? (Guide: *Unity.*)

b. Do all portions of the essay serve as tributaries into this theme, thus giving unity to the writing? If not, what are the exceptions?

4a. Which of the standard techniques of introduction does the author use? (Guide: *Introductions.*)

b. Why do they seem particularly well chosen, considering the basic purpose of this exposition?

5a. The last sentence is a good example of at least one standard technique of closing. (Guide: *Closings.*) What is it?

b. Suggest a different kind of closing and compare the relative effectiveness of the two.

6. Which of the patterns of exposition already studied does Sheehy employ in paragraph 10?

7. In your opinion, would any of her statements have benefited by further qualification? (Guide: *Qualification.*) If so, explain why.

Diction and Vocabulary

1. Illustrate the meaning of the following terms by use of one or more examples from this selection.

a. Colloquialism. (Guide: *Colloquial Expressions.*)

b. Simile. (Guide: *Figures of Speech.*)

c. Cliché. (Guide: *Clichés.*)

2. What is a "social pariah" (par. 7)?

3. Considering this exposition's original purpose, why do you think the author used few, if any, "dictionary-type" words?

Suggestions for Writing and Discussion

1. The author says most people assume that the increase in prostitution is related to an increased use of drugs. How logical does this assumption appear to you? Explain.

2. Explore parallels in other, more legitimate fields in which motivation may be provided by the "upwardly mobile, middle class, American pie dream" (par. 5).

3. In view of the five reasons for a girl's becoming a prostitute—all seeming to be fairly common desires—why is it that even more girls do not engage in prostitution?

4. Which of her five reasons do you think would also apply to the thriving business (in some cities especially) of male prostitution? Are there other reasons that apply here?

5. How logical and/or just do you consider the move in many areas toward "equal guilt" laws, whereby the male is considered as guilty as the prostitute he employs?

6. Should there even *be* laws prohibiting prostitution?

7. The word "prostitution" is often used with broader meaning than in Sheehy's analysis—e.g., "prostitution of talent" or "prostitution of science." Select one such usage and examine motivations in terms of this author's "upward mobility" theories.

(NOTE: Suggestions for topics requiring development by analysis of CAUSE AND EFFECT are on page 213, at the end of this section.)

NANCY MAIRS

NANCY MAIRS was born in Long Beach, California, in 1943. She graduated from Wheaton College in 1964 and worked from 1966 to 1972 as a technical editor at the Smithsonian Astrophysical Observatory, the MIT Press, and Harvard Law School. She has lived in Tucson, Arizona, since 1972. Mairs has been a teacher of composition in both high school and college and has received an M.F.A. in creative writing and a Ph.D. in English literature. A volume of her poems, *In All the Rooms of the Yellow House* (1984), was given first prize for poetry in the Western States Book Awards. A volume of her essays entitled *Plaintext: Deciphering a Woman's Life* appeared in 1986.

On Being a Scientific Booby

In this essay from *Plaintext*, Nancy Mairs looks back at her freshman college course in biology and forward toward her daughter's college career. Mairs's discussion of her difficult experiences in biology class should be easy to understand for any student who has struggled with a particular teacher or course. In addition to cause and effect, the essay makes use of comparison and examples.

My daughter is dissecting a chicken. Her first. Her father, whose   1
job this usually is, has been derelict in his duties, and my hands
are now too weak to dissect much more than a zucchini. If she
wants dinner (and she does), she will make this pale, flabby carcass into eight pieces I can fit into the skillet. I act as coach. To
encourage her, I tell her that her great-great-grandfather was a
butcher. This is true, not something I have made up to con her into
doing a nasty job.

Now that she's gotten going, she is having a wonderful time. She has made the chicken crow and flap and dance all over the cutting board, and now it lies quiet under her short, strong fingers as she slices the length of its breastbone. She pries back the ribs and peers into the cavity. "Oh, look at its mesenteries!" she cries. I tell her I thought mesentery was something you got from drinking the water in Mexico. She pokes at some filmy white webs. Mesenteries, she informs me, are the membranes that hold the chicken's organs in place. My organs too. She flips the chicken over and begins to cut along its spine. As her fingers search out joints and the knife severs wing from breast, leg from thigh, she gives me a lesson in the comparative anatomy of this chicken and the frog she and her friend Emily have recently dissected at school.

I am charmed by her enthusiasm and self-assurance. Since she was quite small, she has talked of becoming a veterinarian, and now that she is approaching adulthood, her purpose is growing firmer. During this, her junior year in a special high school, she is taking a college-level introductory course in biology. I took much the same course when I was a freshman in college. But if I entered that course with Anne's self-confidence, and I may very well have done so, I certainly had none of it by the time I wrote the last word of my final examination in my blue book and turned it in the following spring. As the result of Miss White and the quadrat report, I am daunted to the point of dysfunction by the notion of thinking or writing "scientifically."

That woman—damn that woman!—turned me into a scientific cripple, and did so in the name of science at a prestigious women's college that promised to school me in the liberal arts that I might "have life and have it abundantly." And really, I have had it abundantly, so I suppose I oughtn't to complain if it's been a little short in *Paramecia* and *Amanita phalloides* and *Drosophila melanogaster*, whose eyes I have never seen.

Still. Miss White should not have been allowed to teach freshman biology because she had a fatal idiosyncracy (fatal, that is, to the courage of students, not to herself, though I believe she is dead now of some unrelated cause): She could not bear a well-written report. One could be either a writer or a scientist but not both, she told me one November afternoon, the grey light from a tall window sinking into the grain of the dark woodwork in her cramped office in the old Science Building, her fingers flicking the sheets of my latest lab write-up. She was washing her hands of me, I could tell by the weariness of her tone. She didn't even try to make me a scientist. For that matter, she didn't even point to a spot where I'd gone wrong and show me what she wanted instead. She simply wrinkled her nose at the odor of my writing, handed me the sheets, and sent me away. We never had another conference. At the end of the semester, I wrote my quadrat report, and Miss White failed it. She allowed me to rewrite it. I wrote it again, and she failed it again. Neither of us went for a third try.

All the same, I liked my quadrat, which was a twenty-by- 6 twenty plot in the College Woods behind the Library. Mine was drab compared to some others: Pam Weprin's, I remember, had a brook running through it, in which she discovered goldfish. It turned out that her magical discovery had a drab explanation: In a heavy rain the water from Peacock Pond backed up and spilled its resident carp into the brook. Even so, her quadrat briefly held an excitement mine never did. Mine was, in fact, as familiar as a living room, since I had spent large portions of my youth tramping another such woods sixty miles north. The lichen grew on the north side of the trees. In the rain the humus turned black and rank. Afterwards, a fallen log across one corner would sprout ears of tough, pale fungus.

Each freshman biology student received a quadrat. There were 7 enough of us that we had to double up, but I never met my quadrat-mate or even knew her name. It occurs to me now that I ought to have found out, ought to have asked her what she got on her quadrat report, but I was new to failure and knew no ways to profit from it. I simply did as I was told—visited my quadrat to observe its progress through the seasons and wrote up my observations—and then discovered that I had somehow seen and spoken wrong. I wish now that I had kept the report. I wonder exactly what I said in it. Probably something about ears of fungus. Good God.

With a D+ for the first semester I continued, perversely, to 8 like biology, but I also feared it more and more. Not the discipline itself. I pinned and opened a long earthworm, marveling at the delicately tinted organs. I dissected a beef heart, carefully, so as not to spoil it for stuffing and roasting at the biology department's annual beef-heart feast. For weeks I explored the interior of my rat, which I had opened neatly, like the shutters over a window. He was a homely thing, stiff, his fur yellow and matted from formaldehyde, and because he was male, not very interesting. Several students got pregnant females, and I envied them the intricate organs, the chains of bluish-pink fetuses. At the end of each lab, I would reluctantly close the shutters, swaddle my rat in his plastic bag, and slip him back into the crock.

No, biology itself held more fascination and delight than fear. 9 But with each report I grew more terrified of my own insidious poetic nature, which Miss White sniffed out in the simplest statement about planaria or left ventricles. Years later, when I became a technical editor and made my living translating the garbled outbursts of scientists, I learned that I had done nothing much wrong. My understanding was limited, to be sure, but Miss White would have forgiven me ignorance, even stupidity I think, if I had sufficiently muddled the language. As it was, I finished biology with a C−, and lucky I was to get it, since the next year the college raised the passing grade from C− to C. I have always thought, indeed, that the biology department awarded me a passing grade simply so that they wouldn't have to deal with me another year.

And they didn't. Nor did anyone else. I never took another 1 science course, although I surprised myself long afterward by becoming, perforce and precipitously, a competent amateur herpetologist. My husband arrived home one afternoon with a shoebox containing a young bull snake, or gopher snake as this desert variety is called, which he had bought for a quarter from some of his students at a school for emotionally disturbed boys so that they wouldn't try to find out how long a snake keeps wriggling without its head. This was Ferdinand, who was followed by two more bull snakes, Squeeze and Beowulf, and by a checkered garter snake named Winslow J. Tweed, a black racer named Jesse Owens, a Yuma king snake named Hrothgar, and numerous nameless and short-lived blind snakes, tiny and translucent, brought to us by our cats Freya, Burton Rustle, and Vanessa Bell. I grew so knowledgeable that when my baby boa constrictor, Crictor, contracted a respiratory ailment, I found that I was more capable of caring for him than were any of the veterinarians in the city. In fact, I learned, veterinarians do not do snakes; I could find only one to give Crictor the shot of a broad-spectrum antibiotic he needed.

So I do do snakes. I have read scientific treatises on them. I 1 know that the Latin name for the timber rattlesnake is *Crotalus horridus horridus*. I know that Australia has more varieties of venomous snakes than any other continent, among them the lethal sea snakes and the willfully aggressive tiger snake. I know how long one is likely to live after being bitten by a mamba (not long). I read the treatises; but I don't, of course, write them. Although as a technical editor I grew proficient at unraveling snarls in the writing of scientists, I have never, since Miss White, attempted scientific experimentation or utterance.

Aside from my venture into herpetology, I remain a scientific booby. I mind my stupidity. I feel diminished by it. And I know now that it is unnecessary, the consequence of whatever quirk of fate brought me into Miss White's laboratory instead of Miss Chidsey's or Dr. McCoy's. Miss White, who once represented the whole of scientific endeavor to me, was merely a woman with a hobbyhorse. I see through her. Twenty years later, I am now cynical enough to write a quadrat report badly enough to pass her scrutiny, whereas when I had just turned seventeen I didn't even know that cynicism was an option—knowledge that comes, I suppose, from having life abundantly. I've learned, too, that Miss White's bias, though unusually strong, was not peculiar to herself but arose from a cultural rift between the humanities and the sciences resulting in the assumption that scientists will naturally write badly, that they are, in fact, rhetorical boobies. Today I teach technical writing. My students come to me terrified of the word-world from which they feel debarred, and I teach them to breach the boundaries in a few places, to step with bravado at least a little way inside. Linguistic courage is the gift I can give them. 12

In return, they give me gifts that I delight in—explanations of vortex centrifuges, evaluations of copper-smelting processes, plans for extracting gums from paloverde beans. These help me compensate for my deficiencies, as do the works of the popularizers of science. Carl Sagan, Loren Eiseley, Lewis Thomas and his reverential reflections subtitled *Notes of a Biology Watcher,* Stephen Jay Gould, James Burke and Jacob Bronowski, Pierre Teilhard de Chardin, John McPhee, who has made me love rocks, Isaac Asimov, Elaine Morgan. I watch television too. *Nova, Odyssey, The Undersea World of Jacques Cousteau, The Body in Question.* But always I am aware that I am having translated for me the concepts of worlds I will never now explore for myself. I stand with my toes on the boundaries, peering, listening. 13

Anne has done a valiant job with the chicken. She's had a little trouble keeping its pajamas on, and one of the thighs has a peculiar trapezoidal shape, but she's reduced it to a workable condition. I brown it in butter and olive oil. I press in several cloves 14

of garlic and then splash in some white wine. As I work, I think
of the worlds Anne is going to explore. Some of them are listed in
the college catalogues she's begun to collect: "Genetics, Energet-
ics, and Evolution"; "Histology of Animals"; "Vertebrate Endo-
crinology"; "Electron Microscopy"; "Organic Synthesis"; "Animal Morphogenesis."

Anne can write. No one has yet told her that she can be a   1
scientist or a writer but not both, and I trust that no one ever will.
The complicated world can ill afford such lies to its children. As
she plunges from my view into the thickets of calculus, embryol-
ogy, and chemical thermodynamics, I will wait here for her to send
me back messages. I love messages.

Meanings and Values

1a.   Summarize Miss White's view of the relationship between scien-
      tists and writers, that is, between science and good writing.

 b.   Summarize the author's view of the relationship.

2a.   Identify the causes that led to the author's becoming "a scientific
      cripple."

 b.   Point out evidence in the story that indicates that the author is not
      quite the "scientific booby" she claims to be.

3.   What is the "cultural rift" that Mairs discusses in paragraph 12?
      To what extent do your experiences confirm or fail to confirm the
      existence of such a split?

4.   Are many readers likely to recognize the authors and television
      programs mentioned in paragraph 13? What effect are these refer-
      ences likely to have on readers who recognize most or all of them?
      On readers who recognize few or none of them?

Expository Techniques

1a.   What incident does Mairs use to open the essay?

 b.   How is it related to the subject and theme of the essay? (See Guide
      to Terms: *Unity.*)

2.   In what ways are the opening and closing of the essay related?
      (Guide: *Introductions, Closings.*)

3.   Discuss how the essay makes use of the following patterns:

 a.   narrative

 b.   comparison

 c.   example

4.   Despite the presence of these other patterns, why should this piece be classified as a cause-effect essay?

Diction and Vocabulary

1a.   The names of some of the snakes and cats in paragraph 10 are allusions. Identify as many of the allusions as you can. (Guide: *Figures of Speech.*)

 b.   What do these allusions suggest about the author's attitude toward both language and science?

2a.   Identify the metaphor in the closing paragraph. (Guide: *Figures of Speech.*)

 b.   Why is it appropriate for this essay?

3a.   In what ways is the diction in paragraphs 6 and 8 characteristic of a writer (and poet) rather than a scientist? (Guide: *Diction.*)

 b.   How might the diction be altered to turn the passages into good scientific writing?

4a.   Is an understanding of the scientific terms the author uses necessary to grasp the meaning of the essay?

 b.   If not, what roles do they play?

5.   If you do not understand the following phrases, consult a dictionary: "daunted to the point of dysfunction" (par. 3); "perforce and precipitously" (par. 10); "a scientific booby" (par. 12); "a woman with a hobbyhorse" (par. 12).

Suggestions for Writing and Discussion

1.   In what ways do your experiences in science classes resemble or differ from the author's?

2.   Why are science magazines and television shows so popular?

3.   Prepare an essay of your own telling how a particular class or teacher made you love (or hate) an area of study.

(NOTE: Suggestions for topics requiring development by analysis of CAUSE AND EFFECT are on page 213, at the end of this section.)

SUSAN PERRY AND JIM DAWSON

SUSAN PERRY is a former staff writer for Time-Life, Inc., and now works full-time as a free-lance writer specializing in health, business, and women's issues. Her articles have appeared in such publications as *Ms.*, the *Washington Post,* and the *Minneapolis Star.* JAMES DAWSON is a science reporter who writes regularly for the *Minneapolis Star-Tribune.* Recently Perry and Dawson co-authored *The Secrets Our Body Clocks Reveal* (1988).

What's Your Best Time of Day?

This essay, published as a magazine article, was drawn from *The Secrets Our Body Clocks Reveal.* The piece opens with examples of some puzzling behaviors, looks at their causes in the rhythms of our bodies, then examines some further effects of these rhythms. Along the way it provides some practical advice for taking the best advantage of the biological patterns that help govern our lives. As might be expected, the authors draw on a variety of patterns to accomplish these tasks, including classification, process, and the use of examples.

Every fall, Jane, a young mother and part-time librarian, begins to   1
eat more and often feels sleepy. Her mood is also darker, especially when she awakens in the morning; it takes all her energy just to drag herself out of bed. These symptoms persist until April, when warmer weather and longer days seem to lighten her mood and alleviate her cravings for food and sleep.

Joseph, a 48-year-old engineer for a Midwestern computer   2
company, feels cranky early in the morning. But as the day progresses, he becomes friendlier and more accommodating.

All living organisms, from mollusks to men and women, ex- 3
hibit biological rhythms. Some are short and can be measured in
minutes or hours. Others last days or months. The peaking of
body temperature, which occurs in most people every evening, is
a daily rhythm. The menstrual cycle is a monthly rhythm. The increase in sexual drive in the autumn—not in the spring, as poets
would have us believe—is a seasonal, or yearly, rhythm.

The idea that our bodies are in constant flux is fairly new— 4
and goes against traditional medical training. In the past, many
doctors were taught to believe the body has a relatively stable, or
homeostatic, internal environment. Any fluctuations were considered random and not meaningful enough to be studied.

As early as the 1940s, however, some scientists questioned the 5
homeostatic view of the body. Franz Halberg, a young European
scientist working in the United States, noticed that the number of
white blood cells in laboratory mice was dramatically higher and
lower at different times of day. Gradually, such research spread to
the study of other rhythms in other life forms, and the findings
were sometimes startling. For example, the time of day when a
person receives X-ray or drug treatment for cancer can affect treatment benefits and ultimately mean the difference between life and
death.

This new science is called chronobiology, and the evidence 6
supporting it has become increasingly persuasive. Along the way,
the scientific and medical communities are beginning to rethink
their ideas about how the human body works, and gradually what
had been considered a minor science just a few years ago is being
studied in major universities and medical centers around the
world. There are even chronobiologists working for the National
Aeronautics and Space Administration, as well as for the National
Institutes of Health and other government laboratories.

With their new findings, they are teaching us things that can 7
literally change our lives—by helping us organize ourselves so we
can work *with* our natural rhythms rather than against them. This
can enhance our outlook on life as well as our performance at work
and play.

Because they are easy to detect and measure, more is known 8
of daily—or circadian (Latin for "about a day")—rhythms than
other types. The most obvious daily rhythm is the sleep/wake
cycle. But there are other daily cycles as well: temperature, blood

pressure, hormone levels. Amid these and the body's other changing rhythms, you are simply a different person at 9 A.M. than you are at 3 P.M. How you feel, how well you work, your level of alertness, your sensitivity to taste and smell, the degree with which you enjoy food or take pleasure in music—all are changing throughout the day.

Most of us seem to reach our peak of alertness around noon. Soon after that, alertness declines, and sleepiness may set in by midafternoon.

Your short-term memory is best during the morning—in fact, about 15 percent more efficient than at any other time of day. So, students, take heed: when faced with a morning exam, it really does pay to review your notes right before the test is given.

Long-term memory is different. Afternoon is the best time for learning material that you want to recall days, weeks or months later. Politicians, business executives or others who must learn speeches would be smart to do their memorizing during that time of day. If you are a student, you would be wise to schedule your more difficult classes in the afternoon, rather than in the morning. You should also try to do most of your studying in the afternoon, rather than late at night. Many students believe they memorize better while burning the midnight oil because their short-term recall is better during the wee hours of the morning than in the afternoon. But short-term memory won't help them much several days later, when they face the exam.

By contrast, we tend to do best on cognitive tasks—things that require the juggling of words and figures in one's head—during the morning hours. This might be a good time, say, to balance a checkbook.

Your manual dexterity—the speed and coordination with which you perform complicated tasks with your hands—peaks during the afternoon hours. Such work as carpentry, typing or sewing will be a little easier at this time of day.

What about sports? During afternoon and early evening, your coordination is at its peak, and you're able to react the quickest to an outside stimulus—like a baseball speeding toward you at home plate. Studies have also shown that late in the day, when your body temperature is peaking, you will *perceive* a physical workout to be easier and less fatiguing—whether it actually is or not. That means you are more likely to work harder during a late-afternoon or early-evening workout, and therefore benefit more from it. Studies involving swimmers, runners, shot-putters and rowing crews have shown consistently that performance is better in the evening than in the morning.

In fact, all of your senses—taste, sight, hearing, touch and smell—may be at their keenest during late afternoon and early evening. That could be why dinner usually tastes better to us than breakfast and why bright lights irritate us at night. 15

Even our perception of time changes from hour to hour. Not only does time seem to fly when you're having fun, but it also seems to fly even faster if you are having that fun in the late afternoon or early evening, when your body temperature is also peaking. 16

While all of us follow the same general pattern of ups and downs, the exact timing varies from person to person. It all depends on how your "biological" day is structured—how much of a morning or night person you are. The earlier your biological day gets going, the earlier you are likely to enter—and exit—the peak times for performing various tasks. An extreme morning person and an extreme night person may have circadian cycles that are a few hours apart. 17

Each of us can increase our knowledge about our individual rhythms. Learn how to listen to the inner beats of your body; let them set the pace of your day. You will live a healthier—and happier—life. As no less an authority than the Bible tells us, "To every thing there is a season, and a time to every purpose under heaven." 18

Meanings and Values

1. In what ways are the patterns illustrated or discussed in the first three paragraphs similar to each other?

2. According to the explanations in this essay, what are the best times to undertake the following activities, and why:

   a. play a sport

   b. balance a checkbook

   c. learn a speech

   d. prepare for an exam

Expository Techniques

1.   What functions do the examples that open the essay perform for readers? (Guide: *Introductions.*)

2a. Where in the essay do the authors use classification and for what purposes is it employed?

  b. Where and for what purposes do the authors use process analysis?

3.   Would this essay be more effective if discussions of the causes and the effects were more clearly separated? Why, or why not? (Guide: *Evaluation.*)

4.   Discuss the arrangement of paragraphs 9–12, paying special attention to parallel structures and transitions within and between paragraphs. (Guide: *Unity, Parallel Structure.*)

Diction and Vocabulary

1.   In what ways does the diction in paragraphs 1 and 2 emphasize the contrasts being illustrated? (Guide: *Diction.*)

2.   Discuss how the authors provide explanations of the following scientific or otherwise unfamiliar terms in the text so that readers will not have to pause to look them up: homeostatic (par. 4); circadian (8); cognitive tasks (12); manual dexterity (13).

3.   Does the allusion that concludes the essay seem appropriate? Why, or why not? Try looking up the passage in the Bible (Ecclesiastes 3:1) to see if its original meaning is similar to the one it has in the context of this essay.

Suggestions for Writing and Discussion

1.   Do your experiences confirm what the authors say about the cycles that guide our behavior? Provide examples that either support or contradict the essay's conclusions.

2.   How might typical academic or work schedules be altered to take into account the patterns described in this selection? What common practices seem particularly in need of change given the information provided here?

(NOTE: Suggestions for topics requiring development by analysis of CAUSE AND EFFECT follow.)

Writing Suggestions for Section 6
Cause and Effect

Analyze the immediate and ultimate causes and/or effects of one of the following subjects, or another suggested by them. (Be careful that your analysis does not develop into a mere listing of superficial "reasons.")

1. The ethnic makeup of a neighborhood.
2. Some *minor* discovery or invention.
3. The popularity of some modern singer or other celebrity.
4. The popularity of some fad of clothing or hair style.
5. The widespread fascination for antique cars (or guns, furniture, dishes, etc.).
6. The widespread enjoyment of fishing or hunting.
7. Student cheating.
8. Too much pressure (on you or an acquaintance) for good school grades.
9. Your being a member of some minority ethnic or religious group.
10. Your association, as an outsider, with members of such a group.
11. The decision of some close acquaintance to enter the religious life.
12. Some unreasonable fear or anxiety that afflicts you or someone you know well.
13. The reluctance of many women today to enter what used to be primarily women's professions such as nursing.
14. Your tendency toward individualism.
15. The popularity of computer games.
16. The mainstreaming of handicapped children.
17. The appeal of careers that promise considerable financial rewards.
18. The appeal of a recent movie or current television series.
19. The willingness of some people to sacrifice personal relationships for professional success.
20. The disintegration of a marriage or family.
21. A family's move (or reluctance to move) to a new home.
22. A candidate's success in a local or national election.

7

Using *Definition* to Help Explain

Few writing faults can cause a more serious communication block between writer and reader than using key terms that can have various meanings or shades of meaning. To be useful rather than detrimental, such terms must be adequately defined.

Of the two basic types of definition, only one is our special concern as a pattern of exposition. But the other, the simpler form, is often useful to clarify meanings of concrete or noncontroversial terms. This simple process is similar to that used most in dictionaries: either providing a synonym (for example, cinema: a motion picture), or placing the word in a class and then showing how it differs from others of the same class (for example, metheglin: an alcoholic liquor made of fermented honey—here the general class is "liquor," and the differences between metheglin and other liquors are that it is "alcoholic" and "made of fermented honey").

Berne, for instance, sees the need to define several of his key terms in the process of classifying—e.g., viscerotonic endomorph, somatotonic mesomorph, and cerebrotonic ectomorph; and Reed offers a definition of "Western civilization" as a basis for his discussion of a multinational culture.

With many such abstract, unusual, or coined terms, typical readers are too limited by their own experiences and opinions (and no two sets are identical) for writers to expect understanding of the exact sense in which the terms are used. They have a right, of course, to use such abstract words any way they choose—as long as their readers know what that way is. The importance of making this meaning clear becomes crucial when the term is used as a key element of the overall explanation. And sometimes the term being defined is even more than a key element: it may be the subject itself, either for purposes of explanation or argument.

Extended definition, unlike the simple, dictionary type, follows no set and formal pattern. Often readers are not even aware of the process. Because it is an integral part of the overall subject, extended definition is written in the same tone as the rest of the exposition (or argument), usually with an attempt to interest the readers, as well as to inform or persuade them.

There are some expository techniques peculiar to definition alone. The purpose may be served by giving the background of the term. Or the definition may be clarified by negation, sometimes called "exclusion" or "differentiation," by showing what is *not* meant by the term. Still another way is to enumerate the characteristics of what is defined, sometimes isolating an essential one for special treatment.

To demonstrate the possibilities in these patterns, we can use the term *juvenile delinquency*, which might need defining in some contexts since it certainly means different things to different people. (Where do we draw the line, for instance, between "childish pranks" and antisocial behavior, or between delinquent and nondelinquent experimentation with sex or marijuana?) We might show how attitudes toward juvenile crime have changed: "youthful high spirits" was the label for some of our grandfathers' activities that would be called "delinquency" today. Or we could use negation, eliminating any classes of juvenile wrongdoing not considered delinquency in the current discussion. Or we could simply list characteristics of the juvenile delinquent or isolate one of these—disrespect for authority or lack of consideration for other people—as a universal.

But perhaps the most dependable techniques for defining are the basic expository patterns already studied. Writers could illustrate their meaning of *juvenile delinquency* by giving *examples* from their own experience, from newspaper accounts, or from other sources. (Every one of the introductions to the eleven sections of this book, each a definition, relies greatly on illustration by example.) They could analyze the subject by *classification* of types or degrees of delinquency. They could use the process of *comparison* and *contrast*, perhaps between delinquent and nondelinquent youth. Showing the *causes* and *effects* of juvenile crime could help explain their attitudes toward it, and hence its meaning for them. They might choose to use *analogy*, perhaps comparing the child to a

young tree growing grotesque because of poor care and attention.
Or a step-by-step analysis of the *process* by which a child becomes
delinquent might, in some cases, help explain the intended
meaning.

Few extended definitions would use all these methods, but the
extent of their use must always depend on three factors: (1) the
term itself, since some are more elusive and subject to misunderstanding than others; (2) the function the term is to serve in the
writing, since it would be foolish to devote several pages to defining a term that serves only a casual or unimportant purpose; and
(3) the prospective reader-audience, since writers want to avoid
insulting the intelligence or background of their readers, yet want
to go far enough to be sure of their understanding.

But this, of course, is a basic challenge in any good writing—
analyzing the prospective readers and writing for the best effect
on *them*.

Sample Paragraph (Annotated)

We are tipped off in the first sentence to what will be defined.

Some of the *characteristics*.

(Irony by understate-
ment.)

Negation, or *exclusion*, to
let us know what is not
meant.

Background of the term.

One rare treat the visitor can anticipate is an introduction to Ilona Valley
sorghum molasses—on hot biscuits, or
in taffy or gingerbread, to name a few
of the delights. Rich in iron, moreover,
molasses with sulphur is still a standard spring tonic in some older families. (This is generally considered less
delightful than taffy.) But sorghum
molasses must never, never be confused with ordinary storebought molasses. The latter is typically made of
sugar cane from which much of the
sugar has been boiled off and removed. ("Blackstrap" has given up
practically *all* the sugar.) But Valley
molasses is made of sorghum, a different plant entirely, akin to Indian corn
but containing a sweet pith in the stalk.
Introduced here by the Caseys, it
must have found an ideal climate and

Another important *characteristic*.

Process analysis to help define.

soil; most ranches now have at least a small patch of sorghum. Of four known varieties, only one, sugar (or saccharin) sorghum, is used for making molasses—really a syrup, as all the sugar is left in it. Harvested in late summer, ground or chopped by hand or machine, it is then boiled in vats over outdoor fires. The stirring, straining, fire-tending, and jugging are an all-hands operation, but the result has

(An example, used to illustrate the general, abstract term *prestige*.)

wide prestige: several folks who grew up here (one as far away as Tokyo) have a few gallons shipped to them every fall.

Sample Paragraph (Definition)

This is *orienteering*, a mixture of marathon, hike, and scavenger hunt, a cross-country race in which participants must locate a series of markers set in unfamiliar terrain by means of map and compass. The course, which may range from an acre of city park to twenty square miles of wilderness, is dotted with anywhere from four to fifteen "controls," red-and-white flags whose general locations are marked on the map by small circles. At each control there is a paper punch that produces a distinctive pattern on a card the racer carries. In most events the order in which the card must be punched is fixed; the route taken to reach each control, however, is up to the participant.

Excerpt from "Marathoning with Maps" by Linton Robinson from *Science*, published by The American Association for the Advancement of Science. Reprinted by permission.

MARIE WINN

MARIE WINN was born in Czechoslovakia, and emigrated with
her family to the United States, where she attended the New
York City schools. She was graduated from Radcliffe College
and also attended Columbia University. Winn has written
eleven books, all of them about children, and been a frequent
contributor to the *New York Times* and various other newspapers
and periodicals. Her most recent books are *Children Without
Childhood* (1983) and *Unplugging the Plug-In Drug* (1987).

Television Addiction

"Television Addiction" is the title of a chapter in Marie Winn's
highly regarded book *The Plug-In Drug* (1977), and our selection
is an excerpt from that chapter. It will be seen that a careful definition of the term *addiction,* and a careful application of it to TV
viewing, particularly by the young, is of utmost importance to
the author's main point, as indicated by the book's title. It is a
fairly typical use of extended definition.

The word "addiction" is often used loosely and wryly in conversa- 1
tion. People will refer to themselves as "mystery book addicts" or
"cookie addicts." E. B. White writes of his annual surge of interest
in gardening: "We are hooked and are making an attempt to kick
the habit." Yet nobody really believes that reading mysteries or
ordering seeds by catalogue is serious enough to be compared with
addictions to heroin or alcohol. The word "addiction" is here used
jokingly to denote a tendency to overindulge in some pleasurable
activity.

People often refer to being "hooked on TV." Does this, too, 2
fall into the lighthearted category of cookie eating and other plea-

219

sures that people pursue with unusual intensity, or is there a kind of television viewing that falls into the more serious category of destructive addiction?

When we think about addiction to drugs or alcohol, we frequently focus on negative aspects, ignoring the pleasures that accompany drinking or drug-taking. And yet the essence of any serious addiction is a pursuit of pleasure, a search for a "high" that normal life does not supply. It is only the inability to function without the addictive substance that is dismaying, the dependence of the organism upon a certain experience and an increasing inability to function normally without it. Thus a person will take two or three drinks at the end of the day not merely for the pleasure drinking provides, but also because he "doesn't feel normal" without them.

An addict does not merely pursue a pleasurable experience and need to experience it in order to function normally. He needs to *repeat* it again and again. Something about that particular experience makes life without it less than complete. Other potentially pleasurable experiences are no longer possible, for under the spell of the addictive experience, his life is peculiarly distorted. The addict craves an experience and yet he is never really satisfied. The organism may be temporarily sated, but soon it begins to crave again.

Finally a serious addiction is distinguished from a harmless pursuit of pleasure by its distinctly destructive elements. A heroin addict, for instance, leads a damaged life: his increasing need for heroin in increasing doses prevents him from working, from maintaining relationships, from developing in human ways. Similarly an alcoholic's life is narrowed and dehumanized by his dependence on alcohol.

Let us consider television viewing in the light of the conditions that define serious addictions.

Not unlike drugs or alcohol, the television experience allows the participant to blot out the real world and enter into a pleasurable and passive mental state. The worries and anxieties of reality are as effectively deferred by becoming absorbed in a television program as by going on a "trip" induced by drugs or alcohol. And just as alcoholics are only inchoately aware of their addiction, feeling that they control their drinking more than they really do ("I can cut it out any time I want—I just like to have three or four drinks before dinner"), people similarly overestimate their control over television watching. Even as they put off other activities to spend hour after hour watching television, they feel they could easily resume living in a different, less passive style. But somehow or other while the television set is present in their homes, the click doesn't sound. With television pleasures available, those other experiences seem less attractive, more difficult somehow.

A heavy viewer (a college English instructor) observes: 8

"I find television almost irresistible. When the set is on, I can-   9 not ignore it. I can't turn it off. I feel sapped, will-less, enervated. As I reach out to turn off the set, the strength goes out of my arms. So I sit there for hours and hours."

The self-confessed television addict often feels he "ought" to   10 do other things—but the fact that he doesn't read and doesn't plant his garden or sew or crochet or play games or have conversations means that those activities are no longer as desirable as television viewing. In a way a heavy viewer's life is as imbalanced by his television "habit" as a drug addict's or an alcoholic's. He is living in a holding pattern, as it were, passing up the activities that lead to growth or development or a sense of accomplishment. This is one reason people talk about their television viewing so ruefully, so apologetically. They are aware that it is an unproductive experience, that almost any other endeavor is more worthwhile by any human measure.

Finally it is the adverse effect of television viewing on the lives   11 of so many people that defines it as a serious addiction. The television habit distorts the sense of time. It renders other experiences vague and curiously unreal while taking on a greater reality for itself. It weakens relationships by reducing and sometimes eliminating normal opportunities for talking, for communicating.

And yet television does not satisfy, else why would the viewer   12 continue to watch hour after hour, day after day? "The measure of health," writes Lawrence Kubie, "is flexibility . . . and especially the freedom to cease when sated."[1] But the television viewer can never be sated with his television experiences—they do not provide the true nourishment that satiation requires—and thus he finds that he cannot stop watching.

[1]Lawrence Kubie, *Neurotic Distortion and the Creative Process* (Lawrence: University of Kansas Press, 1958).

Meanings and Values

1. Would you classify this as formal or informal writing? Why? (See Guide to Terms: *Essay.*)

2. Is it primarily objective or subjective? Why? (Guide: *Objective/Subjective.*)

3. Using our three-question method, evaluate this selection, giving particular attention to the third question. (Guide: *Evaluation.*)

4a. What do you think would be Winn's reply to the assertion that television is such an important element in contemporary culture that time spent watching it is seldom wasted?

  b. Do you think you would agree with her answer? Explain.

Expository Techniques

1a. What is the first technique of definition used in this selection? Where is it used?

  b. Why is it important to get this aspect of the subject over first?

2a. Which paragraphs are devoted to an enumeration of the characteristics of addiction?

  b. What are the characteristics of addiction, according to the author?

3a. What major pattern of exposition does the latter half of the selection utilize?

  b. How important is definition of the term prior to this development? Why?

  c. Would it have been better if the author had presented a more orderly, point-by-point discussion of this latter material? Why, or why not?

Diction and Vocabulary

1a. Is there anything distinctive about Winn's diction, as demonstrated in this piece? (Guide: *Diction.*) (You may wish to compare it with that of Wolfe in Section 4.)

  b. Does your answer to question 1a indicate that Winn's style is inferior in some way? Explain.

2. Use the dictionary as necessary to understand the meanings of the following words: wryly (par. 1); organism (3); sated (4); inchoately (7); enervated (9).

Suggestions for Writing and Discussion

1.   Even assuming that a person has a terrible TV habit, what does it really matter (to the person or to others) whether the habit qualifies as an addiction?

2.   What other pastimes can you think of that fit, or nearly fit, Winn's criteria for addiction? Do they have any redeeming qualities that TV viewing does not offer?

3.   Why do people often worry about the amount of time spent watching TV but seldom about the amount of time spent reading books or magazines? Explain.

(NOTE: Suggestions for topics requiring development by use of DEFINITION are on page 242, at the end of this section.)

D. H. LAWRENCE

DAVID HERBERT LAWRENCE (1885–1930), British novelist, poet, essayist, and playwright, was for many years a controversial literary figure because of his frank and, for his time, obsessive treatment of sex in some of his novels. The son of a coal miner,
Lawrence began his career as a schoolmaster, and with the success of his first novel, *The White Peacock* (1911), he decided to live
by writing. His books include *Sons and Lovers* (1913), *The Rainbow*
(1915), *Women in Love* (1921), and *Lady Chatterly's Lover* (1928).
Lawrence has been admired by many for his insightful and artistic power in prose. E. M. Forster referred to him as ''the greatest
imaginative novelist of our generation.''

Pornography

''Pornography'' (editors' title) is excerpted from *Pornography and
Obscenity*, first published in 1930. Providing us with one man's
definition of a still highly controversial term, this selection also
illustrates the naturalness and vivid spontaneity of style characteristic of Lawrence's writing.

What is pornography to one man is the laughter of genius to
another.

The word itself, we are told, means ''pertaining to harlots''—
the graph of the harlot. But nowadays, what is a harlot? If she was
a woman who took money from a man in return for going to bed
with him—really, most wives sold themselves, in the past, and
plenty of harlots gave themselves, when they felt like it, for nothing. If a woman hasn't got a tiny streak of harlot in her, she's a
dry stick as a rule. And probably most harlots had somewhere a
streak of womanly generosity. Why be so cut and dried? The law

is a dreary thing, and its judgments have nothing to do with life. . . .

One essay on pornography, I remember, comes to the conclu- 3 sion that pornography in art is that which is calculated to arouse sexual desire, or sexual excitement. And stress is laid on the fact, whether the author or artist *intended* to arouse sexual feelings. It is the old vexed question of intention, become so dull today, when we know how strong and influential our unconscious intentions are. And why a man should be held guilty of his conscious inten- tions, and innocent of his unconscious intentions, I don't know, since every man is more made up of unconscious intentions than of conscious ones. I am what I am, not merely what I think I am.

However! We take it, I assume, that *pornography* is something 4 base, something unpleasant. In short, we don't like it. And why don't we like it? Because it arouses sexual feelings?

I think not. No matter how hard we may pretend otherwise, 5 most of us rather like a moderate rousing of our sex. It warms us, stimulates us like sunshine on a grey day. After a century or two of Puritanism, this is still true of most people. Only the mob-habit of condemning any form of sex is too strong to let us admit it natu- rally. And there are, of course, many people who are genuinely repelled by the simplest and most natural stirrings of sexual feel- ing. But these people are perverts who have fallen into hatred of their fellowmen; thwarted, disappointed, unfulfilled people, of whom, alas, our civilisation contains so many. And they nearly always enjoy some unsimple and unnatural form of sex excite- ment, secretly.

Even quite advanced art critics would try to make us believe 6 that any picture or book which had "sex appeal" was *ipso facto* a bad book or picture. This is just canting hypocrisy. Half the great poems, pictures, music, stories, of the whole world are great by virtue of the beauty of their sex appeal. Titian or Renoir, the Song of Solomon or *Jane Eyre*, Mozart or "Annie Laurie," the loveliness is all interwoven with sex appeal, sex stimulus, call it what you will. Even Michelangelo, who rather hated sex, can't help filling the Cornucopia with phallic acorns. Sex is a very powerful, benefi- cial and necessary stimulus in human life, and we are all grateful when we feel its warm, natural flow through us, like a form of sunshine. . . .

Then what is pornography, after all this? It isn't sex appeal or 7 sex stimulus in art. It isn't even a deliberate intention on the part of the artist to arouse or excite sexual feelings. There's nothing wrong with sexual feelings in themselves, so long as they are straightforward and not sneaking or sly. The right sort of sex stimulus is invaluable to human daily life. Without it the world grows grey. I would give everybody the gay Renaissance stories to read; they would help to shake off a lot of grey self-importance, which is our modern civilised disease.

But even I would censor genuine pornography, rigorously. It would not be very difficult. In the first place, genuine pornography is almost always underworld, it doesn't come into the open. In the second, you can recognise it by the insult it offers, invariably, to sex and to the human spirit. [8]

Pornography is the attempt to insult sex, to do dirt on it. This is unpardonable. Take the very lowest instance, the picture postcard sold underhand, by the underworld, in most cities. What I have seen of them have been of an ugliness to make you cry. The insult to the human body, the insult to a vital human relationship! Ugly and cheap they make the human nudity, ugly and degraded they make the sexual act, trivial and cheap and nasty. [9]

It is the same with the books they sell in the underworld. They are either so ugly they make you ill, or so fatuous you can't imagine anybody but a cretin or a moron reading them, or writing them. [10]

It is the same with the dirty limericks that people tell after dinner, or the dirty stories one hears commercial travellers telling each other in a smoke-room. Occasionally there is a really funny one, that redeems a great deal. But usually they are just ugly and repellent, and the so-called "humour" is just a trick of doing dirt on sex. [11]

Now the human nudity of a great many modern people is just ugly and degraded, and the sexual act between modern people is just the same, merely ugly and degrading. But this is nothing to be proud of. It is the catastrophe of our civilisation. I am sure no other civilisation, not even the Roman, has showed such a vast proportion of ignominious and degraded nudity, and ugly, squalid dirty sex. Because no other civilisation has driven sex into the underworld, and nudity to the W.C. [12]

The intelligent young, thank heaven, seem determined to alter in these two respects. They are rescuing their young nudity from [13] the stuffy, pornographical hole-and-corner underworld of their elders, and they refuse to sneak about the sexual relation. This is a change the elderly grey ones of course deplore, but it is in fact a very great change for the better, and a real revolution.

But it is amazing how strong is the will in ordinary, vulgar people, to do dirt on sex. It was one of my fond illusions, when I was young, that the ordinary healthy-seeming sort of men in railway carriages, or the smoke-room of an hotel or a pullman, were healthy in their feelings and had a wholesome rough devil-may-care attitude towards sex. All wrong! All wrong! Experience teaches that common individuals of this sort have a disgusting attitude towards sex, a disgusting contempt of it, a disgusting desire to insult it. If such fellows have intercourse with a woman, they triumphantly feel that they have done her dirt, and now she is lower, cheaper, more contemptible than she was before. 14

It is individuals of this sort that tell dirty stories, carry indecent picture postcards, and know the indecent books. This is the great pornographical class—the really common men-in-the-street and women-in-the-street. They have as great a hate and contempt of sex as the greyest Puritan, and when an appeal is made to them, they are always on the side of the angels. They insist that a film-heroine shall be a neuter, a sexless thing of washed-out purity. They insist that real sex-feeling shall only be shown by the villain or villainess, low lust. They find a Titian or a Renoir really indecent, and they don't want their wives and daughters to see it. 15

Why? Because they have the grey disease of sex-hatred, coupled with the yellow disease of dirt-lust. The sex functions and the excrementory functions in the human body work so close together, yet they are, so to speak, utterly different in direction. Sex is a creative flow, the excrementory flow is towards dissolution, decreation, if we may use such a word. In the really healthy human being the distinction between the two is instant, our profoundest instincts are perhaps our instincts of opposition between the two flows. 16

But in the degraded human being the deep instincts have gone dead, and then the two flows become identical. *This* is the secret of really vulgar and of pornographical people: the sex flow and the excrement flow is the same to them. It happens when the psyche deteriorates, and the profound controlling instincts collapse. Then sex is dirt and dirt is sex, and sexual excitement becomes a playing 17 with dirt, and any sign of sex in a woman becomes a show of her dirt. This is the condition of the common, vulgar human being whose name is legion, and who lifts his voice and it is the *Vox populi, vox Dei.* And this is the source of all pornography.

Meanings and Values

1.   Does this selection better illustrate subjective or objective writing? (See Guide to Terms: *Objective/Subjective.*) Justify your answer, citing specific examples.

2.   Would you classify it as formal or informal writing? (Guide: *Essay.*) Why?

3a.   Do you think that a person should, in general, be held responsible for "unconscious intentions" (par. 3)?

 b.   Does the law do so?

4a.   Does it seem to you that the author may be overgeneralizing in the last sentence of paragraph 5?

 b.   If such forms of sex excitement are enjoyed "secretly," how could he know enough about the matter to make such a broad assertion?

5.   What, if anything, is paradoxical in the fact that the type of men described early in paragraph 14 have the "grey disease" (par. 16)? (Guide: *Paradox.*)

Expository Techniques

1a.   In developing his definition of pornography, Lawrence uses negation, or exclusion. What is negated?

 b.   Which paragraphs are devoted to negation?

 c.   Why do you suppose he considers them important enough for so much attention? Do you agree?

2a.   Which of the other methods of extended definition does he use?

 b.   In which paragraphs may they be found?

3.   In your estimation, are rhetorical questions overused in this selection? (Guide: *Rhetorical Questions.*) Be prepared to justify your answer.

4a.   Cite examples of as many as possible of the standard methods of achieving emphasis. (Guide: *Emphasis.*)

 b.   What, to you, is the overall effect?

5.   Several of the most noticeable features of Lawrence's style are also

matters of syntax. (Guide: *Style/Tone* and *Syntax.*) Illustrate as many of these as possible by examples from the writing.

Diction and Vocabulary

1a.   In the second paragraph is a metaphor that is also a cliché. (Guide: *Clichés.*) What is it?

  b.   How, if at all, can its use be justified?

2.   Cite at least two other examples of metaphor and one of simile. (Guide: *Figures of Speech.*)

3.   What is the meaning of W.C. (par. 12)?

4a.   What is the meaning of *ipso facto* (par. 6)?

  b.   Why is it italicized?

5.   What is the meaning of *"Vox populi, vox Dei"* (par. 17)?

6a.   In at least five paragraphs Lawrence uses a euphemism. (Guide: *Connotation/Denotation.*) What is it?

  b.   In which paragraphs do you find it used?

  c.   If sex-hatred is the "grey disease," why do you suppose Lawrence chose "yellow" to describe the disease of "dirt-lust"?

7.   How do you account for the unusual spelling of several words in this essay, e.g., *grey* and *civilisation?*

8.   Consult your dictionary as necessary for the meaning of the following words: canting, phallic (par. 6); fatuous, cretin (10); ignominious (12).

Suggestions for Writing and Discussion

1.   Select one or more of the artists or works of art listed in paragraph 6, analyze, and explain fully why you agree or disagree that "the loveliness is all interwoven with sex appeal [or] sex stimulus."

2.   The "intelligent young" of 1930 (par. 13) are now the gray "establishment" of parents and grandparents against whom the intelligent young of the 1960s and 1970s staged their so-called sexual revolution. Trace the process by which such an ironic reversal came about. Do you believe this is an inevitable result of generation-aging—e.g., will *your* children and grandchildren also be engaging in sexual revolution? Is there a sexual revolution of sorts going on now? Why?

3.   Both of the author's "negated" definitions have been used repeatedly by others in the attempt to get a fair and workable *legal* distinction between pornography and nonpornography. Usually these at-

tempts failed, and no one felt that the problem had been really solved. How well would Lawrence's definition work as a legal definition—perhaps with some modification you can suggest?

4.   What, if anything, do you think should be done about "hard-core" pornography?

(NOTE: Suggestions for topics requiring development by use of DEFINITION are on page 242, at the end of this section.)

PERRI KLASS

PERRI KLASS is both a physician, currently a resident in pediatrics, and a writer. She is the author of numerous articles and stories in such publications as the *New York Times, Self, Esquire, Vogue, Mademoiselle, Christopher Street,* and the *Boston Globe Magazine.* In addition, she has written a regular column, "Vital Signs," for *Discover* magazine. Her three books are *Recombinations* (1985), *I Am Having an Adventure* (1986), and *A Not Entirely Benign Procedure: Four Years as a Medical Student* (1987).

Anatomy and Destiny

Feminism is a term that continues to have "various meanings or shades of meaning" for both women and men. In this essay, first published in *Ms.,* Perri Klass considers some of its meanings—historical, practical, and idealistic—in settings that were once the almost exclusive preserves of men: medical school and the practice of medicine.

When I was a medical student, writing about being a medical student, I had two different editors ask me whether professors had taught anatomy with *Playboy* pinups instead of diagrams, or lecturers had made offensive jokes about women. There seemed to be a sort of common knowledge about the medical school experience that my articles didn't incorporate. In fact, I went through medical school without encountering that sort of nonsense, and if a lecturer did occasionally try a would-be witty, would-be provocative remark about women, he got roundly hissed for his trouble—it's very satisfying to hiss a lecturer, and few of them keep their composure well during the process.

There were, however, other, more subtle, ways in which medical school made me aware that I and my kind were newcomers.

There was, above all, the unending parade of male lecturers. There was the pervasive (and almost unconscious) practice of using the generic *he* for the doctor in any clinical anecdote, and the generic *she* for the patient (provided it wasn't prostate trouble, of course). I can still remember a day when one of our rare female lecturers said to us something on the order of, "So one day someone will come in with these symptoms, and you'll get an orthopedist to look at the patient with you, and she'll tell you such and such," and the women in the audience burst into applause.

So we hissed sexist jokes and we applauded the use of the female pronoun. Did that mean that the women with whom I went to medical school considered themselves feminists? I can't say, but I do know this: many of us felt poised, as women entering a traditionally (and sometimes militantly) male profession, between gratitude to the women who had fought their way through before us on the one hand, and a desire to identify with our new brotherhood on the other.

Most people who go to medical school want very badly to be doctors. It takes a great deal of effort to get to medical school, let alone to get through. Wanting to be a doctor means identifying with the people up ahead of you, the group you are trying to join, and up until very recently, that group has been a brotherhood, in every sense of the word. For some women, the word *feminist* may have been unwelcome, a reminder that they might never be fully accepted into that brotherhood, an awkward and public attempt to make an ideology out of a fact of life. And yet, I think my class was still close enough to the pioneers who had gone before for us to understand that we owed our opportunity, our comparatively easy path, entirely to those resolute embattled pioneers. The graffiti in the women's bathroom in the dormitory at my medical school read, "Every time you sit down here, thank the women who have come before you."

I have taken for granted that I was a feminist ever since I was in junior high school, but I have never seen myself as a banner-carrier. Certainly in college and in graduate school there were women who would have considered me a fellow traveler at best: because I did not live a truly politically correct life, because I was not more active in women's causes. I never minded this and it never kept me from considering myself a feminist; others could carry the banners but I would march; I would acknowledge the debt I owed to other women and to the Women's Movement. I was a feminist, but I was not The Feminist.

When I got to medical school, I discovered that I was a radical feminist. By medical school standards I was in fact The Feminist, or one of them. It didn't take much; there was almost no one person, and certainly no group, to carry the banner or smile patronizingly at my lack of seriousness. I found myself running the medical school women's association, along with a friend. Our activities were far short of revolutionary; we used to invite speakers to come and talk once a week. We covered topics of obvious relevance to women—battered women, midwifery—and also medical topics that we thought might be relevant—alcoholism, child abuse—and we also invited a number of women physicians to come talk about their training and their lives. The talks were generally very well attended, by both female and male students, and they were fun, but not particularly radical. Still, one day when I and a couple of other women from our class were talking to the women who had directed the organization before us about possible speakers and other activities (develop a women's medical directory of the area? get involved with a study that was being done of the medical school's failure to give tenure to women?), one of my classmates said abruptly that she didn't want to help run the organization since it was clear that the group was going to be headed by some radical people. It wasn't that I minded the label. I was vaguely thrilled to find myself finally something other than a weak-minded fellow traveler. But it was disconcerting not to know when I was doing something "extreme."

I was once called to the office of the director of medical school admissions along with the heads of some other student groups to discuss his concern because the women's organization was writing to female applicants, offering encouragement and information, even offering to put them up when they came for interviews. He pointed out that the Hispanic and black student groups were making similar offers to their constituents, and he wanted to put a stop to all these separate letters. Among other things, he said, it just wasn't fair—no one was writing to the white men. There was a pause, and then I said, in unison with one of the other students present, "And yet, somehow they keep coming!" The lesson, in the end, was that medicine is fundamentally a conservative world, that medical students as a group are a far more conservative context for any kind of political thinking than college students or graduate students.

Most female medical students, as I remember, were highly aware of the sex ratios on the hospital teams on which they worked. And I remember a sense of betrayal when a female resident or attending physician proved ineffective, unpleasant, uninspiring. I also remember how different it felt the first time I was ever in an operating room with an all-female group: the orthopedic resident, the surgical intern, the medical student (me), the scrub nurse, *and* the patient. And in fact it was nothing like the usual operating room drama; there was less yelling, more courtesy, more collegiality and less strict hierarchy. That distinction has held up in a fair number of operating rooms since then.

You can't help feeling these differences, whatever the association you choose to claim with feminism. However wary you may be of the word, medical school is an educational experience, and one of the courses everyone gets, like it or not, is an introduction to sexual politics. Many of the men, of course, don't quite realize it's going on.

Now I am doing a residency in pediatrics, a field that has traditionally had a relatively high percentage of women. In my own program there are many female residents. When the list of interns came out for next year, several of us reviewed with fascination the list of the people who would take over our position at the very bottom of the totem pole. Only later did we realize that none of us had thought to count how many of the new interns were male and how many female—the most striking evidence, we all agreed, that we are in a situation where that really isn't an issue. When half or more of the residents are female, a female resident doesn't feel she is by definition on probation. Polarizations of male and female doctor styles are acknowledged; residents are regularly twitted for being macho.

Many of the young female doctors I work with today would call themselves feminists. Their feminism involves a sense of entitlement, and that is also valuable. In a way the victory is the sense of entitlement, the feeling that you belong. You need both—you need a balance of a rock-hard confidence that you belong in medicine, and also an awareness that you only got there because the women ahead of you battered down the doors. With that confidence and that awareness, the hope is you can enjoy your position, preserve it for those who will come next, and also preserve the challenge to the traditional style that is one of the greatest contributions women bring to medicine.

Meanings and Values

1. Why might some women in medical school prefer not to be called ''feminists''?

2. How does the ''all-female'' operating room the author describes in paragraph 8 differ from other operating rooms according to her?

3. What kind of feminist does the author define herself as in paragraph 5?

4a. According to whose standards was Klass ''a radical feminist'' (par. 6)?

  b. In your opinion, do the activities she describes in paragraphs 6 and 7 justify the label? Be ready to defend your answer.

5. If the purpose of this essay is not to define ''feminist'' in a general sense, what is its purpose (or purposes)? (See Guide to Terms: *Purpose*.)

Expository Techniques

1. Where in this selection does Klass make clear her intention to consider the meanings of feminism in a particular professional context?

2a. What examples does Klass offer of her feminist activities in medical school?

  b. In what ways does she qualify her presentation to indicate that she does not consider her activities to have been especially radical? (Guide: *Qualification*.)

3a. Having explained the need for feminism in medical school and given examples of the changes that come with the presence of women, why would Klass spend the last three paragraphs describing some of the successful effects of the feminist movement on the profession?

  b. Do these paragraphs threaten the unity of the essay in any way? (Guide: *Unity*.)

  c. How, if at all, do they extend the definition of *feminism* Klass develops in the course of the piece?

  d. In what way do they constitute an effective conclusion? (Guide: *Closings*.)

4. What use does the author make of definition by negation and by enumeration of characteristics in paragraphs 5–8?

Diction and Vocabulary

1a.   Discuss the use of diction in paragraph 1 to convey the writer's view of a lecturer who makes sexist remarks. (Guide: *Diction.*)

b.   How does the author use irony in paragraph 7 to answer the director's concern about the lack of fairness to white males? (Guide: *Irony.*)

2a.   Contrast the positive denotations and connotations of the diction in paragraph 11 with the uncertain or negative meanings conveyed by the diction in paragraph 4. (Guide: *Connotation and Denotation.*)

b.   What thematic concerns do the differences in diction highlight?

3.   If you do not know the meaning of any of the following words, look them up in the dictionary: pervasive, generic, prostate, orthopedist (par. 2); militantly (3); ideology, embattled (4); patronizingly, midwifery (6); collegiality (8); entitlement (11).

Suggestions for Writing and Discussion

1.   Look over the articles in a recent edition of the magazine *Ms.* Would Klass's essay be considered radical or moderate if it appeared in the context of the articles you examined? If it appeared in a recent edition of *Glamour? National Review?*

2.   How, if at all, does your understanding of feminism differ from Klass's?

3.   To what extent has our society gone beyond a need for feminism? Or was there ever a need for the feminist movement?

(NOTE: Suggestions for topics requiring development by use of DEFINITION are on page 242, at the end of this section.)

MICHAEL KORDA

MICHAEL KORDA was born in London in 1933, and he served with
the Royal Air Force from 1952 to 1954. After holding various editorial positions with Simon and Schuster, book publishers,
Korda is now editor-in-chief. He is also an author in his own
right. His books are *Male Chauvinism: How It Works* (1973), *Power:
How to Get It, How to Use It* (1975), *Charmed Lives* (1979), and the
novels *Worldly Goods* (1982) and *Queenie* (1985).

What It Takes to Be a Leader

"What It Takes to Be a Leader," first published in *Newsweek*, is
hardly a detailed set of instructions, but it is a forthright statement of qualities (and circumstances) that seem to the author to
be most associated with leadership. Point by point he builds his
definition and, in so doing, illustrates some interesting uses of
this pattern of exposition.

At a moment when we are waiting to see whether we have elected
a President or a leader,[1] it is worth examining the differences between the two. For not every President is a leader, but every time
we elect a President we hope for one, especially in times of doubt
and crisis. In easy times we are ambivalent—the leader, after all,
makes demands, challenges the status quo, shakes things up.

Leadership is as much a question of timing as anything else.
The leader must appear on the scene at a moment when people
are looking for leadership, as Churchill did in 1940, as Roosevelt
did in 1933, as Lenin did in 1917. And when he comes, he must
offer a simple, eloquent message.

Great leaders are almost always great simplifiers, who cut
through argument, debate and doubt to offer a solution everybody

1

2

3

"What It Takes to Be a Leader" by Michael Korda from *Newsweek*, January 5, 1981.
Reprinted by permission of Michael Korda.

[1]"What It Takes to Be a Leader" was published on January 5, 1981, before Reagan had taken office. What Korda has to say is still relevant, however.

can understand and remember. Churchill warned the British to expect "blood, toil, tears and sweat"; FDR told Americans that "the only thing we have to fear is fear itself"; Lenin promised the war-weary Russians peace, land and bread. Straightforward but potent messages.

We have an image of what a leader ought to be. We even recognize the physical signs: leaders may not necessarily be tall, but they must have bigger-than-life, commanding features—LBJ's nose and ear lobes, Ike's broad grin. A trademark also comes in handy: Lincoln's stovepipe hat, JFK's rocker. We expect our leaders to stand out a little, not to be like ordinary men. Half of President Ford's trouble lay in the fact that, if you closed your eyes for a moment, you couldn't remember his face, figure or clothes. A leader should have an unforgettable identity, instantly and permanently fixed in people's minds.

It also helps for a leader to be able to do something most of us can't: FDR overcame polio; Mao swam the Yangtze River at the age of 72. We don't want our leaders to be "just like us." We want them to be like us but better, special, more so. Yet if they are *too* different, we reject them. Adlai Stevenson was too cerebral. Nelson Rockefeller, too rich.

Even television, which comes in for a lot of knocks as an image builder that magnifies form over substance, doesn't altogether obscure the qualities of leadership we recognize, or their absence. Television exposed Nixon's insecurity, Humphrey's fatal infatuation with his own voice.

A leader must know how to use power (that's what leadership is about), but he also has to have a way of showing that he does. He has to be able to project firmness—no physical clumsiness (like Ford), no rapid eye movements (like Carter).

A Chinese philosopher once remarked that a leader must have the grace of a good dancer, and there is a great deal of wisdom to this. A leader should know how to appear relaxed and confident. His walk should be firm and purposeful. He should be able, like Lincoln, FDR, Truman, Ike and JFK, to give a good, hearty, belly laugh, instead of the sickly grin that passes for good humor in Nixon or Carter. Ronald Reagan's training as an actor showed to good effect in the debate with Carter, when by his easy manner and apparent affability, he managed to convey the impression that in fact he was the President and Carter the challenger.

If we know what we're looking for, why is it so difficult to 9 find? The answer lies in a very simple truth about leadership. People can only be led where they want to go. The leader follows, though a step ahead. Americans *wanted* to climb out of the Depression and needed someone to tell them they could do it, and FDR did. The British believed that they could still win the war after the defeats of 1940, and Churchill told them they were right.

A leader rides the waves, moves with the tides, understands 10 the deepest yearnings of his people. He cannot make a nation that wants peace at any price go to war, or stop a nation determined to fight from doing so. His purpose must match the national mood. His task is to focus the people's energies and desires, to define them in simple terms, to inspire, to make what people already want seem attainable, important, within their grasp.

Above all, he must dignify our desires, convince us that we 11 are taking part in the making of great history, give us a sense of glory about ourselves. Winston Churchill managed, by sheer rhetoric, to turn the British defeat and the evacuation of Dunkirk in 1940 into a major victory. FDR's words turned the sinking of the American fleet at Pearl Harbor into a national rallying cry instead of a humiliating national scandal. A leader must stir our blood, not appeal to our reason.

For this reason, businessmen generally make poor leaders. 12 They tend to be pragmatists who think that once you've explained why something makes sense, people will do it. But history shows the fallacy of this belief. When times get tough, people don't want to be told what went wrong, or lectured, or given a lot of complicated statistics and plans (like Carter's energy policy) they don't understand. They want to be moved, excited, inspired, consoled, uplifted—in short, led!

A great leader must have a certain irrational quality, a stub- 13 born refusal to face facts, infectious optimism, the ability to convince us that all is not lost even when we're afraid it is. Confucious suggested that while the advisers of a great leader should be as cold as ice, the leader himself should have fire, a spark of divine madness.

He won't come until we're ready for him, for the leader is like 14 a mirror, reflecting back to us our own sense of purpose, putting into words our own dreams and hopes, transforming our needs and fears into coherent policies and programs.

Our strength makes him strong; our determination makes him 1! determined; our courage makes him determined; our courage makes him a hero; he is, in the final analysis, the symbol of the best in us, shaped by our own spirit and will. And when these qualities are lacking in us, we can't produce him; and even with all our skill at image building, we can't fake him. He is, after all, merely the sum of us.

Meanings and Values

1. Precisely what is meant by the allegation that, for some people, the television appearance of a leader or would-be leader "magnifies form over substance" (par. 6)?

2a. Is this selection mostly specific or general? Why? (See Guide to Terms: *Specific/General*.)

 b. Where, if at all, does it change in this respect?

3. Can the various references to presidents be classified as rhetorical allusions? Why, or why not? (Guide: *Figures of Speech*.)

4. Is this a formal, informal, or familiar essay? Why? (Guide: *Essay*.)

5a. How can a leader *follow* "a step *ahead*" (par. 9)?

 b. Is this statement a paradox? Why, or why not? (Guide: *Paradox*.)

6. The author seems to classify Johnson as a leader (par. 4). How, then, can you account for Johnson's loss of support for United States involvement in Vietnam?

7. Has the country found out yet whether we "elected a President or a leader" (par. 1)? Which did we elect?

8. Do Korda's criteria apply only to "good" leaders? Or can they also apply to evil leaders, coming forth when people are ready for them? If the latter, use at least one example (not necessarily in the United States) to illustrate.

Expository Techniques

1a. Which two methods of definition has Korda used extensively?

 b. Why, if at all, do they work well together?

 c. Cite at least one paragraph in which both are used.

2a. What third method of definition is used in paragraph 12? Explain.

 b. Cite other minor uses of this method.

3. Is the last sentence of paragraph 11 an example of parallel structure? Why, or why not? (Guide: *Parallel Structure*.)

4. Does paragraph 14 contain a logical comparison, an analogy, or a

simile? Why do you so classify it? (Guide: *Analogy* and *Figures of Speech.*)

5a. How successful do you consider Korda's closing? Why? (Guide: *Closings.*)

b. Which, if any, of the standard methods of closing does he use?

Diction and Vocabulary

1a. What kind of figures of speech are found in paragraph 10? (Guide: *Figures of Speech.*)

b. What kind are found in paragraph 13?

2. In paragraph 15, does Korda use the word "symbol" in exactly the same sense as described in this book? (Guide: *Symbol.*) If not, what is the difference?

3. Use the dictionary as necessary to become familiar with the following words: ambivalent, status quo (par. 1); cerebral (5); pragmatists, fallacy (12).

Suggestions for Writing and Discussion

1. Select one of the numerous characteristics of a leader (as Korda sees them) to discuss further. Organize your ideas to present a coherent oral or written composition.

2. If you prefer, disagree with the author on one or more of the characteristics, but try to keep your discussion nonpolitical.

3. Clarify (as though for someone slow to grasp such subtleties) and build upon the paradox in paragraph 9.

4. Is there any reason to assume that a woman would be less likely than a man to possess all these qualities of good leadership? Discuss fully—and fairly.

5. What do you consider the possibility of a young man's deliberately *developing* all of the characteristics and then becoming president?

(NOTE: Suggestions for topics requiring development by use of DEFINITION follow.)

Writing Suggestions for Section 7
Definition

Develop a composition for a specified purpose and audience, using whatever methods and expository patterns will help convey a clear understanding of your meaning of one of the following terms:

1. Country music.
2. Conscience.
3. Religion.
4. Bigotry.
5. Success.
6. Empathy.
7. Family.
8. Hypocrisy.
9. Humor.
10. Sophistication.
11. Naiveté.
12. Cowardice.
13. Wisdom.
14. Integrity.
15. Morality.
16. Greed.
17. Social poise.
18. Intellectual (the person).
19. Pornography (if your opinions differ appreciably from D. H. Lawrence's).
20. Courage.
21. Patriotism.
22. Equality (or equal opportunity).
23. Loyalty.
24. Stylishness (in clothing or behavior).
25. Fame.

8

Explaining with the Help of *Description*

Exposition, as well as argument, can be made more vivid, and hence more understandable, with the support of description. Most exposition does contain some elements of description, and at times description carries almost the entire burden of the explanation, becoming a basic pattern for the expository purpose.

Description is most useful in painting a word-picture of something concrete, such as a scene or a person. Its use is not restricted, however, to what we can perceive with our senses; we can also describe (or attempt to describe) an abstract concept, such as an emotion or a quality or a mood. But most attempts to describe fear, for instance, still resort to the physical—a "coldness around the heart," perhaps—and in such concrete ways communicate the abstract to the reader.

In its extreme forms, description is either *objective* or *impressionistic* (subjective), but most of its uses are somewhere between these extremes. Objective description is purely factual, uncolored by any feelings of the author; it is the type used for scientific papers and most business reports. But impressionistic description, as the term implies, at least tinges the purely factual with the author's personal impressions; instead of describing how something *is*, objectively, the author describes how it *seems*, subjectively. Such a description might refer to the "blazing heat" of an August day. Somewhat less impressionistic would be "extreme heat." But the scientist would describe it precisely as "115 degrees Fahrenheit," and this would be purely objective reporting, unaffected by the impressions of the author. (No examples of the latter are included in this section, but many textbooks for other courses utilize the technique of pure objective description, as do encyclopedias. The Petrunkevitch essay in Section 5 provides some good examples of objective description, although not entirely unmixed with colorful impressionistic details.)

The first and most important job in any descriptive endeavor is to select the details to be included. There are usually many from which to choose, and writers must constantly keep in mind the kind of picture they want to paint with words—for *their* purpose and *their* audience. Such a word-picture need not be entirely visual; in this respect writers have more freedom than artists, for writers can use strokes that will add the dimensions of sound, smell, and even touch. Such strokes, if made to seem natural enough, can help create a vivid and effective image in the reader's mind.

Most successful impressionistic description focuses on a single *dominant impression.* Of the many descriptive details ordinarily available for use, the author selects those that will help create a mood or atmosphere or emphasize a feature or quality. But more than the materials themselves are involved, for even diction can often assist in creating the desired dominant impression. Sometimes syntax is also an important factor, as in the use of short, hurried sentences to help convey a sense of urgency or excitement.

Actual structuring of passages is perhaps less troublesome in description than in most of the other patterns. But some kind of orderliness is needed for the sake of both readability and a realistic effect. (Neither objective nor impressionistic description can afford not to be realistic, in one manner or another.) In visual description, orderliness is usually achieved by presenting details as the eye would find them—that is, as arranged in space. We could describe a person from head to toe, or vice versa, or begin with the most noticeable feature and work from there. A scenic description might move from near to far or from far to near, from left to right or from right to left. It might also start with a broad, overall view, gradually narrowing to a focal point, probably the most significant feature of the scene. These are fairly standard kinds of description; but as the types and occasions for using description vary widely, so do the possibilities for interesting treatment. In many cases, writers are limited only by their own ingenuity.

But ingenuity should not be allowed to produce *excessive* description, an amazingly certain path to reader boredom. A few well-chosen details are better than profusion. Economy of words is desirable in any writing, and description is no exception. Appropriate use of figurative language and careful choice of strong nouns and verbs will help prevent the need for strings of modifiers, which are wasteful and can seem amateurish.

Even for the experienced writer, however, achieving good description remains a constant challenge; the beginner should not expect to attain this goal without working at it.

Sample Paragraph (Annotated)

Leads off with impressionistic details. "Barren," "junk-cluttered," and "tired" all are how the area is perceived by the author.

Background information.

Transitional, between background and coming description.

"Leans toward the gulch" is an objective detail (how it is); "to keep watch . . ." is purely impressionistic (how it seems).

These are mostly objective details, but selected no doubt to contribute to a dominant impression of poverty, dejection.

Along South Road, after miles of barren hills and crossing Suicide Creek, the road rounds a bend and levels along a junk-cluttered ravine; and there is Rejoice, lined up in one tired row of buildings facing Colman's Gulch. According to legend, both gulch and town owe their names to Ezra Colman, who had come to settle. Ezra and his wife, Ivy, were just plodding along when Ez found a rock he thought was gold. Mrs. Colman asked how to help, and he shouted to get the hell out of the way, to go rejoice unto the Lord or something. By the time his gold fever eased (with no gold but quite a pile of rocks), Ivy had planted potatoes, so that's where they built a cabin. It still stands there back of Nettie's Gas, still the straightest building in town; but that's not saying much: most of Rejoice leans toward the gulch, as though to keep watch on Ezra's rocks. There's one block of mostly empty stores and a church, another four blocks of houses. Large or small, they are all unpainted and have broken windows stuffed with faded jeans. Each has a cat dozing against the door, and children spiritlessly playing drag-race in a rusty heap in the yard. But Re-

"Fragrant," which is *impressionistic.*

Primarily *objective,* but meant as contrast to the *dominant impression,* perhaps making the dismal scene more poignant by contrast to roses.

joice is fragrant: rose vines, gone wild, blooming pink everywhere, climbing over every sagging barn and stump and even the Galilee Church and the old Colman cabin.

Sample Paragraph (Description)

It's no winter without an ice storm. When Robert Frost gazed at bowed-over birch trees and tried to think that boys had bent them playing, he knew better: "Ice-storms do that." They do that and a lot more, trimming disease and weakness out of the tree—the old tree's friend, as pneumonia used to be the old man's. Some of us provide life-support systems for our precious shrubs, boarding them over against the ice, for the ice storm takes the young or unlucky branch or birch as well as the rotten or feeble. One February morning we look out our windows over yards and fields littered with kindling, small twigs and great branches. We look out at a world turned into one diamond, ten thousand carats in the line of sight, twice as many facets. What a dazzle of spinning refracted light, spider webs of cold brilliance attacking our eyeballs! All winter we wear sunglasses to drive, more than we do in summer, and never so much as after an ice storm, with its painful glaze reflecting from maple and birch, granite boulder and stone wall, turning electric wires into bright silver fila-

ments. The snow itself takes on a crust
of ice, like the finish of a clay pot,
that carries our weight and sends us
swooping and sliding. It's worth
your life to go for the mail. Until sand
and salt redeem the highway, Route
4 is quiet. We cancel the appointment
with the dentist, stay home, and
marvel at the altered universe, knowing that midday sun will strip ice
from tree and roof and restore our ordinary white winter world.

SHARON CURTIN

> SHARON CURTIN, a native of Douglas, Wyoming, was raised in a
> family of ranchers and craftspeople. Curtin, a feminist and polit-
> ical leftist, has worked as a nurse in New York and California
> but now devotes most of her time to writing and to operating a
> small farm in Virginia.

Aging in the Land of the Young

> "Aging in the Land of the Young" is the first part of Curtin's
> article by that title, as it appeared in the *Atlantic* in July 1972. It
> is largely a carefully restructured composite of portions of her
> book *Nobody Ever Died of Old Age,* also published in 1972. It illus-
> trates the subjective form of description, generally known as im-
> pressionistic description.

Old men, old women, almost 20 million of them. They constitute   1
10 percent of the total population, and the percentage is steadily
growing. Some of them, like conspirators, walk all bent over, as if
hiding some precious secret, filled with self-protection. The body
seems to gather itself around those vital parts, folding shoulders,
arms, pelvis like a fading rose. Watch and you see how fragile old
people come to think they are.

Aging paints every action gray, lies heavy on every move-   2
ment, imprisons every thought. It governs each decision with a
ruthless and single-minded perversity. To age is to learn the feeling
of no longer growing, of struggling to do old tasks, to remember
familiar actions. The cells of the brain are destroyed with thou-

sands of unfelt tiny strokes, little pockets of clotted blood wiping out memories and abilities without warning. The body seems slowly to give up, randomly stopping, sometimes starting again as if to torture and tease with the memory of lost strength. Hands become clumsy, frail transparencies, held together with knotted blue veins.

Sometimes it seems as if the distance between your feet and 3
the floor were constantly changing, as if you were walking on shifting and not quite solid ground. One foot down, slowly, carefully force the other foot forward. Sometimes you are a shuffler, not daring to lift your feet from the uncertain earth but forced to slide hesitantly forward in little whispering movements. Sometimes you are able to "step out," but this effort—in fact the pure exhilaration of easy movement—soon exhausts you.

The world becomes narrower as friends and family die or 4
move away. To climb stairs, to ride in a car, to walk to the corner, to talk on the telephone; each action seems to take away from the energy needed to stay alive. Everything is limited by the strength you hoard greedily. Your needs decrease, you require less food, less sleep, and finally less human contact; yet this little bit becomes more and more difficult. You fear that one day you will be reduced to the simple acts of breathing and taking nourishment. This is the ultimate stage you dread, the period of helplessness and hopelessness, when independence will be over.

There is nothing to prepare you for the experience of growing 5
old. Living is a process, an irreversible progression toward old age and eventual death. You see men of eighty still vital and straight as oaks; you see men of fifty reduced to gray shadows in the human landscape. The cellular clock differs for each one of us, and is profoundly affected by our own life experiences, our heredity, and perhaps most important, by the concepts of aging encountered in society and in oneself.

The aged live with enforced leisure, on fixed incomes, subject 6
to many chronic illnesses, and most of their money goes to keep a roof over their heads. They also live in a culture that worships youth.

A kind of cultural attitude makes me bigoted against old 7
people; it makes me think young is best; it makes me treat old people like outcasts.

Hate that gray? Wash it away!   8
Wrinkle cream.   9
Monkey glands.   10
Face-lifting.   11
Look like a bride again.   12
Don't trust anyone over thirty.   13
I fear growing old.   14
Feel Young Again!   15

I am afraid to grow old—we're all afraid. In fact, the fear of   16
growing old is so great that every aged person is an insult and a
threat to the society. They remind us of our own death, that our
body won't always remain smooth and responsive, but will someday betray us by aging, wrinkling, faltering, failing. The ideal way
to age would be to grow slowly invisible, gradually disappearing,
without causing worry or discomfort to the young. In some ways
that does happen. Sitting in a small park across from a nursing
home one day, I noticed that the young mothers and their children
gathered on one side, and the old people from the home on the
other. Whenever a youngster would run over to the "wrong" side,
chasing a ball or just trying to cover all the available space, the old
people would lean forward and smile. But before any communication could be established, the mother would come over, murmur-
ing embarrassed apologies, and take her child back to the "young"
side.

Now, it seemed to me that the children didn't feel any particu-   17
lar fear and the old people didn't seem to be threatened by the
children. The division of space was drawn by the mothers. And
the mothers never looked at the old people who lined the other
side of the park like so many pigeons perched on the benches.
These well-dressed young matrons had a way of sliding their eyes
over, around, through the old people; they never looked at them
directly. The old people may as well have been invisible; they had
no reality for the youngsters, who were not permitted to speak to
them, and they offended the aesthetic eye of the mothers.

My early experiences were somewhat different; since I   18
grew up in a small town, my childhood had more of a nineteenth-
century flavor. I knew a lot of old people, and considered some of
them friends. There was no culturally defined way for me to "re-

late'' to old people, except the rules of courtesy which applied to all adults. My grandparents were an integral and important part of the family and of the community. I sometimes have a dreadful fear that mine will be the last generation to know old people as friends, to have a sense of what growing old means, to respect and understand man's mortality and his courage in the face of death. Mine may be the last generation to have a sense of living history, of stories passed from generation to generation, of identity established by family history.

Meanings and Values

1.   What is the general tone of this writing? (See Guide to Terms: *Style/Tone.*)

2.   If you find it depressing to read about aging, try to analyze why (especially in view of the fact that you are very likely many years from the stage of ''a fading rose'').

3.   Why do you suppose it is more likely to be the mothers than the children who shun old people (pars. 16–17)?

4a.   Has this author avoided the excesses of sentimentality? (Guide: *Sentimentality.*)

  b.   If not, where does she fail? If she does avoid sentimentality, try to discover how.

Expository Techniques

1a.   Why should this writing be classed as primarily impressionistic, rather than objective?

  b.   What is the dominant impression?

2a.   Analyze the role that selection of details plays in creating the dominant impression.

  b.   Provide examples of the type of details that could have been included but were not.

  c.   Are such omissions justifiable?

3a.   Paragraph 5 ends the almost pure description to begin another phase of the writing. What is it?

  b.   How has the author provided for a smooth transition between the two? (Guide: *Transition.*)

4a.   What particular method of gaining emphasis has been used effectively in one portion of the selection? (Guide: *Emphasis.*)

b.   How might the material have been presented if emphasis were not desired?

5.   Which previously studied patterns of exposition are also used in this writing? Cite paragraphs where each may be found.

Diction and Vocabulary

1a.   The author sometimes changes person—e.g., "they" to "you" after paragraph 2. Analyze where the changes occur.

b.   What justification, if any, can you find for each change?

2a.   Which two kinds of figures of speech do you find used liberally to achieve this description? (Guide: *Figures of Speech*.)

b.   Cite three or more examples of each.

c.   As nearly as you can tell, are any of them clichés? (Guide: *Clichés*.)

Suggestions for Writing and Discussion

1.   If Curtin is correct in her fears expressed in the last two sentences, what could be the consequences for society in general?

2.   Discuss the pros and cons of placing senile old people in rest homes, rather than letting them live alone or taking them to live with the family. What other alternatives, if any, does the family have?

3.   If you know some very old person who (apparently) is not as affected by aging as the ones the author describes, what seems to account for this difference?

4.   If many people at age sixty-five to seventy-five are still efficient at their jobs, as is often argued, what practical reasons are there for forcing retirement at that age?

(NOTE: Suggestions for topics requiring development by use of DESCRIPTION are on page 278, at the end of this section.)

JOYCE MAYNARD

JOYCE MAYNARD was born in 1953 and spent her childhood in
Durham, New Hampshire, where her father taught at the
nearby University of New Hampshire. At 19, while she was still
a sophomore at Yale University, her first book appeared: *Looking
Backward: A Chronicle of Growing Up Old in the Sixties* (1973).
Maynard was a reporter for the *New York Times* and currently
writes a syndicated newspaper column. She also writes monthly
for *Mademoiselle* and *Harrowsmith* magazines and has published
a novel, *Baby Love* (1981). Many of her columns were reprinted
in the recent collection *Domestic Affairs* (1988).

The Yellow Door House

Permanence, continuity, and change are some of the ideas explored through description in this essay, originally published as
one of the author's columns. Comparison plays an important
part in the exposition as well, particularly in juxtaposing Maynard's memories of the house with its present reality.

I've known only two homes in my life: the one I live in now, with   1
my husband and children, and another one, just sixty miles from
here, where I grew up. My father's dead now, and even before
that, my parents were divorced and my mother moved away from
our old house. But though she rents the house out nine months of
the year and hasn't spent a winter there for thirteen years, she
hasn't sold our old house yet. It's still filled with our old belongings from our old life. And though my mother has another house
now, and a good life, with another man, in a new place, she still
comes back to the old house for a couple of months every summer.

Every year I ask her, "Have you considered putting the house on the market?" And every summer the answer is "not yet."

My children call the place where I grew up the yellow door house. They love the place, with its big, overgrown yard, the old goldfish pond, the brick walkway, the white picket fence. On the front door there's a heavy brass knocker my sons like to bang on to announce their arrival for visits with their grandmother, and French windows on either side that I was always cautioned against breaking as a child. (As now I caution my children.) There's a brass mail slot I used to pass messages through to a friend waiting on the other side. Now my daughter Audrey does the same.

It's a big house, a hip-roofed colonial, with ceilings higher than anybody needs, and a sweeping staircase rising up from the front hall, with a banister that children more adventurous than my sister and I (mine, for instance) are always tempted to slide on. There are plants everywhere, paintings my father made, Mexican pottery, and a band of tin Mexican soldiers—one on horseback, one playing the flute, one the tuba. We bought those soldiers on the first trip I ever made to New York City. They cost way too much, but my mother said we could get them if we took the bus home instead of flying. So we did.

One room of the yellow door house is wood paneled and lined with books. There used to be a big overstuffed armchair in it that I'd settle into with my cookies and milk, when I came home from school, to do my homework or watch "Leave It to Beaver." (That chair is in my house now.) There's a porch with a swing out back, and a sunny corner in the kitchen where I always ate my toast—grilled in the oven, sometimes with cinnamon sugar and sometimes jam, but always the way my mother made it, buttered on both sides. My mother is a wonderful, natural cook, who would announce, on a typical night, three different dessert possibilities, all homemade. Now I wouldn't think of eating a third piece of blueberry pie. But the old habits return when I walk into my mother's kitchen. The first thing I do is go see what's in the refrigerator.

It's been fourteen years since I lived in the yellow door house, but I could still make my way around it blindfolded. There are places where the house could use some work now, and my mother never was the best housekeeper. I open a drawer in the big Welsh dresser in the dining room, looking for a safety pin, and so much spills out (though not safety pins) that I can't close it again. A person can choose from five different kinds of cookies in this house. There's a whole closetful of fabric scraps and antique lace. Eight teapots. But no yardstick, no light bulbs, no scissors.

My children's favorite place in the house is the attic. The front 6 half used to be the studio where my father painted, at night, when he came home from his job as an English teacher. The paintings and paints are long gone now; but my father was a lover of art supplies and hopelessly extravagant when it came to acquiring them, so every once in a while, even now, thirteen years since he's been here, I'll come upon a box of unopened pastels, or watercolor pencils, or the kind of art gum eraser he always used. I'll pick up a stub of an oil pastel and hold it up to my nose, and a wave of feeling will wash over me that almost makes my knees weak. Cadmium yellow light. Cerulean blue. Suddenly I'm ten years old again, sitting on the grass in a field a couple of miles down the road from here, with a sketch pad on my lap and my father beside me, drawing a picture of Ski Jump Hill.

Beyond the room that was my father's studio is the part of our 7 attic where my mother—a hoarder, like me—has stored away just about every toy we ever owned, and most of our old dresses. A ripped Chinese umbrella, a broken wicker rocker, a hooked rug she started and never finished, an exercise roller, purchased around 1947, meant to undo the damage of all those blueberry pies. Songs I wrote when I was nine. My sister's poems. My mother's notes from college English class. My father's powerfully moving proclamations of love to her, written when she was eighteen and he was thirty-eight, when she was telling him she couldn't marry him and he was telling her she must.

Every time we come to the yellow door house to visit, Audrey 8 and Charlie head for the attic—and though we have mostly cleaned out my old Barbies now (and a Midge doll, whose turned-up nose had been partly nibbled off by mice), we never seem to reach the end of the treasures: My homemade dollhouse furniture (I packed it away, room by room, with notes enclosed, to the daughter I knew I would someday have, describing how I'd laid out the rooms.) An old wooden recorder. A brass doll bed. Wonderfully detailed doll clothes my mother made for us every Christmas (at the time, I longed for store-bought). One year she knit a sweater, for a two-inch-tall bear, using toothpicks for knitting needles. Another year she sewed us matching skirts from an old patchwork quilt.

The little town where I grew up (and where I used to know just about everyone) has been growing so fast that my mother hardly knows anyone on our street anymore. A house like hers has become so desirable that within days of her arrival this summer, my mother got a call from a realtor asking if she'd be interested in selling. He named as a likely asking price a figure neither one of us could believe. My parents bought the house, thirty years ago, for a fifth of that amount, and still, they sometimes had to take out loans to meet the mortgage payments.

For years now, I have been telling my mother that it makes little sense to hold on to the yellow door house (and to worry about tenants, make repairs, put away the Mexican tin soldiers every Labor Day and take them out again every Fourth of July). But I suddenly realized, hearing about this realtor's call, that when the day comes that my mother sells the house, I will be deeply shaken. I doubt if I will even want to drive down our old street after that, or even come back to the town, where I scarcely know anybody anymore. I don't much want to see some other family inventing new games, new rituals, in our house. Don't want to know where they put their Christmas tree, or what sort of paintings they hang on their walls. It would be crazy—impossible—to pack up and haul away all those dress-up clothes and bits of costume jewelry and boxes of old book reports and crumbs of pastels. But neither do I relish the thought of someday having to throw them out.

My mother's yellow door house is a perfect place to play hide-and-seek, and last weekend, when I was there visiting with my three children, that's what my two sons and I did. I found a hiding place in the wood-paneled room, behind the couch. I scrunched myself up so small that several minutes passed without my sons' finding me, even though they passed through the room more than once.

Many families have rented the house since my mother ceased to make it her full-time home, but the smell—I realized—hasn't changed. Listening to my children's voices calling out to me through the rooms, I studied a particular knothole in the paneling, and it came back to me that this knothole had always reminded me of an owl. I ran my finger over the wood floors and the upholstery on the side of the couch, and noted the dust my mother has always tended to leave in corners. I heard the sewing machine whirring upstairs: my mother, sewing doll clothes with Audrey. I smelled my mother's soup on the stove. And for a moment, I wanted time to freeze.

But then I let myself make a small noise. "We found you, we found you," my boys sang out, falling into my arms. And then we all had lunch, with my mother's chocolate chip cookies for dessert—and headed back to the house I live in now. Whose door is green. 13

Meanings and Values

1. Where in the opening paragraph does Maynard introduce the themes of change and continuity?

2. List the kinds of memories the objects in the attic call up in the author's mind (pars. 6–8).

3. What does the author believe will be lost if her mother sells the house?

4a. What is meant by the phrase "I wanted time to freeze" in paragraph 12?

b. What actions does the author take in the next paragraph that undermine this wish and the values implied by it?

Expository Techniques

1a. Identify the subjects Maynard describes in each of the paragraphs following the opening.

b. Do these paragraphs generally focus on a single scene (or subject) or on several? Be ready to support your answer with examples from the text.

c. Can the descriptions in paragraphs 4 and 10 be considered unified? Why, or why not? (See Guide to Terms: *Unity.*)

2a. What use does Maynard make of comparison in paragraphs 2, 12, and 13 to convey themes of continuity, permanence, and change?

Diction and Vocabulary

1a. Identify the concrete diction in paragraph 6 and discuss how it contributes to the effectiveness of the passage. (Guide: *Evaluation.*)

b.   What are the technical terms used in the passage, and how do they contribute to its effect? (Guide: *Diction.*)

2a. Why does the author mention the television program "Leave It to Beaver" (par. 4)?

b.   In what ways has her life been similar to the life of the family depicted in the series?

c.   In what ways has it differed?

Suggestions for Writing and Discussion

1.   Do many people today have a chance to return to the homes and apartments in which they grew up? Is it likely that many spent their entire childhoods living in a single house or apartment? How are the childhood memories of people whose families moved often likely to differ from those of Maynard? Are their values likely to differ also?

2.   Prepare an essay describing one or more places where you lived as a child. In the course of the description deal with questions of change, loss, growth, continuity, and related matters.

(NOTE: Suggestions for topics requiring development by use of DESCRIPTION are on page 278, at the end of this section.)

E. B. WHITE

E. B. WHITE, distinguished essayist, was born in Mount Vernon, New York, in 1899 and died in 1985 in North Brooklin, Maine. A graduate of Cornell University, White worked as a reporter and advertising copywriter, and in 1926 he joined the staff of the *New Yorker* magazine. After 1937 he did most of his writing at his farm in Maine, for many years contributing a regular column, "One Man's Meat," to *Harper's* magazine and freelance editorials for the "Notes and Comments" column of the *New Yorker*. White also wrote children's books, two volumes of verse, and, with James Thurber, *Is Sex Necessary?* (1929). With his wife Katherine White, he compiled *A Subtreasury of American Humor* (1941). Collections of his own essays include *One Man's Meat* (1942), *The Second Tree from the Corner* (1953), *The Points of My Compass* (1962), and *Essays of E. B. White* (1977). In 1959 he revised and enlarged William Strunk's *The Elements of Style,* a textbook still widely used in college classrooms. White received many honors and writing awards for his crisp, highly individual style and his sturdy independence of thought.

Once More to the Lake

In this essay White relies primarily on description to convey his sense of the passage of time and the power of memory. The vivid scenes and the clear yet expressive prose in this essay are characteristic of his writing.

August 1941

One summer, along about 1904, my father rented a camp on a lake   1
in Maine and took us all there for the month of August. We all got
ringworm from some kittens and had to rub Pond's Extract on our

arms and legs night and morning, and my father rolled over in a canoe with all his clothes on; but outside of that the vacation was a success and from then on none of us ever thought there was any place in the world like that lake in Maine. We returned summer after summer—always on August 1 for one month. I have since become a salt-water man, but sometimes in summer there are days when the restlessness of the tides and the fearful cold of the sea water and the incessant wind that blows across the afternoon and into the evening make me wish for the placidity of a lake in the woods. A few weeks ago this feeling got so strong I bought myself a couple of bass hooks and a spinner and returned to the lake where we used to go, for a week's fishing and to revisit old haunts.

I took along my son, who had never had any fresh water up his nose and who had seen lily pads only from train windows. On the journey over to the lake I began to wonder what it would be like. I wondered how time would have marred this unique, this holy spot—the coves and streams, the hills that the sun set behind, the camps and the paths behind the camps. I was sure that the tarred road would have found it out, and I wondered in what other ways it would be desolated. It is strange how much you can remember about places like that once you allow your mind to return into the grooves that lead back. You remember one thing, and that suddenly reminds you of another thing. I guess I remembered clearest of all the early mornings, when the lake was cool and motionless, remembered how the bedroom smelled of the lumber it was made of and of the wet woods whose scent entered through the screen. The partitions in the camp were thin and did not extend clear to the top of the rooms, and as I was always the first up I would dress softly so as not to wake the others, and sneak out into the sweet outdoors and start out in the canoe, keeping close along the shore in the long shadows of the pines. I remembered being very careful never to rub my paddle against the gunwale for fear of disturbing the stillness of the cathedral.

The lake had never been what you would call a wild lake. There were cottages sprinkled around the shores, and it was in farming country although the shores of the lake were quite heavily wooded. Some of the cottages were owned by nearby farmers, and you would live at the shore and eat your meals at the farmhouse. That's what our family did. But although it wasn't wild, it was a fairly large and undisturbed lake and there were places in it that, to a child at least, seemed infinitely remote and primeval.

I was right about the tar: it led to within half a mile of the 4
shore. But when I got back there, with my boy, and we settled into
a camp near a farmhouse and into the kind of summertime I had
known, I could tell that it was going to be pretty much the same
as it had been before—I knew it, lying in bed the first morning,
smelling the bedroom and hearing the boy sneak quietly out and
go off along the shore in a boat. I began to sustain the illusion that
he was I, and therefore, by simple transposition, that I was my
father. This sensation persisted, kept cropping up all the time we
were there. It was not an entirely new feeling, but in this setting
it grew much stronger. I seemed to be living a dual existence. I
would be in the middle of some simple act, I would be picking up
a bait box or laying down a table fork, or I would be saying something, and suddenly it would be not I but my father who was saying the words or making the gesture. It gave me a creepy sensation.

We went fishing the first morning. I felt the same damp moss 5
covering the worms in the bait can, and saw the dragonfly alight
on the tip of my rod as it hovered a few inches from the surface of
the water. It was the arrival of this fly that convinced me beyond
any doubt that everything was as it always had been, that the years
were a mirage and that there had been no years. The small waves
were the same, chucking the rowboat under the chin as we fished
at anchor, and the boat was the same boat, the same color green
and the ribs broken in the same places, and under the floorboards
the same fresh-water leavings and débris—the dead helgramite,
the wisps of moss, the rusty discarded fishhook, the dried blood
from yesterday's catch. We stared silently at the tips of our rods,
at the dragonflies that came and went. I lowered the tip of mine
into the water, tentatively, pensively dislodging the fly, which
darted two feet away, poised, darted two feet back, and came to
rest again a little farther up the rod. There had been no years between the ducking of this dragonfly and the other one—the one
that was part of memory. I looked at the boy, who was silently
watching his fly, and it was my hands that held his rod, my eyes
watching. I felt dizzy and didn't know which rod I was at the end
of.

We caught two bass, hauling them in briskly as though they 6
were mackerel, pulling them over the side of the boat in a busi-
nesslike manner without any landing net, and stunning them with
a blow on the back of the head. When we got back for a swim

before lunch, the lake was exactly where we had left it, the same number of inches from the dock, and there was only the merest suggestion of a breeze. This seemed an utterly enchanted sea, this lake you could leave to its own devices for a few hours and come back to, and find that it had not stirred, this constant and trust-worthy body of water. In the shallows, the dark, water-soaked sticks and twigs, smooth and old, were undulating in clusters on the bottom against the clean ribbed sand, and the track of the mus-sel was plain. A school of minnows swam by, each minnow with its small individual shadow, doubling the attendance, so clear and sharp in the sunlight. Some of the other campers were in swim-ming, along the shore, one of them with a cake of soap, and the water felt thin and clear and unsubstantial. Over the years there had been this person with the cake of soap, this cultist, and here he was. There had been no years.

Up to the farmhouse to dinner through the teeming, dusty   7
field, the road under our sneakers was only a two-track road. The middle track was missing, the one with the marks of the hooves and the splotches of dried, flaky manure. There had always been three tracks to choose from in choosing which track to walk in; now the choice was narrowed down to two. For a moment I missed terribly the middle alternative. But the way led past the tennis court, and something about the way it lay there in the sun reas-sured me; the tape had loosened along the backline, the alleys were green with plantains and other weeds, and the net (installed in June and removed in September) sagged in the dry noon, and the whole place steamed with midday heat and hunger and empti-ness. There was a choice of pie for dessert, and one was blueberry and one was apple, and the waitresses were the same country girls, there having been no passage of time, only the illusion of it as in a dropped curtain—the waitresses were still fifteen; their hair had been washed, that was the only difference—they had been to the movies and seen the pretty girls with the clean hair.

Summertime, oh, summertime, pattern of life indelible, the   8
fade-proof lake, the woods unshatterable, the pasture with the sweetfern and the juniper forever and ever, summer without end; this was the background, and the life along the shore was the de-sign, their tiny docks with the flagpole and the American flag float-ing against the white clouds in the blue sky, the little paths over the roots of the trees leading from camp to camp and the paths leading back to the outhouses and the can of lime for sprinkling,

and at the souvenir counters at the store the miniature birch-bark canoes and the postcards that showed things looking a little better than they looked. This was the American family at play, escaping the city heat, wondering whether the newcomers in the camp at the head of the cove were "common" or "nice," wondering whether it was true that the people who drove up for Sunday dinner at the farmhouse were turned away because there wasn't enough chicken.

It seemed to me, as I kept remembering all this, that those times and those summers had been infinitely precious and worth saving. There had been jollity and peace and goodness. The arriving (at the beginning of August) had been so big a business in itself, at the railway station the farm wagon drawn up, the first smell of the pine-laden air, the first glimpse of the smiling farmer, and the great importance of the trunks and your father's enormous authority in such matters, and the feel of the wagon under you for the long ten-mile haul, and at the top of the last long hill catching the first view of the lake after eleven months of not seeing this cherished body of water. The shouts and cries of the other campers when they saw you, and the trunks to be unpacked, to give up their rich burden. (Arriving was less exciting nowadays, when you sneaked up in your car and parked it under a tree near the camp and took out the bags and in five minutes it was all over, no fuss, no loud wonderful fuss about trunks.)

Peace and goodness and jollity. The only thing that was wrong now, really, was the sound of the place, an unfamiliar nervous sound of the outboard motors. This was the note that jarred, the one thing that would sometimes break the illusion and set the years moving. In those other summertimes all motors were inboard; and when they were at a little distance, the noise they made was a sedative, an ingredient of summer sleep. They were one-cylinder and two-cylinder engines, and some were make-and-break and some were jump-spark, but they all made a sleepy sound across the lake. The one-lungers throbbed and fluttered, and the twin-cylinder ones purred and purred, and that was a quiet sound, too. But now the campers all had outboards. In the daytime, in the hot mornings, these motors made a petulant, irritable sound; at night, in the still evening when the afterglow lit the water, they whined about one's ears like mosquitoes. My boy loved our rented outboard, and his great desire was to achieve single-handed mastery over it, and authority, and he soon learned

9

10

the trick of choking it a little (but not too much), and the adjustment of the needle valve. Watching him I would remember the things you could do with the old one-cylinder engine with the heavy flywheel, how you could have it eating out of your hand if you got really close to it spiritually. Motorboats in those days didn't have clutches, and you would make a landing by shutting off the motor at the proper time and coasting in with a dead rudder. But there was a way of reversing them, if you learned the trick, by cutting the switch and putting it on again exactly on the final dying revolution of the flywheel, so that it would kick back against compression and begin reversing. Approaching a dock in a strong following breeze, it was difficult to slow up sufficiently by the ordinary coasting method, and if a boy felt he had complete mastery over his motor, he was tempted to keep it running beyond its time and then reverse it a few feet from the dock. It took a cool nerve, because if you threw the switch a twentieth of a second too soon you would catch the flywheel when it still had speed enough to go up past center, and the boat would leap ahead, charging bull-fashion at the dock.

We had a good week at the camp. The bass were biting well and the sun shone endlessly, day after day. We would be tired at night and lie down in the accumulated heat of the little bedrooms after the long hot day and the breeze would stir almost imperceptibly outside and the smell of the swamp drift in through the rusty screens. Sleep would come easily and in the morning the red squirrel would be on the roof, tapping out his gay routine. I kept remembering everything, lying in bed in the mornings—the small steamboat that had a long rounded stern like the lip of a Ubangi, and how quietly she ran on the moonlight sails, when the older boys played their mandolins and the girls sang and we ate doughnuts dipped in sugar, and how sweet the music was on the water in the shining night, and what it had felt like to think about girls then. After breakfast we would go up to the store and the things were in the same place—the minnows in a bottle, the plugs and spinners disarranged and pawed over by the youngsters from the boys' camp, the Fig Newtons and the Beeman's gum. Outside, the road was tarred and cars stood in front of the store. Inside, all was just as it had always been, except there was more Coca-Cola and not so much Moxie and root beer and birch beer and sarsaparilla. We would walk out with the bottle of pop apiece and sometimes the pop would backfire up our noses and hurt. We explored the streams, quietly, where the turtles slid off the sunny logs and dug their way into the soft bottom; and we lay on the town wharf and fed worms to the tame bass. Everywhere we went I had trouble making out which was I, the one walking at my side, the one walking in my pants.

One afternoon while we were there at that lake a thunderstorm came up. It was like the revival of an old melodrama that I had seen long ago with childish awe. The second-act climax of the drama of the electrical disturbance over a lake in America had not changed in any important respect. This was the big scene, still the big scene. The whole thing was so familiar, the first feeling of oppression and heat and a general air around camp of not wanting to go very far away. In mid-afternoon (it was all the same) a curious darkening of the sky, and a lull in everything that had made life tick; and then the way the boats suddenly swung the other way at their moorings with the coming of a breeze out of the new quarter, and the premonitory rumble. Then the kettle drum, then the snare, then the bass drum and cymbals, then crackling light against the dark, and the gods grinning and licking their chops in the hills. Afterward the calm, the rain steadily rustling in the calm lake, the return of light and hope and spirits, and the campers running out in joy and relief to go swimming in the rain, their bright cries perpetuating the deathless joke about how they were getting simply drenched, and the children screaming with delight at the new sensation of bathing in the rain, and the joke about getting drenched linking the generations in a strong indestructible chain. And the comedian who waded in carrying an umbrella.

When the others went swimming, my son said he was going in, too. He pulled his dripping trunks from the line where they had hung all through the shower and wrung them out. Languidly, and with no thought of going in, I watched him, his hard little body, skinny and bare, saw him wince slightly as he pulled up around his vitals the small, soggy, icy garment. As he buckled the swollen belt, suddenly my groin felt the chill of death.

Meanings and Values

   1a.   Why does White decide to return to the lake?

     b.   Can the lake be considered a personal symbol for White? (See Guide to Terms: *Symbol*.)

     c.   If so, what does it symbolize?

2a. In what ways have the lake and its surroundings remained the same since White's boyhood? Be specific.

b.   In what ways have they changed?

3a. At one point in the essay White says, "I seemed to be living a dual existence" (par. 4). What is the meaning of this statement?

b.   How does this "dual existence" affect his point of view in the essay? (Guide: *Point of View.*)

c.   Is the "dual existence" emphasized more in the first half of the essay or the second half? Why?

4a. Where would you place this essay on an objective-to-subjective continuum? (Guide: *Objective/Subjective.*)

b.   Is this a formal or an informal essay? Explain. (Guide: *Essay.*)

5a. After spending a day on the lake, White remarks, "There had been no years" (par. 6). What other direct or indirect comments does he make about time and change? Be specific.

b.   How are these comments related to the central theme of the essay? (Guide: *Unity.*)

6a. What is the tone of the essay? (Guide: *Style/Tone.*)

b.   Does the tone change or remain the same throughout the essay?

7a. What is meant by the closing phrase of the essay, "suddenly my groin felt the chill of death" (par. 13)?

b.   Is this an appropriate way to end the essay? Why, or why not?

Expository Techniques

1a. If you agree that the lake is a personal symbol for White, explain how he enables readers to understand its significance. (Guide: *Symbol.*)

b.   Is he successful in doing this? (Guide: *Evaluation.*)

2a. In the first part of the essay White focuses on the unchanged aspects of the lake; in the second part he begins acknowledging the passage of time. Where does this shift in attitude take place?

b.   What strategies, including transitional devices, does White use to signal to the reader the shift in attitude? Be specific.

3.   How does White use the discussion of outboard motors and inboard motors (par. 10) to summarize the differences between life at the lake in his youth and at the time of his return with his son? Explain.

4.   Many of the descriptive passages in this essay convey a dominant impression, usually an emotion or mood. Choose a paragraph

from the essay and discuss how the author's choice of details, variety of syntax, and diction help create a dominant impression. Be specific. (Guide: *Syntax and Diction.*)

5a. In many places the author combines description and comparison. Select a passage from the essay and discuss in detail how he combines the patterns.

  b. In what ways is the combination of description and comparison appropriate to the theme and the point of view of the essay?

6. White has often been praised for the clarity and variety of his prose style. To what extent are these qualities the result of syntax and of the variety of strategies he uses to achieve emphasis? (Choose a sample paragraph, such as 6, 9, or 12, to illustrate your answer.) (Guide: *Emphasis* and *Syntax.*)

Diction and Vocabulary

1. To what extent are the qualities of White's style mentioned in your answer to question 6 of "Expository Techniques" matters of diction? (Guide: *Diction.*)

2a. How much do the connotations of the words used in paragraph 8 contribute to the dominant impression the author is trying to create? (Guide: *Connotation/Denotation.*)

  b. In paragraph 10?

3a. Why would the author refer to the person with the cake of soap as "this cultist" (par. 6)?

  b. In what sense can a tennis court steam "with midday heat and hunger and emptiness" (par. 7)?

4. What kind of paradox is presented in this passage: ". . . the waitresses were the same country girls, there having been no passage of time, only the illusion of it as in a dropped curtain—the waitresses were still fifteen; their hair had been washed, that was the only difference—they had been to the movies and seen the pretty girls with the clean hair" (par. 7)? (Guide: *Paradox.*)

5a. Is the diction in this passage sentimental: "Summertime, oh, summertime, pattern of life indelible, the fade-proof lake, the woods unshatterable, the pasture with the sweetfern and the juniper forever and ever, summer without end. . . ." (par. 8)? (Guide: *Sentimentality.*)

  b. If so, why would the author choose to use this style in the passage?

  c. Does the passage contain an allusion? If so, what is alluded to and why? (Guide: *Figures of Speech.*)

6.   Study the author's uses of the following words, consulting the dictionary as needed: incessant, placidity (par. 1); gunwale (2); primeval (3); transposition (4); helgramite, pensively (5); petulant (10); premonitory (12); languidly (13).

Suggestions for Writing and Discussion

1.   Choose some place you remember from your childhood and have seen recently, and write a description of it comparing its present appearance with your memories of it.

2.   Prepare a description of some object or place that symbolizes the passage of time and try to control the tone of your description so it reflects your attitudes toward time and change.

3.   Discuss your relationship with your parents (or your children) insofar as that relationship includes experiences similar to the ones White describes in "Once More to the Lake."

4.   If you have taken a summer vacation like the one recorded by White, compare your experiences and the setting to those in the essay. How much has our civilization—and our vacations—changed since the time of the events in the essay?

(NOTE: Suggestions for topics requiring development by use of DESCRIPTION are on page 278, at the end of this section.)

GEORGE SIMPSON

GEORGE SIMPSON, born in Virginia in 1950, received his B.A. in journalism from the University of North Carolina. He has been employed at *Newsweek* since 1972 and in 1978 became public affairs director for that magazine. Before joining *Newsweek,* Simpson worked for two years as a writer and editor for the *Carolina Financial Times* in Chapel Hill, North Carolina, and as a reporter for the *News-Gazette* in Lexington, Virginia. He received the Best Feature Writing award from Sigma Delta Chi in 1972 for a five-part investigative series on the University of North Carolina football program. He has written stories for the *New York Times, Sport, Glamour,* the *Winston-Salem Journal,* and *New York.*

The War Room at Bellevue

"The War Room at Bellevue" was first published in *New York* magazine. The author chose, for good reason, to stay strictly within a time sequence as he described the emergency ward. This essay is also noteworthy for the cumulative descriptive effect, which was accomplished almost entirely with objective details.

Bellevue. The name conjures up images of an indoor war zone: the wounded and bleeding lining the halls, screaming for help while harried doctors in blood-stained smocks rush from stretcher to stretcher, fighting a losing battle against exhaustion and the crushing number of injured. "What's worse," says a longtime Bellevue nurse, "is that we have this image of being a hospital only for . . ." She pauses, then lowers her voice; "for crazy people."

Though neither battlefield nor Bedlam is a valid image, there is something extraordinary about the monstrous complex that spreads for five blocks along First Avenue in Manhattan. It is said best by the head nurse in Adult Emergency Service: "If you have any chance for survival, you have it here." Survival—that is why they come. Why do injured cops drive by a half-dozen other hospitals to be treated at Bellevue? They've seen the Bellevue emergency team in action.

9:00 P.M. It is a Friday night in the Bellevue emergency room. The after-work crush is over (those who've suffered through the day, only to come for help after the five-o'clock whistle has blown) and it is nearly silent except for the mutter of voices at the admitting desk, where administrative personnel discuss who will go for coffee. Across the spotless white-walled lobby, ten people sit quietly, passively, in pastel plastic chairs, waiting for word of relatives or to see doctors. In the past 24 hours, 300 people have come to the Bellevue Adult Emergency Service. Fewer than 10 percent were true emergencies. One man sleeps fitfully in the emergency ward while his heartbeat, respiration, and blood pressure are monitored by control consoles mounted over his bed. Each heartbeat trips a tiny bleep in the monitor, which attending nurses can hear across the ward. A half hour ago, doctors in the trauma room withdrew a six-inch stiletto blade from his back. When he is stabilized, the patient will be moved upstairs to the twelve-bed Surgical Intensive Care Unit.

9:05 P.M. An ambulance backs into the receiving bay, its red and yellow lights flashing in and out of the lobby. A split second later, the glass doors burst open as a nurse and an attendant roll a mobile stretcher into the lobby. When the nurse screams, "Emergent!" the lobby explodes with activity as the way is cleared to the trauma room. Doctors appear from nowhere and transfer the bloodied body of a black man to the treatment table. Within seconds his clothes are stripped away, revealing a tiny stab wound in his left side. Three doctors and three nurses rush around the victim, each performing a task necessary to begin treatment. Intravenous needles are inserted into his arms and groin. A doctor draws blood for the lab, in case surgery is necessary. A nurse begins inserting a catheter into the victim's penis and continues to feed in tubing until the catheter reaches the bladder. Urine flows through the tube into a plastic bag. Doctors are glad not to see blood in the urine. Another nurse records pulse and blood pressure.

The victim is in good shape. He shivers slightly, although the trauma room is exceedingly warm. His face is bloodied, but shows no major lacerations. A third nurse, her elbow propped on the treatment table, asks the man a series of questions, trying to quickly outline his medical history. He answers abruptly. He is drunk. His left side is swabbed with yellow disinfectant and a doctor injects a local anesthetic. After a few seconds another doctor inserts his finger into the wound. It sinks in all the way to the knuckle. He begins to rotate his finger like a child trying to get a marble out of a milk bottle. The patient screams bloody murder and tries to struggle free.

Meanwhile in the lobby, a security guard is ejecting a derelict 6 who has begun to drink from a bottle hidden in his coat pocket. "He's a regular, was in here just two days ago," says a nurse. "We checked him pretty good then, so he's probably okay now. Can you believe those were clean clothes we gave him?" The old man, blackened by filth, leaves quietly.

9:15 P.M. A young Hispanic man interrupts, saying his preg- 7 nant girl friend, sitting outside in his car, is bleeding heavily from her vagina. She is rushed into an examination room, treated behind closed doors, and rolled into the observation ward, where, much later in the night, a gynecologist will treat her in a special room—the same one used to examine rape victims. Nearby, behind curtains, the neurologist examines an old white woman to determine if her headaches are due to head injury. They are not.

9:45 P.M. The trauma room has been cleared and cleaned mer- 8 cilessly. The examination rooms are three-quarters full—another overdose, two asthmatics, a young woman with abdominal pains. In the hallway, a derelict who has been sleeping it off urinates all over the stretcher. He sleeps on while attendants change his clothes. An ambulance—one of four that patrol Manhattan for Bellevue from 42nd Street to Houston, river to river—delivers a middle-aged white woman and two cops, the three of them soaking wet. The woman has escaped from the psychiatric floor of a nearby hospital and tried to drown herself in the East River. The cops fished her out. She lies on a stretcher shivering beneath white blankets. Her eyes stare at the ceiling. She speaks clearly when an administrative worker begins routine questioning. The cops are given hospital gowns and wait to receive tetanus shots and gamma globulin—a hedge against infection from the befouled river water. They will hang around the E.R. for another two hours, telling their story to as many as six other policemen who show up to hear it. The woman is rolled into an examination room, where a male

nurse speaks gently: "They tell me you fell into the river." "No,"
says the woman, "I jumped. I have to commit suicide." "Why?"
asks the nurse. "Because I'm insane and I can't help [it]. I have to
die." The nurse gradually discovers the woman has a history of
psychological problems. She is given dry bedclothes and placed
under guard in the hallway. She lies on her side, staring at the
wall.

The pace continues to increase. Several more overdose victims
arrive by ambulance. One, a young black woman, had done a
striptease on the street just before passing out. A second black
woman is semiconscious and spends the better part of her time
at Bellevue alternately cursing at and pleading with the doctors.
Attendants find a plastic bottle coated with methadone in the
pocket of a Hispanic O.D. The treatment is routinely the same, and
sooner or later involves vomiting. Just after doctors begin to treat
the O.D., he vomits great quantities of wine and methadone in all
directions. "Lovely business, huh?" laments one of the doctors. A
young nurse confides that if there were other true emergencies,
the overdose victims would be given lower priority. "You can't
help thinking they did it to themselves," she says, "while the others
are accident victims."

10:30 P.M. A policeman who twisted his knee struggling with
an "alleged perpetrator" is examined and released. By 10:30, the
lobby is jammed with friends and relatives of patients in various
stages of treatment and recovery. The attendant who also functions
as a translator for Hispanic patients adds chairs to accommodate
the overflow. The medical walk-in rate stays steady—between
eight and ten patients waiting. A pair of derelicts, each with battered
eyes, appear at the admitting desk. One has a dramatically
swollen face laced with black stitches.

11:00 P.M. The husband of the attempted suicide arrives. He
thanks the police for saving his wife's life, then talks at length with
doctors about her condition. She continues to stare into the void
and does not react when her husband approaches her stretcher.

Meanwhile, patients arrive in the lobby at a steady pace. A
young G.I. on leave has lower-back pains; a Hispanic man complains
of pains in his side; occasionally parents hurry through the
adult E.R. carrying children to the pediatric E.R. A white woman
of about 50 marches into the lobby from the walk-in entrance.
Dried blood covers her right eyebrow and upper lip. She begins to

perform. "I was assaulted on 28th and Lexington, I was," she says grandly, "and I don't have to take it *anymore*. I was a bride 21 years ago and, God, I was beautiful then." She has captured the attention of all present. "I was there when the boys came home— on Memorial Day—and I don't have to take this kind of treatment."

As midnight approaches, the nurses prepare for the shift change. They must brief the incoming staff and make sure all reports are up-to-date. One young brunet says, "Christ, I'm gonna go home and take a shower—I smell like vomit." 13

11:50 P.M. The triage nurse is questioning an old black man about chest pains, and a Hispanic woman is having an asthma attack, when an ambulance, its sirens screaming full tilt, roars into the receiving bay. There is a split-second pause as everyone drops what he or she is doing and looks up. Then all hell breaks loose. Doctors and nurses are suddenly sprinting full-out toward the trauma room. The glass doors burst open and the occupied stretcher is literally run past me. Cops follow. It is as if a comet has whooshed by. In the trauma room it all becomes clear. A half-dozen doctors and nurses surround the lifeless form of a Hispanic man with a shotgun hole in his neck the size of your fist. Blood pours from a second gaping wound in his chest. A respirator is slammed over his face, making his chest rise and fall as if he were breathing. "No pulse," reports one doctor. A nurse jumps on a stool and, leaning over the man, begins to pump his chest with her palms. "No blood pressure," screams another nurse. The ambulance driver appears shaken. "I never thought I'd get here in time," he stutters. More doctors from the trauma team upstairs arrive. Wrappings from syringes and gauze pads fly through the air. The victim's eyes are open yet devoid of life. His body takes on a yellow tinge. A male nurse winces at the gunshot wound. "This guy really pissed off somebody," he says. This is no ordinary shooting. It is an execution. IV's are jammed into the body in the groin and arms. One doctor has been plugging in an electrocardiograph and asks everyone to stop for a second so he can get a reading. "Forget it," shouts the doctor in charge. "No time." "Take it easy, Jimmy," someone yells at the head physician. It is apparent by now that the man is dead, but the doctors keep trying injections and finally they slit open the chest and reach inside almost up to their elbows. They feel the extent of the damage and 14 suddenly it is all over. "I told 'em he was dead," says one nurse, withdrawing. "They didn't listen." The room is very still. The doctors are momentarily disgusted, then go on about their business. The room clears quickly. Finally there is only a male nurse and the still-warm body, now waxy-yellow, with huge ribs exposed on both sides of the chest and giant holes in both sides of the neck. The nurse speculates that this is yet another murder in a Hispanic political struggle that has brought many such victims to Bellevue. He marvels at the extent of the wounds and repeats, "This guy was really blown away."

Midnight. A hysterical woman is hustled through the lobby into an examination room. It is the dead man's wife, and she is nearly delirious. "I know he's dead, I know he's dead," she screams over and over. Within moments the lobby is filled with anxious relatives of the victim, waiting for word on his condition. The police are everywhere asking questions, but most people say they saw nothing. One young woman says she heard six shots, two louder than the other four. At some point, word is passed that the man is, in fact, dead. Another woman breaks down in hysterics; everywhere young Hispanics are crying and comforting each other. Plainclothes detectives make a quick examination of the body, check on the time of pronouncement of death, and begin to ask questions, but the bereaved are too stunned to talk. The rest of the uninvolved people in the lobby stare dumbly, their injuries suddenly paling in light of a death.

12:30 A.M. A black man appears at the admissions desk and says he drank poison by mistake. He is told to have a seat. The ambulance brings in a young white woman, her head wrapped in white gauze. She is wailing terribly. A girl friend stands over her, crying, and a boyfriend clutches the injured woman's hands, saying, "I'm here, don't worry, I'm here." The victim has fallen downstairs at a friend's house. Attendants park her stretcher against the wall to wait for an examination room to clear. There are eight examination rooms and only three doctors. Unless you are truly an emergency, you will wait. One doctor is stitching up the eyebrow of a drunk who's been punched out. The friends of the woman who fell down the stairs glance up at the doctors anxiously, wondering why their friend isn't being treated faster.

1:10 A.M. A car pulls into the bay and a young Hispanic asks if a shooting victim has been brought here. The security guard blurts out, "He's dead." The young man is stunned. He peels his tires leaving the bay.

1:20 A.M. The young woman of the stairs is getting stitches in a small gash over her left eye when the same ambulance driver who brought in the gunshot victim delivers a man who has been stabbed in the back on East 3rd Street. Once again the trauma room goes from 0 to 60 in five seconds. The patient is drunk, which helps him endure the pain of having the catheter inserted through his penis into his bladder. Still he yells, "That hurts like a bastard," then adds sheepishly, "Excuse me, ladies." But he is not prepared for what comes next. An X-ray reveals a collapsed right lung. After just a shot of local anesthetic, the doctor slices open his side and inserts a long plastic tube. Internal bleeding had kept the lung pressed down and prevented it from reinflating. The tube releases the pressure. The ambulance driver says the cops grabbed the guy who ran the eight-inch blade into the victim's back. "That's not the one," says the man. "They got the wrong guy." A nurse reports that there is not much of the victim's type blood available at the hospital. One of the doctors says that's okay, he won't need surgery. Meanwhile blood pours from the man's knife wound and the tube in his side. As the nurses work, they chat about personal matters, yet they respond immediately to orders from either doctor. "How ya doin'?" the doctor asks the patient. "Okay," he says. His blood spatters on the floor.

So it goes into the morning hours. A Valium overdose, a woman who fainted, a man who went through the windshield of his car. More overdoses. More drunks with split eyebrows and chins. The doctors and nurses work without complaint. "This is nothing, about normal, I'd say," concludes the head nurse. "No big deal."

Meanings and Values

1a.   What is the author's point of view? (See Guide to Terms: *Point of View.*)

   b.   How is this reflected by the tone? (Guide: *Style/Tone.*)

2a.   Does Simpson ever slip into sentimentality—a common failing when describing the scenes of death and tragedy? (Guide: *Sentimentality.*)

   b.   If so, where? If not, how does he avoid it?

3a.   Cite at least six facts learned from reading this piece that are told, not in general terms, but by specific, concrete details—e.g., that a high degree of cleanliness is maintained at Bellevue, illustrated by "the spotless white-walled lobby" (par. 3) and "the trauma room has been cleared and cleaned mercilessly" (par. 8).

b.   What are the advantages of having facts presented in this way?

Expository Techniques

1.   How do you think the author went about selecting details, from among the thousands that must have been available to him?

2a.   Do you consider the writing to be primarily objective or impressionistic?

b.   Clarify any apparent contradictions.

c.   What is the dominant impression, if any?

3.   What is the value of using a timed sequence in such a description?

4.   Does it seem to you that any of this description is excessive—i.e., unnecessary to the task at hand?

5a.   List, in skeletal form, the facts learned about the subject from reading the two-paragraph introduction.

b.   How well does it perform the three basic purposes of an introduction? (Guide: *Introductions*.)

6a.   What is the significance of the rhetorical question in paragraph 2? (Guide: *Rhetorical Questions*.)

b.   Why is it rhetorical?

7.   Is the short closing effective? (Guide: *Closings*.) Why, or why not?

Diction and Vocabulary

1a.   Cite the clichés in paragraphs 4, 5, 8, and 14. (Guide: *Clichés*.)

b.   What justification, if any, can you offer for their use?

2.   Cite the allusion in paragraph 2, and explain its meaning and source. (Guide: *Figures of Speech*.)

3a.   Simpson uses some slang and other colloquialisms. Cite as many of these as you can. (Guide: *Colloquial Expressions*.)

b.   Is their use justified? Why, or why not?

4.   Why is "alleged perpetrator" placed in quotation marks (par. 10)?

Suggestions for Writing and Discussion

1.   Explain why "neither battlefield nor Bedlam is a valid image" of the emergency room at Bellevue (pars. 1, 2).

2.   Do you think it is right and /or understandable that O.D.'s should be given lower priorities than "true emergencies" (par. 9)? Defend your views.

3.   If you have had a job that to the outsider might seem hectic or hazardous, or both, were the personnel also able to "chat about personal matters" while the work was in progress? What were the circumstances?

(NOTE: Suggestions for topics requiring development by use of DESCRIPTION follow.)

Writing Suggestions for Section 8
Description

1. Primarily by way of impressionistic description that focuses on a single dominant impression, show and explain the mood, or atmosphere, of one of the following:

   a. A country fair.
   b. A ball game.
   c. A rodeo.
   d. A wedding.
   e. A funeral.
   f. A busy store.
   g. A ghost town.
   h. A cave.
   i. A beach in summer (or winter).
   j. An antique shop.
   k. A party.
   l. A family dinner.
   m. A traffic jam.
   n. Reveille.
   o. An airport (or a bus depot).
   p. An automobile race (or a horse race).
   q. A home during one of its rush hours.
   r. The last night of Christmas shopping.
   s. A natural scene at a certain time of day.
   t. The campus at examination time.
   u. A certain person at a time of great emotion—e.g., joy, anger, grief.

2. Using objective description as your basic pattern, explain the functional qualities or the significance of one of the following:

   a. A house for sale.
   b. A public building.
   c. A dairy barn.
   d. An ideal workshop (or hobby room).
   e. An ideal garage.
   f. A fast-food restaurant.
   g. The layout of a town (or airport).
   h. The layout of a farm.
   i. A certain type of boat.

9

Using *Narration* as an Expository Technique

Attempts to classify the functions of narration seem certain to develop difficulties and end in arbitrary and sometimes fuzzy distinctions. These need not distress us, however, if we remember that narration remains narration—a factual or fictional report of a sequence of events—and that our only reason for trying to divide it into categories is to find some means of studying its uses.

In a sense, as we have already seen in Section 5, exposition by process analysis makes one important, if rather narrow, use of narration, since it explains in sequence how specific steps lead to completion of some process. At the other extreme is narration that has very little to do with exposition: the story itself is the important thing, and instead of a series of steps leading obviously to a completed act, events *develop* out of each other and build suspense, however mild, through some kind of conflict. This use of narration includes the novel and short story, as well as some news and sports reporting. Because we are studying exposition, however, we must avoid getting too involved with these uses of narration; they require special techniques, the study of which would require a whole course or, in fact, several courses.

Between the extremes of a very usable analysis of process and very intriguing narration for the story's sake—and often seeming to blur into one or the other—is narration for *explanation's* sake, to explain a concept that is more than process and that might have been explained by one of the other patterns of exposition. Here only the form is narrative; the function is expository.

Fortunately, the average student seldom needs to use narration for major explanatory purposes, as it has been used in each of the following selections. But to learn the handling of even minor or localized narration, the best procedure (short of taking several college courses, or at least one that concentrates on the narrative form) is simply to observe how successful writers use it to perform various functions. Localized narration can sometimes be helpful in developing any of the other major patterns of exposition—e.g., as in the Buckley essay (Section 1) or Catton's (Section 3).

The most common problems can be summarized as follows:

1. *Selection of details.* As in writing description, the user of narration always has far more details available than can or should be used. Good unity demands the selection of only those details that are most relevant to the purpose and the desired effect.

2. *Time order.* The writer can use straight chronology, relating events as they happen (the usual method in minor uses of narration), or the flashback method, leaving the sequence temporarily in order to go back and relate some now-significant happening of a time prior to the main action. If flashback is used, it should be deliberate and for a valid reason—not merely because the episode was neglected at the beginning.

3. *Transitions.* The lazy writer of narration is apt to resort to the transitional style of a three-year-old: ". . . and then we . . . and then she . . . and then we . . . ." Avoiding this style may tax the ingenuity, but invariably the result is worth the extra investment of time and thought.

4. *Point of view.* This is a large and complex subject if dealt with fully, as a course in narration would do. Briefly, however, the writer should decide at the beginning whether the reader is to experience the action through a character's eyes (and ears and brain) or from an overall, objective view. This decision makes a difference in how much can be told, whose thoughts or secret actions can be included. The writer must be consistent throughout the narrative and include only information that could logically be known through the adopted point of view.

5. *Dialogue.* Presumably the writer already knows the mechanics of using quotations. Beyond these, the problems are to make conversation as natural-sounding as possible and yet to keep it from rambling through many useless details—to keep the narrative moving forward by *means* of dialogue.

As in most patterns of writing, the use of expository narration is most likely to be successful if the writer constantly keeps the purpose and audience in mind, remembering that the only reason for using the method in the first place—for doing *any* writing—is to communicate ideas. Soundness, clarity, and interest are the best means of attaining this goal.

Sample Paragraph (Annotated)

The author has used a straight sequential time order and selected only those details that will carry the narrative forward.

The overall point of view is objective, not seen through the eyes of any of the characters. There is no dialogue.

("Kid": a colloquialism.)

The Valley was dense with fir when Joseph Casey brought his wife and eleven children upriver on a crude log raft. They landed in a storm on a gravel spit, but the raft broke up and headed, in pieces, back toward the sea with most of their belongings. But Joe Casey saved his tools, and the older boys built a cabin—not much of one, but the first house in Ilona Valley. After several trips back to the settlement for supplies, Casey managed to set up a sawmill, and from then on the family prospered. (Bayport was growing, providing a good market for lumber.) But Mrs. Casey was a city person and never got used to flies and babies. Soon after the youngest, little Ben, wandered off into the woods one day, never to be seen again, Lula Casey, now forty-six and sure she was pregnant again, became hysterical. Casey tried to be comforting: he patted her stomach and said the new kid would be a fine replacement for little lost Ben. This ended the shrieking; but sometime that night Lula got up, took the new oar-boat, and apparently rowed frantically for hours upstream, against the current. The boat came merrily back downstream, empty, passing the Casey place at sunrise. And days later the boys found the body in the backwa-

ter brush at the mouth of what later
was known as Suicide Creek.

Sample Paragraph (Narration)

For anyone who has looked up
from the sullen South Georgia shore
[island near Antarctica] towards the
soaring, razor-edged peaks and the
terrible chaos of glaciers topped by
swirling clouds and scoured by
mighty winds, the knowledge of the
crossing made by these three men
adds a wider dimension to an already
awe-inspiring sight. How they did it,
God only knows, but they crossed the
island in thirty-six hours. They were
fortunate that the weather held, although many times great banks of
fog rolled in from the open sea, creeping towards them over the snow and
threatening to obscure their way. Confronted by precipices of ice and walls
of rock they had often to retrace their
steps adding many miles to the journey. They walked almost without rest.
At one point they sat down in an icy
gully, the wind blowing the drift
around them, and so tired were they
that Worsely and Crean fell asleep immediately. Shackleton, barely able to
keep himself awake, realized that to
fall asleep under such conditions
would prove fatal. After five minutes
he woke the other two, saying that
they had slept for half an hour.

Edwin Mickleburgh, *Beyond the Frozen Sea: Visions of Antarctica*. New York: St. Martin's Press, 1987.

MARTIN GANSBERG

MARTIN GANSBERG, born in Brooklyn, New York, in 1920, received a Bachelor of Social Sciences degree from St. John's University. He has been an editor and reporter for the *New York Times* since 1942, including a three-year period as editor of its international edition in Paris. He also served on the faculty of Fairleigh Dickinson University. Gansberg has written for many magazines, including *Diplomat, Catholic Digest, Facts,* and *U.S. Lady.*

38 Who Saw Murder Didn't Call the Police

"38 Who Saw Murder . . ." was written for the *New York Times* in 1964, and for obvious reasons it has been anthologized frequently since then. Cast in a deceptively simple news style, it still provides material for serious thought, as well as a means of studying the use and technique of narration.

For more than half an hour 38 respectable, law-abiding citizens in Queens watched a killer stalk and stab a woman in three separate attacks in Kew Gardens. 1

Twice their chatter and the sudden glow of their bedroom lights interrupted him and frightened him off. Each time he returned, sought her out, and stabbed her again. Not one person telephoned the police during the assault; one witness called after the woman was dead. 2

That was two weeks ago today. 3

Still shocked is Assistant Chief Inspector Frederick M. Lussen, in charge of the borough's detectives and a veteran of 25 years of 4 homicide investigations. He can give a matter-of-fact recitation on many murders. But the Kew Gardens slaying baffles him—not because it is a murder, but because the "good people" failed to call the police.

"As we have reconstructed the crime," he said, "the assailant had three chances to kill this woman during a 35-minute period. He returned twice to complete the job. If we had been called when he first attacked, the woman might not be dead now."

This is what the police say happened beginning at 3:20 A.M. in the staid, middle-class, tree-lined Austin Street area:

Twenty-eight-year-old Catherine Genovese, who was called Kitty by almost everyone in the neighborhood, was returning home from her job as manager of a bar in Hollis. She parked her red Fiat in a lot adjacent to the Kew Gardens Long Island Rail Road Station, facing Mowbray Place. Like many residents of the neighborhood, she had parked there day after day since her arrival from Connecticut a year ago, although the railroad frowns on the practice.

She turned off the lights of her car, locked the door, and started to walk the 100 feet to the entrance of her apartment at 82–70 Austin Street, which is in a Tudor building, with stores in the first floor and apartments on the second.

The entrance to the apartment is in the rear of the building because the front is rented to retail stores. At night the quiet neighborhood is shrouded in the slumbering darkness that marks most residential areas.

Miss Genovese noticed a man at the far end of the lot, near a seven-story apartment house at 82–40 Austin Street. She halted. Then, nervously, she headed up Austin Street toward Lefferts Boulevard, where there is a call box to the 102nd Police Precinct in nearby Richmond Hill.

She got as far as a street light in front of a bookstore before the man grabbed her. She screamed. Lights went on in the 10-story apartment house at 82–67 Austin Street, which faces the bookstore. Windows slid open and voices punctuated the early-morning stillness.

Miss Genovese screamed: "Oh, my God, he stabbed me! Please help me! Please help me!"

From one of the upper windows in the apartment house, a man called down: "Let that girl alone!"

The assailant looked up at him, shrugged and walked down 14
Austin Street toward a white sedan parked a short distance away.
Miss Genovese struggled to her feet.

Lights went out. The killer returned to Miss Genovese, now 15
trying to make her way around the side of the building by the parking lot to get to her apartment. The assailant stabbed her again.

"I'm dying!" she shrieked. "I'm dying!" 16

Windows were opened again, and lights went on in many 17
apartments. The assailant got into his car and drove away. Miss
Genovese staggered to her feet. A city bus, Q–10, the Lefferts Boulevard line to Kennedy International Airport, passed. It was 3:35
A.M.

The assailant returned. By then, Miss Genovese had crawled 18
to the back of the building, where the freshly painted brown doors
to the apartment house held out hope for safety. The killer tried
the first door; she wasn't there. At the second door, 82–62 Austin
Street, he saw her slumped on the floor at the foot of the stairs.
He stabbed her a third time—fatally.

It was 3:50 by the time the police received their first call, from 19
a man who was a neighbor of Miss Genovese. In two minutes they
were at the scene. The neighbor, a 70-year-old woman, and
another woman were the only persons on the street. Nobody else
came forward.

The man explained that he had called the police after much 20
deliberation. He had phoned a friend in Nassau County for advice
and then he had crossed the roof of the building to the apartment
of the elderly woman to get her to make the call.

"I didn't want to get involved," he sheepishly told the police. 21

Six days later, the police arrested Winston Moseley, a 29-year- 22
old business-machine operator, and charged him with homicide.
Moseley had no previous record. He is married, has two children
and owns a home at 133–19 Sutter Avenue, South Ozone Park,
Queens. On Wednesday, a court committed him to Kings County
Hospital for psychiatric observation.

When questioned by the police, Moseley also said that he had 23
slain Mrs. Annie May Johnson, 24, of 146–12 133rd Avenue, Ja-
maica, on Feb. 29 and Barbara Kralik, 15, of 174–17 140th Avenue,
Springfield Gardens, last July. In the Kralik case, the police are
holding Alvin L. Mitchell, who is said to have confessed to that
slaying.

The police stressed how simple it would have been to have gotten in touch with them. "A phone call," said one of the detectives, "would have done it." The police may be reached by dialing "O" for operator or SPring 7–3100.

Today witnesses from the neighborhood, which is made up of one-family homes in the $35,000 to $60,000 range with the exception of the two apartment houses near the railroad station, find it difficult to explain why they didn't call the police.

A housewife, knowingly if quite casually, said, "We thought it was a lover's quarrel." A husband and wife both said, "Frankly, we were afraid." They seemed aware of the fact that events might have been different. A distraught woman, wiping her hands on her apron, said, "I didn't want my husband to get involved."

One couple, now willing to talk about that night, said they heard the first screams. The husband looked thoughtfully at the bookstore where the killer first grabbed Miss Genovese.

"We went to the window to see what was happening," he said, "but the light from our bedroom made it difficult to see the street." The wife, still apprehensive, added: "I put out the light and we were able to see better."

Asked why they hadn't called the police, she shrugged and replied: "I don't know."

A man peeked out from the slight opening in the doorway to his apartment and rattled off an account of the killer's second attack. Why hadn't he called the police at the time? "I was tired," he said without emotion. "I went back to bed."

It was 4:25 A.M. when the ambulance arrived to take the body of Miss Genovese. It drove off. "Then," a solemn police detective said, "the people came out."

Meanings and Values

1a. What is Gansberg's central (expository) theme?

 b. How might he have developed this theme without using narration at all? Specify what patterns of exposition he could have used instead.

 c. Would any of them have been as effective as narration *for the purpose?* Why, or why not?

2. Show how this selection could be used as an illustration in an ex-

planatory discussion of abstract and concrete writing. (See Guide to Terms: *Concrete/Abstract*.)

3a.   Why has this narrative account of old news (the murder made its only headlines in 1964) retained its significance to this day?

b.   Are you able to see in this event a paradigm of any larger condition or situation? If so, explain, using examples as needed to illustrate your ideas.

4.   If you have read Wolfe's essay (Sec. 4), do you think Dr. Hall would have been very surprised at this New York case of noninvolvement? Why, or why not?

Expository Techniques

1a.   What standard introductory technique is exemplified in the first paragraph? (Guide: *Introductions*.)

b.   How effective do you consider it?

c.   If you see anything ironic in the fact stated there, explain the irony. (Guide: *Irony*.)

2a.   Where does the main narration begin?

b.   What, then, is the function of the preceding paragraphs?

3a.   Study several of the paragraph transitions within the narration itself to determine Gansberg's method of advancing the time sequence (to avoid overuse of ''and then''). What is the technique?

b.   Is another needed? Why, or why not?

4a.   What possible reasons do you see for the predominant use of short paragraphs in this piece?

b.   Does this selection lose any effectiveness because of the short paragraphs?

5.   Undoubtedly, the author selected with care the few quotations from witnesses that he uses. What principle or principles do you think applied to his selection?

6.   Explain why you think the quotation from the ''solemn police detective'' was, or was not, deliberately and carefully chosen to conclude the piece. (Guide: *Closings*.)

7a.   Briefly identify the point of view of the writing. (Guide: *Point of View*.)

b.   Is it consistent throughout?

c.   Show the relation, as you see it, between this point of view and the author's apparent attitude toward his subject matter.

8a.   Does he permit himself any sentimentality? If so, where? (Guide: *Sentimentality*.)

b.   If not, specifically what might he have included that would have slipped into melodrama or sentimentality?

Diction and Vocabulary

1a.   Why do you think the author used no difficult words in this narration?

b.   Do you find the writing at all belittling to college people because of this fact? Why, or why not?

Suggestions for Writing and Discussion

1.   Use both developed and undeveloped examples to show the prevalence, among individuals, of an anti-involvement attitude today. Or, if you prefer, show that this accusation is unjustified.

2.   If this narration can be regarded as a paradigm (see question 3b of "Meanings and Values"), select one example from the larger subject and develop it on whatever theme you choose. Your example could be from international affairs, if you like (and if you don't mind becoming the center of a controversy)—e.g., the recent cries of "Murder!" from numerous small countries. If you prefer, go into more distant (and therefore less controversial) history for your example.

3.   If such a crime as the Genovese murder were happening in an area or a situation where police were not so instantly available, what do you think an observer should do about it? What would *you* do? Justify your stand fully.

(NOTE: Suggestions for topics requiring development by NARRATION are on page 312, at the end of this section.)

BRENDA PETERSON

BRENDA PETERSON, a novelist and essayist, was born in 1950 on a forest ranger station in the Sierra Nevada Mountains. As a child she lived in many different places, especially in the Southeast. Currently, she lives in Seattle. Peterson received a B.A. in 1972 from the University of California—Davis. From 1972 to 1976 she worked as an editorial assistant at the *New Yorker* magazine. She has taught creative writing at Arizona State University and now works as an environmental writer. Her first novel, *River of Light,* appeared in 1978, and her second, *Becoming the Enemy,* was published in 1988.

Stuff as Dreams Are Made On

"Stuff as Dreams Are Made On" first appeared in *The Weekly,* in Seattle, Washington. The essay is a particularly good example of the use of narration for expository purposes. Though the narrative is certainly interesting on its own, Peterson makes clear throughout the selection that her larger aim is to convey to readers an understanding of the patterns she sees governing our experiences.

The first time I believed that dream-life might be as important as   1
daily life was the year we lived across the street from the Atlantic Ocean and a dream saved my brother's life. I was 7 and shared a bedroom with my baby brother. At night, radiators steaming, ocean waves as intimate and steady as our own breathing, I'd lie in my little bed, one arm stretched out through the wooden bars of my brother's crib. In rhythm to a lullaby my grandfather had inherited from his mammy and passed along to me, I'd sing and pat my brother's small back like a miniature island across which

"Stuff as Dreams Are Made On" by Brenda Peterson from *The Weekly,* March 3, 1986. Reprinted by permission of the author.

soon both our dreams would stretch out and into some vast ocean
of sleep.

> *Sail, baby, sail*
> *Out across the sea*
> *Only don't forget to sail*
> *Back again to me*

I'd sing, pat that sweetly powdered back, and we'd both tack off
into the night wind.

But one night my brother drifted too far. Of course, I was far
away, too. I was in a dream that took much of its realistic detail
from the Revere Beach amusement park we passed every day on
our way to school in that run-down suburb of Boston. In the dream
was the same cockamamied roller coaster, the submarine sandwich
stand where we always squandered our allowances, and the Big
Tent.

The Big Tent was really big; in fact, it looked like the King-
dome. And I was even smaller than a child. I was more the size of
my infant brother. In my dream I flew straight into this Big Tent,
not bothering with a ticket; even in a dream it seemed this was the
wrong thing to do. A carnival barker called, "Everyone with tickets
can leave," and the crowd stampeded out. I soon saw why: A giant fat lady, kind of like a King Kong in pink tights and red polka-
dot panties, crashed into the Big Tent, making right for me. I gazed
up and saw the ceiling was now a wide, polka-dot whiteness de-
scending and I screamed until I couldn't breathe. Down, down
came the bottom and then I was snuffed out, suffocated by spa-
cious, spotted silk.

My screams summoned my father, who was immediately beside my bed. But then he started screaming, too. He threw my robe
toward me; it thwacked the air, its plaid wool wrapping around
my head, mummy-like. I couldn't hear what Father was yelling—
something about ice and the baby basin we used to give my
brother baths. Barefooted, I ran for the ice and basin, returning to
find my father holding my brother aloft. The baby was blue, naked, stretched flat and rigid; he was no longer a body, but a board
with familiar bumps.

Father laid my brother in the basin and packed him in three
trays of ice. To this day I cannot hear the sound of champagne

bottles in a bucket without wincing, because that was the sound of my brother's body convulsing under ice.

"Make your hand into a lobster claw," my father ordered and then he used my fingers like pincers to pull my brother's tongue out, holding it tightly. It felt like the time I'd unshelled a snail and been horrified to see that wobbly creature so very vulnerable without his hard, outer sheath; it hurt me to look at it for long.   6

But I could not help looking at my brother's body. He jerked with so much power I knew then that we must be more than a physical presence. For what moved through him, and by connection us, could only be called a great current. The only thing I'd ever felt as powerful as my baby brother's energy was an undertow that once took me until I breathed water. I had not died in the Atlantic Ocean undertow, nor did my brother from his sudden high fever's convulsion.   7

But the doctor said he would have died within minutes had it not been for my nightmare that woke Father.   8

"What did you dream, anyway?" the doctor asked as he lay a supple, still sleeping baby back in the crib. My brother was no longer blue; he even cooed in his sleep like a mourning dove.   9

"I dreamed the fat lady sat down on me," I said.   10

"You were suffocating, then?" the doctor asked in a calm voice. "Well, so was your brother." Then he explained about babies and swallowing tongues.   11

I didn't like all the details. I tuned the doctor out and went back to sleep, only to find the Big Tent waiting for me. But this time I climbed up a chair as high as a mountain. As the fat lady moved to sit down on me again I yelled up to her. She noticed me as she might a gnat, but she didn't sit down. Instead she leaned over, and her face, as big as a planet, loomed. Then she was laughing, crossing her tree-trunk arms as she waited for me to explain myself. I wasn't afraid anymore but I also didn't know how to talk to the fat lady with her way up there and me way down on my wooden plateau. So we both simply waited, one for the other.   12

For years the Big Tent and fat lady waited for me. Every October around the date of my brother's long-ago fever, I used to have the same nightmare.   13

From the age of 7 and that life-saving dream, I've developed the habit of asking myself questions before I go to bed at night,   14 hoping my dreams might answer. Once I asked a dreamy question about a potential lover and was told by a brusque dream friend, who vaguely resembled my biology teacher, Mrs. Chopsky, that I needed new socks because mine were so thick my feet didn't touch ground. Of course, Mrs. Chopsky was right—love, or the longing for it, had ungrounded me so that my dreams had to step right in and be more realistic.

Recently after many years' absence, the fat lady visited me again in my dreams. This time she was out of costume, out of the Big Tent. In fact, she was no longer the cartoon that my fear had first made of her. She was fully present and even though I was still smaller, I met her. I cannot say yet that I am comfortable with her, even in my dreams. I tell myself often that I am too small for the big picture, perhaps the Big Tent. But she will wait for me as she always has.

She waits for me the way I am learning to wait for myself before I take those conscious plunges into my unconscious depths, my own dreams. She waits for me much the way that the Atlantic Ocean waited all during long New England winters for us children to again enter her commanding waves, mindful of the undertow.

And when I think of dreaming, I believe that my dreams live alongside my daily life the way that ocean moved right across the busy street from our apartment house. We lived as children on the edge of infinity; we live as adults on the edge of our dreams. Perhaps we don't need any other vessel to go where we need to go. With sleep as our ship, we can sail, we can sail.

Meanings and Values

1a.   In your own words, summarize briefly the events of the night on which the author first dreamed of the Big Tent and the fat lady.

   b.   What events from other periods of time are also presented in the essay? Explain the relationship of these other events to the narrative presented in paragraphs 1–12.

2.   Where in the opening paragraph is the central theme of the essay stated? (See Guide to Terms: *Unity*.)

3a.   Explain what the author means when she says, "he jerked with so much power I knew then that we must be more than a physical presence. For what moved through him, and by connection us, could only be called a great current" (par. 7).

b.   Explain how these statements and the rest of paragraph 7 reinforce or extend the statement of the essay's central theme in paragraph 1.

c.   Would the author be likely to agree that dreams are simply fantasies, the products of our imaginations at work on materials provided by our emotions and daily experiences? Drawing on the essay, explain why you believe she would be likely to agree or disagree.

4a.   What does the fat lady symbolize? (Guide: *Symbol.*)

b.   What symbolic meanings does the author attribute to the Atlantic Ocean in paragraph 16?

c.   In what ways are the two symbols—the Fat Lady and the Atlantic Ocean—lined in the course of the essay?

Expository Techniques

1.   Where in the essay, in addition to paragraph 1, does the author discuss the central theme more or less directly?

2a.   What elements do the opening and closing paragraphs of this essay (pars. 1 and 17) have in common?

b.   What strategies does the author employ in the introduction? (Guide: *Introductions.*)

c.   In the conclusion? (Guide: *Closings.*)

3a.   In what ways do the episodes presented in paragraphs 13, 14, and 15 reinforce the central theme?

b.   Can they be considered as parts or extensions of the main narrative presented in pars. 1–12? Why? If not, how does the author prevent them from disrupting the unity of the essay? (Guide: *Unity.*)

Diction and Vocabulary

1a.   Identify the concrete details Peterson employs in paragraph 3 to create a vivid and dramatic picture of the fat lady. (Guide: *Concrete/Abstract.*)

b.   What figure of speech does she employ in this description? (Guide: *Figures of Speech.*)

2.   Discuss how the diction in paragraphs 4 and 5 contributes to the sense of urgency the author wishes to convey and to a sense of danger and horror in the episode. (Guide: *Diction.*)

3.   Identify the similes in paragraph 6 and discuss the likely effect on readers. (Guide: *Figures of Speech.*)

4a. What parallels in syntax and diction are there among paragraphs 1, 7, and 17? (Guide: *Syntax, Parallel Structure.*)

 b. What purposes do these parallels serve?

5. If you are unfamiliar with the meaning of any of the following words, consult your dictionary as necessary: cockamamied (par. 2); pincers (6); undertow (7); brusque (14).

Suggestions for Writing and Discussion

1. The interpretation of dreams interests many people. One good place to begin discussion is with a description of one or two of your dreams whose meaning you think you understand and that have helped you form at least a tentative idea of how to interpret dreams.

2. Traumatic events in childhood often shape our values and our ways of viewing the world. Choose one such event as the basis for an essay that conveys your outlook on people, events, or values.

3. Events involving siblings or close relatives often provide an excellent basis for narrative essays because we are close enough to the happenings to describe them in detail yet removed enough to be able to generalize about their meaning. Select an event you remember vividly and share its meaning with readers.

(NOTE: Suggestions for topics requiring development by NARRATION are on page 312, at the end of this section.)

GEORGE ORWELL

GEORGE ORWELL (1903–1950), whose real name was Eric Blair, was a British novelist and essayist, well known for his satire. He was born in India and educated at Eton in England; he was wounded while fighting in the Spanish Civil War. Later he wrote the books *Animal Farm* (1945), a satire on Soviet history, and *1984* (1949), a vivid picture of life in a projected totalitarian society. He was, however, also sharply aware of injustices in democratic societies and was consistently socialistic in his views. Many of Orwell's essays are collected in *Critical Essays* (1946), *Shooting an Elephant and Other Essays* (1950), and *Such, Such Were the Joys* (1953).

A Hanging

"A Hanging" is typical of Orwell's essays in its setting—Burma—and in its subtle but biting commentary on colonialism, on capital punishment, even on one aspect of human nature itself. Although he is ostensibly giving a straightforward account of an execution, the author masterfully uses descriptive details and dialogue to create atmosphere and sharply drawn characterizations. The essay gives concrete form to a social message that is often delivered much less effectively in abstract generalities.

It was in Burma, a sodden morning of the rains. A sickly light, like   1
yellow tinfoil, was slanting over the high walls into the jail yard.
We were waiting outside the condemned cells, a row of sheds
fronted with double bars, like small animal cages. Each cell measured about ten feet by ten and was quite bare within except for a
plank bed and a pot for drinking water. In some of them brown,

silent men were squatting at the inner bars, with their blankets draped round them. These were the condemned men, due to be hanged within the next week or two.

One prisoner had been brought out of his cell. He was a Hindu, a puny wisp of a man, with a shaven head and vague liquid eyes. He had a thick, sprouting mustache, absurdly too big for his body, rather like the mustache of a comic man on the films. Six tall Indian warders were guarding him and getting him ready for the gallows. Two of them stood by with rifles and fixed bayonets, while the others handcuffed him, passed a chain through his handcuffs and fixed it to their belts, and lashed his arms tight to his sides. They crowded very close about him, with their hands always on him in a careful, caressing grip, as though all the while feeling him to make sure he was there. It was like men handling a fish which is still alive and may jump back into the water. But he stood quite unresisting, yielding his arms limply to the ropes, as though he hardly noticed what was happening.

Eight o'clock struck and a bugle call, desolately thin in the wet air, floated from the distant barracks. The superintendent of the jail, who was standing apart from the rest of us, moodily prodding the gravel with his stick, raised his head at the sound. He was an army doctor, with a grey toothbrush mustache and a gruff voice. "For God's sake, hurry up, Francis," he said irritably. "The man ought to have been dead by this time. Aren't you ready yet?"

Francis, the head jailer, a fat Dravidian in a white drill suit and gold spectacles, waved his black hand. "Yes sir, yes sir," he bubbled. "All iss satisfactorily prepared. The hangman iss waiting. We shall proceed."

"Well, quick march, then. The prisoners can't get their breakfast till this job's over."

We set out for the gallows. Two warders marched on either side of the prisoner, with their rifles at the slope; two others marched close against him, gripping him by arm and shoulder, as though at once pushing and supporting him. The rest of us, magistrates and the like, followed behind. Suddenly, when we had gone ten yards, the procession stopped short without any order or warning. A dreadful thing had happened—a dog, come goodness knows whence, had appeared in the yard. It came bounding among us with a loud volley of barks and leapt round us wagging its whole body, wild with glee at finding so many human beings together. It was a large woolly dog, half Airedale, half pariah. For a moment it pranced around us, and then, before anyone could stop it, it had made a dash for the prisoner, and jumping up tried to lick his face. Everybody stood aghast, too taken aback even to grab the dog.

"Who let that bloody brute in here?" said the superintendent   7
angrily. "Catch it, someone!"

A warder detached from the escort, charged clumsily after the dog, but it danced and gambolled just out of his reach, taking everything as part of the game. A young Eurasian jailer picked up a handful of gravel and tried to stone the dog away, but it dodged the stones and came after us again. Its yaps echoed from the jail walls. The prisoner, in the grasp of the two warders, looked on incuriously, as though this was another formality of the hanging. It was several minutes before someone managed to catch the dog. Then we put my handkerchief through its collar and moved off once more, with the dog still straining and whimpering.

It was about forty yards to the gallows. I watched the bare   9
brown back of the prisoner marching in front of me. He walked clumsily with his bound arms, but quite steadily, with that bobbing gait of the Indian who never straightens his knees. At each step his muscles slid neatly into place, the lock of hair on his scalp danced up and down, his feet printed themselves on the wet gravel. And once, in spite of the men who gripped him by each shoulder, he stepped lightly aside to avoid a puddle on the path.

It is curious; but till that moment I had never realized what it   10
means to destroy a healthy, conscious man. When I saw the prisoner step aside to avoid the puddle, I saw the mystery, the unspeakable wrongness, of cutting a life short when it is in full tide. This man was not dying, he was alive just as we are alive. All the organs of his body were working—bowels digesting food, skin renewing itself, nails growing, tissues forming—all toiling away in solemn foolery. His nails would still be growing when he stood on the drop, when he was falling through the air with a tenth-of-a-second to live. His eyes saw the yellow gravel and the grey walls, and his brain still remembered, foresaw, reasoned—even about puddles. He and we were a party of men walking together, seeing, hearing, feeling, understanding the same world; and in two minutes, with a sudden snap, one of us would be gone—one mind less, one world less.

The gallows stood in a small yard, separate from the main grounds of the prison, and overgrown with tall prickly weeds. It was a brick erection like three sides of a shed, with planking on top, and above that two beams and a crossbar with the rope dangling. The hangman, a greyhaired convict in the white uniform of the prison, was waiting beside his machine. He greeted us with a servile crouch as we entered. At a word from Francis the two warders, gripping the prisoner more closely than ever, half led, half pushed him to the gallows and helped him clumsily up the ladder. Then the hangman climbed up and fixed the rope round the prisoner's neck.

We stood waiting, five yards away. The warders had formed in a rough circle round the gallows. And then, when the noose was fixed, the prisoner began crying out to his god. It was a high, reiterated cry of "Ram! Ram! Ram! Ram!" not urgent and fearful like a prayer or cry for help, but steady, rhythmical, almost like the tolling of a bell. The dog answered the sound with a whine. The hangman, still standing on the gallows, produced a small cotton bag like a flour bag and drew it down over the prisoner's face. But the sound, muffled by the cloth, still persisted, over and over again: "Ram! Ram! Ram! Ram! Ram!"

The hangman climbed down and stood ready, holding the lever. Minutes seemed to pass. The steady, muffled crying from the prisoner went on and on, "Ram! Ram! Ram!" never faltering for an instant. The superintendent, his head on his chest, was slowly poking the ground with his stick; perhaps he was counting the cries, allowing the prisoner a fixed number—fifty, perhaps, or a hundred. Everyone had changed colour. The Indians had gone grey like bad coffee, and one or two of the bayonets were wavering. We looked at the lashed, hooded man on the drop, and listened to his cries—each cry another second of life; the same thought was in all our minds; oh, kill him quickly, get it over, stop that abominable noise!

Suddenly the superintendent made up his mind. Throwing up his head he made a swift motion with his stick. "Chalo!" he shouted almost fiercely.

There was a clanking noise, and then dead silence. The prisoner had vanished, and the rope was twisting on itself. I let go of the dog, and it galloped immediately to the back of the gallows; but when it got there it stopped short, barked, and then retreated into a corner of the yard, where it stood among the weeds, looking timorously out at us. We went round the gallows to inspect the prisoner's body. He was dangling with his toes pointed straight downwards, very slowly revolving, as dead as a stone.

The superintendent reached out with his stick and poked the 16 bare brown body; it oscillated slightly. *"He's* all right," said the superintendent. He backed out from under the gallows, and blew out a deep breath. The moody look had gone out of his face quite suddenly. He glanced at his wrist-watch. "Eight minutes past eight. Well, that's all for this morning, thank God."

The warders unfixed bayonets and marched away. The dog, 17 sobered and conscious of having misbehaved itself, slipped after them. We walked out of the gallows yard, past the condemned cells with their waiting prisoners, into the big central yard of the prison. The convicts, under the command of warders armed with lathis, were already receiving their breakfast. They squatted in long rows, each man holding a tin pannikin, while two warders with buckets marched around ladling out rice; it seemed quite a homely, jolly scene, after the hanging. An enormous relief had come upon us now that the job was done. One felt an impulse to sing, to break into a run, to snigger. All at once everyone began chattering gaily.

The Eurasian boy walking beside me nodded towards the way 18 we had come, with a knowing smile: "Do you know, sir, our friend (he meant the dead man) when he heard his appeal had been dismissed, he pissed on the floor of his cell. From fright. Kindly take one of my cigarettes, sir. Do you not admire my new silver case, sir? From the boxwallah, two rupees eight annas. Classy European style."

Several people laughed—at what, nobody seemed certain. 19

Francis was walking by the superintendent, talking garru- 20 lously: "Well, sir, all has passed off with the utmost satisfactoriness. It was all finished—flick! Like that. It iss not always so—oah, no! I have known cases where the doctor wass obliged to go beneath the gallows and pull the prissoner's legs to ensure decease. Most disagreeable!"

"Wriggling about, eh? That's bad," said the superintendent. 21

"Ach, sir, it iss worse when they become refractory! One man, I recall, clung to the bars of hiss cage when we went to take him out. You will scarcely credit, sir, that it took six warders to dislodge him, three pulling at each leg. We reasoned with him, 'My dear fellow,' we said, 'think of all the pain and trouble you are causing to us!' But no, he would not listen! Ach, he wass very troublesome!''

I found that I was laughing quite loudly. Everyone was laughing. Even the superintendent grinned in a tolerant way. "You'd better all come out and have a drink," he said quite genially. "I've got a bottle of whisky in the car. We could do with it."

We went through the big double gates of the prison into the road. "Pulling at his legs!" exclaimed a Burmese magistrate suddenly, and burst into a loud chuckling. We all began laughing again. At that moment Francis' anecdote seemed extraordinarily funny. We all had a drink together, native and European alike, quite amicably. The dead man was a hundred yards away.

Meanings and Values

1. What was the real reason for the superintendent's impatience?
2. On first impression it may have seemed that the author gave undue attention to the dog's role in this narrative.
   a. Why was the episode such a "dreadful thing" (par. 6)?
   b. Why did the author think it worth noting that the dog was excited at "finding so many human beings together"?
   c. Of what significance was the dog's trying to lick the prisoner's face?
3. Explain how the prisoner's stepping around a puddle could have given the author a new insight into what was about to happen (par. 10).
4. Why was there so much talking and laughing after the hanging was finished?
5. What is the broadest meaning of Orwell's last sentence?

Expository Techniques

1. Cite examples of both objective and impressionistic description in the first paragraph.
2a. What is the primary time order used in this narrative?
   b. If there are any exceptions, state where.
3. Considering the relatively few words devoted to them, several of the characterizations in this essay are remarkably vivid—a result,

obviously, of highly discriminating selection of details from the multitude of those that must have been available to the author. For each of the following people, list the character traits that we can observe, and state whether these impressions come to us through details of description, action, and/or dialogue.

a. The prisoner.

b. The superintendent.

c. Francis.

d. The Eurasian boy.

4a. Why do you think the author included so many details of the preparation of the prisoner (par. 2)?

b. Why did he include so many details about the dog and his actions?

c. What is gained by the assortment of details in paragraph 10?

5. The tone of writing such as this can easily slip into sentimentality or even melodrama without the author's realizing what is happening. (See Guide to Terms: *Sentimentality*.) Select three places in this narrative where a less-skilled writer might have had such trouble, and note by what restraints Orwell prevented sentimentality.

Diction and Vocabulary

1. A noteworthy element of Orwell's style is his occasional use of figurative language. Cite six metaphors and similes, and comment on their choice and effectiveness.

2. Orwell was always concerned with the precise effects that words could give to meaning and style.

a. Cite at least six nonfigurative words that seem to you particularly well chosen for their purpose.

b. Show what their careful selection contributes to the description of atmosphere or to the subtle meanings of the author.

c. How is this attention to diction a matter of style? (Guide: *Style/ Tone.*)

Suggestions for Writing and Discussion

1. Select *one* of the points of controversy over capital punishment and present both sides with equal objectivity.

2. Consider the dilemma of a person whose "duty" seems to require one course of action and "conscience" just the opposite course. Use concrete illustrations to show how serious such dilemmas can be.

3.   Examine the moral right, or lack of it, of the people of one country to impose their laws on the people of another country.

4.   Discuss one benefit of colonialism to the people colonized. Use specific illustrations.

5.   Explain how, in your own experience, a seemingly minor incident led to much deeper insight into a matter not fully understood before.

(NOTE: Suggestions for topics requiring development by NARRATION are on page 312, at the end of this section.)

ANNIE DILLARD

ANNIE DILLARD was born in 1945 in Pittsburgh, Pennsylvania.
She received a B.A. and an M.A. from Hollins College. Formerly
a professor of English at Western Washington State College, she
now teaches at Wesleyan University. Her book, *Pilgrim at Tinker
Creek* (1974), based on her experiences living in the Roanoke Valley of Virginia, was awarded the Pulitzer Prize for general nonfiction. She has also published a book of poems, *Tickets for a
Prayer Wheel* (1974); two volumes of literary criticism, *Living by
Fiction* (1982) and *Conversations with Chinese Writers* (1984); and
two collections of brief narratives and meditations on nature and
experience, *Holy the Firm* (1978) and *Teaching a Stone to Talk*
(1982). Her most recent book is *An American Childhood* (1987).

Prologue

In this essay, a chapter from the opening section of *An American
Childhood*, Dillard uses parallel narratives to show how she and
her father awoke to consciousness of themselves and their values. Such awakenings are often turning points, but as this essay
shows through comparison, their meaning often differs from
person to person.

In 1955, when I was ten, my father's reading went to his head.   1

My father's reading during that time, and for many years be-   2
fore and after, consisted for the most part of *Life on the Mississippi*.
He was a young executive in the old family firm, American Standard; sometimes he traveled alone on business. Traveling, he
checked into a hotel, found a bookstore, and chose for the night's
reading, after what I fancy to have been long deliberation, yet
another copy of *Life on the Mississippi*. He brought all these books
home. There were dozens of copies of *Life on the Mississippi* on the
living-room shelves. From time to time, I read one.

Down the Mississippi hazarded the cub riverboat pilot, down the Mississippi from St. Louis to New Orleans. His chief, the pilot Mr. Bixby, taught him how to lay the boat in her marks and dart between points; he learned to pick a way fastidiously inside a certain snag and outside a shifting shoal in the black dark; he learned to clamber down a memorized channel in his head. On tricky crossings the leadsmen sang out the soundings, so familiar I seemed to have heard them the length of my life: "Mark four! . . . Quarter-less-four! . . . Half three! . . . Mark three! . . . Quarter-less . . ." It was an old story.

When all this reading went to my father's head, he took action. From Pittsburgh he went down the river. Although no one else that our family knew kept a boat on the Allegheny River, our father did, and now he was going all the way with it. He quit the firm his great-grandfather had founded a hundred years earlier down the river at his family's seat in Louisville, Kentucky; he sold his own holdings in the firm. He was taking off for New Orleans.

New Orleans was the source of the music he loved: Dixieland jazz, O Dixieland. In New Orleans men would blow it in the air and beat it underfoot, the music that hustled and snapped, the music whose zip matched his when he was a man-about-town at home in Pittsburgh, working for the family firm; the music he tapped his foot to when he was a man-about-town in New York for a few years after college working for the family firm by day and by night hanging out at Jimmy Ryan's on Fifty-second Street with Zutty Singleton, the black drummer who befriended him, and the rest of the house band. A certain kind of Dixieland suited him best. They played it at Jimmy Ryan's, and Pee Wee Russell and Eddie Condon played it too—New Orleans Dixieland chilled a bit by its journey up the river, and smoothed by its sojourns in Chicago and New York.

Back in New Orleans where he was headed they would play the old stuff, the hot, rough stuff—bastardized for tourists maybe, but still the big and muddy source of it all. Back in New Orleans where he was headed the music would smell like the river itself, maybe, like a thicker, older version of the Allegheny River at Pittsburgh, where he heard the music beat in the roar of his boat's inboard motor; like a thicker, older version of the wide Ohio River at Louisville, Kentucky, where at his family's summer house he'd spent his boyhood summers mucking about in boats.

Getting ready for the trip one Saturday, he roamed around 7 our big brick house snapping his fingers. He had put a record on: Sharkey Bonano, "Li'l Liza Jane." I was reading Robert Louis Stevenson on the sunporch: *Kidnapped.* I looked up from my book and saw him outside; he had wandered out to the lawn and was standing in the wind between the buckeye trees and looking up at what must have been a small patch of wild sky. Old Low-Pockets. He was six feet four, all lanky and leggy; he had thick brown hair and shaggy brows, and a mild and dreamy expression in his blue eyes.

When our mother met Frank Doak, he was twenty-seven: 8 witty, boyish, bookish, unsnobbish, a good dancer. He had grown up an only child in Pittsburgh, attended Shady Side Academy, and Washington and Jefferson College in Pennsylvania, where he studied history. He was a lapsed Presbyterian and a believing Republican. "Books make the man," read the blue bookplate in all his books. "Frank Doak." The bookplate's woodcut showed a square-rigged ship under way in a steep following sea. Father had hung around jazz in New York, and halfheartedly played the drums; he had smoked marijuana, written poems, begun a novel, painted in oils, imagined a career as a riverboat pilot, and acted for more than ten seasons in amateur and small-time professional theater. At American Standard, Amstan Division, he was the personnel manager.

But not for long, and never again; Mother told us he was quit- 9 ting to go down the river. I was sorry he'd be leaving the Manufacturers' Building downtown. From his office on the fourteenth floor, he often saw suicides, which he reported at dinner. The suicides grieved him, but they thrilled us kids. My sister Amy was seven.

People jumped from the Sixth Street bridge into the Allegheny 10 River. Because the bridge was low, they shinnied all the way up the steel suspension cables to the bridge towers before they jumped. Father saw them from his desk in silhouette, far away. A man vigorously climbed a slanting cable. He slowed near the top, where the cables hung almost vertically; he paused on the stone tower, seeming to sway against the sky, high over the bridge and the river below. Priests, firemen, and others—presumably family members or passersby—gathered on the bridge. In about half the cases, Father said, these people talked the suicide down. The ones who jumped kicked off from the tower so they'd miss the bridge, and fell tumbling a long way down.

Pittsburgh was a cheerful town, and had far fewer suicides than most other cities its size. Yet people jumped so often that Father and his colleagues on the fourteenth floor had a betting pool going. They guessed the date and time of day the next jumper would appear. If a man got talked down before he jumped, he still counted for the betting pool, thank God; no manager of American Standard ever wanted to hope, even in the smallest part of himself, that the fellow would go ahead and jump. Father said he and the other men used to gather at the biggest window and holler, ''No! Don't do it, buddy, don't!'' Now he was leaving American Standard to go down the river, and he was a couple of bucks in the hole.

While I was reading *Kidnapped* on this Saturday morning, I heard him come inside and roam from the kitchen to the pantry to the bar, to the dining room, the living room, and the sunporch, snapping his fingers. He was snapping the fingers of both hands, and shaking his head, to the record—''Li'l Liza Jane''—the sound that was beating, big and jivey, all over the house. He walked lightly, long-legged, like a soft-shoe hoofer barely in touch with the floor. When he played the drums, he played lightly, coming down soft with the steel brushes that sounded like a Slinky falling, not making the beat but just sizzling along with it. He wandered into the sunporch, unseeing; he was snapping his fingers lightly, too, as if he were feeling between them a fine layer of Mississippi silt. The big buckeyes outside the glass sunporch walls were waving.

A week later, he bade a cheerful farewell to us—to Mother, who had encouraged him, to us oblivious daughters, ten and seven, and to the new baby girl, six months old. He loaded his twenty-four-foot cabin cruiser with canned food, pushed off from the dock of the wretched boat club that Mother hated, and pointed his bow downstream, down the Allegheny River. From there it was only a few miles to the Ohio River at Pittsburgh's point, where the

Monongahela came in. He wore on westward down the Ohio; he watched West Virginia float past his port bow and Ohio past his starboard. It was 138 river miles to New Martinsville, West Virginia, where he lingered for some races. Back on the move, he tied up nights at club docks he'd seen on the charts; he poured himself water for drinks from dockside hoses. By day he rode through locks, twenty of them in all. He conversed with the lockmasters, those lone men who paced silhouetted in overalls on the concrete lock-chamber walls and threw the big switches that flooded or drained the locks: "Hello, up there!" "So long, down there!"

He continued down the river along the Kentucky border with Ohio, bumping down the locks. He passed through Cincinnati. He moved along down the Kentucky border with Indiana. After 640 miles of river travel, he reached Louisville, Kentucky. There he visited relatives at their summer house on the river. 14

It was a long way to New Orleans, at this rate another couple of months. He was finding the river lonesome. It got dark too early. It was September; people had abandoned their pleasure boats for the season; their children were back in school. There were no old salts on the docks talking river talk. People weren't so friendly as they were in Pittsburgh. There was no music except the dreary yacht-club jukeboxes playing "How Much Is That Doggie in the Window?" Jazz had come up the river once and for all; it wasn't still coming, he couldn't hear it across the water at night rambling and blowing and banging along high and tuneful, sneaking upstream to Chicago to get educated. He wasn't free so much as loose. He was living alone on beans in a boat and having witless conversations with lockmasters. He mailed out sad postcards. 15

From phone booths all down the Ohio River he talked to Mother. She told him that she was lonesome, too, and that three children—maid and nanny or no—were a handful. She said, further, that people were starting to talk. She knew Father couldn't bear people's talking. For all his dreaminess, he prized respectability above all; it was our young mother, whose circumstances bespoke such dignity, who loved to shock the world. After only six weeks, then—on the Ohio River at Louisville—he sold the boat and flew home. 16

I was just waking up then, just barely. Other things were changing. The highly entertaining new baby, Molly, had taken up residence in a former guest room. The great outer world hove into 17 view and began to fill with things that had apparently been there all along: mineralogy, detective work, lepidopterology, ponds and streams, flying, society. My younger sister Amy and I were to start at private school that year: the Ellis School, on Fifth Avenue. I would start dancing school.

Children ten years old wake up and find themselves here, discover themselves to have been here all along; is this sad? They wake like sleepwalkers, in full stride; they wake like people brought back from cardiac arrest or from drowning: *in medias res,* surrounded by familiar people and objects, equipped with a hundred skills. They know the neighborhood, they can read and write English, they are old hands at the commonplace mysteries, and yet they feel themselves to have just stepped off the boat, just converged with their bodies, just flown down from a trance, to lodge in an eerily familiar life already well under way.

I woke in bits, like all children, piecemeal over the years. I discovered myself and the world, and forgot them, and discovered them again. I woke at intervals until, by that September when Father went down the river, the intervals of waking tipped the scales, and I was more often awake than not. I noticed this process of waking, and predicted with terrifying logic that one of these years not far away I would be awake continuously and never slip back, and never be free of myself again.

Consciousness converges with the child as a landing tern touches the outspread feet of its shadow on the sand: precisely, toe hits toe. The tern folds its wings to sit; its shadow dips and spreads over the sand to meet and cup its breast.

Like any child, I slid into myself perfectly fitted, as a diver meets her reflection in a pool. Her fingertips enter the fingertips on the water, her wrists slide up her arms. The diver wraps herself in her reflection wholly, sealing it at the toes, and wears it as she climbs rising from the pool, and ever after.

I never woke, at first, without recalling, chilled, all those other waking times, those similar stark views from similarly lighted precipices: dizzying precipices from which the distant, glittering world revealed itself as a brooding and separated scene—and so let slip a queer implication, that I myself was both observer and observable, and so a possible object of my own humming awareness.

Whenever I stepped into the porcelain bathtub, the bath's hot water sent a shock traveling up my bones. The skin on my arms pricked up, and the hair rose on the back of my skull. I saw my own firm foot press the tub, and the pale shadows waver over it, as if I were looking down from the sky and remembering this scene forever. The skin on my face tightened, as it had always done whenever I stepped into the tub, and remembering it all drew a swinging line, loops connecting the dots, all the way back. You again.

Meanings and Values

1. How do the father's reading activities (pars. 2 and 3) contrast with his life as a businessman?

2. In the context of the essay, what does this phrase mean: "my father's reading went to his head" (par. 1)?

3. Tell how each of the following reacted (or would be likely to react) to the actions of the father in leaving his young family for a trip on the river:

   a. His wife.

   b. The author as a child.

   c. Neighbors and friends (i.e., "people" [par. 16]).

   d. Most readers of the essay.

   e. The author as an adult.

4. In what ways is the story of the "jumpers" (pars. 9–11) parallel to and different from the narrative of the father?

5. In your own words, summarize what you believe the author wants us to think her father learned about himself and his values from the trip on the river.

Expository Techniques

1a. Which part of this essay is devoted primarily to the narrative of the father?

  b. To the narrative of the author as a child?

2a. From what narrative are the events presented in paragraph 3 taken?

  b. Which paragraphs other than paragraph 3 provide background information for the father's story (including events prior to the main narrative)?

3. Which paragraphs in the story of the author as a child are devoted mainly to presenting events and which to generalizing about them? Which mix telling and generalizing?

4. Discuss how the author manages in paragraph 16 to explain her father's reasons for returning home and to suggest what he had learned about himself—without generalizing directly about either.

5. From what point of view or points of view is this essay narrated? Be ready to provide examples to support your answer. (See Guide to Terms: *Point of View* and the introduction to Section 9, p. 280.)

Diction and Vocabulary

1a. Compare the diction in paragraphs 15 and 19. In which is the diction more concrete and specific? More abstract and general? Identify words and phrases that support your conclusion. (Guide: *Concrete/Abstract, Specific/General.*)

 b. Paragraph 15 is part of the narrative of the author's father and paragraph 19 is from the narrative of the author as a child. What differences in the purposes of these two segments of the essay are reflected in their diction? (Guide: *Purpose.*)

2. Identify the similes in paragraphs 20 and 21 and discuss the ways in which the author's use of these figures of speech are appropriate or inappropriate to her purpose in these sections of the essay. (Guide: *Purpose.*)

3. Do some of the details in the conclusion (par. 22) call up memories of your own experiences, either as a child or as an adult? Describe your memories briefly and identify the details that prompt them.

4a. What does the term *in medias res* (par. 18) mean? Does its use here add to or detract from the effectiveness of the writing?

 b. If you do not know the meaning of any of the following terms, look them up in the dictionary: hazarded, marks, shoal, soundings (par. 3); bastardized (6); hoofer (12); salts (15); hove, lepidopterology (17); tern (20).

Suggestions for Writing and Discussion

1. Our earliest childhood memories are often of events that involve a growing awareness of ourselves and others. Such events and what they reveal about the way humans develop can make good subjects for expository essays.

2. How are readers who grew up in relatively affluent surroundings likely to respond to this essay? How are readers who grew up in families with modest means (or less) likely to respond? Does the

author take into account the social class of her family in recreating or commenting on the events in the narrative?

3.   What common activities do men undertake to escape from responsibilities or act out in middle age the dreams of their youth? What common activities do women undertake?

(NOTE: Suggestions for topics requiring development by NARRATION follow.)

Writing Suggestions for Section 9
Narration

Use narration as at least a partial pattern (e.g., in developed examples or in comparison) for one of the following expository themes or another suggested by them. Avoid the isolated personal account that has little broader significance. Remember, too, that development of the essay should itself make your point, without excessive moralizing.

1. People can still succeed without a college education.
2. The frontiers are not all gone.
3. When people succeed in communicating, they can learn to get along with each other.
4. Even with "careful" use of capital punishment, innocent people can be executed.
5. Sports don't always build character.
6. Physical danger can make us more aware of ourselves and our values.
7. Conditioning to the realities of the job is as important to the police officer as professional training.
8. It is possible for employees themselves to determine when they have reached their highest level of competence.
9. Wartime massacres are not a new development.
10. "Date rape" or sexual harassment on the job are devastating and generally unexpected.
11. Both heredity and environment shape personality.
12. Physical and mental handicaps can be overcome in some ways, but they are still a burden.
13. Toxic wastes pose a problem for many communities.
14. Hunting is a worthwhile and challenging sport.
15. Lack of money places considerable stress on a family or a marriage.
16. Exercise can become an obsession.
17. People who grow up in affluent surroundings don't understand what it is like to worry about money, to be hungry, or to live in a dangerous neighborhood.
18. Some jobs are simply degrading, either because of the work or because of the fellow workers.

10

Reasoning by Use
of *Induction* and *Deduction*

Induction and deduction, important as they are in argumentation, may also be useful methods of exposition. They are often used simply to explain a stand or conclusion, without any effort or need to win converts.

Induction is the process by which we accumulate evidence until, at some point, we can make the "inductive leap" and thus reach a useful *generalization.* The science laboratory employs this technique; hundreds of tests and experiments and analyses may be required before the scientist will generalize, for instance, that a disease is caused by a certain virus. It is also the primary technique of the prosecuting attorney who presents pieces of inductive evidence, asking the jury to make the inductive leap and conclude that the accused did indeed kill the victim.

Even the commonplace "process of elimination" also may be considered a form of induction. If it can be shown, for instance, that "A" does not have the strength to swing the murder weapon, that "B" was in a drunken sleep at the time of the crime, and that "C" had recently become blind and could not have found her way to the boathouse, then we may be ready for the inductive leap, that the foul deed must have been committed by "X," the only other person on the island. (The use of this kind of induction implies an added obligation, of course, to make certain that all the possibilities but *one* have been eliminated: if we fail to note that "Y," a visitor on a neighboring island, and his boat were unaccounted for that evening, then our conclusion is invalid.)

On a more personal level, of course, we all learned to use induction at a very early age. We may have disliked the taste of orange juice, winter squash, and carrots, and we were not too young to make a generalization: orange-colored food tastes bad.

Whereas induction is the method of reaching a potentially useful generalization (for example, Professor Melville always gives an "F" to students who cut his class three times), *deduction* is the method of *using* such a generality, now accepted as a fact (for example, if we cut this class again today, we will get an "F"). Working from a generalization already formulated—by ourselves, by someone else, or by tradition—we may deduce that a specific thing or circumstance that fits into the generality will act the same. Hence, if convinced that orange-colored food tastes bad, we will be reluctant to try pumpkin pie.

A personnel manager may have discovered over the years that electronics majors from Central College are invariably well trained in their field. His induction may have been based on the evidence of observations, records, and the opinions of fellow Rotary members; and, perhaps without realizing it, he has made the usable generalization about the training of Central College electronics majors. Later, when he has an application from Nancy Ortega, a graduate of Central College, his *d*eductive process will probably work as follows: Central College turns out well-trained electronics majors; Ortega was trained at Central; therefore, Ortega must be well trained. Here he has used a generalization to apply to a specific case.

Put in this simplified form (which, in writing, it seldom is),[1] the deductive process is also called a "syllogism"—with the beginning generality known as the "major premise" and the specific that fits into the generality known as the "minor premise." For example:

---

[1]Neither induction nor deduction is confined to a particular order of presentation. If we use specific evidence to *reach* a generalization, it is induction regardless of which part is stated first in a written or spoken account. (Very likely, both a prosecutor's opening remarks and a medical researcher's written reports first present their generalizations and then the inductive evidence by which they have been reached.) But if we use a generality in which to *place* a specific, it is still deduction, however stated. (Hence the reasoning of the personnel manager might be: "Ortega must be well trained because she was educated at C.C., and there's where they really know how to do it.")

Major premise—Orange-colored food is not fit to eat.
Minor premise—Pumpkin pie is orange-colored.
Conclusion—Pumpkin pie is not fit to eat.

Frequently, however, the validity of one or both of the premises may be questionable, and here is one of the functions of *induction*: to give needed support—with evidence such as opinions of experts, statistics, and results of experiments or surveys—to the *deductive* syllogism, whether stated or implied. Deductive reasoning, in whatever form presented, is only as sound as both its premises. The child's conviction that orange-colored food is not fit to eat was not necessarily true; therefore, the conclusion about pumpkin pie is not very trustworthy. The other conclusions, that we will automatically get an "F" by cutting Melville's class and that Ortega is well trained in electronics, can be only as reliable as the original generalizations that were used as deductive premises. If the generalizations themselves were based on flimsy or insufficient evidence, any future deduction using them is likely to be erroneous.

These two faults are common in induction: (1) the use of *flimsy* evidence—mere opinion, hearsay, or analogy, none of which can support a valid generalization—instead of verified facts or opinions of reliable authorities; and (2) the use of *too little* evidence, leading to a premature inductive leap.

The amount of evidence needed in any situation depends, of course, on purpose and audience. The success of two Central College graduates might be enough to convince some careless personnel director that all Central electronics graduates would be good employees, but two laboratory tests would not convince medical researchers that they had learned anything worthwhile about a disease-causing virus. The authors of the Declaration of Independence, in justifying their argument for rebellion to a wide variety of readers and listeners, explained why they considered the king tyrannical, by listing twenty-eight despotic acts of his government, each of which was a verifiable fact, a matter of public record.

Induction and deduction are highly logical processes, and any trace of weakness can seriously undermine an exposition that depends on their reasonableness. (Such weakness can, of course, be even more disastrous in argument.) Although no induction or deduction ever reaches absolute, 100 percent certainty, we should try to get from these methods as high a degree of *probability* as possible. (We can never positively prove, for instance, that the sun will rise in the east tomorrow, but thousands of years of inductive observation and theorizing make the fact extremely probable—and certainly sound enough for any working generalization.)

Students using induction and deduction in compositions, essay examinations, or term papers—showing that Stephen Crane was a naturalistic writer, or that our national policies are unfair to revolutionary movements—should always assume that they will have a skeptical audience that wants to know the logical basis for *all* generalizations and conclusions.

Sample Paragraph (Annotated)

The basic structure of the professor's article is *inductive*.

Each of these *inductive generalizations* helps explain the residents' satisfaction with life in the Valley.

(A full report needs to contain much more evidence, of course, in order to be convincing.)

Ever since Joseph Casey and his family built the first house in Ilona Valley, outsiders (and some residents, too) have wondered why people enjoy living here. Just last year, a professor from Bayport State College wrote an article for the Casey *Enquirer* explaining how people from the Valley feel about the area. Drawing on interviews with both new and longtime residents, he reported that most people like the physical beauty of the Valley and the many opportunities for hiking and fishing. Many of them admit that a big city like Bayport offers a lot more in the way of social and cultural activities, but they claim that performances of the Casey Community Symphony and the Riverton Chorus, plus the Valley Fair, dances sponsored by local groups, and the Summerfest give them plenty to do throughout the year. People with families praise the traditional values of Valley society, and just about everyone thinks the clean water and air of the region make it a healthful place to live. Most of all, residents like the Valley because its relative isolation has created a close-knit community where people can depend on each other.

The last inductive generalization becomes the *major premise* for a *deductive syllogism*.

Ilona Valley's special qualities, the professor concluded, depend upon its isolation, and he warned that since this

Minor premise.

isolation would be destroyed by the new four-lane highway the State is once again proposing, Valley resi-

Conclusion.

dents should continue to oppose the highway as effectively as they have in the past.

(NOTE: This is formal writing, with a logical progression of ideas and no use of such informalities as first-person pronouns, contractions, or colloquial expressions.)

Sample Paragraph (Induction)

Roaming the site, I can't help noticing that when men start cooking, the hardware gets complicated. Custom-built cookers—massive contraptions of cast iron and stainless steel—may cost $15,000 or more; they incorporate the team's barbecue philosophy. "We burn straight hickory under a baffle," Jim Garts, coleader of the Hogaholics, points out as he gingerly opens a scorching firebox that vents smoke across a water tray beneath a 4-by-8-foot grill. It's built on a trailer the size of a mobile home. Other cookers have been fashioned from a marine diesel engine; from a '76 Datsun, with grilling racks instead of front seats, a chimney above the dash, and coals under the hood; and as a 15-foot version of Elvis Presley's guitar (by the Graceland Love Me Tenderloins). It's awesome ironmongery.

Daniel Cohen, "Cooking-off for fame and fortune," *Smithsonian*, September 1988, p. 132.

Sample Paragraph (Deduction)

It is an everyday fact of life that competitors producing similar products assert that their own goods or services are better than those of their rivals. Every product advertised—from pain relievers to fried chicken—is claimed to be better than its competitors. If all these companies sued for libel, the courts would be so overloaded with cases that they would grind to a halt. For years courts dismissed criticisms of businesses, products, and performances as expressions of opinion. When a restaurant owner sued a guidebook to New York restaurants for giving his establishment a bad review, he won a $20,000 verdict in compensatory damages and $5 in punitive damages. But this was overturned by the court of appeals. The court held that, with the exception of one item, the allegedly libelous statements were expressions of opinion, not fact. Among these statements were that the "dumplings, on our visit, resembled bad ravioli . . . chicken with chili was rubbery and the rice . . . totally insipid. . . ." Obviously, it would be impossible to prove the nature of the food served at that particular meal. What is tender to one palate may be rubbery to another.

The one misstatement of fact, that the Peking duck was served in one dish instead of three, was in my opinion, a minor and insignificant part of the entire review. Had the review of the restaurant been considered as a whole . . . , this small misstatement of fact would have been treated as *de minimis*. That is a well-established doctrine requiring that minor matters not be considered by the courts. In this case, the court held that the restaurant was a public figure and had failed to prove actual malice.

LESTER C. THUROW

LESTER C. THUROW, born in 1938 in Montana, graduated from
Williams College (magna cum laude), Balliol College, Oxford
(where he earned an M.A.), and Harvard University (M.A. and
Ph.D.). He has taught economics and done research at Harvard,
the Kennedy School of Government, and the Institute of Politics, and is currently dean of the Sloan School of Management
at the Massachusetts Institute of Technology. He has been a TV
commentator, has testified before Congress, and has served as
consultant to government agencies and private corporations. He
has written numerous books and articles for professional journals and popular magazines, including *The Nation* and *Newsweek*.

Why Women Are Paid Less Than Men

"Why Women Are Paid Less Than Men" uses a form of induction to prepare for a logical syllogism. The phenomenon Thurow
addresses is puzzling and, for many people, a distressing pattern as well. In the course of the exposition, Thurow considers
several alternate explanations before offering his own. As you
read this essay, pay attention not only to the reasoning but also
to the strength and validity of the evidence, qualities that may
have changed since the essay was written. This selection was
first published in *The New York Times*.

In the 40 years from 1939 to 1979 white women who work full time
have with monotonous regularity made slightly less than 60 percent as much as white men. Why?

Over the same time period, minorities have made substantial
progress in catching up with whites, with minority women making
even more progress than minority men.

Black men now earn 72 percent as much as white men (up 16   3
percentage points since the mid-1950's) but black women earn 92
percent as much as white women. Hispanic men make 71 percent
of what their white counterparts do, but Hispanic women make 82
percent as much as white women. As a result of their faster progress, fully employed black women make 75 percent as much as
fully employed black men while Hispanic women earn 68 percent
as much as Hispanic men.

This faster progress may, however, end when minority   4
women finally catch up with white women. In the bible of the New
Right, George Gilder's "Wealth and Poverty," the 60 percent is
just one of Mother Nature's constants like the speed of light or the
force of gravity.

Men are programmed to provide for their families economi-   5
cally while women are programmed to take care of their families
emotionally and physically. As a result men put more effort into
their jobs than women. The net result is a difference in work intensity that leads to that 40 percent gap in earnings. But there is no
discrimination against women—only the biological facts of life.

The problem with this assertion is just that. It is an assertion   6
with no evidence for it other than the fact that white women have
made 60 percent as much as men for a long period of time.

"Discrimination against women" is an easy answer but it also   7
has its problems as an adequate explanation. Why is discrimination
against women not declining under the same social forces that are
leading to a lessening of discrimination against minorities? In recent years women have made more use of the enforcement provi-
sions of the Equal Employment Opportunities Commission and
the courts than minorities. Why do the laws that prohibit discrimination against women and minorities work for minorities but not
for women?

When men discriminate against women, they run into a prob-   8
lem. To discriminate against women is to discriminate against your
own wife and to lower your own family income. To prevent
women from working is to force men to work more.

When whites discriminate against blacks, they can at least   9
think that they are raising their own incomes. When men discrimi-

nate against women they have to know that they are lowering their own family income and increasing their own work effort.

While discrimination undoubtedly explains part of the male-female earnings differential, one has to believe that men are monumentally stupid or irrational to explain all of the earnings gap in terms of discrimination. There must be something else going on.

Back in 1939 it was possible to attribute the earnings gap to large differences in educational attainments. But the educational gap between men and women has been eliminated since World War II. It is no longer possible to use education as an explanation for the lower earnings of women.

Some observers have argued that women earn less money since they are less reliable workers who are more apt to leave the labor force. But it is difficult to maintain this position since women are less apt to quit one job to take another and as a result they tend to work as long, or longer, for any one employer. From any employer's perspective they are more reliable, not less reliable, than men.

Part of the answer is visible if you look at the lifetime earnings profile of men. Suppose that you were asked to predict which men in a group of 25-year-olds would become economically successful. At age 25 it is difficult to tell who will be economically successful and your predictions are apt to be highly inaccurate.

But suppose that you were asked to predict which men in a group of 35-year-olds would become economically successful. If you are successful at age 35, you are very likely to remain successful for the rest of your life. If you have not become economically successful by age 35, you are very unlikely to do so later.

The decade between 25 and 35 is when men either succeed or fail. It is the decade when lawyers become partners in the good firms, when business managers make it onto the "fast track," when academics get tenure at good universities, and when blue collar workers find the job opportunities that will lead to training opportunities and the skills that will generate high earnings.

If there is any one decade when it pays to work hard and to be consistently in the labor force, it is the decade between 25 and 35. For those who succeed, earnings will rise rapidly. For those who fail, earnings will remain flat for the rest of their lives.

But the decade between 25 and 35 is precisely the decade when women are most apt to leave the labor force or become part-

time workers to have children. When they do, the current system
of promotion and skill acquisition will extract an enormous lifetime
price.

This leaves essentially two avenues for equalizing male and   18
female earnings.

Families where women who wish to have successful careers,   19
compete with men, and achieve the same earnings should alter
their family plans and have their children either before 25 or after
35. Or society can attempt to alter the existing promotion and skill
acquisition system so that there is a longer time period in which
both men and women can attempt to successfully enter the labor
force.

Without some combination of these two factors, a substantial   20
fraction of the male-female earnings differentials are apt to persist
for the next 40 years, even if discrimination against women is eliminated.

Meanings and Values

1a. What is the author's point of view? (See Guide to Terms: *Point of View.*)

b. How could you best describe the tone of the selection? (Guide: *Style/Tone.*)

c. What, if anything, does the point of view have to do with the tone?

2. Is this selection best described as formal, informal, or familiar? Why? (Guide: *Essay.*)

3a. What is the central theme? (Guide: *Unity.*)

b. Do all parts of the selection flow into the theme, as tributaries into a river?

c. Does the essay have unity?

4. Does it seem to you that Thurow's reasoning is valid in paragraphs 8–9? Why, or why not?

5. Do you see any contradiction between the author's reasoning in paragraph 12 and his eventual conclusions in paragraphs 15–17? Explain.

Expository Techniques

1. How effectively do the first two paragraphs fulfill the three necessary functions of a good introduction? (Guide: *Introductions.*)

2. In which paragraph, or paragraphs, do we find the first minor use of the inductive process?

3a. Draw up a simple chart, showing the main inductive points and the paragraphs devoted to each point.

 b. By what other term is this kind of induction sometimes known?

 c. What appear to be the special limitations, if any, of this kind of induction?

4. A logical syllogism representing the author's reasoning in paragraphs 15–17 would have as a major premise something like this: Between the ages of twenty-five and thirty-five is the period when most people get into line for success, if they are to make it at all.

 a. What, then, would be his minor premise?

 b. From these two premises, what conclusion can logically be reached, completing the syllogism?

 c. Is this an inductive or a deductive process?

5. Which other pattern of exposition already studied is apparent throughout this essay?

6a. Which of the standard techniques of closing are used in the last three paragraphs?

 b. How effectively are they used?

Diction and Vocabulary

1a. What are the distinctive characteristics, if any, of Thurow's style in diction or syntax? (Guide: *Style/Tone, Diction,* and *Syntax.*)

 b. What justification can you see for this style?

2. What reason, or reasons, can you see for the author's using a relatively simple vocabulary, with no "dictionary-type" words?

Suggestions for Writing and Discussion

1. Discuss possible reasons black and Hispanic women are doing better in relation to black and Hispanic men, respectively, than white women in relation to white men. Why does the same twenty-five to thirty-five explanation not apply to black and Hispanic women?

2. Do you see any logic at all in the first two sentences of paragraph 5? If so, explain your view.

3. Discuss—agreeing, disagreeing, or explaining—this statement from paragraph 14: "If you have not become economically successful by age 35, you are very unlikely to do so later."

4. Would anything be gained by women having their families either before age twenty-five or after age thirty-five, as suggested in para-

graph 19? Or do you think a several-year period away from their careers *any* time during their productive years would have the same effect? Explain.

5. So, what *is* the answer to the pay discrepancy dilemma?

(NOTE: Suggestions for topics requiring development by INDUCTION and DEDUC-TION are on page 341, at the end of this section.)

ISHMAEL REED

Born in Buffalo in 1938, ISHMAEL REED attended public schools in the city and the University of Buffalo. At present, he lives in Oakland, California. Reed is a prolific writer whose works include novels, plays, essays, and songs. In addition, he works as a television producer, magazine editor, and publisher. He has also taught at Harvard, Yale, and Dartmouth and is currently a lecturer at the University of California at Berkeley. Two of Reed's books have been nominated for National Book Awards, and in 1978 the Studio Museum in Harlem awarded him the Lewis H. Michaux Literary Prize. Among his publications are *The Free Lance Pall Bearers* (1967), *Mumbo Jumbo* (1978), and *Reckless Eyeballing* (1986) (novels); *Conjure* (1972) and *Catechism of D Neoamerican Hoodoo Church* (1970) (poems); and *Shrovetide in New Orleans* (1979) and *Writin' is Fightin'* (1988) (essays).

America: The Multinational Society

"America: The Multinational Society" is an ambitious but nonetheless clearly structured and easily followed essay. The selection opens with a line of inductive reasoning ending in a generalization. Then it employs a mirror image of the process, an inductive "process of elimination" of sorts, designed to disprove competing generalizations. Following this, the essay undertakes a third line of inductive reasoning ending in a generalization that becomes the basis for an informal syllogism. Despite this, most readers should have little trouble understanding Reed's reasoning, though they may reject his conclusions. His energetic, imaginative style may likewise please some readers and irritate others.

At the annual Lower East Side Jewish Festival yesterday, a Chinese woman ate a pizza slice in front of Ty Thuan Duc's Vietnamese   1 grocery store. Beside her a Spanish-speaking family patronized a cart with two signs: "Italian Ices" and "Kosher by Rabbi Alper." And after the pastrami ran out, everybody ate knishes.

(*New York Times*, 23 June 1983)

On the day before Memorial Day, 1983, a poet called me to describe a city he had just visited. He said that one section included mosques, built by the Islamic people who dwelled there. Attending his reading, he said, were large numbers of Hispanic people, forty thousand of whom lived in the same city. He was not talking about a fabled city located in some mysterious region of the world. The city he'd visited was Detroit.

A few months before, as I was leaving Houston, Texas, I heard it announced on the radio that Texas's largest minority was Mexican American, and though a foundation recently issued a report critical of bilingual education, the taped voice used to guide the passengers on the air trams connecting terminals in Dallas Airport is in both Spanish and English. If the trend continues, a day will come when it will be difficult to travel through some sections of the country without hearing commands in both English and Spanish; after all, for some western states, Spanish was the first written language and the Spanish style lives on in the western way of life.

Shortly after my Texas trip, I sat in an auditorium located on the campus of the University of Wisconsin at Milwaukee as a Yale professor—whose original work on the influence of African cultures upon those of the Americas has led to his ostracism from some monocultural intellectual circles—walked up and down the aisle, like an old-time southern evangelist, dancing and drumming the top of the lectern, illustrating his points before some serious Afro-American intellectuals and artists who cheered and applauded his performance and his mastery of information. The professor was "white." After his lecture, he joined a group of Milwaukeeans in a conversation. All of the participants spoke Yoruban, though only the professor had ever traveled to Africa.

One of the artists told me that his paintings, which included African and Afro-American mythological symbols and imagery, were hanging in the local McDonald's restaurant. The next day I went to McDonald's and snapped pictures of smiling youngsters eating hamburgers below paintings that could grace the walls of any of the country's leading museums. The manager of the local McDonald's said, "I don't know what you boys are doing, but I like it," as he commissioned the local painters to exhibit in his restaurant.

Such blurring of cultural styles occurs in everyday life in the United States to a greater extent than anyone can imagine and is probably more prevalent than the sensational conflict between people of different backgrounds that is played up and often encouraged by the media. The result is what the Yale professor, Robert Thompson, referred to as a cultural bouillabaisse, yet members of the nation's present educational and cultural Elect still cling to the notion that the United States belongs to some vaguely defined entity they refer to as "Western civilization," by which they mean, presumably, a civilization created by the people of Europe, as if Europe can be viewed in monolithic terms. Is Beethoven's Ninth Symphony, which includes Turkish marches, a part of Western civilization, or the late nineteenth- and twentieth-century French paintings, whose creators were influenced by Japanese art? And what of the cubists, through whom the influence of African art changed modern painting, or the surrealists, who were so impressed with the art of the Pacific Northwest Indians that, in their map of North America, Alaska dwarfs the lower forty-eight in size?

Are the Russians, who are often criticized for their adoption of "Western" ways by Tsarist dissidents in exile, members of Western civilization? And what of the millions of Europeans who have black African and Asian ancestry, black Africans having occupied several countries for hundreds of years? Are these "Europeans" members of Western civilization, or the Hungarians, who originated across the Urals in a place called Greater Hungary, or the Irish, who came from the Iberian Peninsula?

Even the notion that North America is part of Western civilization because our "system of government" is derived from Europe is being challenged by Native American historians who say that the founding fathers, Benjamin Franklin especially, were actually influenced by the system of government that had been adopted by the Iroquois hundreds of years prior to the arrival of large numbers of Europeans.

Western civilization, then, becomes another confusing category like Third World, or Judeo-Christian culture, as man attempts to impose his small-screen view of political and cultural reality upon a complex world. Our most publicized novelist recently said that Western civilization was the greatest achievement of mankind, an attitude that flourishes on the street level as scribbles in public restrooms: "White Power," "Niggers and Spics Suck," or "Hitler was a prophet," the latter being the most telling, for wasn't Adolph Hitler the archetypal monoculturalist who, in his pig-headed arrogance, believed that one way and one blood was so pure that it had to be protected from alien strains at all costs? Where did such an attitude, which has caused so much misery and depression in our national life, which has tainted even our noblest achievements, begin? An attitude that caused the incarceration of Japanese-American citizens during World War II, the persecution of Chicanos and Chinese Americans, the near-extermination of the Indians, and the murder and lynchings of thousands of Afro-Americans.

Virtuous, hardworking, pious, even though they occasionally would wander off after some fancy clothes, or rendezvous in the woods with the town prostitute, the Puritans are idealized in our schoolbooks as "a hardy band" of no-nonsense patriarchs whose discipline razed the forest and brought order to the New World (a term that annoys Native American historians). Industrious, responsible, it was their "Yankee ingenuity" and practicality that created the work ethic. They were simple folk who produced a number of good poets, and they set the tone for the American writing style, of lean and spare lines, long before Hemingway. They worshiped in churches whose colors blended in with the New England snow, churches with simple structures and ornate lecterns. [10]

The Puritans were a daring lot, but they had a mean streak. They hated the theater and banned Christmas. They punished people in a cruel and inhuman manner. They killed children who disobeyed their parents. When they came in contact with those whom they considered heathens or aliens, they behaved in such a bizarre and irrational manner that this chapter in the American history comes down to us as a late-movie horror film. They exterminated the Indians, who taught them how to survive in a world unknown to them, and their encounter with the calypso culture of Barbados resulted in what the tourist guide in Salem's Witches' House refers to as the Witchcraft Hysteria. [11]

The Puritan legacy of hard work and meticulous accounting led to the establishment of a great industrial society; it is no won- [12]

der that the American industrial revolution began in Lowell, Massachusetts, but there was the other side, the strange and paranoid attitudes toward those different from the Elect.

The cultural attitudes of that early Elect continue to be voiced in everyday life in the United States: the president of a distinguished university, writing a letter to the *Times,* belittling the study of African civilizations; the television network that promoted its show on the Vatican art with the boast that this art represented "the finest achievements of the human spirit." A modern up-tempo state of complex rhythms that depends upon contacts with an international community can no longer behave as if it dwelled in a "Zion Wilderness" surrounded by beasts and pagans.

When I heard a schoolteacher warn the other night about the invasion of the American educational system by foreign curriculums, I wanted to yell at the television set, "Lady, they're already here." It has already begun because the world is here. The world has been arriving at these shores for at least ten thousand years from Europe, Africa, and Asia. In the late nineteenth and early twentieth centuries, large numbers of Europeans arrived, adding their cultures to those of the European, African, and Asian settlers who were already here, and recently millions have been entering the country from South America and the Caribbean, making Yale Professor Bob Thompson's bouillabaisse richer and thicker.

One of our most visionary politicians said that he envisioned a time when the United States could become the brain of the world, by which he meant the repository of all of the latest advanced information systems. I thought of that remark when an enterprising poet friend of mine called to say that he had just sold a poem to a computer magazine and that the editors were delighted to get it because they didn't carry fiction or poetry. Is that the kind of world we desire? A humdrum homogenous world of all brains but no heart, no fiction, no poetry; a world of robots with human attendants bereft of imagination, of culture? Or does North America deserve a more exciting destiny? To become a place where the cultures of the world crisscross. This is possible because the United States is unique in the world: The world is here.

Meanings and Values

1a. What inductive generalization based on the opening paragraphs of the essay does Reed offer in paragraph 6?

b.   What generalization representing the views of the "present educational and cultural Elect" does he offer in the same paragraph?

c.   Summarize in your own words the inductive generalization presented in paragraph 12.

2.   In several places in the essay, especially in paragraph 9, Reed directs some harsh comments at those who reach conclusions about American culture that differ from his. Are these comments likely to alienate a majority of his readers? If not, what in the tone and content of his remarks keeps them from seeming unacceptable? (See Guide to Terms: *Tone.*)

3a. Some elements of this section are characteristic of a formal essay and others of an informal essay. Identify elements belonging to each category. (Guide: *Essay.*)

b.   In what ways does this mixing of qualities add to or detract from the effectiveness of the selection? (Guide: *Evaluation.*)

Expository Techniques

1a. Evaluate the quality of the inductive evidence that Reed presents in paragraphs 1–5. Is it believable or flimsy? Is there enough evidence to justify the leap to a generalization? (See Introduction to Section 10.)

b.   Evaluate the quality of the evidence presented in paragraphs 6–8 that the author uses to undermine the conclusion that there is a "'Western civilization' . . . created by the people of Europe" (par. 6).

2.   Identify the generalization in paragraph 9 that the author calls into question.

3.   Should the quotation that begins the essay be considered part of the pattern of reasoning or simply a device to get the reader's attention? Explain.

4.   What role do the rhetorical questions in paragraph 6 play? (Guide: *Rhetorical Questions.*)

Diction and Vocabulary

1.   Locate the paragraphs in which the word "Elect" appears and discuss the ways in which Reed uses it to link the outlook of the Puritans to that of people who believe that American culture is (or ought to be) homogeneous and "Western."

2.   Discuss the use Reed makes of diction in establishing both the positive and negative qualities of the Puritans. (Guide: *Diction.*)

3.   In discussing the contributions of various cultures to American society and elsewhere in the essay, Reed uses a number of terms that

readers may find unfamiliar. If you do not know what some of these words mean, look them up in the dictionary: knishes (par. 1); Yoruban (4); bouillabaisse, monolithic (6); Urals (7); archetypal, incarceration (9); patriarchs (10); Zion (13); bereft (15).

Suggestions for Writing and Discussion

1. If you have taken or are taking a course in Western civilization or Western literature, explain why you think Reed's criticisms do or do not apply to the content and perspective of the course.

2. What ethnic groups or cultures (including those discussed by Reed) do you believe are excluded from mainstream American culture? Are some of the cultures that Reed discusses actually a part of what most of us consider American culture?

3. Should high school and college curriculums pay more attention to African and Asian cultures?

4. If you belong to an ethnic group or culture that you believe is excluded from mainstream American society, prepare a paper explaining the special and different features of the culture.

(NOTE: Suggestions for topics requiring development by INDUCTION and DEDUCTION are on page 341, at the end of this section.)

PETER FARB

Peter Farb (1929–1980) was born in New York and attended Vanderbilt University and Columbia University. Farb was a respected environmentalist and expert on the land and people of North and South America. His books include *Face of North America* (1963), *Man's Rise to Civilization as Shown by the Indians of North America* (1968), *Word Play: What Happens When People Talk* (1973), and (with George Armelagos) *Consuming Passions* (1980). Farb served as consultant to the Smithsonian Institution, as curator of American Indian Cultures at the Riverside Museum in New York City, and as visiting lecturer in English at Yale. He was a fellow of the American Association for the Advancement of Science and a member of numerous scientific societies.

In Other Words

This essay, a section of a chapter with the same title in *Word Play*, illustrates how inductive reasoning can lead to a generalization that in turn becomes the basis for a process of deduction. In the course of the essay Farb manages to cover a wide variety of topics—from "thinking" horses to elementary education—and to demonstrate their surprising but logical relationships.

Early in this century, a horse named Hans amazed the people of   1
Berlin by his extraordinary ability to perform rapid calculations in
mathematics. After a problem was written on a blackboard placed
in front of him, he promptly counted out the answer by tapping
the low numbers with his right forefoot and multiples of ten with
his left. Trickery was ruled out because Hans's owner, unlike owners of other performing animals, did not profit financially—and
Hans even performed his feats whether or not the owner was pres-

ent. The psychologist O. Pfungst witnessed one of these performances and became convinced that there had to be a more logical
explanation than the uncanny intelligence of a horse.

Because Hans performed only in the presence of an audience
that could see the blackboard and therefore knew the correct answer, Pfungst reasoned that the secret lay in observation of the
audience rather than of the horse. He finally discovered that as
soon as the problem was written on the blackboard, the audience
bent forward very slightly in anticipation to watch Hans's forefeet.
As slight as that movement was, Hans perceived it and took it as
his signal to begin tapping. As his taps approached the correct
number, the audience became tense with excitement and made almost imperceptible movements of the head—which signaled Hans
to stop counting. The audience, simply by expecting Hans to stop
when the correct number was reached, had actually told the animal when to stop. Pfungst clearly demonstrated that Hans's intelligence was nothing but a mechanical response to his audience,
which unwittingly communicated the answer by its body language.

The "Clever Hans Phenomenon," as it has come to be known,
raises an interesting question. If a mere horse can detect uninten-
tional and extraordinarily subtle body signals, might they not also
be detected by human beings? Professional gamblers and con men
have long been known for their skill in observing the body-
language cues of their victims, but only recently has it been shown
scientifically that all speakers constantly detect and interpret such
cues also, even though they do not realize it.

An examination of television word games several years ago
revealed that contestants inadvertently gave their partners body-
language signals that led to correct answers. In one such game,
contestants had to elicit certain words from their partners, but they
were permitted to give only brief verbal clues as to what the words
might be. It turned out that sometimes the contestants also gave
body signals that were much more informative than the verbal
clues. In one case, a contestant was supposed to answer *sad* in
response to his partner's verbal clue of *happy*—that is, the correct
answer was a word opposite to the verbal clue. The partner giving
the *happy* clue unconsciously used his body to indicate to his fellow
contestant that an opposite word was needed. He did that by shift-

ing his body and head very slightly to one side as he said *happy*, then to the other side in expectation of an opposite word.

Contestants on a television program are usually unsophisti- 5 cated about psychology and linguistics, but trained psychological experimenters also unintentionally flash body signals which are sometimes detected by the test subjects—and which may distort the results of experiments. Hidden cameras have revealed that the sex of the experimenter, for example, can influence the responses of subjects. Even though the films showed that both male and female experimenters carried out the experiments in the same way and asked the same questions, the experimenters were very much aware of their own sex in relation to the sex of the subjects. Male experimenters spent 16 percent more time carrying out experiments with female subjects than they did with male subjects; similarly, female experimenters took 13 percent longer to go through experiments with male subjects than they did with female subjects. The cameras also revealed that chivalry is not dead in the psychological experiment; male experimenters smiled about six times as often with female subjects as they did with male subjects.

The important question, of course, is whether or not such 6 nonverbal communication influences the results of experiments. The answer is that it often does. Psychologists who have watched films made without the knowledge of either the experimenters or the subjects could predict almost immediately which experimenters would obtain results from their subjects that were in the direction of the experimenters' own biases. Those experimenters who seemed more dominant, personal, and relaxed during the first moments of conversation with their subjects usually obtained the results that they secretly hoped the experiments would yield. And they somehow communicated their secret hopes in a completely visual way, regardless of what they said or their paralanguage when they spoke. That was made clear when these films were shown to two groups, one of which saw the films without hearing the sound track while the other heard only the sound track without seeing the films. The group that heard only the voices could not accurately predict the experimenters' biases—but those who saw the films without hearing the words immediately sensed whether or not the experimenters were communicating their biases.

A person who signals his expectations about a certain kind of behavior is not aware that he is doing so—and usually he is indignant when told that his experiment was biased—but the subjects themselves confirm his bias by their performances. Such bias in experiments has been shown to represent self-fulfilling prophecies. In other words, the experimenters' expectations about the results of the experiment actually result in those expectations coming true. That was demonstrated when each of twelve experimenters was given five rats bred from an identical strain of laboratory animals. Half of the experimenters were told that their rats could be expected to perform brilliantly because they had been bred especially for high intelligence and quickness in running through a maze. The others were told that their rats could be expected to perform very poorly because they had been bred for low intelligence. All the experimenters were then asked to teach their rats to run a maze.

Almost as soon as the rats were put into the maze it became clear that those for which the experimenters had high expectations would prove to be the better performers. And the rats which were expected to perform badly did in fact perform very badly, even though they were bred from the identical strain as the excellent performers. Some of these poor performers did not even budge from their starting positions in the maze. The misleading prophecy about the behavior of the two groups of rats was fulfilled—simply because the two groups of experimenters unconsciously communicated their expectations to the animals. Those experimenters who anticipated high performance were friendlier to their animals than those who expected low performance; they handled their animals more, and they did so more gently. Clearly, the predictions of the experimenters were communicated to the rats in subtle and unintended ways—and the rats behaved accordingly.

Since animals such as laboratory rats and Clever Hans can detect body-language cues, it is not surprising that human beings are just as perceptive in detecting visual signals about expectations for performance. It is a psychological truth that we are likely to speak to a person whom we expect to be unpleasant in such a way that we force him to act unpleasantly. But it has only recently become apparent that poor children—often black or Spanish-speaking—perform badly in school because that is what their teachers expect of them, and because the teachers manage to convey that expectation by both verbal and nonverbal channels. True to the teachers' prediction, the black and brown children probably will do poorly—not necessarily because children from minority groups are capable only of poor performance, but because poor performance has been expected of them. The first grade may be the place where teachers anticipate poor performances by children of certain racial, economic, and cultural backgrounds—and where the teachers actually teach these children how to fail.

Evidence of the way the "Clever Hans Phenomenon" works 10 in many schools comes from a careful series of experiments by psychologist Robert Rosenthal and his co-workers at Harvard University. They received permission from a school south of San Francisco to give a series of tests to the children in the lower grades. The teachers were blatantly lied to. They were told that the test was a newly developed tool that could predict which children would be "spurters" and achieve high performance in the coming year. Actually, the experimenters administered a new kind of IQ test that the teachers were unlikely to have seen previously. After IQ scores were obtained, the experimenters selected the names of 20 percent of the children completely at random. Some of the selected children scored very high on the IQ test and others scored low, some were from middle-class families and others from lower-class. Then the teachers were lied to again. The experimenters said that the tests singled out this 20 percent as the children who could be expected to make unusual intellectual gains in the coming year. The teachers were also cautioned not to discuss the test results with the pupils or their parents. Since the names of these children had been selected completely at random, any difference between them and the 80 percent not designated as "spurters" was completely in the minds of the teachers.

All the children were given IQ tests again during that school 11 year and once more the following year. The 20 percent who had been called to the attention of their teachers did indeed turn in the high performances expected of them—in some cases dramatic increases of 25 points in IQ. The teachers' comments about these children also were revealing. The teachers considered them more happy, curious, and interesting than the other 80 percent—and they predicted that they would be successes in life, a prophecy

they had already started to fulfill. The experiment plainly showed
that children who are expected to gain intellectually do gain and
that their behavior improves as well.

The results of the experiment are clear—but the explanation   1
for the results is not. It might be imagined that the teachers simply
devoted more time to the children singled out for high expectations, but the study showed that was not so. Instead, the influence
of the teachers upon these children apparently was much more
subtle. What the teachers said to them, how and when it was said,
the facial expressions, gestures, posture, perhaps even touch that
accompanied their speech—some or all of these things must have
communicated that the teachers expected improved performance
from them. And when these children responded correctly, the
teachers were quicker to praise them and also more lavish in their
praise. Whatever the exact mechanism was, the effect upon the
children who had been singled out was dramatic. They changed
their ideas about themselves, their behavior, their motivation, and
their learning capacities.

The lesson of the California experiment is that pupil perfor-   1:
mance does not depend so much upon a school's audio-visual
equipment or new textbooks or enriching trips to museums as it does
upon teachers whose body language communicates high expectations for the pupils—even if the teacher thinks she "knows" that
a black, a Puerto Rican, a Mexican-American, or any other disadvantaged child is fated to do poorly in school. Apparently, reme-
dial instruction in our schools is misdirected. It is needed more by
the middle-class teachers than by the disadvantaged children.

Meanings and Values

1a.   What generalizations does Farb arrive at in paragraph 3?

  b.   Can this be considered the central theme of the essay? (See Guide
       to Terms: *Unity.*)

  c.   If not, what is the central theme?

2.   In your own words, define the "Clever Hans Phenomenon."

3.   Where would you place this essay on an objective-to-subjective
      continuum? (Guide: *Objective/Subjective.*)

4.   Are Farb's explanations of the behavior of TV contestants and of
      psychological experimenters convincing? Why, or why not?

5.   Is the amount of evidence Farb supplies to support his conclusions appropriate for the subject and the purpose of the essay? If not, is more needed, or would even less have been satisfactory? Explain.

6.   What does the example of the laboratory rats contribute to the reader's understanding of nonverbal behavior and its effects?

7.   Is there something paradoxical about the behavior of the teachers as reported in paragraph 9? If so, what is the paradox? (Guide: *Paradox.*)

8a.   The research on the effects of teachers' expectations on children's behavior involved lying to the subjects of the research. Do you think the lying makes the results of the research unreliable? Explain.

b.   In what ways does this research differ from that involving rats?

Expository Techniques

1a.   What process of reasoning is represented by Pfungst's study of Clever Hans?

b.   What process is represented by paragraphs 1–3 of the essay?

c.   What process by paragraph 4? By paragraphs 5–6? 7–8? 9–13?

2a.   Are the discussions of each of the different topics in this essay clearly related to the central theme? (Guide: *Unity.*)

b.   If not, which sections of the essay damage its unity?

c.   What transitional devices does the author use to create coherence in the selection? (Guide: *Transitions* and *Coherence.*)

3a.   Why does Farb take up the topic of the effect of nonverbal behavior in the classroom *after* he discusses the other topics?

b.   Is there any logic behind the arrangement of the topics in this essay? Explain.

4.   At what points in the essay does the author take into account possible objections to his conclusions, and how does he answer them?

5.   How would this essay have to be changed to make it into an argument proposing changes in the way teachers deal with students? (Guide: *Argument.*)

Diction and Vocabulary

1a.   What is "body language" (par. 2)?

b.   What are "self-fulfilling prophecies" (par. 7)?

c.   If you do not know what "paralanguage" means, look up the prefix ''para'' in the dictionary and try to explain the use of the word in paragraph 6.

2a. Identify some of the places in this essay where Farb makes use of qualifications and explain their functions. (Guide: *Qualification.*)

b. What is the function of the rhetorical question in paragraph 3? (Guide: *Rhetorical Questions.*)

Suggestions for Writing and Discussion

1. If Farb is correct in his conclusions about the importance of teachers' expectations, what steps can we take to improve teaching? Be specific in your recommendations, and be ready to defend them.

2. In what situations other than those described in the essay can self-fulfilling prophecies affect us? Explain.

3. Does anything in your experience confirm what Farb has to say about either self-fulfilling prophecies or the importance of nonverbal communication? Describe your experiences in detail.

4. How much lying, if any, is justified in scientific experiments like those described in the essay? In medical experiments? Develop your answer into an essay.

5. Speculate on the long-term effects on the children whose elementary teachers are told, rightly or wrongly, that they are highly intelligent.

(NOTE: Suggestions for topics requiring development by INDUCTION and DEDUCTION follow.)

Writing Suggestions for Section 10
Induction and *Deduction*

Choose one of the following unformed topics and shape your central theme from it. This could express the view you prefer or an opposing view. Develop your composition primarily by use of induction, alone or in combination with deduction. Unless otherwise directed by your instructor, be completely objective and limit yourself to exposition, rather than engaging in argumentation.

1. Little League baseball (or the activities of 4-H clubs, Boy Scouts, Girl Scouts, etc.) as a molder of character.
2. Conformity as an expression of insecurity.
3. Pop music as a mirror of contemporary values.
4. The status symbol as a motivator to success.
5. The liberal arts curriculum and its relevance to success in a career.
6. Student opinion as the guide to better educational institutions.
7. The role of public figures (including politicians, movie stars, and business people) in shaping attitudes and fashions.
8. The values of education, beyond dollars and cents.
9. Knowledge and its relation to wisdom.
10. The right of individuals to select the laws they obey.
11. Television commercials as a molder of morals.
12. The "other" side of one ecological problem.
13. The value of complete freedom from worry.
14. The threat of nuclear war and public policy.
15. Raising mentally retarded children at home.
16. Fashionable clothing as an expression of power (or a means of attaining status).

11

Using Patterns for *Argument*

Argument and exposition have many things in common. They both use the basic patterns of exposition; they share a concern for the audience; and they often deal with similar subjects, including social trends (changing relationships between men and women, the growth of the animal rights movement), recent developments (the creation of new strains of plants through genetic manipulation, medical treatment of the terminally ill), and issues of widespread concern (the quality of education, the effects of pollution). As a result, the study of argument is a logical companion to the study of exposition. Yet the two kinds of writing have very different purposes.

Expository writing shares information and ideas; it explores issues and explains problems. In exposition we select facts and ideas to give an accurate picture of a subject and arrange them as clearly as we can, emphasizing features likely to interest readers. To explain the importance of knowing how to use computers, for instance, an essay might provide examples of the roles of computers in business, industry, education, and research; it might describe the uses of computers for personal budgeting, record-keeping, and entertainment; and it might emphasize that more everyday tasks than we realize are already heavily dependent on computers.

Argumentative writing, however, has a different motivation. It asks readers to choose one side of an issue or take a particular action, whether it be to buy a product, vote for a candidate, or build a new highway. In argument we select facts and ideas that provide strong support for our point of view and arrange this evidence in the most logical and persuasive order, taking care to provide appropriate background information and to acknowledge and refute opposing points of view. The evidence we choose is determined to a great extent by the attitudes and needs of the people we are trying to convince. For example, suppose we want to argue successfully that a high school or college ought to give all students advanced training in computer use. Our essay would need to provide examples of benefits to students that are great enough to justify the considerable expenses for equipment and staff. (Examples of greatly increased job opportunities and improved learning skills would make good evidence; discussions of how computers can be used for personal recordkeeping and managing household finances would not be likely to persuade school officials facing tight budgets.) And an effective essay would also answer possible objections to the proposal: Will only a limited number of students really benefit from advanced computer training? Are computers developing so rapidly that only large businesses and specialized institutes can afford to provide up-to-date training?

At the heart of an argumentative essay is the opinion we want readers to share or the action we want them to take. In argument this central theme is called the *thesis* or *proposition* and is often expressed concisely in a *thesis statement* designed to alert readers to the point of the argument. Some writers like to arrive at a sharply focused thesis early in the process of composing and use it to guide the selection and arrangement of evidence. Others settle on a tentative ("working") thesis, which they revise as the essay takes shape. In either case, checking frequently to see that factual evidence and supporting ideas or arguments are clearly linked to the thesis is a good way for writers to make sure their finished essays are coherent, unified arguments.

The purpose of a simple argumentative essay often falls into one of three categories. Some essays ask readers to agree with a value judgment ("The present city government is corrupt and ineffective"). Others propose a specific action ("Money from the student activity fee at this college should be used to establish and staff a fitness program available to all students"). And still others advance an opinion quite different from that held by most people ("Contrary to what many people believe, investing in stocks and bonds is not just for the wealthy—it is for people who want to become wealthy, too"). In situations calling for more complex arguments, however, writers should feel free to combine these purposes as long as the relationship among them is made clear to the reader. In a complex argument, for instance, we might *first* show that the city government is inefficient and corrupt and *then* argue that it is better to change the city charter to eliminate the opportunities for the abuse of power than it is to try to vote a new party into office or to support a reform faction within the existing political "machine."

Another distinction is normally made between *logical argument* (usually called, simply, *argument*) and *persuasive argument* (usually termed *persuasion*). Whereas logical argument appeals to reason, persuasive argument appeals to the emotions. The aim of both, however, is to convince, and they are nearly always blended into whatever mixture seems most likely to do the convincing. After all, reason and emotion are both important human elements—and we may have to persuade someone even to listen to our logic. The emphasis on one or the other, of course, should depend on the subject and the audience.

Some authorities make a slightly different distinction: they say we argue merely to get people to change their minds, and we use persuasion to get them to *do* something about it—for example, to vote a Republican ticket, not just agree with the party platform. But this view is not entirely inconsistent with the other. We can hardly expect to change a *mind* by emotional appeal, but we can hope to get someone to *act* because of it.

The choice of supporting evidence for an argument depends in part on the subject and in part on the audience and situation. There is a good deal of evidence to support the argument that industry should turn to labor-saving machines and new work arrangements to increase its competitiveness. Company executives looking for ways to increase profits are likely to find almost all of this evidence persuasive, but workers and union leaders worried about loss of jobs and cuts in wages will probably be harder to persuade. Writers addressing the second group would need to choose evidence to show that industrial robots and work rules calling for fewer people would lead to increased sales, not lower wages and fewer jobs. And if the changes might actually cause layoffs, writers would have to show that without the changes a company might be forced to shut down entirely, throwing everyone out of work.

Variety in evidence gives the writer a chance to present an argument fully and at the same time helps persuade readers. Examples, facts and figures, statements from authorities, personal experience or the experience of other people—all these can be valuable sources of support. The basic patterns of exposition, too, can be viewed as ways to support arguments. For instance, to persuade people to take sailing (hang-gliding, skin-diving) lessons, we might tell the story of the inexperienced sailor who almost drowned even though she was sailing in a "safe" boat on a small lake. Or we might combine this narrative with a discussion of how lack of knowledge causes sailing accidents, with a classification of the dangers facing beginning sailors, or with examples of things that can go wrong while sailing. Most writers choose to combine patterns on the grounds that variety helps convince readers, just as three pieces of evidence are more convincing than one—as long as all three point to the same conclusion.

All the expository patterns can also be used to arrange factual evidence and supporting ideas or arguments, though some patterns are more useful than others. Entire arguments structured as narratives are rare, except for stories designed to show what the world will be like if we do not change our present nuclear, military, or technological policies. But example, comparison and contrast, cause and effect, definition, and induction or deduction are frequently used to organize arguments. A series of *examples* can be an effective way of showing that a government social policy does not work and in fact hurts the people it is supposed to serve. *Cause and effect* can organize argument over who is to blame for a problem or over the possible consequences of a new program. *Comparison* and *contrast* can guide choices among competing products, among ways of disposing of toxic waste, or among directions for national economic policy. *Definition* is helpful when a controversy hinges on the interpretation of a key term or when the meaning of an important word is itself the subject of disagreement. *Induction* and *deduction* are useful in argument because they provide the kind of careful, logical reasoning necessary to convince many readers, especially those who may at first have little sympathy for the writer's opinion.

An argument need not be restricted to a single pattern. The choice of a pattern or a combination of patterns depends on the subject, the specific purpose, and the kinds of evidence needed to convince the audience to which the essay is directed. Some arguments about complicated, significant issues make use of so many patterns that they can be called *complex arguments.*

In addition to using the patterns of exposition, most argumentative essays also arrange evidence according to its potential impact on the audience. Three of the most common arrangements are ascending order, refutation-proof, and con-pro. In *ascending order,* the strongest, most complex, or most emotionally moving evidence comes last, where it can build on the rest of the evidence in the essay and is likely to have the greatest impact on the reader. *Refutation-proof* acknowledges opposing points of view early in the essay and then goes on to show why the author's outlook is superior. *Con-pro* presents an opposing point of view and then refutes it, continuing until all opposition has been dealt with and all positive arguments voiced; this strategy is particularly useful when there is strong opposition to the writer's thesis. The strategies can be combined, of course, as in a refutation-proof essay that builds up to its strongest evidence.

Accuracy and fairness in argument are not only morally correct, they can also be a means of persuasion. Accuracy in the use of facts, figures, quotations, and references can encourage readers to trust what an author has to say. And writers who are able to acknowledge and refute opposing arguments fairly and without hostility add strength to their own arguments and may even win the respect of those who disagree with them.

But the most important elements of effective argument are careful choice of evidence and clear, logical reasoning. It is never possible to arrive at absolute proof—argument, after all, assumes that there are at least two sides to the matter under discussion— yet a carefully constructed case will convince many readers. At the same time, a flaw in logic can undermine an otherwise reasonable argument and destroy a reader's confidence in its conclusions. The introduction to Section 10, ''Reasoning by Use of *Induction* and *Deduction,*'' discusses some important errors to avoid in reasoning or in choosing evidence. Here are some others:

—*Post hoc ergo propter hoc* (''After this therefore because of this'')— Just because one thing happened *after* does not mean that the first event caused the second. In arguing without detailed supporting evidence that a recent drop in the crime rate is the result of a newly instituted anticrime policy, a writer might be committing this error because there are other equally plausible explanations: a drop in the unemployment rate, for example, or a reduction in the number of people in the fifteen to twenty-five age bracket, the segment of the population that is responsible for a high proportion of all crimes.

—*Begging the question*—A writer "begs the question" when he or she assumes the truth of something that is still to be proven. An argument that begins this way, "The recent, unjustified rise in utility rates should be reversed by the state legislature," assumes that the rise is "unjustified," though this important point needs to be proven.

—*Ignoring the question*—A writer may "ignore the question" by shifting attention away from the issue at hand to some loosely related or even irrelevant matter: for example, "Senator Jones's plan for encouraging new industries cannot be any good because in the past he has opposed tax cuts for corporations" (this approach shifts attention away from the merits of Senator Jones's proposal). A related problem is the *ad hominem* (toward the person) argument, which substitutes a personal attack for a discussion of the issue in question.

In composing argumentative essays, therefore, writers need to pay attention not only to what is necessary to convince an audience but also to the integrity of the evidence and arguments they advance in support of a thesis.

Sample Paragraph (Annotated)

The issue stated briefly with a suggestion of the kind of arguments the state has advanced to justify the highway.

Once again the state is proposing to build a four-lane highway through Ilona Valley, from one end to the other, and on through the state forest to join up with I-5 beyond. The state claims this project will improve the quality of life in the valley. Valley residents argue

Thesis statement

that the state should not waste tax dollars on an uneconomical project that will adversely affect those who supplied the dollars in the first place. The

Ilona Predisposition District has already marshalled most of the arguments against the project: (1) The road will cut a wide swath through some of the most productive farm land in the state. (2) One hundred fifty-nine residences and business places will be demolished. (3) The road will open up the valley to all the undesirable elements of the country at large, dooming its solid, law-abiding character. (4) Safety of children and old people will be continually threatened by increased traffic and speed. (5) The valley will be ruined aesthetically by litter and gas stations and junk-food drive-ins. (6) The road could be built further north with little community loss and far less expense (figures at hand). Valley residents hope the state will listen carefully to their arguments because they are worried about the kind of confrontation that might occur if the bulldozers turn up one day and start tearing up their land and homes.

Evidence and *supporting arguments.* (These six points will themselves need much more evidence, of course, in presenting the actual argument.)

Sample Paragraphs (Argument)

Still, the nearly two decades since Congress created Earth Day have left no doubt that our system of environmental regulation badly needs an overhaul. Overloaded with unrealistic deadlines and sweeping legislation during the 1970s, battered by budget cuts during the '80s, the Environmental Protection Agency now needs to devise a regulatory approach that's flexible and effective, and that relies as much on market-based incentives as rigid penalties. As perverse as this may sound, the EPA needs to stop trying to ban pollution and start letting companies pay for the privilege of polluting.

The basic idea is to turn pollution into a cost that, like any other expense, the company will want to minimize. This can be done directly by imposing a fee or tax on the pollutants released into the environment. It can be done indirectly by making companies pay for pollution permits. The government could even auction off the permits (a nice "revenue enhancer"). Alternatively, companies with low pollution levels could sell pollution rights to companies with poorer controls—financially rewarding the "clean" companies and penalizing the laggards. All of these schemes would force companies to pay for their pollution, giving them an incentive to find and use the most cost-effective preventive technology.

From "Grime and Punishment," *The New Republic,* February 20, 1989. Reprinted by permission.

ANNA QUINDLEN

ANNA QUINDLEN is a reporter and writer best known for her "Life in the 30s" column which appeared in *The New York Times* from 1986–1988 and was nationally syndicated. After graduating from Barnard College in 1974 she worked as a general assignment and city hall reporter at *The New York Times,* as writer of the "About New York" column, and finally as deputy metropolitan editor. At present she is working on a novel and along with her husband taking care of their three sons.

Execution

Few issues have been argued as extensively in writing as the death penalty, yet this essay, originally a newspaper column, is fresh both in outlook and technique. Student writers might note that in choosing to build much of the essay around an extended example, Quindlen acknowledges the importance of specificity and concreteness in persuasive writing. Of particular interest, too, are her use of examples drawn from two sources likely to be familiar to readers: newspaper reporting and television.

Ted Bundy and I go back a long way, to a time when there was a   1
series of unsolved murders in Washington State known only as
the Ted murders. Like a lot of reporters, I'm something of a crime
buff. But the Washington Ted murders—and the ones that followed in Utah, Colorado, and finally in Florida, where Ted Bundy
was convicted and sentenced to die—fascinated me because I could
see myself as one of the victims. I looked at the studio photographs

of young women with long hair, pierced ears, easy smiles, and I read the descriptions: polite, friendly, quick to help, eager to please. I thought about being approached by a handsome young man asking for help, and I knew if I had been in the wrong place at the wrong time I would have been a goner. By the time Ted finished up in Florida, law enforcement authorities suspected he had murdered dozens of young women. He and the death penalty seemed made for each other.

The death penalty and I, on the other hand, seem to have nothing in common. But Ted Bundy has made me think about it all over again, now that the outlines of my sixties liberalism have been filled in with a decade as a reporter covering some of the worst back alleys in New York City and three years as a mother who, like most, would lay down her life for her kids. Simply put, I am opposed to the death penalty. I would tell that to any judge or lawyer undertaking the voir dire[1] of jury candidates in a state in which the death penalty can be imposed. That is why I would be excused from such a jury. In a rational, completely cerebral way, I think the killing of one human being as punishment for the killing of another makes no sense and is inherently immoral.

But whenever my response to an important subject is rational and completely cerebral, I know there is something wrong with it—and so it is here. I have always been governed by my gut, and my gut says I am hypocritical about the death penalty. That is, I do not in theory think that Ted Bundy, or others like him, should be put to death. But if my daughter had been the one clubbed to death as she slept in a Tallahassee sorority house, and if the bite mark left in her buttocks had been one of the prime pieces of evidence against the young man charged with her murder, I would with the greatest pleasure kill him myself.

The State of Florida will not permit the parents of Bundy's victims to do that, and, in a way, that is the problem with an emotional response to capital punishment. The only reason for a death penalty is to exact retribution. Is there anyone who really thinks that it is a deterrent, that there are considerable numbers of criminals out there who think twice about committing crimes because of the sentence involved? The ones I have met in my professional

---

[1]Examination of the competence of a prospective juror (Editors' note).

duties have either sneered at the justice system, where they can exchange one charge for another with more ease than they could return a shirt to a clothing store, or they have simply believed that it is the other guy who will get caught, get convicted, get the stiffest sentence. Of course, the death penalty would act as a deterrent by eliminating recidivism, but then so would life without parole, albeit at greater taxpayer expense.

5   I don't believe deterrence is what most proponents seek from the death penalty anyhow. Our most profound emotional response is to want criminals to suffer as their victims did. When a man is accused of throwing a child from a high-rise terrace, my emotional—some might say hysterical—response is that he should be given an opportunity to see how endless the seconds are from the thirty-first story to the ground. In a civilized society that will never happen. And so what many people want from the death penalty, they will never get.

6   Death is death, you may say, and you would be right. But anyone who has seen someone die suddenly of a heart attack and someone else slip slowly into the clutches of cancer knows that there are gradations of dying.

7   I watched a television reenactment one night of an execution by lethal injection. It was well done; it was horrible. The methodical approach, people standing around the gurney waiting, made it more awful. One moment there was a man in a prone position; the next moment that man was gone. On another night I watched a television movie about a little boy named Adam Walsh, who disappeared from a shopping center in Florida. There was a reenactment of Adam's parents coming to New York, where they appeared on morning talk shows begging for their son's return, and in their hotel room, where they received a call from the police saying that Adam had just been found: not all of Adam, actually, just his severed head, discovered in the waters of a Florida canal. There is nothing anyone could do that is bad enough for an adult who took a six-year-old boy away from his parents, perhaps tortured, then murdered him and cut off his head. Nothing at all. Lethal injection? The electric chair? Bah.

8   And so I come back to the position that the death penalty is wrong, not only because it consists of stooping to the level of the killers, but also because it is not what it seems. Just before one of Ted Bundy's execution dates was postponed pending further

appeals, the father of his last known victim, a twelve-year-old girl, said what almost every father in his situation must feel. "I wish they'd bring him back to Lake City," said Tom Leach of the town where Kimberly Leach lived and died, "and let us all have at him." But the death penalty does not let us all have at him in the way Mr. Leach seems to mean. What he wants is for something as horrifying as what happened to his child to happen to Ted Bundy. And that is impossible.

Meanings and Values

1a.   According to Quindlen, what two purposes do people believe the death penalty can serve?

b.   Does she believe it can effectively serve either purpose?

2a.   Tell what you think the phrase "sixties liberalism" is likely to mean to most readers. (See Guide to Terms: *Connotation and Denotation*.)

b.   Does the essay provide any clear evidence that Quindlen is either liberal or conservative in her political and social outlook? If so, what is the evidence?

3.   How does the author try to show that she is not unthinking and naive in her opposition to the death penalty and is, in fact, entitled to speak with authority?

4a.   How does Quindlen answer one of the most common arguments made on behalf of capital punishment, that it helps deter crime?

b.   Explain why you find her answer satisfactory or unsatisfactory.

Argumentative Techniques

1.   Why does the author wait until the second paragraph to state the thesis of the essay?

2a.   Identify the examples Quindlen presents in paragraphs 1, 3, 5, 6, and 7.

b.   To what extent do the examples in paragraphs 1, 3, and 7 function as a refutation? (Guide: *Refutation*.)

c.   How successful is the author in convincing readers that these examples accurately represent her view of the complexity of the issue and are more than simply strategies to refute opposing arguments? Be ready to support your evaluation with examples from the text. (Guide: *Evaluation*.)

3.   Tell how the essay uses comparison in paragraphs 1–3 and 6.

Diction and Vocabulary

1a. In the fourth paragraph, Quindlen argues against using the death penalty as a deterrent. How does the wording of the second sentence exclude opposing arguments?

 b. What flaw in logic, if any, does this assertion contain? (See Introduction to Chapter 11, pp. 347–48.)

2a. Identify several instances of colloquial expressions in this essay that keep it from being completely formal. (Guide: *Colloquial Expressions.*)

 b. Does the colloquial language add to or detract from the effectiveness of the essay? How? (Guide: *Evaluation.*)

 c. What effect are technical terms such as *voir dire* (par. 2) and *recidivism* (par. 4) likely to have on readers?

Suggestions for Writing and Discussion

1. Have TV specials and docudramas, such as those mentioned in the essay, become important forces shaping our moral outlooks? Discuss some programs that you or your classmates remember, identifying their moral perspectives and considering their likely effects on viewers.

2. To what extent is punishment of any sort a deterrent for crime? Are some punishments more effective than others? Besides deterrence, what ends can punishment serve?

3. Prepare an essay arguing for (or against) a mandatory life sentence without parole as an alternative for capital punishment.

(NOTE: Suggestions for topics requiring development by use of ARGUMENT are on page 426, at the end of this section.)

JUDITH JENKINS GEORGE

> JUDITH JENKINS GEORGE is Associate Professor of Health, Physical Education, and Recreation at De Pauw University. She has coached field hockey and other sports for twenty-four years.

Women Coaches Are an Endangered Species

> In the opening of this opinion essay from *The New York Times,*
> the author observes that despite the remarkable achievements
> of women athletes in the last decade and the growth of opportunities for women to participate in sports, there are now fewer
> women coaches in college athletics than there were in the mid–
> 1970s. Using a variety of examples, she argues that discrimination and lack of equal opportunity have caused the problem, and
> she proposes strong steps to overcome it.

As you sit in the stands at Fenway Park or Shea Stadium and your 1
eye drifts to the third base coaching box, do you ever see a woman?
No. At first base? No. Do you ever see a woman manager in the
dugout? Of course not.

The same thing is pretty much true on collegiate baseball dia- 2
monds. But, more significantly, it is true in collegiate gyms, where
women and men—separately—play basketball.

Whatever happened to the dream of women taking their place 3
alongside men in athletic leadership, especially on the court?

In the mid–70's, the dreamers among us envisioned growing 4
numbers of women coaches and women in athletic administration.
Today, although women have more opportunities to participate in

sports, they have fewer opportunities to coach and administer collegiate athletic programs.

A nationwide study by Vivian Acosta and Linda Carpenter, 5
both professors in the department of physical education at Brooklyn College, shows that women coached more than 90 percent of all female collegiate teams in 1972 compared with only 48 percent today. In 1972, more than 90 percent of women's collegiate athletic programs were administered by women; today, only 16 percent are.

The indignities and sexism that women in athletics must cope 6
with should cause a national uproar, but the complacent public routinely accepts subtle, even blatant, discrimination in sports.

Here are two examples. 7

The Indiana High School Men's and Women's Basketball As- 8
sociation requires that, during coaches' clinics, coaches of boys' teams sit on the main level of Lawrence Central Gymnasium in Indianapolis while the coaches of girls' teams, 70 percent of whom are men, are relegated to the balcony.

Wilma Rudolph, the only woman to have received the Na- 9
tional College Athletic Association's silver anniversary award, was sent a form letter from the NCAA stating that all recipients of that distinguished honor must submit a publicity photo of themselves with coat and tie.

It's no secret that the patriarchal sports world is insensitive to 10
females. What's surprising is that women in athletics quietly accept the fact that very little media attention is given to women's sports, ignore reports of inequities in women's collegiate athletic programs and allow themselves to be satisfied with such token patronage assignments as assistant coaching jobs or academic advisers to men's (revenue producing) college teams.

Jean Lenti Ponsetto, associate athletic director at DePaul Uni- 11
versity in Chicago, says in an issue of The NCAA News that women are entitled to have the best coaches, whether male or female. That's true. But nationwide, why isn't there one female coach of a men's collegiate basketball team?

Coaching is the first rung in the ladder that leads to other vo- 12
cational opportunities in athletics. Without being a coach, a woman cannot become an athletic director or avail herself of opportunities in professional sports.

My 1987 study of Indiana collegiate athletes found that 55 percent of the 516 female athletes polled were interested in coaching
but that very few were being guided into coaching ranks.

While female athletes are acceptable to male athletes, the female stepping into the coaching arena threatens the old-boy network.

One notable exception to the rule is the naming of Phyllis
Holmes as 1988 president of the National Association of Intercolle-
giate Athletics.

The few women coaches in athletics have little time to think
about larger issues such as recruiting more women coaches. Moreover, coaching jobs are tenuous enough without rocking the boat
with what some might see as zany feminist ideas. In any case,
young women are not being attracted to coaching, largely because
there are so few role models.

We live in the age of Florence Griffith-Joyner's 100-meter dash
world record and Mary Decker Slaney's dedication to middle-
distance training and motherhood. Women are expected to compete and to stretch their physical range, as men do. It is time that
women refuse to be satisfied with token coaching jobs and administrative morsels.

In high schools and colleges, women must develop support
for female sports leadership in their communities. Toward that
end, they should work with athletic directors, school administra-
tions and service and professional organizations to bring about
needed changes.

Furthermore, women should not hesitate to cause a stir in athletic circles. They need to follow the example of the Black Coaches
Association, a collegiate organization, and use a consolidated female network to help each other find jobs and serve as a pressure
group for the recognition of women coaches.

In addition, they must be willing to use lawsuits, affirmative
action and boycotts to protest discrimination.

It is time for women to leave the stands, to enter first- and
third-base coaching boxes and to sit on the bench.

Meanings and Values

1a.   In your own words, state the causes George identifies for the rela-
      tively small number of women coaches.

b. What examples and statistics does the author offer to support her argument that the athletic establishment makes it difficult for women to become coaches?

c. Tell why you find this evidence either persuasive or unpersuasive. (See Guide to Terms: *Evaluation*.)

2. What is the main purpose (or purposes) of this essay? (Guide: *Purpose*.)

3a. Which examples in this essay appeal to readers' emotions (including anger and pride)? (See Introduction to Chapter 11, p. 345.)

b. Given the purpose of the selection, are the appeals to emotion appropriate or inappropriate? Why?

Argumentative Techniques

1. In which paragraphs does the author acknowledge and refute opposing arguments? (Guide: *Refutation*.)

2a. What parts of this essay are devoted to identifying a problem?

b. To offering value judgments about its causes?

c. To proposing actions to solve it?

3a. The central theme of this essay is stated several times in somewhat different forms, most notably in paragraph 6 and in the last sentence of paragraph 17. To what extent does the problem-solution structure of the essay necessitate this strategy?

b. Explain why you believe that the sentences in paragraphs 6 and 17 should be considered either two different thesis statements or simply variations on the essay's central proposition. (Guide: *Thesis*.)

Diction and Vocabulary

1. Tell what use the author makes of rhetorical questions in paragraphs 1, 3, and 11. (Guide: *Rhetorical Questions*.)

2. Discuss the denotative and connotative meanings of the following phrases (Guide: *Connotation* and *Denotation*):

a. "relegated to the balcony" (par. 8)

b. "patriarchal sports world" (par. 10)

c. "token coaching jobs and administrative morsels" (par. 17)

3a. Why can the language in the concluding paragraph be considered metaphoric even though the language of the opening paragraph which it echoes has a literal intent? (Guide: *Figures of Speech*.)

b. Is this use of language an effective device for concluding the essay? Why, or why not? (Guide: *Closings*.)

Suggestions for Writing and Discussion

1. If you have any experiences in athletics that support or contradict George's argument, draw on them in preparing an essay of your own that responds to the issues raised in "Women Coaches Are an Endangered Species."

2. Are women's athletic programs treated fairly at the college you attend? Should they receive support equal to that of men's sports?

3. Is it appropriate for men's athletic programs such as football and basketball to receive the most financial and administrative support at those schools where they produce considerable revenue? How are other athletic programs helped or hurt by the dominance of these sports?

4. What steps other than those suggested by George might be undertaken to increase coaching and administrative opportunities for women?

(NOTE: Suggestions for topics requiring development by use of ARGUMENT are on page 426, at the end of this section.)

GEORGIE ANNE GEYER

GEORGIE ANNE GEYER was born in 1935 in Chicago, Illinois, and attended Northwestern University, from which she received a B.S. in 1956. From 1964 to 1975 she was a foreign correspondent for the *Chicago Daily News* and since then has been a nationally syndicated newspaper columnist and a frequent guest on public television's "Washington Week in Review." Her essays appear often in magazines such as *The Atlantic, The New Republic, The Progressive, The Nation,* and *Wildlife,* and her books include *The New Latins: Fateful Change in South and Central America* (1970) and *The Young Russians* (1970).

Drugs: Facing the Responsibility

Central to the effectiveness of "Drugs: Facing the Responsibility" (editors' title), one of Geyer's syndicated columns, is her use of cause and effect to present a fresh perspective on an issue about which many readers are likely to have already made up their minds. Her subject is the use of illegal drugs, a habit that one suspects all too many of her readers either practice, condone, or simply ignore. To give her arguments force she presents in vivid detail some consequences of the drug trade that users and opponents of drug use alike seldom consider because they are outside our routine experience.

Go ahead, pick up the marijuana cigarette. It's an "innocent" vice,   1
after all. It's a victimless crime, and it gives you such a good
feeling.

    Go ahead—have some cocaine before dinner and laugh at the   2
squares. You'll have a high like you've never had before, made

Reprinted by permission of Georgia Anne Geyer.

even more intense by thinking about what your proper old mom and dad would say about it.

Go ahead—young and not-so-young America: Take your drugs, which are transforming the world. But do me one favor, will you? Cut out the hypocrisy.

As you so fashionably smoke your marijuana cigarette, or as you so genteelly sniff your cocaine, for just one moment think of the square brown faces of the Bolivian Indians whose country you are destroying. Or think of the body of Rodrigo Lara Bonilla, the upright and courageous Colombian minister of justice who was riddled with bullets by drug "czars" a year ago. Or of Enrique Camarena Salazar, the American drug enforcement agent kidnapped in Mexico.

Can you honestly tell me that you are not the one who is destroying Bolivia? Or that you were not the clean hand behind the dirty hand that killed Lara? Or that you weren't the one responsible for Camarena's kidnapping—and the swiftly developing breakdown of neighboring Mexico because of drugs?

Let me tell you about these countries.

Bolivia is a vast, high, glorious plateau of purples, pinks and browns, where the descendants of the great Inca Empire live strange and (to us) wondrous lives. When the winds and rains sweep across the Altiplano, the Indians stand on little piles of rocks and wave palm leaves to drive the storms away.

Bolivia was once a hopeful country, despite its poverty. It had the single great non-Marxist democratic revolution in South America, in 1954, and was doing well—until the drug trade came and so destroyed its institutions that it now is in the thrall of anarchy.

Colombia is another glorious Andean country, but more gray and heavy in its traditional Spanish spirit. The Colombians had terrible years of what they called "la Violencia" in the 1950s, in which upward of 200,000 people were killed in cruel countryside fighting that was a blend of banditry and Marxism. Still, because Colombia had a truly dedicated leadership class in politics and in the military, amazingly they were able to overcome this period.

Now this valiant country is slipping into the quicksand as drug "families" (an obnoxious use of the word) are rapidly taking over the country, destabilizing the government and the judicial system. No one can be sure whether Colombia will continue as the stable and hopeful democracy—or even the country—it has been.

Mexico, of course, is the country that had the first great rev- 11
olution in Latin America in general, in 1910 and 1911. It has been
the area's hope, a country of vast energies with an open future.

Today, it has many problems—terrible corruption, civil wars 12
on its southern borders, immense overpopulation, economic
breakdown and debt problems. But if it didn't have the drug problem—the north of Mexico now is virtually ruled by drug dealers—
it probably could "make it." With these drug dealers, it's all a
toss-up.

At this point, I think I know what you will say. You will argue 13
that it is their fault. The drugs are illegal; let their governments
clean them up. Forgive me if I differ emphatically with this rationalization. Governments are fragile; states are not forever, particularly with struggling countries like these.

You want the decent people down there to die trying to control 14
the drug traffic—while you won't even deny yourself a momentary
kick. No, the fault is yours; the drug trade primarily is yours, and
thus it is all of ours, as Americans. It arises out of your essential
narcissism. The blood is on your hands first.

Funny—out of your selfishness, you have unleashed a compel- 15
ling new force in the world. *The Washington Post* calls it "a revolutionary political force of global dimensions," referring to the geopolitical force of the trade whose drugs now reach an estimated 25
million Americans. No one ever said that "revolutions" were all
good. Many take mankind backward, particularly when they have
to do with drugs. The opium wars of the 19th century put the final
seal on the destruction of the China of that time (an epoch they
are still only working their way out of). The Inca Indians of the
Andes turned to chewing the soporific coca leaf to forget the
Spanish conquest (and are still numbed by its effects). In many
parts of the Middle East, hashish is the drug of historic forget-
fulness.

Those peoples had drugs forced upon them—or took them to 16
obliterate wrenching historical experiences. You are wantonly taking them, and in the process—make no mistake about it—blithely
destroying whole cultures and countries.

It's funny—15 and 20 years ago, young Americans flocked to 17
join the Peace Corps to help build up those countries. Now it is
your generation of Americans who are staying home and destroying them.

Meanings and Values

1a.   List the harmful effects of drug use that Geyer presents in this essay as support for her thesis.

 b.   What arguments *for* drug use does she mention either directly or indirectly in the essay, and where are they mentioned?

2a.   Do the arguments for drug use focus primarily on its personal consequences, and do those against it focus primarily on its consequences for other people—its social and political consequences?

 b.   If so, explain why Geyer is or is not justified in referring to the attitudes of drug users as ''hypocrisy'' (par. 3) and their actions as ''selfishness'' (par. 15).

 c.   If not, into what categories (if any) do the arguments fall, and in what ways do the groupings justify or fail to justify her opinion of drug users?

3a.   Did the effects described in paragraphs 4–5 and the accompanying claim that drug users are responsible seem farfetched after you first read it? Why?

 b.   If not, did they seem reasonable after you read the supporting evidence in paragraphs 6–12?

 c.   What kinds of evidence presented in these paragraphs seemed particularly convincing—or unconvincing? (See Guide to Terms: *Argument, Evaluation.*)

4a.   The opening paragraphs appear to be addressed primarily to drug users. What evidence is there in the opening and in the rest of the essay that it is addressed as well to people who do not use drugs but tolerate their use and to people who strongly oppose the use of illegal drugs?

 b.   What use could be made of this essay by people who already oppose illegal drugs because of what their use does to individuals and to our society?

Argumentative Techniques

1a.   To what extent can the sentence ''Cut out the hypocrisy'' in paragraph 3 be considered a thesis statement? (Guide: *Thesis.*)

 b.   In what paragraph later in the essay is the thesis presented at greater length?

 c.   Why do you think the author chose to announce her thesis more than once in the essay?

 d.   Is the strategy effective? Why, or why not? (Guide: *Evaluation.*)

2a.   What does the descriptive detail in paragraph 7 contribute to the argument?

b.   What other kinds of support does Geyer employ in paragraphs 8–12 and 15? (Guide: *Argument.*)

3.   Besides cause and effect, what pattern(s) does the author use to present supporting evidence and arguments in paragraphs 7 and 8? 9 and 10? 15?

4a.   Can the questions in paragraph 5 be considered rhetorical questions? Why, or why not? (Guide: *Rhetorical Questions.*)

b.   What role do they play in alerting readers to the organization of the essay?

c.   What other functions do they perform?

5a.   Where in the essay does Geyer acknowledge opposing arguments?

b.   How does she refute them? (Guide: *Refutation.*)

6.   How is parallel structure used in the opening paragraphs to attract the audience's attention and to emphasize points the author wishes to make? (Guide: *Parallel Structure, Emphasis.*)

Diction and Vocabulary

1.   Define "victimless crime" as the term is used in paragraph 1.

2a.   What comment on the attitudes of drug users does the author make in paragraph 4 through the diction? (Guide: *Diction.*)

b.   What words does she use elsewhere in the paragraph to make plain her view of the consequences of drug users' behavior and to emphasize the contrast between the intentions and the ultimate effects?

3.   Discuss how Geyer uses repetition of related words to add emphasis to paragraph 14. (Guide: *Emphasis.*)

4a.   In what sense is the word "funny" in paragraphs 15 and 17 used? Is the use ironic in any way? (Guide: *Irony.*)

b.   What other word or phrase could have been used in these places to achieve the author's purpose?

5.   If you do not know the meaning of some of the following words, look them up in your dictionary: genteelly, czars (par. 4); Inca (7); thrall, anarchy (8); destabilizing (10); rationalization (13); narcissism (14); geopolitical, epoch, soporific, coca, hashish (15); obliterate, wrenching, wantonly, blithely (16).

Suggestions for Writing and Discussion

1.   Discuss whether making marijuana, cocaine, and perhaps other drugs legal would eliminate the problems Geyer describes. Would legalization have harmful effects of its own?

2.   Prepare an essay in which you argue that some illegal or immoral
      practice that many people indulge in and others are willing to ig-
      nore (cheating on income tax, illegal betting, drinking and driving,
      for example) has consequences that should make people change
      their attitudes and behavior.

(NOTE: Suggestions for topics requiring development by use of ARGUMENT are on
page 426, at the end of this section.)

ARGUMENT THROUGH COMPARISON AND CONTRAST

EDWARD ABBEY

EDWARD ABBEY was born in Pennsylvania in 1927 and died in
1989. He attended the University of Michigan. After having
worked as a park ranger and forest fire lookout, he became a
full-time writer, publishing novels and essays. Much of the time
he wrote about the American West, especially its rivers and des-
serts. Like Thoreau, to whom he is often compared, Abbey was
concerned with the beauty, power, and integrity of the natural
world, qualities he felt are endangered by the industrial and
commercial forces in our society. Among his writings are *The
Monkey Wrench Gang* (1975) (a novel) and collections of his essays
and journals: *Desert Solitaire* (1968), *The Journey Home: Some
Words in Defense of the American West* (1977), *Abbey's Road* (1979),
Down the River (1982), *Beyond the Wall* (1984), and *One Life at a
Time, Please* (1988). His essays appeared frequently in magazines
such as *Geo, National Geographic, The New York Times Magazine,
Harper's, Rolling Stone, Backpacker, Mother Earth News, City Lights
Review,* and *Architectural Digest.*

The Damnation of a Canyon

In "The Damnation of a Canyon," an essay from *Beyond the
Wall*, Abbey uses a comparison focused on a familiar scene, a
recreational lake formed by a dam, in order to advance his argument about the impact of development on natural beauty and
what he calls elsewhere the "question of muscle and will versus
motors and money." The essay employs a number of other patterns as well, and is marked throughout by Abbey's distinctive
voice, which ranges in tone from irreverant, cranky, and even
insulting to formal, rational, and even poetic—all in praise and
defense of the lands and rivers.

There was a time when, in my search for essences, I concluded   1
that the canyonland country has no heart. I was wrong. The canyonlands did have a heart, a living heart, and that heart was Glen
Canyon and the golden, flowing Colorado River.

In the summer of 1959 a friend and I made a float trip in little   2
rubber rafts down through the length of Glen Canyon, starting at
Hite and getting off the river near Gunsight Butte—The Crossing
of the Fathers. In this voyage of some 150 miles and ten days our
only motive power, and all that we needed, was the current of the
Colorado River.

In the summer and fall of 1967 I worked as a seasonal park   3
ranger at the new Glen Canyon National Recreation Area. During
my five-month tour of duty I worked at the main marina and headquarters area called Wahweap, at Bullfrog Basin toward the upper
end of the reservoir, and finally at Lee's Ferry downriver from Glen
Canyon Dam. In a number of powerboat tours I was privileged to
see almost all of our nation's newest, biggest and most impressive
''recreational facility.''

Having thus seen Glen Canyon both before and after what we   4
may fairly call its damnation, I feel that I am in a position to evaluate the transformation of the region caused by construction of the
dam. I have had the unique opportunity to observe firsthand some
of the differences between the environment of a free river and a
power-plant reservoir.

One should admit at the outset to a certain bias. Indeed I am   5
a ''butterfly chaser, googly eyed bleeding heart and wild conservative.'' I take a dim view of dams; I find it hard to learn to love
cement; I am poorly impressed by concrete aggregates and statistics in the cubic tons. But in this weakness I am not alone, for I
belong to that ever-growing number of Americans, probably a
good majority now, who have become aware that a fully industrial-
ized, thoroughly urbanized, elegantly computerized social system
is not suitable for human habitation. Great for machines, yes: But
unfit for people.

Lake Powell, formed by Glen Canyon Dam, is not a lake. It is   6
a reservoir, with a constantly fluctuating water level—more like a
bathtub that is never drained than a true lake. As at Hoover (or
Boulder) Dam, the sole practical function of this impounded water
is to drive the turbines that generate electricity in the powerhouse
at the base of the dam. Recreational benefits were of secondary

importance in the minds of those who conceived and built this dam. As a result the volume of water in the reservoir is continually being increased or decreased according to the requirements of the Basin States Compact and the power-grid system of which Glen Canyon Dam is a component.

The rising and falling water level entails various conse- 7 quences. One of the most obvious, well known to all who have seen Lake Mead, is the "bathtub ring" left on the canyon walls after each drawdown of water, or what rangers at Glen Canyon call the Bathtub Foundation. This phenomenon is perhaps of no more than aesthetic importance; yet it is sufficient to dispel any illusion one might have, in contemplating the scene, that you are looking upon a natural lake.

Of much more significance is the fact that plant life, because 8 of the unstable water line, cannot establish itself on the shores of the reservoir. When the water is low, plant life dies of thirst; when high, it is drowned. Much of the shoreline of the reservoir consists of near-perpendicular sandstone bluffs, where very little flora ever did or ever could subsist, but the remainder includes bays, coves, sloping hills and the many side canyons, where the original plant life has been drowned and new plant life cannot get a foothold. And of course where there is little or no plant life there is little or no animal life.

The utter barrenness of the reservoir shoreline recalls by con- 9 trast the aspect of things before the dam, when Glen Canyon formed the course of the untamed Colorado. Then we had a wild and flowing river lined by boulder-strewn shores, sandy beaches, thickets of tamarisk and willow, and glades of cottonwoods.

The thickets teemed with songbirds: vireos, warblers, mock- 10 ingbirds and thrushes. On the open beaches were killdeer, sand-pipers, herons, ibises, egrets. Living in grottoes in the canyon walls were swallows, swifts, hawks, wrens and owls. Beaver were common if not abundant: not an evening would pass, in drifting down the river, that we did not see them or at least hear the whack of their flat tails on the water. Above the river shores were the great recessed alcoves where water seeped from the sandstone, nourishing the semitropical hanging gardens of orchid, ivy and columbine, with their associated swarms of insects and birdlife.

Up most of the side canyon, before damnation, there were 11 springs, sometimes flowing streams, waterfalls and plunge pools—

the kind of marvels you can now find only in such small-scale rem-
nants of Glen Canyon as the Escalante area. In the rich flora of
these laterals the larger mammals—mule deer, coyote, bobcat, ring-
tailed cat, gray fox, kit fox, skunk, badger and others—found a
home. When the river was dammed almost all of these things were
lost. Crowded out—or drowned and buried under mud.

The difference between the present reservoir, with its silent
sterile shores and debris-choked side canyons, and the original
Glen Canyon, is the difference between death and life. Glen Canyon was alive. Lake Powell is a graveyard.

For those who may think I exaggerate the contrast between
the former river canyon and the present man-made impoundment,
I suggest a trip on Lake Powell followed immediately by another
boat trip on the river below the dam. Take a boat from Lee's Ferry
up the river to within sight of the dam, then shut off the motor
and allow yourself the rare delight of a quiet, effortless drifting
down the stream. In that twelve-mile stretch of living green, singing birds, flowing water and untarnished canyon walls—sights and
sounds a million years older and infinitely lovelier than the roar of
motorboats—you will rediscover a small and imperfect sampling of
the kind of experience that was taken away from everybody when
the oligarchs and politicians condemned our river for purposes of
their own.

The effects of Glen Canyon Dam also extend downstream,
causing changes in the character and ecology of Marble Gorge and
Grand Canyon. Because the annual spring floods are now a thing
of the past, the shores are becoming overgrown with brush, the
rapids are getting worse where the river no longer has enough
force to carry away the boulders washed down from the lateral
canyons, and the beaches are disappearing, losing sand that is not
replaced.

Lake Powell, though not a lake, may well be as its defenders
assert the most beautiful reservoir in the world. Certainly it has
a photogenic backdrop of buttes and mesas projecting above the
expansive surface of stagnant waters where the speedboats,
houseboats and cabin cruisers ply. But it is no longer a wilderness.
It is no longer a place of natural life. It is no longer Glen Canyon.

The defenders of the dam argue that the recreational benefits
available on the surface of the reservoir outweigh the loss of Indian
ruins, historical sites, wildlife and wilderness adventure. Relying

on the familiar quantitative logic of business and bureaucracy, they assert that whereas only a few thousand citizens even ventured down the river through Glen Canyon, now millions can—or will— enjoy the motorized boating and hatchery fishing available on the reservoir. They will also argue that the rising waters behind the dam have made such places as Rainbow Bridge accessible by pow- erboat. Formerly you could get there only by walking (six miles).

This argument appeals to the wheelchair ethos of the wealthy,   17 upper-middle-class American slob. If Rainbow Bridge is worth seeing at all, then by God it should be easily, readily, immediately available to everybody with the money to buy a big powerboat. Why should a trip to such a place be the privilege only of those who are willing to walk six miles? Or if Pikes Peak is worth getting to, then why not build a highway to the top of it so that anyone can get there? Anytime? Without effort? Or as my old man would say, "By Christ, one man's just as good as another—if not a damn sight better."

Or as ex-Commissioner Floyd Dominy of the U.S. Bureau of   18 Reclamation pointed out poetically in his handsomely engraved and illustrated brochure *Lake Powell: Jewel of the Colorado* (produced by the U.S. Government Printing Office at our expense): "There's something about a lake which brings us a little closer to God." In this case, Lake Powell, about five hundred feet closer. Eh, Floyd?

It is quite true that the flooding of Glen Canyon has opened   19 up to the motorboat explorer parts of side canyons that formerly could be reached only by people able to walk. But the sum total of terrain visible to the eye and touchable by hand and foot has been greatly diminished, not increased. Because of the dam the river is gone, the inner canyon is gone, the best parts of the numerous side canyons are gone—all hidden beneath hundreds of feet of polluted water, accumulating silt, and mounting tons of trash. This portion of Glen Canyon—and who can estimate how many cubic miles were lost?—*is no longer accessible to anybody.* (Except scuba divers.) And this, do not forget, was the most valuable part of Glen Can- yon, richest in scenery, archaeology, history, flora and fauna.

Not only has the heart of Glen Canyon been buried, but many   20 of the side canyons above the fluctuating waterline are now ren- dered more difficult, not easier, to get into. This because the debris brought down into them by desert storms, no longer carried away by the river, must unavoidably build up in the area where flood meets reservoir. Narrow Canyon, for example, at the head of the impounded waters, is already beginning to silt up and to amass huge quantities of driftwood, some of it floating on the surface, some of it half afloat beneath the surface. Anyone who has tried to pilot a motorboat through a raft of half-sunken logs and bloated dead cows will have his own thoughts on the accessibility of these waters.

Hite Marina, at the mouth of Narrow Canyon, will probably have to be abandoned within twenty or thirty years. After that it will be the turn of Bullfrog Marina. And then Rainbow Bridge Marina. And eventually, inevitably, whether it takes ten centuries or only one, Wahweap. Lake Powell, like Lake Mead, is foredoomed sooner or later to become a solid mass of mud, and its dam a waterfall. Assuming, of course, that either one stands that long.

Second, the question of costs. It is often stated that the dam and its reservoir have opened up to the many what was formerly restricted to the few, implying in this case that what was once expensive has now been made cheap. Exactly the opposite is true.

Before the dam, a float trip down the river through Glen Canyon would cost you a minimum of seven days' time, well within anyone's vacation allotment, and a capital outlay of about forty dollars—the prevailing price of a two-man rubber boat with oars, available at any army-navy surplus store. A life jacket might be useful but not required, for there were no dangerous rapids in the 150 miles of Glen Canyon. As the name implies, this stretch of the river was in fact so easy and gentle that the trip could be and was made by all sorts of amateurs: by Boy Scouts, Camp Fire Girls, stenographers, schoolteachers, students, little old ladies in inner tubes. Guides, professional boatmen, giant pontoons, outboard motors, radios, rescue equipment were not needed. The Glen Canyon float trip was an adventure anyone could enjoy, on his own, for a cost less than that of spending two days and nights in a Page motel. Even food was there, in the water: the channel catfish were easier to catch and a lot better eating than the striped bass and rainbow trout dumped by the ton into the reservoir these days. And one other thing: at the end of the float trip you still owned your boat, usable for many more such casual and carefree expeditions.

What is the situation now? Float trips are no longer possible. The only way left for the exploration of the reservoir and what remains of Glen Canyon demands the use of a powerboat. Here you have three options: (1) buy your own boat and engine, the necessary auxiliary equipment, the fuel to keep it moving, the parts and repairs to keep it running, the permits and licenses required for legal operation, the trailer to transport it; (2) rent a boat; or (3) go on a commercial excursion boat, packed in with other sightseers, following a preplanned itinerary. This kind of play is only for the affluent.

The inescapable conclusion is that no matter how one attempts to calculate the cost in dollars and cents, a float trip down Glen Canyon was much cheaper than a powerboat tour of the reservoir. Being less expensive, as well as safer and easier, the float trip was an adventure open to far more people than will ever be able to afford motorboat excursions in the area now. 25

What about the "human impact" of motorized use of the Glen Canyon impoundment? We can visualize the floor of the reservoir gradually accumulating not only silt, mud, waterlogged trees and drowned cattle but also the usual debris that is left behind when the urban, industrial style of recreation is carried into the open country. There is also the problem of human wastes. The waters of the wild river were good to drink, but nobody in his senses would drink from Lake Powell. Eventually, as is already sometimes the case at Lake Mead, the stagnant waters will become too foul even for swimming. The trouble is that while some boats have what are called "self-contained" heads, the majority do not; most sewage is disposed of by simply pumping it into the water. It will take a while, but long before it becomes a solid mass of mud Lake Powell ("Jewel of the Colorado") will enjoy a passing fame as the biggest sewage lagoon in the American Southwest. Most tourists will never be able to afford a boat trip on this reservoir, but everybody within fifty miles will be able to smell it. 26

All of the foregoing would be nothing but a futile exercise in nostalgia (so much water over the dam) if I had nothing constructive and concrete to offer. But I do. As alternate methods of power generation are developed, such as solar, and as the nation establishes a way of life adapted to actual resources and basic needs, so that the demand for electrical power begins to diminish, we can shut down the Glen Canyon power plant, open the diversion tunnels, and drain the reservoir. 27

This will no doubt expose a drear and hideous scene: immense mud flats and whole plateaus of sodden garbage strewn with dead trees, sunken boats, the skeletons of long-forgotten, decomposing 28 water-skiers. But to those who find the prospect too appalling, I say give nature a little time. In five years, at most in ten, the sun and wind and storms will cleanse and sterilize the repellent mess. The inevitable floods will soon remove all that does not belong within the canyons. Fresh green willow, box elder and redbud will reappear; and the ancient drowned cottonwoods (noble monuments to themselves) will be replaced by young of their own kind. With the renewal of plant life will come the insects, the birds, the lizards and snakes, the mammals. Within a generation—thirty years—I predict the river and canyons will bear a decent resemblance to their former selves. Within the lifetime of our children Glen Canyon and the living river, heart of the canyonlands, will be restored to us. The wilderness will again belong to God, the people and the wild things that call it home.

Meanings and Values

1a.   Is the primary purpose of this essay to argue against the Glen Canyon Dam, or is its main purpose somewhat broader? (See Guide to Terms: *Purpose.*)

 b.   If you believe the primary aim is broader, state the essay's purpose in your own words.

2a.   What is the "certain bias" to which Abbey admits in paragraph 5?

 b.   Is he right in assuming that most people share it? Do you?

3a.   Summarize the qualities Abbey found so attractive in Glen Canyon.

 b.   Summarize the corresponding qualities he finds so unattractive in Lake Powell.

4a.   What arguments do defenders of the dam advance in favor of the lake it created?

 b.   How does Abbey attempt to refute these arguments? (Guide: *Refutation.*)

 c.   Are his refutations successful? Why, or why not? (Guide: *Evaluation.*)

5a.   What solution does Abbey offer in paragraphs 27–28?

 b.   How probable are the changes he predicts in the way energy is generated?

 c.   What, if anything, does the last paragraph (28) do to encourage readers to take whatever action they can to help bring about the restoration of areas like Glen Canyon?

Argumentative Techniques

1a. In which paragraph does Abbey make plain his thesis and indicate the primary pattern of development the argument will follow? (Guide: *Thesis.*)

b. Where else in the essay is the thesis stated more or less directly?

2. What is the significance of the title? Does it contribute to the effectiveness of the essay? (Guide: *Evaluation.*)

3. Though comparison is the dominant pattern used to advance the argument in this essay, Abbey also uses a number of other patterns. What are they and where are they used?

4a. How would you describe the tone in paragraphs 17–18 and 26? (Guide: *Style/Tone.*)

b. Does the tone add to or detract from the effectiveness of the argument? Why?

Diction and Vocabulary

1a. How does the diction in paragraphs 9–12 differ from that in most of the remainder of the essay? (Guide: *Diction.*)

b. What is its effect on the reader and how does it contribute to the argument?

c. How does the syntax in these paragraphs contribute to their impact? (Guide: *Syntax.*)

2a. In what ways does the comparison of Lake Powell to a bathtub in paragraphs 6 and 7 help support the thesis of the essay?

b. What comparison is made in paragraph 26 and how does it contribute to the argument?

3a. Describe the contrasts in diction in paragraph 28 and discuss their intended impact on the reader.

b. How does the structure of the sentences in this paragraph reflect the contrasts in diction and the overall comparison pattern of the essay?

4. If you do not know the meaning of some of the following words, look them up in your dictionary: motive (par. 2); bias, aggregates, urbanized (5); impounded (6); aesthetic, dispel (7); perpendicular, flora (8); grottoes, alcoves (10); oligarchs (13); photogenic, buttes, mesas, ply (15); quantitative (16); ethos (17); fauna (19); heads (26).

Suggestions for Writing and Discussion

1. Some people feel that urban renewal or gentrification (the upgrad-
   ing of run-down city districts) destroys intact and thriving, though
   often poor, neighborhoods. Discuss this issue, drawing whatever
   parallels are appropriate with Abbey's comparison of Glen Canyon
   and Lake Powell.

2. If you have been to a recreational site like Lake Powell, compare
   your observations with those made in this essay, and indicate
   whether you think Abbey is being fair or unfair in his description
   of the impact of recreational development.

3. Write an essay about a proposed development project you know
   about (or can learn about through research) and argue for or
   against it.

(NOTE: Suggestions for topics requiring development by use of ARGUMENT are on
page 426, at the end of this section.)

RICHARD LYNN

RICHARD LYNN was born in London, England, in 1930. He received a B.A. from Kings College, Cambridge, in 1953 and was
awarded a Ph.D. in 1956. He has taught at Exeter University;
the Economic and Social Research Institute, Dublin; and is currently a professor of psychology at the University of Ulster.
Among his books are *Personality and National Character* (1971);
An Introduction to the Study of Personality (1971); *The Entrepreneur*
(1974); and, most recently, *Educational Achievement in Japan*
(1988).

Why Johnny Can't Read, but Yoshio Can

This essay was first published in the *National Review*, a magazine
noted for its advocacy of conservative social, economic, and political policies. In the selection, Lynn compares the Japanese
educational system to those of the United States and England in
order to argue for changes in the latter two systems. Of particular interest in this essay is the way the comparison pattern lends
itself to arguments urging the adoption of policies that have
worked in another setting.

There can be no doubt that American schools compare poorly with   1
Japanese schools. In the latter, there are no serious problems with
poor discipline, violence, or truancy; Japanese children take school
seriously and work hard. Japanese educational standards are high,
and illiteracy is virtually unknown.

The evidence of Japan's high educational standards began to   2
appear as long ago as the 1960s. In 1967 there was published the

first of a series of studies of educational standards in a dozen or so economically developed nations, based on tests of carefully drawn representative samples of children. The first study was concerned with achievement in math on the part of 13- and 18-year-olds. In both age groups the Japanese children came out well ahead of their coevals in other countries. The American 13-year-olds came out second to last for their age group; the American 18-year-olds, last. In both age groups, European children scored about halfway between the Japanese and the Americans.

Since then, further studies have appeared, covering science as well as math. The pattern of results has always been the same: the Japanese have generally scored first, the Americans last or nearly last, and the Europeans have fallen somewhere in between. In early adolescence, when the first tests are taken, Japanese children are two or three years ahead of American children; by age 18, approximately 98 per cent of Japanese children surpass their American counterparts.

Meanwhile, under the Reagan Administration, the United States at least started to take notice of the problem. In 1983 the President's report, *A Nation at Risk,* described the state of American schools as a national disaster. A follow-up report issued by the then-secretary of education, Mr. William Bennett, earlier this year[1] claims that although some improvements have been made, these have been "disappointingly slow."

An examination of Japan's school system suggests that there are three factors responsible for its success, which might be emulated by other countries: a strong national curriculum, stipulated by the government; strong incentives for students; and the stimulating effects of competition between schools.

The national curriculum in Japan is drawn up by the Department of Education. It covers Japanese language and literature, math, science, social science, music, moral education, and physical education. From time to time, the Department of Education requests advice on the content of the curriculum from representatives of the teaching profession, industry, and the trade unions.

[1] 1988, the year this essay was first published (Editors' note).

Syllabi are then drawn up, setting out in detail the subject matter that has to be taught at each grade. These syllabi are issued to school principals, who are responsible for ensuring that the stipulated curriculum is taught in their schools. Inspectors periodically check that this is being done.

The Japanese national curriculum ensures such uniformly 7 high standards of teaching that almost all parents are happy to send their children to the local public school. There is no flight into private schools of the kind that has been taking place in America in recent years. Private schools do exist in Japan, but they are attended by less than 1 per cent of children in the age range of compulsory schooling (six to 15 years).

This tightly stipulated national curriculum provides a striking 8 contrast with the decentralized curriculum of schools in America. Officially, the curriculum in America is the responsibility of school principals with guidelines from state education officials. In practice, even school principals often have little idea of what is actually being taught in the classroom.

America and Britain have been unusual in leaving the curricu- 9 lum so largely in the hands of teachers. Some form of national curriculum is used throughout Continental Europe, although the syllabus is typically not specified in as much detail as in Japan. And now Britain is changing course: legislation currently going through Parliament will introduce a national curriculum for England and Wales, with the principal subjects being English, math, science, technology, a foreign language, history and geography, and art, music, and design. It is envisioned that the new curriculum will take up approximately 70 per cent of teaching time, leaving the remainder free for optional subjects such as a second foreign language, or extra science.

Under the terms of the new legislation, schoolchildren are go- 10 ing to be given national tests at the ages of seven, 11, 14, and 16 to ensure that the curriculum has been taught and that children have learned it to a satisfactory standard. When the British national curriculum comes into effect, America will be left as the only major economically developed country without one.

To achieve high educational standards in schools it is neces- 11 sary to have motivated students as well as good teachers. A national curriculum acts as a discipline on teachers, causing them to teach efficiently, but it does nothing to provide incentives for students, an area in which American education is particularly weak.

One of the key factors in the Japanese education system is that secondary schooling is split into two stages. At the age of 11 or 12, Japanese children enter junior high school. After three years there, they take competitive entrance examinations for senior high schools. In each locality there is a hierarchy of public esteem for these senior high schools, from the two or three that are regarded as the best in the area, through those considered to be good or average, down to those that (at least by Japanese standards) are considered to be poor.

The top schools enjoy national reputations, somewhat akin to the famous English schools such as Eton and Harrow. But in England the high fees exacted by these schools mean that very few parents can afford them. Consequently there are few candidates for entry, and the entrance examinations offer little incentive to work for the great mass of children. By contrast, in Japan the elite senior high schools are open to everyone. While a good number of these schools are private (approximately 30 per cent nationwide, though in some major cities the figure is as high as 50 per cent), even these schools are enabled, by government subsidies, to keep their fees within the means of a large proportion of parents. The public schools also charge fees, but these are nominal, amounting to only a few hundred dollars a year, and loans are available to cover both fees and living expenses.

Thus children have every expectation of being able to attend the best school they can qualify for; and, hence, the hierarchical rankings of senior high schools act as a powerful incentive for children preparing for the entrance examinations. There is no doubt that Japanese children work hard in response to these incentives. Starting as early as age ten, approximately half of them take extra tuition on weekends, in the evenings, and in the school holidays at supplementary coaching establishments known as *juku,* and even at that early age they do far more homework than American children. At about the age of 12, Japanese children enter the period of their lives known as *examination hell:* during this time, which lasts fully two years, it is said that those who sleep more than five hours a night have no hope of success, either in school or in life. For, in addition to conferring great social and intellectual status on their students, the elite senior high schools provide a first-rate academic education, which, in turn, normally enables the students to get into one of the elite universities and, eventually, to move into a good job in industry or government.

Although Japanese children are permitted to leave school at the age of 15, 94 per cent of them proceed voluntarily to the senior high schools. Thus virtually all Japanese are exposed in early adolescence to the powerful incentive for academic work represented by the senior-high-school entrance examinations. There is nothing in the school systems of any of the Western countries resembling this powerful incentive.

The prestige of the elite senior high schools is sustained by the extensive publicity they receive from the media. Each year the top hundred or so schools in Japan are ranked on the basis of the percentage of their pupils who obtain entry to the University of Tokyo, Japan's most prestigious university. These rankings are widely reported in the print media, and the positions of the top twenty schools are announced on TV news programs, rather like the scores made by leading sports teams in the United States and Europe. At a local level, more detailed media coverage is devoted to the academic achievements of all the schools in the various localities, this time analyzed in terms of their pupils' success in obtaining entry to the lesser, but still highly regarded, local universities.

Thus, once Japanese 15-year-olds have been admitted to their senior high schools, they are confronted with a fresh set of incentives in the form of entrance examinations to universities and colleges, which are likewise hierarchically ordered in public esteem. After the University of Tokyo, which stands at the apex of the status hierarchy, come the University of Kyoto and ten or so other highly prestigious universities, including the former Imperial Universities in the major provincial cities and the technological university of Hitosubashi, whose standing and reputation in Japan resembles that of the Massachusetts Institute of Technology in the United States.

Below these top dozen institutions stand some forty or so less prestigious but still well-regarded universities. And after these come numerous smaller universities and colleges of varying degrees of standing and reputation.

To some extent the situation in Japan has parallels in the United States and Europe, but there are two factors that make the

15

16

17

18

19

importance of securing admission to an elite university substantially greater in Japan than in the West. In the first place, the entire Japanese system is geared toward providing lifelong employment, both in the private sector and in the civil service. It is practically unheard of for executives to switch from one corporation to another, or into public service and then back into the private sector, as in the United States and Europe. Employees are recruited directly out of college, and, needless to say, the major corporations and the civil service recruit virtually entirely from the top dozen universities. The smaller Japanese corporations operate along the same lines, although they widen their recruitment net to cover the next forty or so universities in the prestige hierarchy. Thus, obtaining entry to a prestigious university is a far more vital step for a successful career in Japan than it is in the United States or Europe.

Secondly, like the elite senior high schools, the elite universities are meritocratic. The great majority of universities are public institutions, receiving substantial government subsidies. Again, as with the senior high schools, fees are quite low, and loans are available to defray expenses. In principle and to a considerable extent in practice, any young Japanese can get into the University of Tokyo, or one of the other elite universities, provided only that he or she is talented enough and is prepared to do the work necessary to pass the entrance examinations. Knowing this, the public believes that *all* the most talented young Japanese go to one of these universities—and, conversely, that anyone who fails to get into one of these schools is necessarily less bright. Avoiding this stigma is, of course, a further incentive for the student to work hard to get in.

The third significant factor responsible for the high educational standards in Japan is competition among schools. This operates principally among the senior high schools, and what they are competing for is academic reputation. The most prestigious senior high school in Japan is Kansei in Tokyo, and being a teacher at Kansei is something like being a professor at Harvard. The teachers' self-esteem is bound up with the academic reputation of their schools—a powerful motivator for teachers to teach well.

In addition to this important factor of self-esteem, there is practical necessity. Since students are free to attend any school they can get into, if a school failed to provide good-quality teaching, it would no longer attract students. In business terms, its customers would fade away, and it would be forced to close. Thus the essential feature of the competition among the Japanese senior high schools is that it exposes the teachers to the discipline of the free-enterprise system. In the case of the public senior high schools, the system can be regarded as a form of market socialism in which the competing institutions are state-owned but nevertheless compete against each other for their customers. Here the Japanese have been successfully operating the kind of system that Mikhail Gorbachev may be feeling his way toward introducing in the Soviet Union. The Japanese private senior high schools add a further capitalist element to the system insofar as they offer their educational services more or less like firms operating in a conventional market.

The problem of how market disciplines can be brought to bear   23
on schools has been widely discussed in America and also in Britain ever since Milton Friedman raised it a quarter of a century or so ago, but solutions such as Friedman's voucher proposal seem as distant today as they did then. Although the proposal has been looked at sympathetically by Republicans in the United States and by Conservatives in Britain, politicians in both countries have fought shy of introducing it. Probably they have concluded that the problems of getting vouchers into the hands of all parents, and dealing with losses, fraud, counterfeits, and so forth, are likely to be too great for the scheme to be feasible.

The Japanese have evolved a different method of exposing   24
schools to market forces. Subsidies are paid directly to the schools on a per-capita basis in accordance with the number of students they have. If a school's rolls decline, so do its incomes, both from subsidies and from fees. This applies to both the public and private senior high schools, although the public schools obviously receive a much greater proportion of their income as subsidies and a smaller proportion from fees.

A similar scheme is being introduced in Britain. The Thatcher   25
government is currently bringing in legislation that will permit public schools to opt out of local-authority control. Those that opt out will receive subsidies from the central government on the basis of the number of students they have. They will then be on their own, to sink or swim.

There is little doubt that this is the route that should be fol-   26 lowed in America. The exposure of American schools to the invigorating stimulus of competition, combined with the introduction of a national curriculum and the provision of stronger incentives for students, would work wonders. Rather than complaining about Japanese aggressiveness and instituting counterproductive protectionist measures, Americans ought to be looking to the source of Japan's power.

Meanings and Values

1.   What is the issue or problem Lynn identifies in paragraphs 1–4?

2.   Summarize briefly the main reasons Lynn offers for the success of the Japanese school system.

3a. How does the curriculum in Japanese schools contrast with those in American and British schools?

b.   How does the Japanese system motivate students to excel, in contrast to the American and British systems?

4a. One possible weakness in this argument is that the author pays little attention to opposing points of view. Think of some reasonable objections a North American reader might have to the Japanese educational system. Try to identify some practical difficulties that stand in the way of the reforms the author proposes based on the Japanese model.

b.   Explain how you think the author might respond to these objections and possible problems.

Argumentative Techniques

1.   What kinds of evidence does the author offer to demonstrate the seriousness of the problem he describes in the opening of the essay? (See Guide to Terms: *Argument*.)

2.   Why might the author have chosen to summarize his main supporting arguments in paragraph 5, early in the essay?

3a. Discuss the strategies Lynn employs in paragraphs 11 and 21, which act as transitions between major segments of the essay. (Guide: *Transition*.)

b.   Tell how these two paragraphs, along with paragraphs 5 and 6, contribute to the overall coherence of the essay. (Guide: *Coherence*.)

4.   How would you describe the tone of the essay? In what ways does it add to the persuasiveness of the argument? (Guide: *Tone*.)

Diction and Vocabulary

1a.   Examine the diction in paragraphs 7, 14, and 22 to decide whether it is designed to appeal primarily to readers' emotions, reason, or both. (See Introduction to Chapter 11, p. 345 and Guide: *Diction.*)

  b.   On the whole, would you characterize the writing in this selection as objective or subjective? Why? (Guide: *Objective/Subjective.*)

2.   Identify the uses Lynn makes of parallel structures and contrasts in diction to emphasize the seriousness of the problem described in paragraphs 2 and 3. (Guide: *Parallel Structure.*)

3.   Point out the transitional devices used in paragraphs to emphasize contrasts between the Japanese educational system and those of Britain and America. (Guide: *Transition.*)

Suggestions for Writing and Discussion

1.   In what other ways do you think North Americans can learn from the economic or social systems of other countries? In discussing this issue, pay particular attention to countries such as Japan that have been especially successful in the last decade.

2.   Prepare an essay in which you take issue with the recommendations in this essay and propose some educational reforms of your own that you believe would be just as effective—or even more so.

3.   Using comparison as a strategy, argue for some solutions to a local problem such as disposal of solid waste, improvement of the transportation system, better administration of school athletics, or control of drug and alcohol abuse.

(NOTE: Suggestions for topics requiring development by use of ARGUMENT are on page 426, at the end of this section.)

BARBARA LAWRENCE

> BARBARA LAWRENCE was born in Hanover, New Hampshire.
> After receiving a B.A. in French literature from Connecticut Col-
> lege, she worked as an editor on *McCall's, Redbook, Harper's Ba-
> zaar,* and the *New Yorker.* During this period she also took an
> M.A. in philosophy from New York University. Currently a pro-
> fessor of humanities at the State University of New York's Col-
> lege at Old Westbury, Lawrence has published criticism, poetry,
> and fiction in *Choice, Commonweal, Columbia Poetry, The New York
> Times,* and the *New Yorker.*

Four-Letter Words Can Hurt You

> "Four-Letter Words Can Hurt You" first appeared in *The New
> York Times* and was later published in *Redbook.* In arguing against
> the "earthy, gut-honest" language often preferred by her stu-
> dents, Lawrence also provides a thoughtful, even scholarly, ex-
> tended definition of *obscenity* itself. To accomplish her purpose,
> the author makes use of several other patterns as well.

Why should any words be called obscene? Don't they all describe   1
natural human functions? Am I trying to tell them, my students
demand, that the "strong, earthy, gut-honest"—or, if they are fans
of Norman Mailer, the "rich, liberating, existential"—language
they use to describe sexual activity isn't preferable to "phony-
sounding, middle-class words like 'intercourse' and 'copulate'?"
"Cop You Late!" they say with fancy inflections and gagging grimaces. "Now, what is *that* supposed to mean?"

Well, what is it supposed to mean? And why indeed should 2 one group of words describing human functions and human organs be acceptable in ordinary conversation and another, describing presumably the same organs and functions, be tabooed—so much so, in fact, that some of these words still cannot appear in print in many parts of the English-speaking world?

The argument that these taboos exist only because of ''sexual 3 hangups'' (middle-class, middle-age, feminist), or even that they are a result of class oppression (the contempt of the Norman conquerors for the language of their Anglo-Saxon serfs), ignores a much more likely explanation, it seems to me, and that is the sources and functions of the words themselves.

The best known of the tabooed sexual words, for example, 4 comes from the German *ficken*, meaning ''to strike''; combined according to Partridge's etymological dictionary *Origins*, with the Latin sexual verb *futuere*: associated in turn with the Latin *fustis*, ''a staff or cudgel''; the Celtic *buc*, ''a point, hence to pierce''; the Irish *bot*, ''the male member''; the Latin *battuere*, ''to beat''; the Gaelic *batair*, ''a cudgeller''; the Early Irish *bualaim*, ''I strike''; and so forth. It is one of what etymologists sometimes called ''the sadistic group of words for the man's part in copulation.''

The brutality of this word, then, and its equivalents (''screw,'' 5 ''bang,'' etc.), is not an illusion of the middle class or a crotchet of Women's Liberation. In their origins and imagery these words carry undeniably painful, if not sadistic, implications, the object of which is almost always female. Consider, for example, what a ''screw'' actually does to the wood it penetrates; what a painful, even mutilating, activity this kind of analogy suggests. ''Screw'' is particularly interesting in this context, since the noun, according to Partridge, comes from words meaning ''groove,'' ''nut,'' ''ditch,'' ''breeding sow,'' ''scrofula'' and ''swelling,'' while the verb, besides its explicit imagery, has antecedent associations to ''write on,'' ''scratch,'' ''scarify,'' and so forth—a revealing fusion of a mechanical or painful action with an obviously denigrated object.

Not all obscene words, of course, are as implicitly sadistic or 6 denigrating to women as these, but all that I know seem to serve a similar purpose: to reduce the human organism (especially the female organism) and human functions (especially sexual and procreative) to their least organic, most mechanical dimension; to sub-

stitute a trivializing or deforming resemblance for the complex human reality of what is being described.

Tabooed male descriptives, when they are not openly denigrating to women, often serve to divorce a male organ or function
from any significant interaction with the female. Take the word
"testes," for example, suggesting "witnesses" (from the Latin
testis) to the sexual and procreative strengths of the male organ;
and the obscene counterpart of this word, which suggests little
more than a mechanical shape. Or compare almost any of the
"rich," "liberating" sexual verbs, so fashionable today among
male writers, with that much-derived Latin word "copulate" ("to
bind or join together") or even that Anglo-Saxon phrase (which
seems to have had no trouble surviving the Norman Conquest)
"make love."

How arrogantly self-involved the tabooed words seem in comparison to either of the other terms, and how contemptuous of the
female partner. Understandably so, of course, if she is only a
"skirt," a "broad," a "chick," a "pussycat" or a "piece." If she
is, in other words no more than her skirt, or what her skirt con-
ceals; no more than a breeder, or the broadest part of her; no more
than a piece of a human being or a "piece of tail."

The most severely tabooed of all the female descriptives, inci-
dentally, are those like a "piece of tail," which suggests (either
explicitly or through antecedents) that there is no significant difference between the female channel through which we are all conceived and born and the anal outlet common to both sexes—a distinction that pornographers have always enjoyed obscuring.

This effort to deny women their biological identity, their individuality, their humanness, is such an important aspect of obscene
language that one can only marvel at how seldom, in an era preoc-
cupied with definitions of obscenity, this fact is brought to our attention. One problem, of course, is that many of the people in the
best position to do this (critics, teachers, writers) are so reluctant
today to admit that they are angered or shocked by obscenity.
Bored, maybe, unimpressed, aesthetically displeased, but—no
matter how brutal or denigrating the material—never angered,
never shocked.

And yet how eloquently angered, how piously shocked many
of these same people become if denigrating language is used about
any minority group other than women; if the obscenities are racial

or ethnic, that is, rather than sexual. Words like "coon," "kike," "spic," "wop," after all, deform identity, deny individuality and humanness in almost exactly the same way that sexual vulgarisms and obscenities do.

No one that I know, least of all my students, would fail to 12 question the values of a society whose literature and entertainment rested heavily on racial or ethnic pejoratives. Are the values of a society whose literature and entertainment rest as heavily as ours on sexual pejoratives any less questionable?

Meanings and Values

1a.   Explain the meaning of *irony* by use of at least one illustration from the latter part of this essay. (See Guide to Terms: *Irony*.)

b.   What kind of irony is it?

2a.   Inasmuch as the selection itself includes many of the so-called "strong, earthy, gut-honest" words, could anyone logically call it obscene? Why, or why not?

b.   To what extent, if at all, does the author's point of view help determine your answer to question 2a? (Guide: *Point of View*.)

3a.   Compose, in your own words, a compact statement of Lawrence's thesis. (Guide: *Thesis*.)

b.   Are all parts of the essay completely relevant to this thesis? Justify your answer.

c.   Does the writing have unity?

4.   Evaluate this composition by use of our three-question system. (Guide: *Evaluation*.)

Argumentative Techniques

1.   What is the purpose of this essay? (Guide: *Purpose*.)

2a.   What objection to her opinion does the author refute in paragraph 3, and how does she refute it? (Guide: *Refutation*.)

b.   Where else in the essay does she refute opposing arguments?

3a.   Are the evidence and supporting arguments in this essay arranged in a refutation-proof pattern?

b.   If not, describe the arrangement of the essay.

4a.   Which of the methods "peculiar to definition alone" (see the introduction to Section 7) does the author employ in developing this essay?

b.   Which of the regular patterns of exposition does she also use?

c.   Explain your reasons and cite examples to justify your answers to
4a and 4b.

5a. Which of the standard techniques of introduction are used?
(Guide: *Introductions.*)

b.   Which methods are used to close the essay? (Guide: *Closing.*)

Diction and Vocabulary

1a. How, if at all, is this discussion of words related to *connotation*?
(Guide: *Connotation/Denotation.*)

b.   To what extent would connotations in this matter depend on the
setting and circumstances in which the words are used? Cite illustrations to clarify your answer.

2.   In view of the fact that the author uses frankly many of the "gut-
honest" words, why do you suppose she plainly avoids others,
such as in paragraphs 4 and 7?

3.   The author says that a "kind of analogy" is suggested by some of
the words discussed (par. 5). If you have studied Section 4 of this
book, does her use of the term *analogy* seem in conflict with what
you believed it to mean? Explain.

4.   Study the author's uses of the following words, consulting the dictionary as needed: existential, grimaces (par. 1); etymological, cudgel (4); sadistic (4–6); crotchet, scrofula, explicit, antecedent, scarify (5); denigrated (5–7, 10–11); aesthetically (10); pejoratives (12).

Suggestions for Writing and Discussion

1.   Why is it the so-called middle class that is so often accused of having sexual hangups—and hence all sorts of sex-related taboos?

2.   Probably most people using obscene language (obscene, at least,
by Lawrence's definition) are not aware of the etymology of the
words. Can they, therefore, be accused of denigrating women—or,
unlike legal matters, is ignorance a suitable defense?

3.   Does the author make a justifiable comparison between obscene
words and ethnic pejoratives? Using illustrations for specificity,
carry the comparison further to show why it is sound, or explain
why you consider it a weak comparison.

(NOTE: Suggestions for topics requiring development by use of ARGUMENT are on
page 426, at the end of this section.)

ARGUMENT THROUGH INDUCTION AND DEDUCTION

LEWIS THOMAS

LEWIS THOMAS (born 1913) attended private schools in New York
and then Princeton University and Harvard Medical School. As
a United States naval officer he took part in the invasion of Oki-
nawa during World War II. After the war he advanced steadily
in medical research, teaching, and administration. A physician,
he has also served in posts at the University of Minnesota and
New York University Medical School and at Yale, Cornell, and
Rockefeller universities. Thomas was president and is now
chancellor of Memorial Sloan-Kettering Cancer Center in New
York. He remains active in committee work, frequently appears
before congressional hearings in Washington, and also serves
on the Harvard Board of Overseers. A lifelong interest in literature and writing led Thomas in 1970 to begin writing a monthly
column for the *New England Journal of Medicine*—a practice that
has evolved into his three collections of essays: *The Lives of a
Cell: Notes of a Biology Watcher* (1974), which has become a steady
best-seller, *The Medusa and the Snail* (1979), and *Late Night
Thoughts on Listening to Mahler's Ninth Symphony* (1983). *The
Youngest Science: Notes of a Medicine-Watcher* (1983) is his personal
account of how medicine has developed as a science and a profession during this century.

Nurses

In this essay, a chapter from *The Youngest Science*, Thomas uses
an inductive pattern to guide his argument. This pattern seems
a natural choice for him because it embodies the kind of reasoning he often uses in his medical research.

When my mother became a registered nurse at Roosevelt Hospital, in 1903, there was no question in anyone's mind about what nurses did as professionals. They did what the doctors ordered. The attending physician would arrive for his ward rounds in the early morning, and when he arrived at the ward office the head nurse would be waiting for him, ready to take his hat and coat, and his cane, and she would stand while he had his cup of tea before starting. Entering the ward, she would hold the door for him to go first, then his entourage of interns and medical students, then she followed. At each bedside, after he had conducted his examination and reviewed the patient's progress, he would tell the nurse what needed doing that day, and she would write it down on the part of the chart reserved for nursing notes. An hour or two later he would be gone from the ward, and the work of the rest of the day and the night to follow was the nurse's frenetic occupation. In addition to the stipulated orders, she had an endless list of routine things to do, all learned in her two years of nursing school: the beds had to be changed and made up with fresh sheets by an exact geometric design of folding and tucking impossible for anyone but a trained nurse; the patients had to be washed head to foot; bedpans had to be brought, used, emptied, and washed; temperatures had to be taken every four hours and meticulously recorded on the chart; enemas were to be given; urine and stool samples collected, labeled, and sent off to the laboratory; throughout the day and night, medications of all sorts, usually pills and various vegetable extracts and tinctures, had to be carried on trays from bed to bed. At most times of the year about half of the forty or so patients on the ward had typhoid fever, which meant that the nurse couldn't simply move from bed to bed in the performance of her duties; each typhoid case was screened from the other patients, and the nurse was required to put on a new gown and wash her hands in disinfectant before approaching the bedside. Patients with high fevers were sponged with cold alcohol at frequent intervals. The late-evening back rub was the rite of passage into sleep.

In addition to the routine, workaday schedule, the nurse was responsible for responding to all calls from the patients, and it was expected that she would do so on the run. Her rounds, scheduled as methodical progressions around the ward, were continually interrupted by these calls. It was up to her to evaluate each situation quickly: a sudden abdominal pain in a typhoid patient might signify intestinal perforation; the abrupt onset of weakness, thirst, and pallor meant intestinal hemorrhage; the coughing up of gross blood by a tuberculous patient was an emergency. Some of the calls came from neighboring patients on the way to recovery; patients on open wards always kept a close eye on each other: the man in the next bed might slip into coma or seem to be dying, or be indeed dead. For such emergencies the nurse had to get word immediately to the doctor on call, usually the intern assigned to the ward, who might be off in the outpatient department or working in the diagnostic laboratory (interns of that day did all the laboratory work themselves; technicians had not yet been invented) or in his room. Nurses were not allowed to give injections or to do such emergency procedures as spinal punctures or chest taps, but they were expected to know when such maneuvers were indicated and to be ready with appropriate trays of instruments when the intern arrived on the ward.

It was an exhausting business, but by my mother's accounts 3 it was the most satisfying and rewarding kind of work. As a nurse she was a low person in the professional hierarchy, always running from place to place on orders from the doctors, subject as well to strict discipline from her own administrative superiors on the nursing staff, but none of this came through in her recollections. What she remembered was her usefulness.

Whenever my father talked to me about nurses and their 4 work, he spoke with high regard for them as professionals. Although it was clear in his view that the task of the nurses was to do what the doctor told them to, it was also clear that he admired them for being able to do a lot of things he couldn't possibly do, had never been trained to do. On his own rounds later on, when he became an attending physician himself, he consulted the ward nurse for her opinion about problem cases and paid careful attention to her observations and chart notes. In his own days of intern training (perhaps partly under my mother's strong influence, I don't know) he developed a deep and lasting respect for the whole nursing profession.

I have spent all of my professional career in close association 5 with, and close dependency on, nurses, and like many of my faculty colleagues, I've done a lot of worrying about the relationship between medicine and nursing. During most of this century the nursing profession has been having a hard time of it. It has been largely, although not entirely, an occupation for women, and sensitive issues of professional status, complicated by the special issue of the changing role of women in modern society, have led to a standoffish, often adversarial relationship between nurses and doctors. Already swamped by an increasing load of routine duties, nurses have been obliged to take on more and more purely administrative tasks: keeping the records in order; making sure the supplies are on hand for every sort of ward emergency; supervising the activities of the new paraprofessional group called LPNs (licensed practical nurses), who now perform much of the bedside work once done by RNs (registered nurses); overseeing ward maids, porters, and cleaners; seeing to it that patients scheduled for X rays are on their way to the X-ray department on time. Therefore, they have to spend more of their time at desks in the ward office and less time at the bedsides. Too late maybe, the nurses have begun to realize that they are gradually being excluded from the one duty which had previously been their most important reward but which had been so taken for granted that nobody mentioned it in listing the duties of a nurse: close personal contact with patients. Along with everything else nurses did in the long day's work, making up for all the tough and sometimes demeaning jobs assigned to them, they had the matchless opportunity to be useful friends to great numbers of human beings in trouble. They listened to their patients all day long and through the night, they gave comfort and reassurance to the patients and their families, they got to know them as friends, they were depended on. To contemplate the loss of this part of their work has been the deepest worry for nurses at large, and for the faculties responsible for the curricula of the nation's new and expanding nursing schools. The issue lies at the center of the running argument between medical school and nursing school administrators, but it is never clearly stated. Nursing education has been upgraded in recent years. Almost all the former hospital schools, which took in high-school graduates and provided an RN certificate after two or three years, have been replaced by schools attached to colleges and universities, with a four-year curriculum leading simultaneously to a bachelor's degree and an RN certificate.

The doctors worry that nurses are trying to move away from their historical responsibilities to medicine (meaning, really, to the doctors' orders). The nurses assert that they are their own profession, responsible for their own standards, coequal colleagues with physicians, and they do not wish to become mere ward administrators or technicians (although some of them, carrying the new and prestigious title of "nurse practitioner," are being trained within nursing schools to perform some of the most complex technological responsibilities in hospital emergency rooms and intensive care units). The doctors claim that what the nurses really want is to become substitute psychiatrists. The nurses reply that they have unavoidable responsibilities for the mental health and well-being of their patients, and that these are different from the doctors' tasks. Eventually the arguments will work themselves out, and some sort of agreement will be reached, but if it is to be settled intelligently, some way will have to be found to preserve and strengthen the traditional and highly personal nurse-patient relationship.

I have had a fair amount of firsthand experience with the issue, having been an apprehensive patient myself off and on over a three-year period on the wards of the hospital for which I work. I am one up on most of my physician friends because of this experience. I know some things they do not know about what nurses do. 7

One thing the nurses do is to hold the place together. It is an astonishment, which every patient feels from time to time, observing the affairs of a large, complex hospital from the vantage point of his bed, that the whole institution doesn't fly to pieces. A hospital operates by the constant interplay of powerful forces pulling away at each other in different directions, each force essential for getting necessary things done, but always at odds with each other. The intern staff is an almost irresistible force in itself, learning medicine by doing medicine, assuming all the responsibility within reach, pushing against an immovable attending and administrative staff, and frequently at odds with the nurses. The attending physicians are individual entrepreneurs trying to run small cottage industries at each bedside. The diagnostic laboratories are feudal fiefdoms, prospering from the insatiable demands for their services from the interns and residents. The medical students are all over the place, learning as best they can and complaining that they are not, as they believe they should be, at the epicenter of everyone's concern. Each individual worker in the place, from the chiefs of surgery to the dieticians to the ward maids, porters, and elevator 8

operators, lives and works in the conviction that the whole appa-
ratus would come to a standstill without his or her individual con-
tribution, and in one sense or another each of them is right.

My discovery, as a patient first on the medical service and later   9
in surgery, is that the institution is held together, *glued* together,
enabled to function as an organism, by the nurses and by nobody
else.

The nurses, the good ones anyway (and all the ones on my   10
floor were good), make it their business to know everything that
is going on. They spot errors before errors can be launched.
They know everything written on the chart. Most important of all,
they know their patients as unique human beings, and they soon
get to know the close relatives and friends. Because of this knowledge, they are quick to sense apprehensions and act on them. The
average sick person in a large hospital feels at risk of getting lost,
with no identity left beyond a name and a string of numbers on a
plastic wristband, in danger always of being whisked off on a litter
to the wrong place to have the wrong procedure done, or worse
still, *not* being whisked off at the right time. The attending physician or the house officer, on rounds and usually in a hurry, can
murmur a few reassuring words on his way out the door, but it
takes a confident, competent, and cheerful nurse, there all day
long and in and out of the room on one chore or another through
the night, to bolster one's confidence that the situation is indeed
manageable and not about to get out of hand.

Knowing what I know, I am all for the nurses. If they are to   11
continue their professional feud with the doctors, if they want their
professional status enhanced and their pay increased, if they infuriate the doctors by their claims to be equal professionals, if they
ask for the moon, I am on their side.

Meanings and Values

1a.   Summarize Thomas's description of the attitudes of doctors
      toward nurses.

 b.   Summarize his view of the special skills and contributions of
      nurses.

 c.   Does he consider nurses the equal of doctors? If not, what is his
      view?

2a.   What is the thesis of this essay? (Guide: *Thesis.*)

 b.   Does it contain a thesis statement?

3a. If Thomas supports changes in the role of nurses, why does he avoid making any specific proposals for altering the status or responsibilities of the profession or its relationship to the medical profession?

  b. If you think that changes are called for, what specific alterations would you suggest?

4a. Does the author acknowledge directly any objections to his view of the role nurses should play in medical treatment? If so, where?

  b. If not, how does he acknowledge and refute opposing points of view?

Argumentative Techniques

1a. Much of the evidence in this essay is personal. Does this add to or detract from its effectiveness? In what ways? (Guide: *Argument.*)

  b. Why is the evidence drawn from the author's own experience also a form of authoritative testimony?

2a. The author waits until well into the essay to explain the issue behind it fully and to make his point of view explicit. Is this approach consistent with the pattern of inductive reasoning used in the essay? How?

  b. What are the major stages of this argument? (Cite specific paragraphs in your answer.)

3. What patterns other than induction are used in this essay, and where are they used?

4a. Are the evidence and supporting ideas in this essay arranged in ascending order, as refutation-proof, as con-pro, or in some combination of these?

  b. Make a rough outline representing the arrangement of the essay.

5a. What do the lists of nurse's duties in paragraphs 1 and 2 contribute to the argument? (Guide: *Unity.*)

  b. Are these lists of duties likely to make many readers lose interest in the selection? Why, or why not? (Guide: *Introductions.*)

  c. Is Thomas able to suggest in the opening paragraph something of the purpose and the thesis of the essay? How?

Diction and Vocabulary

1a. Identify the figures of speech in paragraphs 8 and 9 and tell why the author uses them. (Guide: *Figures of Speech.*)

  b. Why are there more figures of speech in these paragraphs than in other parts of the selection?

2a.   What elements of syntax contribute to the emotional impact of paragraphs 9 and 10? (Guide: *Syntax.*)

b.   In what ways is the vision of the hospital from a patient's perspective in paragraphs 7–10 a preparation for the judgment Thomas delivers in paragraph 11?

c.   What do the parallel structures in paragraph 11 contribute to its impact? (Guide: *Parallel Structure.*)

3a.   Does the last sentence in paragraph 3 contain anything that might be regarded as a paradox? What is it, and why is it paradoxical? (Guide: *Paradox.*)

b.   How does this paradox aid the argument?

4.   How does the diction in this essay help determine the tone, especially in those sections where Thomas speaks of nurses and their relationship to patients? (Guide: *Diction* and *Style/Tone.*)

5.   Use your dictionary as necessary to become familiar with the following words: ward, rounds, entourage, frenetic, tinctures, typhoid fever (par. 1); taps (2); paraprofessional (5); feudal fiefdoms, epicenter (8).

Suggestions for Writing and Discussion

1.   Some people might claim that recent conflicts between doctors and nurses are a result of the rising status of women during the past fifteen years. Do you agree or disagree?

2.   To what extent can the ways women are raised in our society be seen as a preparation for the kind of work nurses do? Can men be expected to perform as well as women in such a profession? Be ready to defend your answer.

3.   Prepare a written or oral composition from the point of view of a nursing director in a large hospital and argue that nurses should be given greater responsibility for running the hospital and caring for patients. Be as specific as you can in your proposals.

4.   A recent report indicates that many female teachers choose not to seek higher-paying administrative jobs because they feel that administrative tasks will deprive them of the experiences of teaching and helping people for which they entered the profession. Comment on this dilemma as it applies to teaching, nursing, and similar professions. (Note: Many male teachers face the same dilemma.)

(NOTE: Suggestions for topics requiring development by use of ARGUMENT are on page 426, at the end of this section.)

THOMAS JEFFERSON

THOMAS JEFFERSON (1743–1826) was born in Virginia, where he spent his childhood and later attended William and Mary College. He became a lawyer, a member of the Virginia House of Burgesses, and a member of the Continental Congress in 1775. His influence as a liberal democrat was always aided by his prolific and forceful writing. During the Revolutionary War he became governor of Virginia. After the war he served the new government in various capacities, including those of special minister to France, secretary of state under Washington, vice-president, and, for two terms, the country's third president. He died on July 4, the fiftieth anniversary of the signing of the Declaration of Independence.

The Declaration of Independence

The Declaration of Independence, written and revised by Jefferson, was later further revised by the Continental Congress, meeting then in Philadelphia. In this way, as Jefferson later remarked, it drew its authority from "the harmonizing sentiments of the day"; it was, when signed on July 4, 1776, "an expression of the American mind." However, the document still retained much of the form and style of Jefferson's writing, and as literature it has long been admired for its lean and forthright prose. We can find no clearer example of the practical combination of deductive and inductive argument.

When in the course of human events, it becomes necessary for one 1
people to dissolve the political bands which have connected them
with another, and to assume among the Powers of the earth, the
separate and equal station to which the Laws of Nature and of
Nature's God entitle them, a decent respect to the opinions of

mankind requires that they should declare the causes which impel them to the separation.

    We hold these truths to be self-evident, that all men are created equal, that they are endowed by their Creator with certain unalienable Rights, that among these are Life, Liberty and the pursuit of Happiness. That to secure these rights, Governments are instituted among Men, deriving their just powers from the consent of the governed. That whenever any Form of Government becomes destructive of these ends, it is the Right of the People to alter or to abolish it, and to institute a new Government, laying its foundation on such principles and organizing its powers in such form, as to them shall seem most likely to effect their Safety and Happiness. Prudence, indeed, will dictate that Governments long established should not be changed for light and transient causes; and accordingly all experience hath shown that mankind are more disposed to suffer, while evils are sufferable, than to right themselves by abolishing the forms to which they are accustomed. But when a long train of abuses and usurpations pursuing invariably the same Object evinces a design to reduce them under absolute Despotism, it is their right, it is their duty, to throw off such government, and to provide new Guards for their future security. Such has been the patient sufferance of these Colonies; and such is now the necessity which constrains them to alter their former Systems of Government. The history of the present King of Great Britain is a history of repeated injuries and usurpations, all having in direct object the establishment of an absolute Tyranny over these States. To prove this, let Facts be submitted to a candid world.

    He has refused his Assent to Laws, the most wholesome and necessary for the public good.

    He has forbidden his Governors to pass Laws of immediate and pressing importance, unless suspended in their operation till his Assent should be obtained; and when so suspended, he has utterly neglected to attend to them.

    He has refused to pass other Laws for the accommodation of large districts of people, unless those people would relinquish the right of Representation in the Legislature, a right inestimable to them and formidable to tyrants only.

    He has called together legislative bodies at places unusual, uncomfortable, and distant from the depository of their Public Records, for the sole purpose of fatiguing them into compliance with his measures.

He has dissolved Representative Houses repeatedly, for 7 opposing with manly firmness his invasions on the rights of the people.

He has refused for a long time, after such dissolutions, to 8 cause others to be elected; whereby the Legislative Powers, incapable of Annihilation, have returned to the People at large for their exercise; the State remaining in the mean time exposed to all the dangers of invasion from without, and convulsions within.

He has endeavored to prevent the population of these States; 9 for that purpose obstructing the Laws of Naturalization of Foreigners; refusing to pass others to encourage their migration hither, and raising the conditions of new Appropriations of Lands.

He has obstructed the Administration of Justice, by refusing 10 his Assent to Laws for establishing Judiciary Powers.

He has made Judges dependent on his Will alone, for the ten- 11 ure of their offices, and the amount and payment of their salaries.

He has erected a multitude of New Offices, and sent hither 12 swarms of Officers to harass our People, and eat out their substance.

He has kept among us, in time of peace, Standing Armies 13 without the consent of our Legislature.

He has affected to render the Military independent of and su- 14 perior to the Civil Power.

He has combined with others to subject us to jurisdictions for- 15 eign to our constitution, and unacknowledged by our laws; giving his Assent to their acts of pretended Legislation:

For quartering large bodies of armed troops among us: 16

For protecting them, by a mock Trial, from Punishment for 17 any Murders which they should commit on the Inhabitants of these States:

For cutting off our Trade with all parts of the world: 18

For imposing Taxes on us without our Consent: 19

For depriving us in many cases, of the benefits of Trial by Jury: 20

For transporting us beyond Seas to be tried for pretended of- 21 fenses:

For abolishing the free System of English Laws in a Neigh- 22 bouring Province, establishing therein an Arbitrary government, and enlarging its boundaries so as to render it at once an example and fit instrument for introducing the same absolute rule into these Colonies:

For taking away our Charters, abolishing our most valuable Laws, and altering fundamentally the Forms of our Governments:

For suspending our own Legislatures, and declaring themselves invested with Power to legislate for us in all cases whatsoever.

He has abdicated Government here, by declaring us out of his Protection and waging War against us.

He has plundered our seas, ravaged our Coasts, burnt our towns and destroyed the Lives of our people.

He is at this time transporting large Armies of foreign Mercenaries to compleat the works of death, desolation and tyranny, already begun with circumstances of Cruelty & perfidy scarcely paralleled in the most barbarous ages, and totally unworthy the Head of a civilized nation.

He has constrained our fellow Citizens taken Captive on the high Seas to bear Arms against their Country, to become the executioners of their friends and Brethren, or to fall themselves by their Hands.

He has excited domestic insurrections amongst us, and has endeavored to bring on the inhabitants of our frontiers, the merciless Indian Savages, whose known rule of warfare, is an undistinguished destruction of all ages, sexes and conditions.

In every stage of these Oppressions We Have Petitioned for Redress in the most humble terms: Our repeated petitions have been answered only by repeated injury. A Prince, whose character is thus marked by every act which may define a Tyrant, is unfit to be the ruler of a free People.

Nor have We been wanting in attention to our British brethren. We have warned them from time to time of attempts by their legislature to extend an unwarrantable jurisdiction over us. We have reminded them of the circumstances of our emigration and settlement here. We have appealed to their native justice and magnanimity and we have conjured them by the ties of our common kindred to disavow these usurpations, which would inevitably interrupt our connections and correspondence. They too have been deaf to the voice of justice and of consanguinity. We must, therefore, acquiesce in the necessity, which denounces our Separation, and hold them, as we hold the rest of mankind, Enemies in War, in Peace Friends.

We, therefore, the Representatives of the United States of America, in General Congress, Assembled, appealing to the Supreme Judge of the world for the rectitude of our intentions, do, in the Name, and by Authority of the good People of these Colonies, solemnly publish and declare, That these United Colonies are, and of Right ought to be, Free and Independent States; that they are Absolved from all Allegiance to the British Crown, and that all political connection between them and the State of Great Britain, is and ought to be totally dissolved; and that as Free and Independent States, they have full power to levy War, conclude Peace, contract Alliances, establish Commerce, and to do all other Acts and Things which Independent States may of right do. And for the support of this Declaration, with a firm reliance on the protection of Divine Providence, we mutually pledge to each other our lives, our Fortunes and our sacred Honor.

Meanings and Values

1.   For what practical reasons (other than the "decent respect to the opinions of mankind"—par. 1) did the Founding Fathers need to explain so carefully their reasons for declaring independence?

2a.   By what justification can this selection be considered an argument?

  b.   Why might it also be classified as exposition?

  c.   Except for study purposes, is there any reason to categorize it at all? Explain.

3.   Many American colonials opposed the break with England and remained loyal to the Crown throughout the struggle for independence. What do you suppose could inspire such loyalty to a king whom most of them had never seen and who had shown little concern for their welfare?

Argumentative Techniques

1.   The basis of the Declaration of Independence is deduction and can therefore be stated as a logical syllogism. The major premise, stated twice in the second paragraph, may be paraphrased as follows: when a government proves to be despotic, it is the people's right and duty to get rid of it. (See the introduction to Section 10, "Reasoning by use of *Induction* and *Deduction*.")

a. What, then, is the minor premise of the syllogism?

b. Where is the syllogism's conclusion set forth? Restate it concisely in your own words.

c. Write this resulting syllogism in standard form.

2. Twenty-eight pieces of inductive evidence are offered as support for one of the deductive premises.

a. Which premise is thus supported?

b. Demonstrate the meaning of "inductive leap" by use of materials from this selection. (Remember that the order of presentation in inductive or deductive writing is merely an arrangement for *arguing,* not necessarily that of the original reasoning.)

3a. Why, according to the document itself, is the other premise not supported by any inductive reasoning?

b. Would everyone agree with this premise? If not, why do you suppose the Founding Fathers did not present inductive evidence to support it?

4. What benefits are gained in the Declaration by the extensive use of parallel structures? (Guide: *Parallel Structure.*)

5. Show as specifically as possible the effects that a "decent respect to the opinions of mankind" apparently had on the selection and use of materials in the Declaration of Independence.

Diction and Vocabulary

1. Select five words or phrases from the Declaration of Independence to demonstrate the value of an awareness of connotation. (Guide: *Connotation/Denotation.*)

2. If you are not already familiar with the following words as they are used in this selection, consult your dictionary for their meanings: impel (par. 1); transient, usurpations, evinces, sufferance, constrains (2); inestimable (5); depository (6); dissolutions (8); mercenaries, perfidy (27); redress (30); magnanimity, conjured, consanguinity, acquiesce (31); rectitude, absolved (32).

Suggestions for Writing and Discussion

1. George Santayana, an American writer and expatriate, called the Declaration of Independence "a salad of illusion." Develop this metaphor into a full-scale analogy to explain his meaning. Without arguing the matter, attempt to assess the truth of his allegation.

2. Select one important similarity or difference between the rebellion of the American colonials and that of some other country in recent

history. Use comparison or contrast to develop a theme on this subject.

3. Compare or contrast any of the Declaration signers with one of the leaders of some other country that more recently severed ties with a colonial power.

4. Give evidence from your knowledge of history to support, or to negate, the following statement by Patrick Henry, one of the signers of the Declaration: ''It is impossible that a nation of infidels or idolators should be a nation of freemen. It is when a people forget God, that tyrants forge their chains. A vitiated state of morals, a corrupted public conscience, is incompatible with freedom.''

(NOTE: Suggestions for topics requiring development by use of ARGUMENT are on page 426, at the end of this section.)

MARTIN LUTHER KING, JR.

MARTIN LUTHER KING, JR. (1929–1968), was a Baptist minister, the president of the Southern Christian Leadership Conference, and a respected leader in the nationwide movement for equal rights for blacks. He was born in Atlanta, Georgia, and earned degrees from Morehouse College (A.B., 1948), Crozer Theological Seminary (B.D., 1951), Boston University (Ph.D., 1955), and Chicago Theological Seminary (D.D., 1957). He held honorary degrees from numerous other colleges and universities and was awarded the Nobel Peace Prize in 1964. Some of his books are *Why We Can't Wait* (1964), *Stride Toward Freedom* (1958), and *Strength to Love* (1963). King was assassinated April 4, 1968, in Memphis, Tennessee.

Letter from Birmingham Jail[1]

This letter, written to King's colleagues in the ministry, is a reasoned explanation for his actions during the civil rights protests in Birmingham. It is a good example of both persuasion and logical argument. Here the two are completely compatible, balancing each other in rather intricate but convincing and effective patterns.

[1]This response to a published statement by eight fellow clergymen from Alabama (Bishop C. C. J. Carpenter, Bishop Joseph A. Durick, Rabbi Hilton L. Grafman, Bishop Paul Hardin, Bishop Holan B. Harmon, the Reverend George M. Murray, the Reverend Edward V. Ramage and the Reverend Earl Stallings) was composed under somewhat constricting circumstances. Begun on the margins of the newspaper in which the statement appeared while I was in jail, the letter was continued on scraps of writing paper supplied by a friendly Negro trusty, and concluded on a pad my attorneys were eventually permitted to leave me. Although the text remains in substance unaltered, I have indulged in the author's prerogative of polishing it for publication.—King's note.

My Dear Fellow Clergymen:

While confined here in the Birmingham city jail, I came across   1
your recent statement calling my present activities "unwise and
untimely." Seldom do I pause to answer criticism of my work and
ideas. If I sought to answer all the criticisms that cross my desk,
my secretaries would have little time for anything other than such
correspondence in the course of the day, and I would have no time
for constructive work. But since I feel that you are men of genuine
good will and that your criticisms are sincerely set forth, I want to
try to answer your statement in what I hope will be patient and
reasonable terms.

I think I should indicate why I am here in Birmingham, since   2
you have been influenced by the view which argues against "outsiders coming in." I have the honor of serving as president of the
Southern Christian Leadership Conference, an organization operating in every southern state, with headquarters in Atlanta, Georgia. We have some eighty-five affiliated organizations across the
South, and one of them is the Alabama Christian Movement for
Human Rights. Frequently we share staff, educational, and financial resources with our affiliates. Several months ago the affiliate
here in Birmingham asked us to be on call to engage in a nonviolent direct-action program if such were deemed necessary. We
readily consented, and when the hour came, we lived up to our
promise. So I, along with several members of my staff, am here
because I was invited here. I am here because I have organizational
ties here.

But more basically, I am in Birmingham because injustice is   3
here. Just as the prophets of the eighth century B.C. left their vil-
lages and carried their "thus saith the Lord" far beyond the
boundaries of their home towns, and just as the Apostle Paul left
his village of Tarsus and carried the gospel of Jesus Christ to the
far corners of the Greco-Roman world, so am I compelled to carry
the gospel of freedom beyond my own home town. Like Paul, I
must constantly respond to the Macedonian call for aid.

Moreover, I am cognizant of the interrelatedness of all commu-   4
nities and states. I cannot sit idly by in Atlanta and not be concerned about what happens in Birmingham. Injustice anywhere is
a threat to justice everywhere. We are caught in an inescapable
network of mutuality, tied in a single garment of destiny. Whatever affects one directly, affects all indirectly. Never again can we
afford to live with the narrow, provincial "outside agitator" idea.

Anyone who lives inside the United States can never be considered an outsider within its bounds.

You deplore the demonstrations taking place in Birmingham. 5
But your statement, I am sorry to say, fails to express a similar concern for the conditions that brought about the demonstrations. I am sure that none of you would want to rest content with the superficial kind of social analysis that deals merely with effects and does not grapple with underlying causes. It is unfortunate that demonstrations are taking place in Birmingham, but it is even more unfortunate that the city's white power structure left the Negro community with no alternative.

In any nonviolent campaign there are four basic steps: collec- 6
tion of the facts to determine whether injustices exist; negotiation; self-purification; and direct action. We have gone through all these steps in Birmingham. There can be no gainsaying the fact that racial injustice engulfs this community. Birmingham is probably the most thoroughly segregated city in the United States. Its ugly record of brutality is widely known. Negroes have experienced grossly unjust treatment in the courts. There have been more unsolved bombings of Negro homes and churches in Birmingham than in any other city in the nation. These are the hard, brutal facts of the case. On the basis of these conditions, Negro leaders sought to negotiate with the city fathers. But the latter consistently refused to engage in good-faith negotiation.

Then, last September, came the opportunity to talk with lead- 7
ers of Birmingham's economic community. In the course of the negotiations, certain promises were made by the merchants—for example, to remove the stores' humiliating racial signs. On the basis of these promises, the Reverend Fred Shuttlesworth and the leaders of the Alabama Christian Movement for Human Rights agreed to a moratorium on all demonstrations. As the weeks and months went by, we realized that we were the victims of a broken promise. A few signs, briefly removed, returned; the others remained.

As in so many past experiences, our hopes had been blasted, 8
and the shadow of deep disappointment settled upon us. We had no alternative except to prepare for direct action, whereby we would present our very bodies as a means of laying our case before the conscience of the local and the national community. Mindful of the difficulties involved, we decided to undertake a process of self-purification. We began a series of workshops on nonviolence,

and we repeatedly asked ourselves: "Are you able to accept blows without retaliating?" "Are you able to endure the ordeal of jail?" We decided to schedule our direct-action program for the Easter season, realizing that except for Christmas, this is the main shopping period of the year. Knowing that a strong economic-withdrawal program would be the by product of direct action, we felt that this would be the best time to bring pressure to bear on the merchants for the needed change.

Then it occurred to us that Birmingham's mayoral election was coming up in March, and we speedily decided to postpone action until after election day. When we discovered that the Commissioner of Public Safety, Eugene "Bull" Connor, had piled up enough votes to be in the run-off, we decided again to postpone action until the day after the run-off so that the demonstrations could not be used to cloud the issues. Like many others, we waited to see Mr. Connor defeated, and to this end we endured postponement after postponement. Having aided in this community need, we felt that our direct-action program could be delayed no longer.

You may well ask, "Why direct action? Why sit-ins, marches, and so forth? Isn't negotiation a better path?" You are quite right in calling for negotiation. Indeed, this is the very purpose of direct action. Nonviolent direct action seeks to create such a crisis and foster such a tension that a community which has constantly refused to negotiate is forced to confront the issue. It seeks so to dramatize the issue that it can no longer be ignored. My citing the creation of tension as part of the work of the nonviolent-resister may sound rather shocking. But I must confess that I am not afraid of the word "tension." I have earnestly opposed violent tension, but there is a type of constructive, nonviolent tension which is necessary for growth. Just as Socrates felt that it was necessary to create a tension in the mind so that individuals could rise from the bondage of myths and half-truths to the unfettered realm of creative analysis and objective appraisal, so must we see the need for nonviolent gadflies to create the kind of tension in society that will help men rise from the dark depths of prejudice and racism to the majestic heights of understanding and brotherhood.

The purpose of our direct-action program is to create a situation so crisis-packed that it will inevitably open the door to negotiation. I therefore concur with you in your call for negotiation. Too long has our beloved Southland been bogged down in a tragic effort to live in monologue rather than dialogue.

One of the basic points in your statement is that the action
that I and my associates have taken in Birmingham is untimely.
Some have asked: "Why didn't you give the new city administration time to act?" The only answer that I can give to this query is
that the new Birmingham administration must be prodded about
as much as the outgoing one, before it will act. We are sadly mistaken if we feel that the election of Albert Boutwell as mayor will
bring the millennium to Birmingham. While Mr. Boutwell is a
much more gentle person than Mr. Connor, they are both segrega-
tionists, dedicated to maintenance of the status quo. I have hoped
that Mr. Boutwell will be reasonable enough to see the futility of
massive resistance to desegregation. But he will not see this without pressure from devotees of civil rights. My friends, I must say
to you that we have not made a single gain in civil rights without
determined legal and nonviolent pressure. Lamentably, it is an historical fact that privileged groups seldom give up their privileges
voluntarily. Individuals may see the moral light and voluntarily
give up their unjust posture; but, as Reinhold Niebuhr has reminded us, groups tend to be more immoral than individuals.

We know through painful experience that freedom is never
voluntarily given by the oppressor; it must be demanded by the
oppressed. Frankly, I have yet to engage in a direct-action campaign that was "well timed" in the view of those who have not
suffered unduly from the disease of segregation. For years now I
have heard the word "Wait!" It rings in the ear of every Negro
with piercing familiarity. This "Wait" has almost always meant
"Never." We must come to see, with one of our distinguished ju-
rists, that "justice too long delayed is justice denied."

We have waited for more than 340 years for our constitutional
and God-given rights. The nations of Asia and Africa are moving
with jetlike speed toward gaining political independence, but we
still creep at horse-and-buggy pace toward gaining a cup of coffee
at a lunch counter. Perhaps it is easy for those who have never felt
the stinging darts of segregation to say, "Wait." But when you
have seen vicious mobs lynch your mothers and fathers at will and
drown your sisters and brothers at whim; when you have seen
hate-filled policemen curse, kick, and even kill your black brothers
and sisters; when you see the vast majority of your twenty million
Negro brothers smothering in an airtight cage of poverty in the
midst of an affluent society; when you suddenly find your tongue

twisted and your speech stammering as you seek to explain to your six-year-old daughter why she can't go to the public amusement park that has just been advertised on television, and see tears welling up in her eyes when she is told that Funtown is closed to colored children, and see ominous clouds of inferiority beginning to form in her little mental sky, and see her beginning to distort her personality by developing an unconscious bitterness toward white people; when you have to concoct an answer for a five-year-old son who is asking, "Daddy, why do white people treat colored people so mean?"; when you take a cross-country drive and find it necessary to sleep night after night in the uncomfortable corners of your automobile because no motel will accept you; when you are humiliated day in and day out by nagging signs reading "white" and "colored"; when your first name becomes "nigger," your middle name becomes "boy" (however old you are) and your last name becomes "John," and your wife and mother are never given the respected title "Mrs."; when you are harried by day and haunted by night by the fact that you are a Negro, living constantly at tiptoe stance, never quite knowing what to expect next, and are plagued with inner fears and outer resentments; when you are forever fighting a degenerating sense of "nobodiness"—then you will understand why we find it difficult to wait. There comes a time when the cup of endurance runs over, and men are no longer willing to be plunged into the abyss of despair. I hope, sirs, you can understand our legitimate and unavoidable impatience.

You express a great deal of anxiety over our willingness to 15 break laws. This is certainly a legitimate concern. Since we so diligently urge people to obey the Supreme Court's decision of 1954 outlawing segregation in the public schools, at first glance it may seem rather paradoxical for us consciously to break laws. One may well ask: "How can you advocate breaking some laws and obeying others?" The answer lies in the fact that there are two types of laws: just and unjust. I would be the first to advocate obeying just laws. One has not only a legal but a moral responsibility to obey just laws. Conversely, one has a moral responsibility to disobey unjust laws. I would agree with St. Augustine that "an unjust law is no law at all."

Now, what is the difference between the two? How does one 16 determine whether a law is just or unjust? A just law is a man-made code that squares with the moral law or the law of God. An unjust law is a code that is out of harmony with the moral law. To put it in the terms of St. Thomas Aquinas: An unjust law is a human law that is not rooted in eternal law and natural law. Any law that uplifts human personality is just. Any law that degrades human personality is unjust. All segregation statutes are unjust because segregation distorts the soul and damages the personality. It gives the segregator a false sense of superiority and the segregated a false sense of inferiority. Segregation, to use the terminology of the Jewish philosopher Martin Buber, substitutes an "I-it" relationship for an "I-thou" relationship and ends up relegating persons to the status of things. Hence segregation is not only politically, economically, and sociologically unsound, it is morally wrong and sinful. Paul Tillich has said that sin is separation. Is not segregation an existential expression of man's tragic separation, his awful estrangement, his terrible sinfulness? Thus it is that I can urge men to obey the 1954 decision of the Supreme Court, for it is morally right; and I can urge them to disobey segregation ordinances, for they are morally wrong.

Let us consider a more concrete example of just and unjust laws. An unjust law is a code that a numerical or power majority group compels a minority group to obey but does not make binding on itself. This is *difference* made legal. By the same token, a just law is a code that a majority compels a minority to follow and that it is willing to follow itself. This is *sameness* made legal.

Let me give another explanation. A law is unjust if it is inflicted on a minority that, as a result of being denied the right to vote, had no part in enacting or devising the law. Who can say that the legislature of Alabama which set up that state's segregation laws was democratically elected? Throughout Alabama all sorts of devious methods are used to prevent Negroes from becoming registered voters, and there are some counties in which, even though Negroes constitute a majority of the population, not a single Negro is registered. Can any law enacted under such circumstances be considered democratically structured?

Sometimes a law is just on its face and unjust in its application. For instance, I have been arrested on a charge of parading without a permit. Now, there is nothing wrong in having an ordinance which requires a permit for a parade. But such an ordinance becomes unjust when it is used to maintain segregation and to deny citizens the First-Amendment privilege of peaceful assembly and protest.

I hope you are able to see the distinction I am trying to point out. In no sense do I advocate evading or defying the law, as would the rabid segregationist. That would lead to anarchy. One who breaks an unjust law must do so openly, lovingly, and with a willingness to accept the penalty. I submit that an individual who breaks a law that conscience tells him is unjust, and who willingly accepts the penalty of imprisonment in order to arouse the conscience of the community over its injustice, is in reality expressing the highest respect for the law. 20

Of course, there is nothing new about this kind of civil disobedience. It was evidenced sublimely in the refusal of Shadrach, Meshach, and Abednego to obey the laws of Nebuchadnezzar, on the ground that a higher moral law was at stake. It was practiced superbly by the early Christians, who were willing to face hungry lions and the excruciating pain of chopping blocks rather than submit to certain unjust laws of the Roman Empire. To a degree, academic freedom is a reality today because Socrates practiced civil disobedience. In our own nation, the Boston Tea Party represented a massive act of civil disobedience. 21

We should never forget that everything Adolf Hitler did in Germany was "legal" and everything the Hungarian freedom fighters did in Hungary was "illegal." It was "illegal" to aid and comfort a Jew in Hitler's Germany. Even so, I am sure that, had I lived in Germany at the time, I would have aided and comforted my Jewish brothers. If today I lived in a Communist country where certain principles dear to the Christian faith are suppressed, I would openly advocate disobeying that country's anti-religious laws. 22

I must make two honest confessions to you, my Christian and Jewish brothers. First, I must confess that over the past few years I have been gravely disappointed with the white moderate. I have almost reached the regrettable conclusion that the Negro's great stumbling block in his stride toward freedom is not the White Citizen's Counciler or the Ku Klux Klanner, but the white moderate, who is more devoted to "order" than to justice; who prefers a negative peace which is the absence of tension to a positive peace which is the presence of justice; who constantly says, "I agree with 23 you in the goal you seek, but I cannot agree with your methods of direct action''; who paternalistically believes he can set the time-table for another man's freedom; who lives by a mythical concept of time and who constantly advises the Negro to wait for a "more convenient season." Shallow understanding from people of good will is more frustrating than absolute misunderstanding from people of ill will. Lukewarm acceptance is much more bewildering than outright rejection.

I had hoped that the white moderate would understand that law and order exist for the purpose of establishing justice and that when they fail in this purpose they become the dangerously struc-tured dams that block the flow of social progress. I had hoped that the white moderate would understand that the present tension in the South is a necessary phase of the transition from an obnoxious negative peace, in which the Negro passively accepted his unjust plight, to a substantive and positive peace, in which all men will respect the dignity and worth of human personality. Actually, we who engage in nonviolent direct action are not the creators of ten-sion. We merely bring to the surface the hidden tension that is already alive. We bring it out in the open, where it can be seen and dealt with. Like a boil that can never be cured so long as it is covered up but must be opened with all its ugliness to the natural medicines of air and light, injustice must be exposed, with all the tension its exposure creates, to the light of human conscience and the air of national opinion, before it can be cured.

In your statement you assert that our actions, even though peaceful, must be condemned because they precipitate violence. But is this a logical assertion? Isn't this like condemning a robbed man because his possession of money precipitated the evil act of robbery? Isn't this like condemning Socrates because his unswerv-ing commitment to truth and his philosophical inquiries precipi-tated the act by the misguided populace in which they made him drink hemlock? Isn't this like condemning Jesus because his unique God-consciousness and never-ceasing devotion to God's will precipitated the evil act of crucifixion? We must come to see that, as the federal courts have consistently affirmed, it is wrong to urge an individual to cease his efforts to gain his basic constitu-tional rights because the quest may precipitate violence. Society must protect the robbed and punish the robber.

I had also hoped that the white moderate would reject the

myth concerning time in relation to the struggle for freedom. I have just received a letter from a white brother in Texas. He writes: "All Christians know that the colored people will receive equal rights eventually, but it is possible that you are in too great a religious hurry. It has taken Christianity almost two thousand years to accomplish what it has. The teachings of Christ take time to come to earth." Such an attitude stems from a tragic misconception of time, from the strangely irrational notion that there is something in the very flow of time that will inevitably cure all ills. Actually, time itself is neutral; it can be used either destructively or constructively. More and more I feel that the people of ill will have used time much more effectively than have the people of good will. We will have to repent in this generation not merely for the hateful words and actions of the bad people, but for the appalling silence of the good people. Human progress never rolls in on wheels of inevitability; it comes through the tireless efforts of men willing to be co-workers with God, and without this hard work, time itself becomes an ally of the forces of social stagnation. We must use time creatively, in the knowledge that the time is always ripe to do right. Now is the time to make real the promise of democracy and transform our pending national elegy into a creative psalm of brotherhood. Now is the time to lift our national policy from the quicksand of racial injustice to the solid rock of human dignity.

You speak of our activity in Birmingham as extreme. At first I was rather disappointed that fellow clergymen would see my non-violent efforts as those of an extremist. I began thinking about the fact that I stand in the middle of two opposing forces in the Negro community. One is a force of complacency, made up in part of Negroes who, as a result of long years of oppression, are so drained of self-respect and a sense of "somebodiness" that they have adjusted to segregation; and in part of a few middle-class Negroes who, because of a degree of academic and economic security and because in some ways they profit by segregation, have become insensitive to the problems of the masses. The other force is one of bitterness and hatred, and it comes perilously close to advocating violence. It is expressed in the various black nationalist groups that are springing up across the nation, the largest and best-known being Elijah Muhammad's Muslim movement. Nourished by the Negro's frustration over the continued existence of racial discrimination, this movement is made up of people who have lost faith in America, who have absolutely repudiated Christianity, and who have concluded that the white man is an incorrigible "devil."

I have tried to stand between these two forces, saying that we need emulate neither the "do-nothingism" of the complacent nor the hatred and despair of the black nationalist. For there is the more excellent way of love and nonviolent protest. I am grateful to God that, through the influence of the Negro church, the way of nonviolence became an integral part of our struggle.

If this philosophy had not emerged, by now many streets of the South would, I am convinced, be flowing with blood. And I am further convinced that if our white brothers dismiss as "rabble-rousers" and "outside agitators" those of us who employ nonviolent direct action, and if they refuse to support our nonviolent efforts, millions of Negroes will, out of frustration and despair, seek solace and security in black-nationalist ideologies—a development that would inevitably lead to a frightening racial nightmare.

Oppressed people cannot remain oppressed forever. The yearning for freedom eventually manifests itself, and that is what has happened to the American Negro. Something within has reminded him of his birthright of freedom, and something without has reminded him that it can be gained. Consciously or unconsciously, he has been caught up by the *Zeitgeist,* and with his black brothers of Africa and his brown and yellow brothers of Asia, South America, and the Caribbean, the United States Negro is moving with a sense of great urgency toward the promised land of racial justice. If one recognizes this vital urge that has engulfed the Negro community, one should readily understand why public demonstrations are taking place. The Negro has many pent-up resentments and latent frustrations, and he must release them. So let him march; let him make prayer pilgrimages to the city hall; let him go on freedom rides—and try to understand why he must do so. If his repressed emotions are not released in nonviolent ways, they will seek expression through violence; this is not a threat but a fact of history. So I have not said to my people, "Get rid of your discontent." Rather, I have tried to say that this normal and healthy discontent can be channeled into the creative outlet of nonviolent direct action. And now this approach is being termed extremist.

But though I was initially disappointed at being categorized as an extremist, as I continued to think about the matter I gradually gained a measure of satisfaction from the label. Was not Jesus an extremist for love: "Love your enemies, bless them that curse you, do good to them that hate you, and pray for them which despite-fully use you, and persecute you." Was not Amos an extremist for justice: "Let justice roll down like waters and righteousness like an everflowing stream." Was not Paul an extremist for the Christian gospel: "I bear in my body the marks of the Lord Jesus." Was not Martin Luther an extremist: "Here I stand; I cannot do otherwise, so help me God." And John Bunyan: "I will stay in jail to the end of my days before I make a butchery of my conscience." And Abraham Lincoln: "This nation cannot survive half slave and half free." And Thomas Jefferson: "We hold these truths to be self-evident, that all men are created equal . . ." So the question is not whether we will be extremists, but what kind of extremists we will be. Will we be extremists for hate or for love? Will we be extremists for the preservation of injustice or for the extension of justice? In that dramatic scene on Calvary's hill three men were crucified. We must never forget that all three were crucified for the same crime—the crime of extremism. Two were extremists for immorality, and thus fell below their environment. The other, Jesus Christ, was an extremist for love, truth, and goodness, and thereby rose above his environment. Perhaps the South, the nation, and the world are in dire need of creative extremists.

I had hoped that the white moderate would see this need. Perhaps I was too optimistic; perhaps I expected too much. I suppose I should have realized that few members of the oppressor race can understand the deep groans and passionate yearnings of the oppressed race, and still fewer have the vision to see that injustice must be rooted out by strong, persistent, and determined action. I am thankful, however, that some of our white brothers in the South have grasped the meaning of this social revolution and committed themselves to it. They are still all too few in quantity, but they are big in quality. Some—such as Ralph McGill, Lillian Smith, Harry Golden, James McBride Dabbs, Anne Braden, and Sarah Patton Boyle—have written about our struggle in eloquent and prophetic terms. Others have marched with us down nameless streets of the South. They have languished in filthy, roach-infested jails, suffering the abuse and brutality of policemen who view them as "dirty nigger-lovers." Unlike so many of their moderate brothers and sisters, they have recognized the urgency of the moment and sensed the need for powerful "action" antidotes to combat the disease of segregation.

Let me take note of my other major disappointment. I have been so greatly disappointed with the white church and its leadership. Of course, there are some notable exceptions. I am not unmindful of the fact that each of you has taken some significant stands on this issue. I commend you, Reverend Stallings, for your Christian stand on this past Sunday, in welcoming Negroes to your worship service on a nonsegregated basis. I commend the Catholic leaders of this state for integrating Spring Hill College several years ago.

But despite these notable exceptions, I must honestly reiterate that I have been disappointed with the church. I do not say this as one of those negative critics who can always find something wrong with the church. I say this as a minister of the gospel, who loves the church; who was nurtured in its bosom; who has been sustained by its spiritual blessings and who will remain true to it as long as the cord of life shall lengthen.

When I was suddenly catapulted into the leadership of the bus protest in Montgomery, Alabama, a few years ago, I felt we would be supported by the white church. I felt that the white ministers, priests, and rabbis of the South would be among our strongest allies. Instead, some have been outright opponents, refusing to understand the freedom movement and misrepresenting its leaders; all too many others have been more cautious than courageous and have remained silent behind the anesthetizing security of stained glass windows.

In spite of my shattered dreams, I came to Birmingham with the hope that the white religious leadership of this community would see the justice of our cause and, with deep moral concern, would serve as the channel through which our just grievances could reach the power structure. I had hoped that each of you would understand. But again I have been disappointed.

I have heard numerous southern religious leaders admonish their worshipers to comply with a desegregation decision because it is the law, but I have longed to hear white ministers declare: "Follow this decree because integration is morally right and because the Negro is your brother." In the midst of blatant injustices inflicted upon the Negro, I have watched white churchmen stand on the sideline and mouth pious irrelevancies and sanctimonious trivialities. In the midst of a mighty struggle to rid our nation of racial and economic injustice I have heard many ministers say: "Those are social issues, with which the gospel has no real concern." And I have watched many churches commit themselves to a completely otherworldly religion which makes a strange, un-Biblical distinction between body and soul, between the sacred and the secular.

I have traveled the length and breadth of Alabama, Mississippi, and all the other southern states. On sweltering summer days and crisp autumn mornings I have looked at the South's beautiful churches with their lofty spires pointing heavenward. I have beheld the impressive outlines of her massive religious-education buildings. Over and over I have found myself asking: "What kind of people worship here? Who is their God? Where were their voices when the lips of Governor Barnett dripped with words of interposition and nullification? Where were they when Governor Wallace gave a clarion call for defiance and hatred? Where were their voices of support when bruised and weary Negro men and women decided to rise from the dark dungeons of complacency to the bright hills of creative protest?" 38

Yes, these questions are still in my mind. In deep disappointment I have wept over the laxity of the church. But be assured that my tears have been tears of love. There can be no deep disappointment where there is not deep love. Yes, I love the church. How could I do otherwise? I am in the rather unique position of being the son, the grandson, and the great-grandson of preachers. Yes, I see the church as the body of Christ. But, oh! How we have blemished and scarred that body through social neglect and through fear of being nonconformists. 39

There was a time when the church was very powerful—in the time when the early Christians rejoiced at being deemed worthy to suffer for what they believed. In those days the church was not merely a thermometer that recorded the ideas and principles of popular opinion; it was a thermostat that transformed the mores of society. Whenever the early Christians entered a town, the people in power became disturbed and immediately sought to convict the Christians for being "disturbers of the peace" and "outside agitators." But the Christians pressed on, in the conviction 40 that they were "a colony of heaven," called to obey God rather than man. Small in number, they were big in commitment. They were too God-intoxicated to be "astronomically intimidated." By their effort and example they brought an end to such ancient evils as infanticide and gladiatorial contests.

Things are different now. So often the contemporary church is a weak, ineffectual voice with an uncertain sound. So often it is an archdefender of the status quo. Far from being disturbed by the presence of the church, the power structure of the average community is consoled by the church's silent—and often even vocal—sanction of things as they are.

But the judgment of God is upon the church as never before. If today's church does not recapture the sacrificial spirit of the early church, it will lose its authenticity, forfeit the loyalty of millions, and be dismissed as an irrelevant social club with no meaning for the twentieth century. Every day I meet young people whose disappointment with the church has turned into outright disgust.

Perhaps I have once again been too optimistic. Is organized religion too inextricably bound to the status quo to save our nation and the world? Perhaps I must turn my faith to the inner spiritual church, the church within the church, as the true *ekklesia*[2] and the hope of the world. But again I am thankful to God that some noble souls from the ranks of organized religion have broken loose from the paralyzing chains of conformity and joined us as active partners in the struggle for freedom. They have left their secure congregations and walked the streets of Albany, Georgia, with us. They have gone down the highways of the South on tortuous rides for freedom. Yes, they have gone to jail with us. Some have been dismissed from their churches, have lost the support of their bishops and fellow ministers. But they have acted in the faith that right defeated is stronger than evil triumphant. Their witness has been the spiritual salt that has preserved the true meaning of the gospel in these troubled times. They have carved a tunnel of hope through the dark mountain of disappointment.

I hope the church as a whole will meet the challenge of this decisive hour. But even if the church does not come to the aid of justice, I have no despair about the future. I have no fear about the

[2]The Greek New Testament word for the early Christian church.—(Editors' note).

outcome of our struggle in Birmingham, even if our motives are at present misunderstood. We will reach the goal of freedom in Birmingham and all over the nation, because the goal of America is freedom. Abused and scorned though we may be, our destiny is tied up with America's destiny. Before the pilgrims landed at Plymouth, we were here. Before the pen of Jefferson etched the majestic words of the Declaration of Independence across the pages of history, we were here. For more than two centuries, our forebears labored in this country without wages; they made cotton king; they built the homes of their masters while suffering gross injustice and shameful humiliation—and yet out of a bottomless vitality they continued to thrive and develop. If the inexpressible cruelties of slavery could not stop us, the opposition we now face will surely fail. We will win our freedom because the sacred heritage of our nation and the eternal will of God are embodied in our echoing demands.

Before closing I feel impelled to mention one other point in your statement that has troubled me profoundly. You warmly commended the Birmingham police force for keeping ''order'' and ''preventing violence.'' I doubt that you would have so warmly commended the police force if you had seen its dogs sinking their teeth into unarmed, nonviolent Negroes. I doubt that you would so quickly commend the policemen if you were to observe their ugly and inhumane treatment of Negroes here in the city jail; if you were to watch them push and curse old Negro women and young Negro girls; if you were to see them slap and kick old Negro men and young boys; if you were to observe them, as they did on two occasions, refuse to give us food because we wanted to sing our grace together. I cannot join you in your praise of the Birmingham police department. 45

It is true that the police have exercised a degree of discipline in handling the demonstrators. In this sense they have conducted themselves rather ''nonviolently'' in public. But for what purpose? To preserve the evil system of segregation. Over the past few years I have consistently preached that nonviolence demands that the means we use must be as pure as the ends we seek. I have tried to make clear that it is wrong to use immoral means to attain moral ends. But now I must affirm that it is just as wrong, or perhaps even more so, to use moral means to preserve immoral ends. Perhaps Mr. Connor and his policemen have been rather nonviolent 46 in public, as was Chief Pritchett in Albany, Georgia, but they have used the moral means of nonviolence to maintain the immoral end of racial injustice. As T. S. Eliot has said, ''The last temptation is the greatest treason: To do the right deed for the wrong reason.''

I wish you had commended the Negro sit-inners and demon-   47
strators of Birmingham for their sublime courage, their willingness to suffer, and their amazing discipline in the midst of great provocation. One day the South will recognize its real heroes. They will be the James Merediths, with the noble sense of purpose that enables them to face jeering and hostile mobs, and with the agonizing loneliness that characterizes the life of the pioneer. They will be old, oppressed, battered Negro women, symbolized in a seventy-two-year-old woman in Montgomery, Alabama, who rose up with a sense of dignity and with her people decided not to ride segregated buses, and who responded with ungrammatical profundity to one who inquired about her weariness: ''My feets is tired, but my soul is at rest.'' They will be the young high school and college students, the young ministers of the gospel and a host of their elders, courageously and nonviolently sitting in at lunch counters and willingly going to jail for conscience' sake. One day the South will know that when these disinherited children of God sat down at lunch counters, they were in reality standing up for what is best in the American dream and for the most sacred values in our Judaeo-Christian heritage, thereby bringing our nation back to those great wells of democracy which were dug deep by the founding fathers in their formulation of the Constitution and the Declaration of Independence.

Never before have I written so long a letter. I'm afraid it is   48
much too long to take your precious time. I can assure you that it would have been much shorter if I had been writing from a comfortable desk, but what else can one do when he is alone in a narrow jail cell, other than write long letters, think long thoughts, and pray long prayers?

If I have said anything in this letter that overstates the truth   49
and indicates an unreasonable impatience, I beg you to forgive me. If I have said anything that understates the truth and indicates my having a patience that allows me to settle for anything less than brotherhood, I beg God to forgive me.

I hope this letter finds you strong in the faith. I also hope that   50
circumstances will soon make it possible for me to meet each of

you, not as an integrationist or a civil-rights leader but as a fellow clergyman and a Christian brother. Let us all hope that the dark clouds of racial prejudice will soon pass away and the deep fog of misunderstanding will be lifted from our fear-drenched communities, and in some not too distant tomorrow the radiant stars of love and brotherhood will shine over our great nation with all their scintillating beauty.

Yours for the cause of Peace and Brotherhood,
MARTIN LUTHER KING, JR.

Meanings and Values

1a. Does King's purpose in this essay go beyond responding to the criticism of the white clergymen?

  b. If so, what is his broader purpose?

2. Reconstruct as many of the arguments in the clergymen's letter as you can by studying King's refutation of their accusations.

3. What arguments are used in the essay to justify the demonstrations?

4. Summarize the distinction King makes between just and unjust laws.

5a. What kind of behavior did King expect from the white moderates?

  b. Why was he disappointed?

6. How does King defend himself and his followers against the accusation that their actions lead to violence?

7. What is the thesis of this essay?

8. Like many other argumentative essays, this was written in response to a specific situation; yet it is widely regarded as a classic essay. What qualities give the essay its broad and lasting appeal?

Argumentative Techniques

1. How does King establish his reasonableness and fairness so that his audience will take the arguments in the essay seriously even if they are inclined at the start to reject his point of view?

2. Identify as many of the expository patterns as you can in this essay and explain what each contributes to the argument. (Guide: *Unity.*)

3a. What standard techniques of refutation are used in this essay to deal with the accusations made by the clergymen? (Guide: *Refutation.*)

b.   Are any other strategies of refutation used in the essay?

4a.   State the argument in paragraph 6 as a syllogism. (See the introduction to Section 10, "Reasoning by Use of *Induction* and *Deduction.*")

b.   Do the same with the argument in paragraphs 15–22.

5.   Identify several examples of inductive argument in this essay.

6.   At what points in the argument does King use several examples, where one would do, in order to strengthen the argument through variety in evidence?

Diction and Vocabulary

1.   Locate an example of each of the following figures of speech in the essay and explain what it contributes to the argument. (Guide: *Figures of Speech.*)

a.   Metaphor.

b.   Allusion.

c.   Simile.

d.   Paradox.

2a.   Discuss what resources of syntax King uses to construct a 29-line sentence in paragraph 14—without confusing the reader. (Guide: *Syntax.*)

b.   Choose a paragraph that displays considerable variety in sentence length and structure and show how King uses variety in sentence style to convey his point. (Guide: *Style/Tone.*)

3.   Choose two paragraphs, each with a different tone, and discuss how the diction of the passages differs and how the diction in each case contributes to the tone. (Guide: *Diction.*)

4.   In many passages King uses the resources of diction and syntax to add emotional impact to logical argument. Choose such a passage and discuss how it mingles logic and emotion.

Suggestions for Writing and Discussion

1.   Use some of King's arguments to construct a defense of a more recent act of protest or to encourage people to protest a policy you consider unjust. Or, if you wish, draw on his arguments to attack a recent protest on the grounds that it does not meet the high standards he sets.

2. Discuss the practical consequences of King's distinction between just and unjust laws.

3. To what extent does the racism against which King was protesting still exist in our society? Has it been replaced by other forms of discrimination?

(NOTE: Suggestions for topics requiring development by use of ARGUMENT follow.)

Writing Suggestions for Section 11
Argument

Choose one of the following topic areas, identify an issue (a conflict or problem) within it, and prepare an essay that tries to convince readers to share your opinion about the issue and to take any
appropriate action. Use a variety of evidence in your essay, and
choose any pattern of development you consider proper for the
topic, for your thesis, and for the intended audience.

1. Gun control.
2. The quality of education in American elementary and secondary
    schools.
3. Treatment of critically ill newborn babies.
4. Hunting.
5. Euthanasia.
6. Censorship in public schools and libraries.
7. College athletics.
8. The problem of toxic waste or a similar environmental problem.
9. Careers versus family responsibilities.
10. The separation of church and state.
11. Law on the drinking age or on drunk driving.
12. Evolution versus creationism.
13. Arms control.
14. Government spending on social programs.
15. The quality of television programming.
16. The impact of divorce.
17. The effects of television viewing on children.
18. Professional sports.
19. Violence in service of an ideal or belief.
20. Scholarship and student loan policies.
21. Low pay for public service and the "helping" professions.
22. Cheating in college courses.
23. Drug and alcohol abuse.
24. Product safety and reliability.
25. Government economic or social policy.

Further Readings

JONATHAN SWIFT (1667–1745), an Anglican clergyman whose English family were longtime residents of Ireland, was Dean of Saint Patrick's in Dublin and also a poet and political pamphleteer. The greatest satirist of his period, Swift was noted for his clear, sharp prose and his effective indignation at social injustices of the day. His best-known works are *The Battle of the Books, Gulliver's Travels, The Tale of a Tub,* and *A Modest Proposal.* The last, written in 1729, remains one of the world's greatest satires[1] and is almost certainly the most vitriolic, grotesque in its details. It was aimed directly at his English compatriots for their oppression of the Irish people. Writing students should remember, however, that effective as satire can be as a rouser of emotions (i.e., as persuasion), it is not a reliable tool of logic (e.g., as in argument).

A Modest Proposal

FOR PREVENTING THE CHILDREN
OF POOR PEOPLE IN IRELAND
FROM BEING A BURDEN TO THEIR PARENTS OR COUNTRY,
AND FOR MAKING THEM BENEFICIAL TO THE PUBLIC

It is a melancholy object to those who walk through this great town[2] or travel in the country, when they see the streets, the roads, and cabin doors, crowded with beggars of the female sex, followed by three, four, or six children, all in rags and importuning every passenger for an alms. These mothers, instead of being able to work for their honest livelihood, are forced to employ all their time in strolling to beg sustenance for their helpless infants, who, as they grow up, either turn thieves for want of work, or leave their dear native country to fight for the Pretender in Spain, or sell themselves to the Barbadoes.[3]

[1]See Guide to Terms: *Satire.*

[2]Dublin.—EDS.

[3]That is, bind themselves to work for a period of years, in order to pay for their transportation to a colony.—EDS.

I think it is agreed by all parties that this prodigious number 2
of children in the arms, or on the backs, or at the heels of their
mothers, and frequently of their fathers, is in the present deplor-
able state of the kingdom a very great additional grievance; and
therefore whoever could find out a fair, cheap, and easy method
of making these children sound, useful members of the common-
wealth would deserve so well of the public as to have his statue
set up for a preserver of the nation.

But my intention is very far from being confined to provide 3
only for the children of professed beggars; it is of a much greater
extent, and shall take in the whole number of infants at a certain
age who are born of parents in effect as little able to support them
as those who demand our charity in the streets.

As to my own part, having turned my thoughts for many 4
years upon this important subject, and maturely weighed the several schemes of other projectors, I have always found them grossly
mistaken in their computation. It is true, a child just dropped from
its dam may be supported by her milk for a solar year, with little
other nourishment; at most not above the value of two shillings,
which the mother may certainly get, or the value in scraps, by her
lawful occupation of begging; and it is exactly at one year old that
I propose to provide for them in such a manner as instead of being
a charge upon their parents or the parish, or wanting food and
raiment for the rest of their lives, they shall on the contrary contribute to the feeding, and partly to the clothing, of many thousands.

There is likewise another great advantage in my scheme, that 5
it will prevent those voluntary abortions, and that horrid practice
of women murdering their bastard children, alas, too frequent
among us, sacrificing the poor innocent babes, I doubt, more to
avoid the expense than the shame, which would move tears and
pity in the most savage and inhuman breast.

The number of souls in this kingdom being usually reckoned 6
one million and a half, of these I calculate there may be about two
hundred thousand couples whose wives are breeders; from which
number I subtract thirty thousand couples who are able to maintain their own children, although I apprehend there cannot be so
many under the present distress of the kingdom; but this being
granted, there will remain an hundred and seventy thousand
breeders. I again subtract fifty thousand for those women who mis-
carry, or whose children die by accident or disease within the year.

There only remain an hundred and twenty thousand children of
poor parents annually born. The question therefore is, how this
number shall be reared and provided for, which, as I have already
said, under the present situation of affairs, is utterly impossible by
all the methods hitherto proposed. For we can neither employ
them in handicraft nor agriculture; we neither build houses (I
mean in the country) nor cultivate land. They can very seldom pick
up a livelihood by stealing till they arrive at six years old, except
where they are of towardly parts; although I confess they learn the
rudiments much earlier, during which time they can however be
looked upon only as probationers, as I have been informed by a
principal gentleman in the country of Cavan, who protested to me
that he never knew above one or two instances under the age of
six, even in a part of the kingdom so renowned for the quickest
proficiency in that art.

I am assured by our merchants that a boy or a girl before
twelve years old is no salable commodity; and even when they
come to this age, they will not yield above three pounds, or three
pounds and half a crown at most on the Exchange; which cannot
turn to account either to the parents or the kingdom, the charge of
nutriment and rags having been at least four times that value.

I shall now therefore humbly propose my own thoughts,
which I hope will not be liable to the least objection.

I have been assured by a very knowing American of my acquaintance in London, that a young healthy child well nursed is
at a year old a most delicious, nourishing, and wholesome food,
whether stewed, roasted, baked, or boiled; and I make no doubt
that it will equally serve in a fricassee or a ragout.

I do therefore humbly offer it to public consideration that of
the hundred and twenty thousand children, already computed,
twenty thousand may be reserved for breed, whereof only one
fourth part to be males, which is more than we allow to sheep,
black cattle, or swine; and my reason is that these children are
seldom the fruits of marriage, a circumstance not much regarded
by our savages, therefore one male will be sufficient to serve four
females. That the remaining hundred thousand may at a year old
be offered in sale to the persons of quality and fortune through the
kingdom, always advising the mother to let them suck plentifully
in the last month, so as to render them plump and fat for a good
table. A child will make two dishes at an entertainment for friends;
and when the family dines alone, the fore or hind quarter will

make a reasonable dish, and seasoned with a little pepper or salt will be very good boiled on the fourth day, especially in winter.

I have reckoned upon a medium that a child just born will weigh twelve pounds, and in a solar year if tolerably nursed increaseth to twenty-eight pounds.   11

I grant this food will be somewhat dear, and therefore very proper for landlords, who, as they have already devoured most of the parents, seem to have the best title to the children.   12

Infant's flesh will be in season throughout the year, but more plentiful in March, and a little before and after. For we are told by a grave author, an eminent French physician,[4] that fish being a prolific diet, there are more children born in Roman Catholic countries about nine months after Lent, than at any other season; therefore, reckoning a year after Lent, the markets will be more glutted than usual, because the number of popish infants is at least three to one in this kingdom; and therefore it will have one other collateral advantage, by lessening the number of Papists among us.   13

I have already computed the charge of nursing a beggar's child (in which list I reckon all cottagers, laborers, and four fifths of the farmers) to be about two shillings per annum, rags included; and I believe no gentleman would repine to give ten shillings for the carcass of a good fat child, which, as I have said, will make four dishes of excellent nutritive meat, when he hath only some particular friend or his own family to dine with him. Thus the squire will learn to be a good landlord, and grow popular among the tenants; the mother will have eight shillings net profit, and be fit for work till she produces another child.   14

Those who are more thrifty (as I must confess the times require) may flay the carcass; the skin of which artificially dressed will make admirable gloves for ladies, and summer boots for fine gentlemen.   15

As to our city of Dublin, shambles may be appointed for this purpose in the most convenient parts of it, and butchers we may be assured will not be wanting; although I rather recommend buying the children alive, and dressing them hot from the knife as we do roasting pigs.   16

A very worthy person, a true lover of his country, and whose virtues I highly esteem, was lately pleased in discoursing on this matter to offer a refinement upon my scheme. He said that many   17

[4]François Rabelais.—EDS.

gentlemen of his kingdom, having of late destroyed their deer, he
conceived that the want of venison might be well supplied by the
bodies of young lads and maidens, not exceeding fourteen years
of age nor under twelve, so great a number of both sexes in every
county being now ready to starve for want of work and service;
and these to be disposed of by their parents, if alive, or otherwise
by their nearest relations. But with due deference to so excellent
a friend and so deserving a patriot, I cannot be altogether in his
sentiments; for as to the males, my American acquaintance assured
me from frequent experience that their flesh was generally tough
and lean, like that of our schoolboys, by continual exercise, and
their taste disagreeable; and to fatten them would not answer the
charge. Then as to the females, it would, I think with humble submission, be a loss to the public, because they soon would become
breeders themselves; and besides, it is not improbable that some
scrupulous people might be apt to censure such a practice (although indeed very unjustly) as a little bordering upon cruelty;
which, I confess, hath always been with me the strongest objection
against any project, how well soever intended.

But in order to justify my friend, he confessed that this expedi-
ent was put into his head by the famous Psalmanazar, a native of
the island Formosa, who came from thence to London above
twenty years ago, and in conversation told my friend that in his
country when any young person happened to be put to death, the
executioner sold the carcass to the persons of quality as a prime
dainty; and that in his time the body of a plump girl of fifteen,
who was crucified for an attempt to poison the emperor, was sold
to his Imperial Majesty's prime minister of state, and other great
mandarins of the court, in joints from the gibbet, at four hundred
crowns. Neither indeed can I deny that if the same use were made
of several plump young girls in this town, who without one single
groat to their fortunes cannot stir abroad without a chair, and appear at the playhouse and assemblies in foreign fineries which they
never will pay for, the kingdom would not be the worse.

Some persons of a desponding spirit are in great concern
about that vast number of poor people who are aged, diseased, or
maimed, and I have been desired to employ my thoughts what
course may be taken to ease the nation of so grievous an encum-
brance. But I am not in the least pain upon that matter, because it
is very well known that they are every day dying and rotting by

cold and famine, and filth and vermin, as fast as can be reasonably expected. And as to the younger laborers, they are now in almost as hopeful a condition. They cannot get work, and consequently pine away for want of nourishment to a degree that if any time they are accidentally hired to common labor, they have not strength to perform it; and thus the country and themselves are happily delivered from the evils to come.

I have too long digressed, and therefore shall return to my subject. I think the advantages by the proposal which I have made are obvious and many, as well as of the highest importance. 20

For first, as I have already observed, it would greatly lessen the number of Papists, with whom we are yearly overrun, being the principal breeders of the nation as well as our most dangerous enemies; and who stay at home on purpose to deliver the kingdom to the Pretender, hoping to take their advantage by the absence of so many good Protestants, who have chosen rather to leave their country than to stay at home and pay tithes against their conscience to an Episcopal curate. 21

Secondly, the poorer tenants will have something valuable of their own, which by law may be made liable to distress, and help to pay their landlord's rent, their corn and cattle being already seized and money a thing unknown. 22

Thirdly, whereas the maintenance of an hundred thousand children, from two years old and upwards, cannot be computed at less than ten shillings a piece per annum, the nation's stock will be thereby increased fifty thousand pounds per annum, besides the profit of a new dish introduced to the tables of all gentlemen of fortune in the kingdom who have any refinement in taste. And the money will circulate among ourselves, the goods being entirely of our own growth and manufacture. 23

Fourthly, the constant breeders, besides the gain of eight shillings sterling per annum by the sale of their children, will be rid of the charge for maintaining them after the first year. 24

Fifthly, this food would likewise bring great custom to taverns, where the vintners will certainly be so prudent as to procure the best receipts for dressing it to perfection, and consequently have their houses frequented by all the fine gentlemen, who justly value themselves upon their knowledge in good eating; and a skillful cook, who understands how to oblige his guests, will contrive to make it as expensive as they please. 25

Sixthly, this would be a great inducement to marriage, which all wise nations have either encouraged by rewards or enforced by laws and penalties. It would increase the care and tenderness of mothers toward their children, when they were sure of a settlement for life to the poor babes, provided in some sort by the public, to their annual profit instead of expense. We should see an honest emulation among the married women, which of them could bring the fattest child to the market. Men would become as fond of their wives during the time of their pregnancy as they are now of their mares in foal, their cows in calf, or sows when they are ready to farrow; nor offer to beat or kick them (as is too frequent a practice) for fear of a miscarriage.

Many other advantages might be enumerated. For instance, the addition of some thousand carcasses in our exportation of barreled beef, the propagation of swine's flesh, and improvements in the art of making good bacon, so much wanted among us by the great destruction of pigs, too frequent at our tables, which are no way comparable in taste or magnificence to a well-grown, fat, yearling child, which roasted whole will make a considerable figure at a lord mayor's feast or any other public entertainment. But this and many others I omit, being studious of brevity.

Supposing that one thousand families in this city would be constant customers for infants' flesh, besides others who might have it at merry meetings, particularly weddings and christenings, I compute that Dublin would take off annually about twenty thousand carcasses, and the rest of the kingdom (where probably they will be sold somewhat cheaper) the remaining eighty thousand.

I can think of no one objection that will possibly be raised against this proposal, unless it should be urged that the number of people will be thereby much lessened in the kingdom. This I freely own, and it was indeed one principal design in offering it to the world. I desire the reader will observe, that I calculate my remedy for this one individual kingdom of Ireland and for no other that ever was, is, or I think ever can be upon earth. Therefore, let no man talk to me of other expedients: of taxing our absentees at five shillings a pound: of using neither clothes nor household furniture except what is of our own growth and manufacture: of utterly rejecting the materials and instruments that promote foreign luxury: of curing the expensiveness of pride, vanity, idleness, and gaming in our women: of introducing a vein of parsimony, prudence, and temperance: of learning to love our country, in the want of which we differ even from Laplanders and the inhabitants of Topinamboo[5]: of quitting our animosities and factions, nor acting any longer like the Jews, who were murdering one another at the very moment their city was taken: of being a little cautious not to sell our country and conscience for nothing: of teaching landlords to have at least one degree of mercy toward their tenants: lastly, of putting a spirit of honesty, industry, and skill into our shopkeepers; who, if a resolution could now be taken to buy only our native goods, would immediately unite to cheat and exact upon us in the price, the measure, and the goodness, nor could ever yet be brought to make one fair proposal of just dealing, though often and earnestly invited to it.[6]

Therefore, I repeat, let no man talk to me of these and the like expedients, till he hath at least some glimpse of hope that there will ever be some hearty and sincere attempt to put them in practice. 30

But as to myself, having been wearied out for many years with offering vain, idle, visionary thoughts, and at length utterly despairing of success, I fortunately fell upon this proposal, which, as it is wholly new, so it hath something solid and real, of no expense and little trouble, full in our own power, and whereby we can incur no danger in disobliging England. For this kind of commodity will not bear exportation, the flesh being of too tender a consistence to admit a long continuance in salt, although perhaps I could name a country which would be glad to eat up our whole nation without it. 31

After all, I am not so violently bent upon my own opinion as to reject any offer proposed by wise men, which shall be found equally innocent, cheap, easy, and effectual. But before something of that kind shall be advanced in contradiction to my scheme, and offering a better, I desire the author or authors will be pleased maturely to consider two points. First, as things now stand, how they will be able to find food and raiment for an hundred thousand useless mouths and backs. And secondly, there being a round million of creatures in human figure throughout this kingdom, whose sole subsistence put into a common stock would leave them in debt 32

[5]A district in Brazil.—Eds.
[6]Swift himself had made these various proposals in previous works.—Eds.

two millions of pounds sterling, adding those who are beggars by profession to the bulk of farmers, cottagers, and laborers, with their wives and children who are beggars in effect; I desire those politicians who dislike my overture, and may perhaps be so bold to attempt an answer, that they will first ask the parents of these mortals whether they would not at this day think it a great happiness to have been sold for food at a year old in this manner I prescribe, and thereby have avoided such a perpetual scene of misfortunes as they have since gone through by the oppression of landlords, the impossibility of paying rent without money or trade, the want of common sustenance, with neither house nor clothes to cover them from the inclemencies of the weather, and the most inevitable prospect of entailing the like or greater miseries upon their breed forever.

I profess, in the sincerity of my heart, that I have not the least personal interest in endeavoring to promote this necessary work, having no other motive than the public good of my country, by advancing our trade, providing for infants, relieving the poor, and giving some pleasure to the rich. I have no children by which I can propose to get a single penny; the youngest being nine years old, and my wife past childbearing.

MARGARET ATWOOD was born in Ottawa, Ontario, in 1939. After attending college in Canada, she went to graduate school at Harvard University. She has had a distinguished career as a novelist, poet, and essayist, and is generally considered to be one of the central figures in contemporary Canadian literature and culture. Atwood's international reputation as a writer rests on her novels, including *The Edible Woman* (1969); *Surfacing* (1972); *Life Before Man* (1979); *Bodily Harm* (1982); *The Handmaid's Tale* (1986); and *Cat's Eye* (1989), and her short stories, including *Bluebeard's Egg and Other Stories* (1986), though she has written poetry, television plays, and children's books as well. Her essays were collected in the volume *Second Words* (1982) and have continued to appear in magazines such as *Ms., Harper's, The Humanist, The New Republic,* and *Architectural Digest.* As an essayist, Atwood frequently writes about issues in contemporary culture and society, including the nature of Canadian culture and relationships between Canada and the United States. In the following essay, taken from *Second Words,* she addresses the question of pornography with a directness and originality that are characteristic of her work.

Pornography

When I was in Finland a few years ago for an international writers' conference, I had occasion to say a few paragraphs in public on the subject of pornography. The context was a discussion of political repression, and I was suggesting the possibility of a link between the two. The immediate result was that a male journalist took several large bites out of me. Prudery and pornography are two halves of the same coin, said he, and I was clearly a prude. What could you expect from an Anglo-Canadian? Afterward, a couple of pleasant Scandinavian men asked me what I had been so worked up about. All "pornography" means, they said, is graphic depictions of whores, and what was the harm in that?

1

Not until then did it strike me that the male journalist and I had two entirely different things in mind. By "pornography," he meant naked bodies and sex. I, on the other hand, had recently been doing the research for my novel *Bodily Harm*, and was still in a state of shock from some of the material I had seen, including the Ontario Board of Film Censors' "outtakes." By "pornography," I meant women getting their nipples snipped off with garden shears, having meat hooks stuck into their vaginas, being disemboweled; little girls being raped; men (yes, there are some men) being smashed to a pulp and forcibly sodomized. The cutting edge of pornography, as far as I could see, was no longer simple old copulation, hanging from the chandelier or otherwise: it was death, messy, explicit and highly sadistic. I explained this to the nice Scandinavian men. "Oh, but that's just the United States," they said. "Everyone knows they're sick." In their country, they said, violent "pornography" of that kind was not permitted on television or in movies; indeed, excessive violence of any kind was not permitted. They had drawn a clear line between erotica, which earlier studies had shown did not incite men to more aggressive and brutal behavior toward women, and violence, which later studies indicated did.

Some time after that I was in Saskatchewan, where, because of the scenes in *Bodily Harm*, I found myself on an open-line radio show answering questions about "pornography." Almost no one who phoned in was in favor of it, but again they weren't talking about the same stuff I was, because they hadn't seen it. Some of them were all set to stamp out bathing suits and negligees, and, if possible, any depictions of the female body whatsoever. God, it was implied, did not approve of female bodies, and sex of any kind, including that practised by bumblebees, should be shoved back into the dark, where it belonged. I had more than a suspicion that *Lady Chatterley's Lover*, Margaret Laurence's *The Diviners*, and indeed most books by most serious modern authors would have ended up as confetti if left in the hands of these callers.

For me, these two experiences illustrate the two poles of the emotionally heated debate that is now thundering around this issue. They also underline the desirability and even the necessity of defining the terms. "Pornography" is now one of those catchalls, like "Marxism" and "feminism," that have become so broad they can mean almost anything, ranging from certain verses in the Bi-

ble, ads for skin lotion and sex tests for children to the contents of
Penthouse, Naughty '90s postcards and films with titles containing
the word *Nazi* that show vicious scenes of torture and killing. It's
easy to say that sensible people can tell the difference. Unfortunately, opinions on what constitutes a sensible person vary.

But even sensible people tend to lose their cool when they   5
start talking about this subject. They soon stop talking and start
yelling, and the name-calling begins. Those in favor of censorship
(which may include groups not noticeably in agreement on other
issues, such as some feminists and religious fundamentalists) ac-
cuse the others of exploiting women through the use of degrading
images, contributing to the corruption of children, and adding to
the general climate of violence and threat in which both women
and children live in this society; or, though they may not give
much of a hoot about actual women and children, they invoke
moral standards and God's supposed aversion to "filth," "smut"
and deviated *preversion,* which may mean ankles.

The camp in favor of total "freedom of expression" often   6
comes out howling as loud as the Romans would have if told they
could no longer have innocent fun watching the lions eat up Christians. It too may include segments of the population who are not
natural bedfellows: those who proclaim their God-given right to
freedom, including the freedom to tote guns, drive when drunk,
drool over chicken porn and get off on videotapes of women being
raped and beaten, may be waving the same anticensorship banner
as responsible liberals who fear the return of Mrs. Grundy, or gay
groups for whom sexual emancipation involves the concept of
"sexual theatre." *Whatever turns you on* is a handy motto, as is *A
man's home is his castle* (and if it includes a dungeon with beautiful
maidens strung up in chains and bleeding from every pore, that's
his business).

Meanwhile, theoreticians theorize and speculators speculate.   7
Is today's pornography yet another indication of the hatred of the
body, the deep mind-body split, which is supposed to pervade
Western Christian society? Is it a backlash against the women's
movement by men who are threatened by uppity female behavior
in real life, so like to fantasize about women done up like outsize
parcels, being turned into hamburger, kneeling at their feet in
slavelike adoration or sucking off guns? Is it a sign of collective
impotence, of a generation of men who can't relate to real women

at all but have to make do with bits of celluloid and paper? Is the
current flood just a result of smart marketing and aggressive promotion by the money men in what has now become a multibillion-
dollar industry? If they were selling movies about men getting their
testicles stuck full of knitting needles by women with swastikas on
their sleeves, would they do as well, or is this penchant somehow
peculiarly male? If so, why? Is pornography a power trip rather
than a sex one? Some say that those ropes, chains, muzzles and
other restraining devices are an argument for the immense power
female sexuality still wields in the male imagination: you don't put
these things on dogs unless you're afraid of them. Others, more
literary, wonder about the shift from the 19th-century Magic
Woman or Femme Fatale image to the lollipop-licker, airhead or
turkey-carcass treatment of women in porn today. The proporners
don't care much about theory; they merely demand product. The
antiporners don't care about it in the final analysis either; there's
dirt on the street, and they want it cleaned up, now.

It seems to me that this conversation, with its *You're-a-prude/*   8
You're-a-pervert dialectic, will never get anywhere as long as we
continue to think of this material as just "entertainment." Possibly
we're deluded by the packaging, the format: magazine, book,
movie, theatrical presentation. We're used to thinking of these
things as part of the "entertainment industry," and we're used to
thinking of ourselves as free adult people who ought to be able to
see any kind of "entertainment" we want to. That was what the
First Choice pay-TV debate was all about. After all, it's only entertainment, right? Entertainment means fun, and only a killjoy
would be antifun. What's the harm?

This is obviously the central question: *What's the harm?* If there   9
isn't any real harm to any real people, then the antiporners can
tsk-tsk and/or throw up as much as they like, but they can't right-
fully expect more legal controls or sanctions. However, the no-
harm position is far from being proven.

(For instance, there's a clear-cut case for banning—as the fed-   1
eral government has proposed—movies, photos and videos that
depict children engaging in sex with adults: real children are used
to make the movies, and hardly anybody thinks this is ethical. The
possibilities for coercion are too great.)

To shift the viewpoint, I'd like to suggest three other models   1
for looking at "pornography"—and here I mean the violent kind.

Those who find the idea of regulating pornographic materials 12
repugnant because they think it's Fascist or Communist or otherwise not in accordance with the principles of an open democratic
society should consider that Canada has made it illegal to dissemi-
nate material that may lead to hatred toward any group because of
race or religion. I suggest that if pornography of the violent kind
depicted these acts being done predominantly to Chinese, to
blacks, to Catholics, it would be off the market immediately, under
the present laws. Why is hate literature illegal? Because whoever
made the law thought that such material might incite real people
to do real awful things to other real people. The human brain is to
a certain extent a computer: garbage in, garbage out. We only hear
about the extreme cases (like that of American multimurderer Ted
Bundy) in which pornography has contributed to the death and/
or mutilation of women and/or men. Although pornography is not
the only factor involved in the creation of such deviance, it certainly has upped the ante by suggesting both a variety of techniques and the social acceptability of such actions. Nobody knows
yet what effect this stuff is having on the less psychotic.

Studies have shown that a large part of the market for all kinds 13
of porn, soft and hard, is drawn from the 16-to-21-year-old population of young men. Boys used to learn about sex on the street, or
(in Italy, according to Fellini movies) from friendly whores, or, in
more genteel surroundings, from girls, their parents, or, once
upon a time, in school, more or less. Now porn has been added,
and sex education in the schools is rapidly being phased out. The
buck has been passed, and boys are being taught that all women
secretly like to be raped and that real men get high on scooping
out women's digestive tracts.

Boys learn their concept of masculinity from other men: is this 14
what most men want them to be learning? If word gets around that
rapists are ''normal'' and even admirable men, will boys feel that
in order to be normal, admirable and masculine they will have to
be rapists? Human beings are enormously flexible, and how they
turn out depends a lot on how they're educated, by the society in
which they're immersed as well as by their teachers. In a society
that advertises and glorifies rape or even implicitly condones it,
more women get raped. It becomes socially acceptable. And at a
time when men and the traditional male role have taken a lot of
flak and men are confused and casting around for an acceptable

way of being male (and, in some cases, not getting much comfort from women on that score), this must be at times a pleasing thought.

It would be naïve to think of violent pornography as just harmless entertainment. It's also an educational tool and a powerful propaganda device. What happens when boy educated on porn meets girl brought up on Harlequin romances? The clash of expectations can be heard around the block. She wants him to get down on his knees with a ring, he wants her to get down on all fours with a ring in her nose. Can this marriage be saved?

Pornography has certain things in common with such addictive substances as alcohol and drugs: for some, though by no means for all, it induces chemical changes in the body, which the user finds exciting and pleasurable. It also appears to attract a "hard core" of habitual users and a penumbra of those who use it occasionally but aren't dependent on it in any way. There are also significant numbers of men who aren't much interested in it, not because they're undersexed but because real life is satisfying their needs, which may not require as many appliances as those of users.

For the "hard core," pornography may function as alcohol does for the alcoholic: tolerance develops, and a little is no longer enough. This may account for the short viewing time and fast turnover in porn theatres. Mary Brown, chairwoman of the Ontario Board of Film Censors, estimates that for every one mainstream movie requesting entrance to Ontario, there is one porno flick. Not only the quantity consumed but the quality of explicitness must escalate, which may account for the growing violence: once the big deal was breasts, then it was genitals, then copulation, then that was no longer enough and the hard users had to have more. The ultimate kick is death, and after that, as the Marquis de Sade so boringly demonstrated, multiple death.

The existence of alcoholism has not led us to ban social drinking. On the other hand, we do have laws about drinking and driving, excessive drunkenness and other abuses of alcohol that may result in injury or death to others.

This leads us back to the key question: what's the harm? Nobody knows, but this society should find out fast, before the saturation point is reached. The Scandinavian studies that showed a connection between depictions of sexual violence and increased impulse toward it on the part of male viewers would be a starting point, but many more questions remain to be raised as well as answered. What, for instance, is the crucial difference between men who are users and men who are not? Does using affect a man's relationship with actual women, and, if so, adversely? Is there a clear line between erotica and violent pornography, or are they on an escalating continuum? Is this a "men versus women" issue, with all men secretly siding with the proporners and all women secretly siding against? (I think not; there *are* lots of men who don't think that running their true love through the Cuisinart is the best way they can think of to spend a Saturday night, and they're just as nauseated by films of someone else doing it as women are.) Is pornography merely an expression of the sexual confusion of this age or an active contributor to it?

Nobody wants to go back to the age of official repression,   20 when even piano legs were referred to as "limbs" and had to wear pantaloons to be decent. Neither do we want to end up in George Orwell's *1984*, in which pornography is turned out by the State to keep the proles in a state of torpor, sex itself is considered dirty and the approved practise it only for reproduction. But Rome under the emperors isn't such a good model either.

If all men and women respected each other, if sex were consid-   21 ered joyful and life-enhancing instead of a wallow in germ-filled glop, if everyone were in love all the time, if, in other words, many people's lives were more satisfactory for them than they appear to be now, pornography might just go away on its own. But since this is obviously not happening, we as a society are going to have to make some informed and responsible decisions about how to deal with it.

ANDREW HOLLERAN

ANDREW HOLLERAN is a novelist and essay writer. His articles
have appeared in *New York Magazine, Christopher Street,* and
other publications. He has published two novels: *Dancer from
the Dance* (1978) and *Nights in Aruba* (1983). A collection of his
essays, *Ground Zero,* was published in 1988. "Bedside Manners"
is taken from it. The essay begins with personal events, but
quickly moves to consider the relationships between sickness
and health and between living and dying that set boundaries on
all human lives. Its movement thus resembles the ripples from
a stone thrown in the water. In the end, Holleran asks readers
to consider not simply the narrower meanings of "the plague"
but also the larger challenges it poses.

Bedside Manners

"There is no difference between men so profound," wrote Scott
Fitzgerald, "as that between the sick and the well."

There are many thoughts that fill someone's head as he walks
across town on a warm July afternoon to visit a friend confined to
a hospital room—and that is one of them. Another occurs to you
as you wait for the light to change and watch the handsome young
basketball players playing on the public court behind a chicken
wire fence: Health is everywhere. The world has a surreal quality
to it when you are on your way to the hospital to visit someone
you care for who is seriously ill: Everyone in it, walking down the
sidewalk, driving by in cars, rushing about on a basketball court
with sweat-stained chests, exhausted faces, and wide eyes, seems
to you extremely peculiar. They are peculiar because they are free:
walking under their own power, nicely dressed, sometimes beautiful. Beauty does not lose its allure under the spell of grief. The
hospital visitor still notices the smooth chests of the athletes in
their cotton shorts as they leap to recover the basketball after it

bounces off the rim. But everything seems strangely quiet—speechless—as if you were watching a movie on television with the sound turned off, as if everyone else in the world but you is totally unaware of something: that the act of walking across York Avenue under one's own power is essentially miraculous.

Every time he enters a hospital, the visitor enters with two simultaneous thoughts: He hates hospitals, and only people working in them lead serious lives. Everything else is selfish. Entering a hospital he always thinks, *I should work for a year as a nurse, an aide, a volunteer helping people, coming to terms with disease and death.* This feeling will pass the moment he leaves the hospital. In reality the visitor hopes his fear and depression are not evident on his face as he walks down the gleaming, silent hall from the elevator to his friend's room. He is trying hard to stay calm.

The door of the room the receptionist downstairs has told the visitor his friend is in is closed—and on it are taped four signs that are not on any of the other doors and are headlined, WARNING. The visitor stops as much to read them as to allow his heartbeat to subside before going in. He knows—from the accounts of friends who have already visited—he must don a robe, gloves, mask, and even a plastic cap. He is not sure if the door is closed because his friend is asleep inside or because the door to this room is always kept closed. So he pushes it open a crack and peers in. His friend is turned on his side, a white mound of bed linen, apparently sleeping.

The visitor is immensely relieved. He goes down the hall and asks a nurse if he may leave the *Life* magazine he brought for his friend and writes a note to him saying he was here. Then he leaves the hospital and walks west through the summer twilight as if swimming through an enchanted lagoon. The next day—once more crossing town—he is in that surreal mood, under a blue sky decorated with a few photogenic, puffy white clouds, certain that no one else knows . . . knows he or she is absurdly, preposterously, incalculably fortunate to be walking on the street. He feels once again that either the sound has been turned off or some other element (his ego, perhaps with all its anger, ambition, jealousy) has been removed from the world. The basketball players are different youths today but just as much worth pausing to look at. He enters the hospital one block east more calmly this time and requests to see his friend—who is allowed only two visitors at a time, and visits lasting no more than ten minutes. He goes upstairs, peeks around the door, and sees his friend utterly awake. The visitor's heart races as he steps back and puts on the gloves, mask, cap, and robe he has been told his friends all look so comical in. He smiles because he hopes the photograph that made him bring the copy of *Life* to the hospital—Russian women leaning against a wall in Leningrad in bikinis and winter coats, taking the sun on a February day—has amused his friend as much as it tickled him.

"Richard?" the visitor says as he opens the door and peeks in. 6 His friend blinks at him. Two plastic tubes are fixed in his nostrils bringing him oxygen. His face is emaciated and gaunt, his hair longer, softer in appearance, wisps rising above his head. But the one feature the visitor cannot get over are his friend's eyes. His eyes are black, huge, and furious. Perhaps because his face is gaunt or perhaps because they really are larger than usual, they seem the only thing alive in his face; as if his whole being were distilled and concentrated, poured, drained, into his eyes. They are shining, alarmed, and—there is no other word—furious. He looks altogether like an angry baby—or an angry old man—or an angry bald eagle.

And just as the hospital visitor is absorbing the shock of these 7 livid eyes, the sick man says in a furious whisper, "Why did you bring me that dreadful magazine? I hate *Life* magazine! With that stupid picture! I wasn't amused! I wasn't amused at all! You should never have brought that dreck into this room!"

The visitor is momentarily speechless: It is the first time in 8 their friendship of ten years that anything abusive or insulting has ever been said; it is as astonishing as the gaunt face in which two huge black eyes burn and shine. But he sits down and recovers his breath and apologizes. The visitor thinks, *He's angry because I haven't visited him till now. He's angry that he's here at all, that he's sick.* And they begin to talk. They talk of the hospital food (which he hates too), of the impending visit of his mother (whose arrival he dreads), of the drug he is taking (which is experimental), and of the other visitors he has had. The patient asks the visitor to pick up a towel at the base of the bed and give it to him. The visitor complies. The patient places it across his forehead—and the visitor, who, like most people, is unsure what to say in this situation, stifles the question he wants to ask, *Why do you have a towel on your forehead?* The patient finally says, "Don't you think I look like

Mother Theresa?'' And the visitor realizes his friend has made a joke—as he did years ago in their house on Fire Island: doing drag with bedspreads, pillow cases, towels, whatever was at hand. The visitor does not smile—he is so unprepared for a joke in these circumstances—but he realizes, with relief, he is forgiven. He realizes what people who visit the sick often learn: It is the patient who puts the visitor at ease. In a few moments his ten minutes are up. He rises and says, ''I don't want to tire you.'' He goes to the door and once beyond it he turns and looks back. His friend says to him, ''I'm proud of you for coming.''

''Oh—!'' the visitor says and shakes his head. ''Proud of *me* for coming!'' he tells a friend later that evening, after he has stripped off his gown and mask and gone home, through the unreal city of people in perfect health. ''Proud of me! Can you imagine! To say that to me, to make *me* feel good! When he's the one in bed!'' The truth is he is proud of himself the next time he visits his friend, for he is one of those people who looks away when a nurse takes a blood test and finds respirators frightening. He is like almost everyone—everyone except these extraordinary people who work in hospitals, he thinks, as he walks into the building. The second visit is easier, partly because it is the second, and partly because the patient is better—the drug has worked.   9

But he cannot forget the sight of those dark, angry eyes and the plastic tubes and emaciated visage—and as he goes home that evening, he knows there is a place whose existence he was not aware of before: the foyer of death. It is a place many of us will see at least once in our lives. Because modern medicine fights for patients who a century ago would have died without its intervention, it has created an odd place between life and death. One no longer steps into Charon's boat to be ferried across the River Styx—ill people are now detained, with one foot in the boat and the other still on shore. It is a place where mercy looks exactly like cruelty to the average visitor. It is a place that one leaves, if one is only a visitor, with the conviction that ordinary life is utterly miraculous, so that, going home from the hospital on the subway, one is filled with things one cannot express to the crowd that walks up out of the station or throngs the street of the block where he lives. But if the people caught in the revolving door between health and death could speak, would they not say—as Patrick Cowley reportedly did as he watched the men dancing to his music while he   10

was fatally ill, "Look at those stupid queens. Don't they *know?*"
Guard your health. It is all you have. It is the thin line that stands
between you and hell. It is your miraculous possession. Do nothing to threaten it. Treat each other with kindness. Comfort your
suffering friends. Help one another. Revere life. Do not throw it
away for the momentous pleasures of lust, or even the obliteration
of loneliness.

Many homosexuals wonder how they will die: where, with
whom. Auden went back to Oxford, Santayana to the Blue Nuns
in Rome. We are not all so lucky. Some men afflicted with AIDS
returned to die in their family's home. Others have died with
friends. Some have died bitterly and repudiated the homosexual
friends who came to see them; others have counted on these
people. Volunteers from the Gay Men's Health Crisis have cooked,
cleaned, shopped, visited, taken care of people they did not even
know until they decided to help. One thing is sure—we are learning how to help one another. We are discovering the strength and
goodness of people we knew only in discotheques or as faces on
Fire Island. We are following a great moral precept by visiting the
sick. We are once again learning the awful truth Robert Penn War-
ren wrote years ago: "Only through the suffering of the innocent
is the brotherhood of man confirmed." The most profound difference between men may well be that between the sick and the well,
but compassionate people try to reach across the chasm and bridge
it. The hospital visitor who conquers his own fear of something
facing us all takes the first step on a journey that others less fearful
than he have already traveled much further on: They are combining eros and agape as they rally round their stricken friends. As
for the courage and dignity and sense of humor of those who are
sick, these are beyond praise, and one hesitates where words are
so flimsy. As for a disease whose latency period is measured in
years, not months, there is no telling which side of the line dividing the sick and the well each of us will be on before this affliction
is conquered. We may disdain the hysteria of policemen and firemen who call for masks, and people who ask if it is safe to ride the
subway, and television crews who will not interview AIDS patients. For they are not at risk—those who are, are fearlessly helping their own. This is the greatest story of the plague.

A Guide to Terms

Abstract (See *Concrete/Abstract.*)
Allusion (See *Figures of Speech.*)
Analogy (See Section 4.)
Argument is writing that uses factual evidence and supporting ideas to convince readers to share the author's opinion on an issue or to take some action the writer considers appropriate or necessary. Like exposition, argument conveys information; however, it does so not to explain but to induce readers to favor one side in a conflict or to choose a particular course of action.

Some arguments appeal primarily to reason, others primarily to emotion. Most, however, mix reason and emotion in whatever way is appropriate for the issue and the audience. (See Section 11.)

Support for an argument can take a number of forms:

1. *Examples*—Real-life examples, or hypothetical examples (used sparingly) can be convincing evidence if they are typical and if the author provides enough of them to illustrate all the major points in the argument or combines them with other kinds of evidence. (See Quindlen, George, Abbey.) Some examples are *specific*, referring to particular people or events. (See Geyer, Quindlen.) Others are *general*, referring to kinds of events or people, usually corresponding in some way to the reader's experiences. (See Thomas.)

2. *Facts and figures*—Detailed information about a subject, particularly if presented in statistical form, can help convince readers by showing that the author's perspective on an issue is consistent with what is known about the subject. (See George,

Lynn.) But facts whose accuracy is questionable or statistics that are confusing can undermine an argument.

    3. *Authority*—Supporting an argument with the ideas or the actual words of someone who is recognized as an expert can be an effective strategy as long as the author can show that the expert is a reliable witness and can combine the expert's opinion with other kinds of evidence that point in the same direction.

    4. *Personal experience*—Examples drawn from personal experience or the experience of friends can be more detailed and vivid (and hence more convincing) than other kinds of evidence, but a writer should use this kind of evidence sparingly because readers may sometimes suspect that it represents no more than one person's way of looking at events. When combined with other kinds of evidence, however, examples drawn from personal experience can be an effective technique for persuasion. (See Thomas, Abbey.)

    In addition, all the basic expository patterns can be used to support an argument. (See Section 11.)

Cause (See Section 6.)

Central Theme (See *Unity.*)

Classification (See Section 2.)

Clichés are tired expressions, perhaps once fresh and colorful, that have been overused until they have lost most of their effectiveness and become trite or hackneyed. The term is also applied, less commonly, to trite ideas or attitudes.

    We may need to use clichés in conversation, of course, where the quick and economical phrase is an important and useful tool of expression—and where no one expects us to be constantly original. We are fortunate, in a way, to have a large accumulation of clichés from which to draw. To describe someone, without straining our originality very much, we can always declare that he is *as innocent as a lamb, as thin as a rail*, or *as fat as a pig;* that he is *as dumb as an ox, as sly as a fox*, or *as wise as an owl;* that he is *financially embarrassed* or *has a fly in the ointment* or *his ship has come in;* or that, *last but not least, in this day and age*, the *Grim Reaper* has taken him to *his eternal reward.* There is indeed *a large stockpile* from which we can draw for ordinary conversation. But the trite expression, written down on paper, is a permanent reminder that the writer is either lazy or not aware of the dullness of stereotypes—or, even more damaging, it is a clue that the ideas themselves may be threadbare, and therefore can be adequately expressed in threadbare language.

Occasionally, of course, a writer can use obvious clichés deliberately (see Sheehy, par. 12; B. Lawrence, par. 1). But usually to be fully effective, writing must be fresh, and should seem to have been written specifically for the occasion. Clichés, however fresh and appropriate at one time, have lost these qualities.

Closings are almost as much of a problem as introductions, and they are equally important. The function of a closing is simply ''to close,'' of course, but this implies somehow tying the entire writing into a neat package, giving the final sense of unity to the whole endeavor, and thus leaving the reader with a sense of satisfaction instead of an uneasy feeling that there ought to be another page. There is no standard length for closings. A short composition may be effectively completed with one sentence—or even without any real closing at all, if the last point discussed is a strong or climactic one. A longer piece of writing, however, may end more slowly, perhaps through several paragraphs.

A few types of weak endings are so common that warnings are in order here. Careful writers will avoid these faults: (1) giving the effect of suddenly tiring and quitting; (2) ending on a minor detail or an apparent afterthought; (3) bringing up a new point in the closing; (4) using any new qualifying remark in the closing (if writers want their opinions to seem less dogmatic or generalized, they should go back to do their qualifying where the damage was done); (5) ending with an apology of any kind (authors who are not interested enough to become at least minor experts in their subject should not be wasting the reader's time).

Of the several acceptable ways of giving the sense of finality to a paper, the easiest is the *summary,* but it is also the least desirable for most short papers. Readers who have read and understood something only a page or two before probably do not need to have it reviewed for them. Such a review is apt to seem merely repetitious. Longer writings, of course, such as research or term papers, may require thorough summaries.

Several other closing techniques are available to writers. The following, which do not represent all the possibilities, are useful in many situations, and they can frequently be employed in combination:

1. *Using word signals*—e.g., *finally, at last, thus, and so, in conclusion,* as well as more original devices suggested by the subject itself. (See Buhler and Graham, Simpson.)

2. *Changing the tempo*—usually a matter of sentence length or pace. This is a very subtle indication of finality, and it is difficult to achieve. (For examples of modified use, see Simpson; Peterson; Walker.)

3. *Restating the central idea* of the writing—sometimes a "statement" so fully developed that it practically becomes a summary itself. (See Catton, Marsh.)

4. *Using climax*—a natural culmination of preceding points or, in some cases, the last major point itself. This is suitable, however, only if the materials have been so arranged that the last point is outstanding. (See Catton, Rettie, B. Lawrence, Walker, Korda.)

5. *Making suggestions,* perhaps mentioning a possible solution to the problem being discussed—a useful technique for exposition as well as for argument, and a natural signal of the end. (See Thurow.)

6. *Showing the topic's significance,* its effects, or the universality of its meaning—a commonly used technique that, if carefully handled, is an excellent indication of closing. (See Buckley, Rettie, Morris, B. Lawrence, Thurow.)

7. *Echoing the introduction*—a technique that has the virtue of improving the effect of unity by bringing the development around full circle, so to speak. The echo may be a reference to a problem posed or a significant expression, quotation, analogy, or symbol used in the introduction or elsewhere early in the composition. (See Buckley, Ehrenreich.)

8. *Using some rhetorical device*—a sort of catchall category, but a good supply source that includes several very effective techniques: pertinent quotations, anecdotes and brief dialogues, metaphors, allusions, ironic comments, and various kinds of witty or memorable remarks. All, however, run the risk of seeming forced and hence amateurish; but properly handled, they make for an effective closing. (See White, Rettie,

Peterson, George, Sheehy, B. Lawrence, Simpson, Geyer, King.)

Coherence is the quality of good writing that results from the presentation of all parts in logical and clear relations.

Coherence and unity are usually studied together and, indeed, are almost inseparable. But whereas unity refers to the relation of parts to the central theme (see *Unity*), coherence refers to their relations with each other. In a coherent piece of writing, each sentence, each paragraph, each major division seems to grow out of those preceding it.

Several transitional devices (see *Transition*) help to make these relations clear, but far more fundamental to coherence is the sound organization of materials. From the first moment of visualizing the subject materials in pattern, the writer's goal must be clear and logical development. If it is, coherence is almost ensured.

Colloquial Expressions are characteristic of conversation and informal writing, and they are normally perfectly appropriate in those contexts. However, most writing done for college, business, or professional purposes is considered "formal" writing; and for such usage, colloquialisms are too informal, too *folksy* (itself a word most dictionaries would label "colloq.").

Some of the expressions appropriate only for informal usage are *kid* (for child), *boss* (for employer), *flunk, buddy, snooze, gym, a lot of, phone, skin flicks, porn*. In addition, contractions such as *can't* and *I'd* are usually regarded as colloquialisms and are never permissible in, for instance, a research or term paper.

Slang is defined as a low level of colloquialism, but it is sometimes placed "below" colloquialism in respectability; even standard dictionaries differ as to just what the distinction is. (Some of the examples in the preceding paragraph, if included in dictionaries at all, are identified both ways.) At any rate, slang generally comprises words either coined or given novel meanings in an attempt at colorful or humorous expression. Slang soon becomes limp with overuse, however, losing whatever vigor it first had. In time, slang expressions either disappear completely or graduate to more acceptable colloquial status and thence, possibly, into standard usage. (That is one way in which our language is constantly changing.) But until their "graduations," slang and colloquialism have an appropriate place in formal writing only if used sparingly and for special effect. Because dictionaries frequently differ in matters of usage, the student should be sure to use a standard edition approved by the instructor. (For further examples, see Viorst; Wolfe; Sheehy; Simpson, pars. 8, 16, 17.)

Comparison (See Section 3.)

Conclusions (See *Closings.*)

Concrete and **Abstract** words are both indispensable to the language, but a good rule in most writing is to use the concrete whenever possible. This policy also applies, of course, to sentences that express only abstract ideas, which concrete examples can often make clearer and more effective. Many expository and argumentative paragraphs are constructed with an abstract topic sentence and its concrete support. (See *Unity.*)

A concrete word names something that exists as an entity in itself, something that can be perceived by the human senses. We can see, touch, hear, and smell a horse—hence *horse* is a concrete word. But a horse's *strength* is not. We have no reason to doubt that strength exists, but it does not have an independent existence: something else must *be* strong or there is no strength. Hence *strength* is an abstract word.

Purely abstract reading is difficult for average readers; with no concrete images provided, they are constantly forced to make their own. Concrete writing helps readers to visualize and is therefore easier and faster to read.

(See *Specific/General* for further discussion.)

Connotation and **Denotation** both refer to the meanings of words. Denotation is the direct, literal meaning as it would be found in a dictionary, whereas connotation refers to the response a word *really* arouses in the reader or listener. (See Wolfe, par. 14; B. Lawrence.)

There are two types of connotation: personal and general. Personal connotations vary widely, depending on the experiences and moods that an individual associates with the word. (This corresponds with personal symbolism; see *Symbol.*) *Waterfall* is not apt to have the same meaning for the happy young honeymooners at Yosemite as it has for the grieving mother whose child has just drowned in a waterfall. General connotations are those shared by many people. *Fireside*, far beyond its obvious dictionary definition, generally connotes warmth and security and good companionship. *Mother*, which denotatively means simply "female parent," means much more connotatively.

A word or phrase considered less distasteful or offensive than a more direct expression is called a *euphemism*, and this is also a matter of connotation. (See Mitford.) The various expressions used instead of the more direct "four-letter words" referring to daily bathroom events are examples of euphemisms. (See Wolfe's "mounting" or D. H. Lawrence's "dirt.") *Remains* is often used instead of *corpse*, and a few newspapers still have people *passing away* and being *laid to rest*, rather than *dying* and being *buried*.

But a serious respect for the importance of connotations goes far beyond euphemistic practices. Young writers can hardly expect to know all the different meanings of words for all their potential readers, but they can at least be aware that words do *have* different meanings. Of course, this is most important in persuasive writing—in political speeches, in advertising copywriting, and in any endeavor where some sort of public image is being created. When President Franklin Roosevelt began his series of informal radio talks, he called them "fireside chats," thus putting connotation to work. An advertising copywriter trying to evoke the feeling of love and tenderness associated with motherhood is not seriously tempted to use *female parent* instead of *mother*.

In exposition, where the primary purpose is to explain, the writer ordinarily tries to avoid words that may have emotional overtones, unless these can somehow be used to increase understanding. In argument, however, a writer may on occasion wish to appeal to the emotions.

Contrast (See Section 3.)

Deduction (See Section 10.)

Denotation (See *Connotation/Denotation*.)

Description (See Section 8.)

Diction refers simply to "choice of words," but, not so simply, it involves many problems of usage, some of which are explained under several other headings in this guide, e.g., *Clichés, Colloquial Expressions, Connotation/Denotation, Concrete/*

Abstract—anything, in fact, that pertains primarily to word choices. But the characteristics of good diction may be more generally classified as follows:

1. *Accuracy*—the choice of words that mean exactly what the author intends.

2. *Economy*—the choice of the simplest and fewest words that will convey the exact meaning intended.

3. *Emphasis*—the choice of fresh, strong words, avoiding clichés and unnecessarily vague or general terms.

4. *Appropriateness*—the choice of words that suit the subject matter, the prospective reader-audience, and the purpose of the writing.

(For contrasts of diction see Abbey, Walker, Eiseley, King, Thomas, Rodriguez, Quindlen.)

Division (See Section 2.)

Effect (See Section 6.)

Emphasis is almost certain to fall *somewhere,* and the author should be the one to decide where. A major point, not some minor detail, should be emphasized.

Following are the most common ways of achieving emphasis. Most of them apply to the sentence, the paragraph, or the overall writing—all of which can be seriously weakened by emphasis in the wrong places.

1. By *position*—the most emphatic position is usually at the end, the second most emphatic at the beginning. (There are a few exceptions, including news stories and certain kinds of scientific reports.) The middle, therefore, should be used for materials that do not deserve special emphasis. (See Buckley, for saving the most significant example until last; Catton, par. 16; and Rettie, for the long witheld revelation of the real central theme.)

A sentence in which the main point is held until the last is called a *periodic sentence,* e.g., "After a long night of suspense and horror, the cavalry arrived." In a *loose sentence,* the main point is disposed of earlier and followed by dependencies, e.g., "The calvary arrived after a long night of suspense and horror." (See Thomas, par. 11, second sentence, for an effective periodic sentence that concludes an essay.)

2. By *proportion*—Ordinarily, but not necessarily, important elements are given the most attention and thus automati-

cally achieve a certain emphasis. (See Rettie for a unique kind of reverse application of this method.)

3. By *repetition*—Words and ideas may sometimes be given emphasis by reuse, usually in a different manner. If not cautiously handled, however, this method can seem merely repetitious, not emphatic. (See D. H. Lawrence.)

4. By *flat statement*—Although an obvious way to achieve emphasis is simply to *tell* the reader what is most important, it is often least effective, at least when used as the only method. Readers have a way of ignoring such pointers as "most important" and "especially true." (See Catton, par. 16; Korda, the last part.)

5. By *mechanical devices*—Emphasis can be achieved by using italics (underlining), capital letters, or exclamation points. But too often these devices are used, however unintentionally, to cover deficiencies of content or style. Their employment can quickly be overdone and their impact lost. (For very limited and therefore especially emphatic use of italics and capitalization, see D. H. Lawrence. Notice the Mitford, with a more emphatic style than most, uses none of these devices.)

6. By *distinctiveness of style*—The author can emphasize subtly with fresh and concrete words or figures of speech, crisp or unusual structures, and careful control of paragraph or sentence lengths. (These methods are used in many essays in this book: see Peterson; Buckley; Twain, who changes style radically for the second half of his essay; Catton; Rettie, par. 19; Wolfe; Thomas, pars. 9–10; Curtin, pars. 7–15.) *Verbal irony* (see *Irony)*, including *sarcasm* (see Buckley) and the rather specialized form known as *understatement*, if handled judiciously, is another valuable means of achieving distinctiveness of style and increasing emphasis. (See Wolfe, Mitford, D. H. Lawrence.)

Essay refers to a brief prose composition on a single topic, usually, but not always, communicating the author's personal ideas and impressions. Beyond this, because of the wide and loose application of the term, no really satisfactory definition has been universally accepted.

Classifications of essay types have also been widely varied and sometimes not very meaningful. One basic and useful distinction, however, is between *formal* and *informal* essays, although many defy classification even in such broad categories as these. It is best to regard the two types as opposite ends of a continuum, along which most essays may be placed.

The formal essay usually develops an important theme through a logical progression of ideas, with full attention to unity and coherence, and in a serious tone. Although the style is seldom completely impersonal, it is literary rather than collo-quial. (For examples of essays that are somewhere near the "formal" end of the continuum, see Buckley, Lynn, Eiseley, Catton, Winn, B. Lawrence, Thurow. Note that the Declaration of Independence, a completely formal document, is not classi-fiable as an "essay" at all.)

The informal, or personal, essay is less elaborately orga-nized and more chatty in style. First-person pronouns, contrac-tions, and other colloquial or even slang expressions are often freely used. Informal essays are less serious is apparent pur-pose than formal essays. Although most do contain a worth-while message or observation of some kind, an important pur-pose of many is to entertain. (See Wolfe, Reed, who treats a serious subject in an informal and idiosyncratic manner.)

The more personal and intimate informal essays may be classifiable as *familiar* essays, although, again, there is no well-established boundary. Familiar essays pertain to the author's own experience, ideas, or prejudices, frequently in a light and humorous style. (See Viorst, Curtin, White, Greene, Mairs.)

Evaluation of a literary piece, as for any other creative endeavor, is meaningful only when based somehow on the answers to three questions: (1) What was the author's purpose? (2) How successfully was it fulfilled? (3) How worthwhile was it?

An architect could hardly be blamed for designing a poor gymnasium if the commission had been to design a library. Similarly, an author who is trying to explain for us why women are paid less than men, as is Thurow, cannot be faulted for failing to make the reader laugh. An author whose purpose is simply to amuse (a worthy goal) should not be condemned for teaching little about trichobothria (as did Petrunkevitch). (Nothing prevents the author from trying to explain pornogra-phy through the use of humor, or trying to amuse by compar-ing two Civil War generals, but in these situations the purpose has changed—and grown almost unbearably harder to achieve.)

An architect who was commissioned to design a gymnasium, and who, in fact, designed one, however, could be justifiably criticized on whether the building is successful and attractive *as a gymnasium*. If an author is trying to show how definitions of feminism are changing (as is Klass), the reader has a right to expect sound reasoning and clear expository prose; and varied, detailed support ought to be expected in an essay that looks at the physical basis of human behavior (Perry and Dawson).

Many things are written and published that succeed very well in carrying out the author's intent—but simply are not worthwhile. Although this is certainly justifiable grounds for unfavorable criticism, readers should first make full allowance for their own limitations and perhaps their narrow range of interests, evaluating the work as nearly as possible from the standpoint of the average reader for whom the writing was intended.

Figures of Speech are short, vivid comparisons, either stated or implied; but they are not literal comparisons (e.g., "Your car is like my car," which is presumably a plain statement of fact). Figures of speech are more imaginative. They imply analogy but, unlike analogy, are used less to inform than to make quick and forceful impressions. All figurative language is a comparison of unlikes, but the unlikes do have some interesting point of likeness, perhaps one never noticed before.

A *metaphor* merely suggests the comparison and is worded as if the two unlikes are the same thing—e.g., "the language of the river" and "was turned to blood" (Twain, par. 1) and "a great chapter in American life" (Catton, par. 1). (For some of the many other examples in this book, see Eiseley, Thomas, King.)

A *simile* (which is sometimes classified as a special kind of metaphor) expresses a similarity directly, usually with the word *like* or *as* (Eiseley, par. 4).

A *personification,* which is actually a special type of either metaphor or simile, is usually classified as a "figure" in its own right. In personification, inanimate things are treated as if they had the qualities or powers of a person. Some people would also label as personification any characterization of inanimate objects as animals, or of animals as humans.

An *allusion* is literally any casual reference, any alluding, to something, but rhetorically it is limited to a figurative reference to a famous or literary person, event, or quotation, and it should be distinguished from the casual reference that has a literal function in the subject matter. Hence casual mention of Judas Iscariot's betrayal of Jesus is merely a reference, but calling a modern traitor a "Judas" is an allusion. A rooster might be referred to as "the Hitler of the barnyard," or a lover as a "Romeo." Many allusions refer to mythological or biblical persons or places. (See Buckley, par. 11; Rettie, title; Wolfe, title and par. 1; Petrunkevitch, par. 9; and Simpson, par. 2, for a discussion of some commonly employed allusions.)

Irony and paradox (both discussed under their own headings) and analogy (see Section 4) are also frequently classed as figures of speech, and there are several other less common types that are really subclassifications of those already discussed.

General (See *Specific/General.*)

Illustration (See Section 1.)

Impressionistic Description (See Section 8.)

Induction (See Section 10.)

Introductions give readers their first impressions, which often turn out to be the lasting ones. In fact, unless an introduction succeeds in somehow attracting a reader's interest, he or she probably will read no further. The importance of the introduction is one reason that writing it is nearly always difficult.

When the writer remains at a loss to know how to begin, it may be a good idea to forget about the introduction for a while and go ahead with the main body of the writing. Later the writer may find that a suitable introduction has suggested itself or even that the way the piece begins is actually introduction enough.

Introductions may vary in length from one sentence in a short composition to several paragraphs or even several pages in longer and more complex expositions and arguments, such as research papers and reports of various kinds.

Good introductions in expository writing have at least three and sometimes four functions:

1. *To identify the subject and set its limitations*, thus building a solid foundation for unity. This function usually includes some indication of the central theme, letting the reader know what point is to be made about the subject. Unlike the other

forms of prose, which can often benefit by some degree of mystery, exposition has the primary purpose of explaining, so the reader has a right to know from the beginning just *what* is being explained.

2. *To interest the readers,* and thus ensure their attention. To be sure of doing this, writers must analyze their prospective readers and the readers' interest in their subject. The account of a new X-ray technique would need an entirely different kind of introduction if written for doctors than if written for the campus newspaper.

3. *To set the tone* of the rest of the writing. (See *Style/Tone.*) Tone varies greatly in writing, just as the tone of a person's voice varies with the person's mood. One function of the introduction is to let the reader know the author's attitude since it may have a subtle but important bearing on the communication.

4. *Frequently,* but not always, *to indicate the plan of organization.* Although seldom important in short, relatively simple compositions and essay examinations, this function of introductions can be especially valuable in more complex papers.

These are the necessary functions of an introduction. For best results, keep these guidelines in mind: (1) Avoid referring to the title, or even assuming that the reader has seen it. Make the introduction do all the introducing. (2) Avoid crude and uninteresting beginnings, such as ''This paper is about. . . .'' (3) Avoid going too abruptly into the main body—smooth transition is at least as important here as anywhere else. (4) Avoid overdoing the introduction, either in length or in extremes of style.

Fortunately, there are many good ways to introduce expository writing (and argumentative writing), and several of the most useful are illustrated by the selections in this book. Many writings, of course, combine two or more of the following techniques for interesting introductions.

1. *Stating the central theme,* which is sometimes fully enough explained in the introduction to become almost a preview-summary of the exposition or argument to come. (See Peterson, Morris, Petrunkevitch, Viorst.)

2. *Showing the significance of the subject,* or stressing its importance. (See Catton, Wolfe, Simpson.)

3. *Giving the background of the subject,* usually in brief form,

in order to bring the reader up to date as early as possible for a better understanding of the matter at hand. (See Buhler and Graham, Lynn.)

4. _"Focusing down" to one aspect of the subject,_ a technique similar to that used in some movies, showing first a broad scope (of subject area, as of landscape) and then progressively narrowing views until the focus is on one specific thing (perhaps the name "O'Grady O'Connor" on a mailbox by a gate— or the silent sufferers on Buckley's train). (See also Rooney, Rettie.)

5. _Using a pertinent rhetorical device_ that will attract interest as it leads into the main exposition—e.g., an anecdote, analogy, allusion, quotation, or paradox. (See Sheehy, Simpson.)

6. _Using a short but vivid comparison or contrast_ to emphasize the central idea. (See Petrunkevitch, Murray.)

7. _Posing a challenging question,_ the answering of which the reader will assume to be the purpose of the writing. (See B. Lawrence, Thurow.)

8. _Referring to the writer's experience with the subject,_ perhaps even giving a detailed account of that experience. Some writings are simply continuations of experience so introduced, perhaps with the expository purpose of making the telling entirely evident only at the end or slowly unfolding it as the account progresses. (See White.)

9. _Presenting a startling statistic or other fact_ that will indicate the nature of the subject to be discussed. (See Thurow.)

10. _Making an unusual statement_ that can intrigue as well as introduce. (See Berne, Wolfe, Sheehy, Gansberg, George.)

11. _Making a commonplace remark_ that can draw interest because of its very commonness in sound or meaning. (See Berne.)

Irony, in its verbal form sometimes classed as a figure of speech, consists of saying one thing on the surface but meaning exactly (or nearly) the opposite—e.g., "this beautiful neighborhood of ours" may mean that it is dump. (For other illustrations, see Wolfe, Mitford, Walker.)

Verbal irony has a wide range of tones, from the gentle, gay, or affectionate to the sharpness of outright _sarcasm_ (see Buckley), which is always intended to cut. It may consist of only a word or phrase, it may be a simple _understatement_ (see

Mitford), or it may be sustained as one of the major components of satire.

Irony can be an effective tool of exposition if its tone is consistent with the overall tone and if the writer is sure that the audience is bright enough to recognize it. In speech, a person usually indicates by voice or eye-expression that he is not to be taken literally; in writing, the words on the page have to speak for themselves. (See Klass, par. 7.)

In addition to verbal irony, there is also an *irony of situation*, in which there is a sharp contradiction between what is logically expected to happen and what does happen—e.g., a man sets a trap for an obnoxious neighbor and then gets caught in it himself. Or the ironic situation may simply be some discrepancy that an outsider can see while those involved cannot. (See Thomas; Sheehy, par. 9; B. Lawrence, pars. 11–12.)

Logical Argument (See Section 11.)

Loose Sentences (See *Emphasis.*)

Metaphor (See *Figures of Speech.*)

Narration (See Section 9.)

Objective writing and **Subjective** writing are distinguishable by the extent to which they reflect the author's personal attitudes or emotions. The difference is usually one of degree, as few writing endeavors can be completely objective or subjective.

Objective writing, seldom used in its pure form except in business or scientific reports, is impersonal and concerned almost entirely with straight narration, with logical analysis, or with the description of external appearances. (For somewhat objective writing, see Berne, Simpson, Thurow, Staples, par. 1.)

Subjective writing (in description called "impressionistic"—see Section 8) is more personalized, more expressive of the beliefs, ideals, or impressions of the author. Whereas in objective writing the emphasis is on the object being written about, in subjective writing the emphasis is on the way the author sees and interprets the object. (For some of the many examples in this book, see Twain, Wolfe, Mitford, Peterson, B. Lawrence, D. H. Lawrence, Staples, after par. 1, Eiseley, Rodriguez, Ehrenreich, Klass.)

Paragraph Unity (See *Unity.*)

Parallel Structure refers in principle to the same kind of "parallelism'' that is studied in grammar: the principle that coordinate elements should have coordinate presentation, as in a pair of a series of verbs, prepositional phrases, gerunds. It is often as much a matter of ''balance'' as it is of parallelism.

But the principle of parallel structure, far from being just a negative ''don't mix'' set of rules, is also a positive rhetorical device. Many writers use it as an effective means of stressing variety of profusion in a group of nouns or modifiers, or of emphasizing parallel ideas in sentence parts, in two or more sentences, or even in two or more paragraphs. At times it can also be useful stylistically, to give a subtle poetic quality to the prose.

(For illustrations of parallel parts within a sentence, see Berne, par. 5; Murray, pars. 21, 26; Wolfe, pars. 1, 4; of parallel sentences themselves, see Berne, par. 4; Catton, par. 14; Jefferson; of both parallel parts and parallel sentences, see Twain, Maynard, Viorst; of parallel paragraphs, see the beginnings of Rettie's paragraphs 6–14; Jefferson.)

Periodic Sentence (See *Emphasis*.)

Persona refers to a character created as the speaker in an essay or the narrator of a story. The attitudes and character of a persona often differ from those of the author, and their persona may be created as a way of submitting certain values or perspectives to examination and criticism. The speaker in Swift's fictitious essay ''A Modest Proposal'' is clearly a persona and advocates actions that the author would consider abhorrent if put into practice.

Personification (See *Figures of Speech*.)

Point of View in *argument* means the author's opinion on an issue or the thesis being advanced in an essay. In *exposition*, however, point of view is simply the position of the author in relation to the subject matter. Rhetorical point of view in exposition has little in common with the grammatical sort and differs somewhat from point of view in fiction.

A ranch in a mountain valley is seen differently by the ranch-hand working at the corral, by the gardener deciding where to plant the petunias, by the artist or poet viewing the ranch from the mountainside, and by the geographer in a plane above, map-sketching the valley in relation to the entire range. It is the same ranch, but the positions and attitudes of the viewers are different.

So it is with expository prose. The position and attitude of the author are the important lens through which the reader sees the subject. Consistency is important, because if the lens is changed without sufficient cause and explanation, the reader will become disconcerted, if not annoyed.

Obviously, since the point of view is partially a matter of attitude, the tone and often the style of writing are closely linked to it. (See *Style/Tone.*)

The expository selections in this book provide examples of numerous points of view. Dillard's and Twain's are those of authority in their own fields of experience; Mitford's is as the debunking prober; Ehrenreich's is that of the angry observer of human behavior. In each of these (and the list could be extended to include all the selections in the book), the subject would seem vastly different if seen from some other point of view.

Process Analysis (See Section 5.)

Purpose that is clearly understood by the author before beginning to write is essential to both unity and coherence. A worthwhile practice, certainly in the training stages, is to write down the controlling purpose before even beginning to outline. Some instructors require both a statement of purpose and a statement of central theme or thesis. (See *Unity, Thesis.*)

The most basic element of a statement of purpose is the commitment to "explain" or, in some assignments, to "convince" (argument). But the statement of purpose, whether written down or only decided upon, goes further—e.g., "to argue that 'dirty words' are logically offensive because of the sources and connotations of the words themselves" (B. Lawrence).

Qualification is the tempering of broad statements to make them more valid and acceptable, the authors themselves admitting the probability of exceptions. This qualifying can be done inconspicuously, to whatever degree needed, by the use of *possibly, nearly always* or *most often, usually* or *frequently, sometimes* or *occasionally.* Instead of saying, "Chemistry is the most valuable field of study," it would probably be more accurate and defensible to say that it is for *some* people, or that it *can* be the most valuable. (For examples of qualification, see Klass.)

Refutation of opposing arguments is an important element in most argumentative essays, especially where the opposition is strong enough or reasonable enough to provide a real alternative to the author's opinion. A refutation consists of a brief summary of the opposing point of view along with a discussion of its inadequacies, a discussion which often helps support the author's own thesis.

Here are three commonly used strategies for refutation:

1. *Pointing out weaknesses in evidence*—If an opposing argument is based on inaccurate, incomplete, or misleading evidence, or if the argument does not take into account some new evidence that contradicts it, then the refutation should point out these weaknesses.

2. *Pointing our errors in logic*—If an opposing argument is loosely reasoned or contains major flaws in logic, then the refutation should point these problems out to the reader.

3. *Questioning the relevance of an argument*—If an opposing argument does not directly address the issue under consideration, than the refutation should point out that even though the argument may well be correct, it is not worth considering because it is not relevant.

Refutations should always be moderate in tone and accurate in representing opposing arguments; otherwise, readers may feel that the writer has treated the opposition unfairly and as a result judge the author's own argument more harshly.

Rhetorical Questions are posed with no expectation of receiving an answer; they are merely structural devices for launching or furthering a discussion or for achieving emphasis. (See Berne's title; Rattie's last sentence; Sheehy; B. Lawrence; D. H. Lawrence; Ehrenreich, par. 1; Quindlen, par. 4.)

Sarcasm (See *Irony.*)

Satire, sometimes called "extended irony," is a literary form that brings wit and humor to the serious task of pointing out frailties or evils of human institutions. It has thrived in Western literature since the time of the ancient Greeks, and English literature of the eighteenth century was particularly noteworthy for the extent and quality of its satire. Broadly, two types are recognized: *Horatian satire*, which is gentle, smiling, and aims to correct by invoking laughter and sympathy, and *Juvenalian satire,* which is sharper and which points with anger, contempt, and/or moral indignation to corruption and evil. (Swift's "A Modest Proposal" belongs in this category.)

Sentimentality, also called *sentimentalism,* is an exaggerated show of emotion, whether intentional or caused by lack of restraint. An author can sentimentalize almost any situation, but the trap is most dangerous when writing of timeworn emotional symbols or scenes—e.g., a broken heart, mother love, a lonely death, the conversion of a sinner. However sincere the author may be, if readers are not fully oriented to the worth and uniqueness of the situation described, they may be either resentful or amused at any attempt to play on their emotions. Sentimentality is, of course, one of the chief characteristics of melodrama. (For examples of writing that, less adeptly handled, could easily have slipped into sentimentality, see Twain, Catton, Thomas, Staples, Curtin, Simpson, Gansberg, Maynard, Greene.)

Simile (See *Figures of Speech.*)

Slang (See *Colloquial Expressions.*)

Specific and **General** terms, and the distinctions between the two, are similar to concrete and abstract terms (as discussed under their own heading), and for our purpose there is no real need to keep the two sets of categories separated. Whether *corporation* is thought of as "abstract" and *Ajax Motor Company* as "concrete," or whether they are assigned to "general" and "specific" categories, the principle is the same: in most writing, *Ajax Motor Company* is better.

But "specific" and "general" are relative terms. For instance, the word *apple* is more specific than *fruit* but less so than *Winesap.* And *fruit,* as general as it certainly is in one respect, is still more specific than *food.* Such relationships are shown more clearly in a series, progressing from general to specific: *food, fruit, apple, Winesap;* or *vehicle, automobile, Ford, Mustang.* Modifiers and verbs can also have degrees of specificity: *bright, red, scarlet;* or *moved, sped, careened.* It is not difficult to see the advantages to the reader—and, of course, to the writer who needs to communicate an idea clearly—in "the scarlet Mustang careened through the pass," instead of "the bright-colored vehicle moved through the pass."

Obviously, however, there are times when the general or the abstract term or statement is essential—e.g., "A balanced diet includes some fruit," or "There was no vehicle in sight." But the use of specific language whenever possible is one of the best ways to improve diction and thus clarity and forcefulness in writing.

(Another important way of strengthening general, abstract writing is, of course, to use examples or other illustrations. See Section 1.)

Style and **Tone** are so closely linked and so often even elements of each other that it is best to consider them together.

But there is a difference. Think of two young men, each with his girlfriend on separate moonlit dates, whispering in nearly identical tender and loving tones of voice. One young man says, "Your eyes, dearest, reflect a thousand sparkling candles of heaven," and the other says, "Them eyes of yours— in this light—they sure do turn me on." Their *tones* were the same; their *styles* considerably different.

The same distinction exists in writing. But, naturally, with more complex subjects than the effect of moonlight on a lover's eyes, there are more complications in separating the two qualities, even for the purpose of study.

The tone is determined by the *attitude* of writers toward their subject and toward their audience. Writers, too, may be tender and loving, but they may be indignant, solemn, playful, enthusiastic, belligerent, contemptuous—the list could be as long as a list of the many "tones of voice." (In fact, wide ranges of tone may be illustrated by essays in this book. Compare, for example, those of the two parts of Twain; Eiseley and Mitford; Abbey and Lynn; Staples and Ehrenreich; Reed and Rodriguez.)

Style, on the other hand, expresses the author's individuality through choices of words (see *Diction*), sentence patterns (see *Syntax*), and selection and arrangement of details and basic materials. (All these elements of style are illustrated in the contrasting statements of the moonstruck lads.) These matters of style are partially prescribed, of course, by the adopted tone, but they are still bound to reflect the writer's personality and mood, education and general background.

(Some of the more distinctive styles—partially affected by and affecting tone—represented by selections in this book are those of Rodriguez, Viorst, Wolfe, Buckley, White, D. H. Lawrence, Eiseley, Quindlen, Staples, Walker, and Abbey.)

Subjective Writing (See *Objective/Subjective.*)

Symbol refers to anything that although real itself also suggests something broader or more significant—not just in greater numbers, however, as a person would not symbolize a group or even humankind itself, although a person might be typical or representative in one or more abstract qualities. On the most elementary level, even words are symbols—e.g., *bear* brings to mind the furry beast itself. But more important is that things, persons, or even acts may also be symbolic, if they invoke abstract concepts, values, or qualities apart from themselves or their own kind. Such symbols, in everyday life as well as in literature and the other arts, are generally classifiable according to three types, which, although terminology differs, we may label *natural, personal,* and *conventional.*

In a natural symbol, the symbolic meaning is inherent in the thing itself. The sunrise naturally suggests new beginnings to most people, an island is almost synonymous with isolation, a cannon automatically suggests war; hence these are natural symbols. It does not matter that some things, by their nature, can suggest more than one concept. Although a valley may symbolize security to one person and captivity to another, both meanings, contradictory as they might seem, are inherent, and in both respects the valley is a natural symbol.

The personal symbol, depending as it does on private experience or perception, is meaningless to others unless they are told about it or allowed to see its significance in context (as in literature). Although the color green may symbolize the outdoor life to the farm boy trapped in the gray city (in this respect perhaps a natural symbol), it can also symbolize romance to the young woman proposed to while wearing her green blouse, or dismal poverty to the woman who grew up in a weathered green shanty; neither of these meanings is suggested by something *inherent* in the color green, so they are personal symbols. Anything at all could take on private symbolic meaning, even the odor of marigolds or the sound of a

A Guide to Terms

lawnmower. The sunrise itself could mean utter despair, instead of fresh opportunities, to the man who has long despised his daily job and cannot find another.

Conventional symbols usually started as personal symbols, but continued usage in life or art permits them to be generally recognized for their broader meanings, which depend on custom rather than any inherent quality—e.g., the olive branch for peace, the flag for love of country, the cross for Christianity, the raised fist for revolutionary power.

Symbols are used less in expository and argumentative writing than in fiction and poetry, but a few authors represented in this book have either referred to the subtle symbolism of others or made use of it in developing their own ideas. Eiseley says that the old men clung to their seats as if they were symbols, Morris mentions ''symbolic battle,'' and symbolism is central to Peterson's discussion of dreams and reality.

Syntax is a very broad term—too broad, perhaps, to be very useful—referring to the arrangement of words in a sentence. Good syntax implies the use not only of correct grammar but also of effective patterns. These patterns depend on sentences with good unity, coherence, and emphasis, on the use of subordination and parallel construction as appropriate, on economy, and on a consistent and interesting point of view. A pleasing variety of sentence patterns is also important in achieving effective syntax.

Theme (See *Unity.*)

Thesis In an argumentative essay, the central theme is often referred to as the *thesis,* and to make sure that readers recognize it, the thesis is often summed up briefly in a *thesis statement.* In a very important sense, the thesis is the center of an argument because the whole essay is designed to make the reader agree with it and, hence, with the author's opinion. (See *Unity.*)

Tone (See *Style/Tone.*)

Transition is the relating of one topic to the next, and smooth transition is an important aid to the coherence of a sentence, a paragraph, or an entire piece of writing. (See *Coherence.*)

The most effective coherence, of course, comes about naturally with sound development of ideas, one growing logically into the next—and that depends on sound organization. But

sometimes beneficial even in this situation, particularly in going from one paragraph to the next, is the use of appropriate
transitional devices.

Readers are apt to be sensitive creatures, easy to lose.
(And, of course, the writers are the real losers since they are
the ones who presumably have something they want to communicate.) If the readers get into a new paragraph and the territory seems familiar, chances are that they will continue. But
if there are no identifying landmarks, they will often begin to
feel uneasy and will either start worrying about their slow comprehension or take a dislike to the author and the subject matter. Either way, a communication block arises, and very likely
the author will soon have fewer readers.

A good policy, then, unless the progression of ideas is ex-
ceptionally smooth and obvious, is to provide some kind of
familiar identification early in the new paragraph, to keep the
reader feeling at ease with the different ideas. The effect is subtle but important. These familiar landmarks or transitional devices are sometimes applied deliberately but more often come
naturally, especially when the prospective reader is kept constantly in mind at the time of writing.

An equally important reason for using some kinds of transitional devices, however, is a logical one: while functioning as
bridges between ideas, they also assist the basic organization
by pointing out the *relationship* of the ideas—and thus contributing still further to readability.

Transitional devices useful for bridging paragraph changes
(and, some of them, to improve transitional flow within paragraphs) may be roughly classified as follows:

1. *Providing an "echo"* from the preceding paragraph.
This may be the repetition of a key phrase or word, or a pronoun referring back to such a word, or a casual reference to an
idea. (See Wolfe, especially from pars. 1 to 2 and 4 to 5; Mitford.) Such an echo cannot be superimposed on new ideas, but
must, by careful planning, be made an organic part of them.

2. *Devising a whole sentence or paragraph* to bridge other important paragraphs or major divisions. (See Lynn; pars. 11, 20,
and 21.)

3. *Using parallel structure* in an important sentence of one
paragraph and the first sentence of the next. This is a subtle

means of making the reader feel at ease in the new surroundings, but it is seldom used because it is much more limited in its potential than the other methods of transition. (See B. Lawrence, pars. 1 to 2.)

4. *Using standard transitional expressions,* most of which have the additional advantage of indicating relationship of ideas. Only a few of those available are classified below, but nearly all the selections in this book amply illustrate such transitional expressions:

Time—soon, immediately, afterward, later, meanwhile, after a while.

Place—nearby, here, beyond, opposite.

Result—as a result, therefore, thus, consequently, hence.

Comparison—likewise, similarly, in such a manner.

Contrast—however, nevertheless, still, but, yet, on the other hand, after all, otherwise.

Addition—also, too, and, and then, furthermore, moreover, finally, first, second, third.

Miscellaneous—for example, for instance, in fact, indeed, on the whole, in other words.

Trite (See *Clichés.*)

Unity in writing is the same as unity in anything else—in a picture, a musical arrangement, a campus organization—and that is a *one*ness, in which all parts contribute to an overall effect.

Many elements of good writing contribute in varying degrees to the effect of unity. Some of these are properly designed introductions and closings; consistency of point of view, tone, and style; sometimes the recurring use of analogy or thread of symbolism; occasionally the natural time boundaries of an experience or event, as in the selections of Rettie, Mitford, Simpson, Gansberg, and Orwell ("A Hanging").

But in most expository and argumentative writing the only dependable unifying force is the *central theme,* which every sentence, every word, must somehow help to support. (The central theme is also called the *central idea* or the *thesis* when pertaining to the entire writing and is almost always called the *thesis* in argument. In an expository or argumentative paragraph it is the same as the *topic sentence,* which may be implied or, if stated, may be located anywhere in the paragraph, but is usually placed first.) As soon as anything appears that is not related to the central idea, there are *two* units instead of one. Hence unity is basic to all other virtues of good writing, even to coherence and emphasis, the other two organic essentials. (See *Coherence, Emphasis.*)

An example of unity may be found in a single river system (for a practical use of analogy), with all its tributaries, big or little, meandering or straight, flowing into the main stream and making it bigger—or at least flowing into another tributary that finds its way to the main stream. This is *one* river system, an example of unity. Now picture another stream nearby that does not empty into the river but goes off in some other direction. There are now two systems, not one, and there is no longer unity.

It is the same way with writing. The central theme is the main river, flowing along from the first capital letter to the last period. Every drop of information or evidence must find its way into this theme-river, or it is not a part of the system. It matters not even slightly if the water is good, the idea-stream perhaps deeper and finer than any of the others: if it is not a tributary, it has no business pretending to be relevant to *this* theme of writing.

And that is why most students are required to state their central idea or thesis, usually in solid sentence form, before even starting to organize their ideas. If the writer can use only tributaries, it is very important to know from the start just what the river is.

To the Student:

Part of our job as educational publishers is to try to improve the textbooks we publish. Thus, when revising, we take into account the experiences of both instructors and students with the previous edition. At some time your instructor will be asked to comment extensively on *Patterns of Exposition* 12, but right now we want to hear from you. After all, though your instructor assigned this book, you are the one who paid for it.

Please help us by completing this questionnaire and returning it to College English, Scott, Foresman/Little, Brown Higher Education, A Division of Scott, Foresman and Company, 1900 East Lake Avenue, Glenview, Illinois 60025.

School _____ Course title _____

Instructor's name _____

Other books assigned _____

	Liked Best				Liked Least	Didn't Read
Rooney, In and of Ourselves We Trust	5	4	3	2	1	_____
Langone, There's Always a Catch	5	4	3	2	1	_____
Staples, Just Walk on By	5	4	3	2	1	_____
Buckley, Why Don't We Complain?	5	4	3	2	1	_____
Ehrenreich, What I've Learned from Men	5	4	3	2	1	_____
Berne, Can People Be Judged by Their Appearance?	5	4	3	2	1	_____
Viorst, What, Me? Showing Off?	5	4	3	2	1	_____
Morris, Territorial Behaviour	5	4	3	2	1	_____
Marsh, Tribes	5	4	3	2	1	_____
Twain, Two Ways of Seeing a River	5	4	3	2	1	_____
Catton, Grant and Lee: A Study in Contrasts	5	4	3	2	1	_____
Croce, Scrambled Eggs and Cross-Purposes	5	4	3	2	1	_____
Rodriguez, Aria	5	4	3	2	1	_____
Walker, Am I Blue?	5	4	3	2	1	_____
Wolfe, O Rotten Gotham—Sliding Down into the Behavioral Sink	5	4	3	2	1	_____
Eiseley, The Brown Wasps	5	4	3	2	1	_____
Rettie, "But a Watch in the Night": A Scientific Fable	5	4	3	2	1	_____
Murray, The Maker's Eye: Revising Your Own Manuscripts	5	4	3	2	1	_____
Buhler and Graham, Give Juggling a Hand!	5	4	3	2	1	_____
Petrunkevitch, The Spider and the Wasp	5	4	3	2	1	_____
Mitford, To Dispel Fears of Live Burial	5	4	3	2	1	_____
Greene, Thirty Seconds	5	4	3	2	1	_____
Sheehy, $70,000 a Year, Tax Free	5	4	3	2	1	_____
Mairs, On Being a Scientific Booby	5	4	3	2	1	_____
Perry and Dawson, What's Your Best Time of Day?	5	4	3	2	1	_____
Winn, Television Addiction	5	4	3	2	1	_____

	Liked Best				Liked Least	Didn't Read
Lawrence, Pornography	5	4	3	2	1	_____
Klass, Anatomy and Destiny	5	4	3	2	1	_____
Korda, What It Takes to Be a Leader	5	4	3	2	1	_____
Curtin, Aging in the Land of the Young	5	4	3	2	1	_____
Maynard, The Yellow Door House	5	4	3	2	1	_____
White, Once More to the Lake	5	4	3	2	1	_____
Simpson, The War Room at Bellevue	5	4	3	2	1	_____
Gansberg, 38 Who Saw Murder Didn't Call the Police	5	4	3	2	1	_____
Peterson, Stuff as Dreams Are Made On	5	4	3	2	1	_____
Orwell, A Hanging	5	4	3	2	1	_____
Dillard, Prologue	5	4	3	2	1	_____
Thurow, Why Women Are Paid Less Than Men	5	4	3	2	1	_____
Reed, America: The Multinational Society	5	4	3	2	1	_____
Farb, In Other Words	5	4	3	2	1	_____
Quindlen, Execution	5	4	3	2	1	_____
George, Women Coaches Are an Endangered Species	5	4	3	2	1	_____
Geyer, Drugs: Facing the Responsibility	5	4	3	2	1	_____
Abbey, The Damnation of a Canyon	5	4	3	2	1	_____
Lynn, Why Johnny Can't Read, but Yoshio Can	5	4	3	2	1	_____
Lawrence, Four-Letter Words Can Hurt You	5	4	3	2	1	_____
Thomas, Nurses	5	4	3	2	1	_____
Jefferson, The Declaration of Independence	5	4	3	2	1	_____
King, Letter from Birmingham Jail	5	4	3	2	1	_____
Swift, A Modest Proposal	5	4	3	2	1	_____
Atwood, Pornography	5	4	3	2	1	_____
Holleran, Bedside Manners	5	4	3	2	1	_____

1. Are there any authors not included whom you would like to see represented? _____

2. Were the biographical sketches and introductions useful? _____
   How might they be improved? _____

3. Will you keep this book for your library? _____

4. Please add any comments or suggestions. _____
   _____

5. May we quote you in our promotional efforts for this book?
   _____ yes _____ no

Date _____ Signature _____

Mailing address _____

NOTES

NOTES

NOTES